MORE BEHIND THE BLUE LAMP

Policing South and South East London

By

David Swinden

Peter Kennison

Alan Moss

Printed and published by
Coppermill Press
Unit 5 Fanton Hall Farm,
Wickford
Essex
SS12 9JF
Tel: 01268 768080
Fax: 01268 768484

© The authors

All rights reserved; no part of this publication may be reproduced, stored in a retrieval system, or transmitted in any form or by any means, electronic, mechanical, photocopying, recording or otherwise without prior written permission of the publisher or a licence permitting copying in the UK issued by the Copyright Licensing Agency Ltd., 90 Tottenham Court Road, London W1P9HE

First published 2011

ISBN 978-0-9546534-3-9

British Library Cataloguing-in-Publication data.
A catalogue record for this book is available from the British Library.

All photographs and illustrations are reproduced by kind courtesy of the Metropolitan Police Historic Collection with the exception of the following;

Peter Kennison 1-5, 7- 17, 19 – 29, 31 - 36, 41, 78, 93 -95, 103, 105, 107, 109, 111 -112, 119 - 120, 125, 134 – 142, 148, 151, 154, 156, 159, 163, 165, 167, 169 – 170, 172 – 175, 179, 184, 192 – 194, 197 – 200, 202, 208, 213 – 216, 218, 222 – 223, 225, 235, 237, 243, 247, 249, 253 - 256, 258 – 259, 261 – 264, 267 – 268, 270, 272, 274 – 279, 281 – 282, 284 – 284, 287, 289, 292 – 295, 298, 300, 302 - 303
David Swinden 102, 149, 152, 161, 182, 187, 207
Alan Moss 43 – 49, 51 – 53, 56 – 57, 59 – 60, 62, 64 -67, 69 -74, 76 – 77, 79, 86, 88- 89,
Chris Lordan 104, 124, 128, 209, 257, 291, 301
Chris Forester 257, 291, 301,
Peter Straighton 80,

Every attempt has been made to credit the source of the photographs used in this book. Any omission's brought to our attention will be corrected in any future publications.

This book is dedicated to the men and women of the Metropolitan Police (past and present) who risk their lives daily in the protection of the public.

Acknowledgements.

The authors are particularly indebted to friends and colleagues, who advised, directed and discussed the research, yet still remained interested. Particular gratitude and thanks are also extended to some special people;

The authors would particularly like to make extra special mention of Maggie **Bird** who sadly passed away in 2010. Maggie was a tireless police historian and a devoted Civil staff member. She helped to re-organise the MPS Historic Collection at Charlton. Maggie helped the authors with newly found information on policing.

Bernard **Brown**– Metropolitan Police Officer (retired) - deserves an extra mention because of his consistent historical research which made our task easier- thank-you Bernie.

A special mention is also made to the late John **Back**- whose research from the 1970's in the Metropolitan Police Service Archives provided us with valuable material. Also Phillip **Barnes-Warden** - Metropolitan Police Historical Collection for his considerable help in discovering new material and photographic skills.

Helen **Barnard** - Friends of the Metropolitan Police Historical Collection
John **Barnie** - Chief Executive of Metropolitan Police Trading Service
Ken **Butler** - Friends of the Metropolitan Police Historical Collection
Sioban **Clark** - Friends of the Metropolitan Police Historical Collection
Jeff **Cowdell** - Staffordshire Police Officer (retired) and badge collector
Michael **Cox** - Historian and postcard enthusiast
Bill **Davidson** - Surveyor Metropolitan Police Service
Tony **Dawson** - Chief Superintendent Metropolitan Police
Paul **Dew** - Metropolitan Police Historical Collection
Chris **Forester** - Friends of the Metropolitan Police Historical Collection
Anna **Gardener** - Metropolitan Police Historical Collection
Sarah **Gould** - London Borough of Merton Library
Charles **Griggs** - Chief Superintendent Metropolitan Police
Richard **Hayes** - Historian and postcard enthusiast
Neville (Spike) **Hughes** - Metropolitan Police Officer (retired) (who sadly passed away in 2008)
Dee **Jupp** - Metropolitan Police Service – London Borough of Merton
Christopher **Lordan** - Metropolitan Police Officer (retired)

Chris **Newman** – Sheerness Historian
Neil **Paterson** -Metropolitan Police Historical Collection
Barnaby **Palmer** - Police history researcher
Terry **Pizzala** - Metropolitan Police Service -Civil Staff (retired)
John **Player**
Bill **Prowse**
Ray **Seal** - Metropolitan Police Service, Museum Charlton (retired)
Peter **Simmons**
Keith **Skinner**
Barbara **Street**
Peter **Straiton** - Metropolitan Police Officer (retired)
Victor Legender **Wilkinson** - Metropolitan Police Officer (retired)
Julieanne **Young**-Metropolitan Police Service Architectural Library,

The Staff of *The Job* Newspaper
The Staff of the London Borough Libraries of Bexley, Bromley, Croydon, Greenwich, Lambeth, Lewisham, Merton, Sutton, Southwark and Wandsworth.

List of Illustrations

No	Description	Page
1	Badge of Rank for Constable	vi
2	Metropolitan Police Constable 1865 -71	vi
3	Badge of Rank for Sergeant	Vii
4	Station Police Sergeant pre 1921	viii
5	Badge of Rank for Station Police Sergeant	viii
6	Victorian Police Superintendent	ix
7	Victorian Police Inspector's Helmet Plate	Ix
8	Police Inspector circa 1906	ix
9	Badge of Rank for Police Inspector pre-1953	ix
10	Police Inspector with flat hat	x
11	Sub-Divisional Police Inspector 1916	x
12	Badge of Rank for Police Inspector	x
13	Badge of Rank for Police Chief Inspector	xi
14	Victorian Police Chief Inspector	xi
15	Helmet Plate for Police Chief Inspector	xii
16	Police Chief Inspector circa 1916	xii
17	Badge of Rank for Police Superintendent Grade 1 pre-1953	xii
18	Victorian Police Superintendent's Helmet	xiii
19	Badge of Rank for Police Superintendent Grade 2 pre-1953	xiii
20	Badge of Rank for Police Superintendent Grade 2 post-1953	xiii
21	Divisional Police Chief Superintendent circa 1936	xiv
22	Badge of Rank for Police Chief Superintendent pre-1953	xiv
23	John Mulvaney Police Chief Superintendent 'H' Division	xv
24	Badge of Rank for Police Chief Superintendent	xv
25	Badge for Chief Constable	xv
26	Chief Constable P. W. Sprules MBE 1939	xvi
27	Badge of Rank for Deputy Police Commander	xvi
28	Badge of Rank for Police Commander	xvi
29	Badge of Police Commander (metal badge)	xvii
30	Uniformed Police Commander	xvii
31	Badge of Rank for Deputy Assistant Commissioner 1946	xvii
32	Badge of Rank for Deputy Assistant Commissioner	xviii
33	Badge of Rank for Deputy Commissioner	xvii
34	Badge of Rank for Commissioner pre 1953	xix
35	Badge of Rank for Commissioner 1980s (metal)	xix
36	Badge of Rank for Commissioner circa 2006	xix
37	Sir Joseph Simpson Commissioner 1958 - 1967	xix
38	Belvedere Police Station 1881-1968	3
39	Rear of Belvedere Police Station	5
40	Belvedere Police Station 1968 – Present day	6
41	Bexleyheath Police Station 1855-1908	7

42	Bexleyheath Police Station 1908-1994	8
43	Bexleyheath Police Rifle Club winners 1913-1914	9
44	'R' Division Police Band	10
45	Crayford Safer Neighbourhood Office	11
46	Bexleyheath Police Station 1994 – Present day	12
47	Bexley Safer Neighbourhood Unit, Old Bexley Primary School	13
48	Erith Police Station 1847-1908	14
49	Erith Police Officers, 1865	15
50	Erith Police Station 1908-2000	17
51	Erith Special Police Constable	18
52	Erith Safer Neighbourhood Unit	19
53	Sidcup Police Station 1842-1902	20
54	Sidcup Police Station 1902-Present day	21
55	Sidcup Police Station 1908	22
56	North Cray Safer Neighbourhood Team Office	23
57	Colyers Safer Neighbourhood Team Office	23
58	Welling Police Office	24
59	Falconwood Safer Neighbourhood Office	25
60	Beckenham Police Station 1875	29
61	Beckenham Police Station 1885-2008	31
62	Elmers End Safer Neighbourhood Team Office	34
63	Biggin Hill Police Station 1970-2006	35
64	Biggin Hill Police Office 2006	36
65	Albermarle Police Office 2008 – present day	36
66	Bromley Police Station 1840-1865	37
67	Bromley Police Station 1865-1915	37
68	Bromley Police Station 1915-2003	38
69	Police Medals	39
70	Bromley Police Station 2003-Present day	42
71	Walpole Road Safer Neighbourhood Office	42
72	Burnt Ash Lane Police Office	43
73	Bromley Police Office	43
74	Chislehurst Police Station 1888-1893	44
75	Chislehurst Police Station 1893-1999	45
76	Chislehurst Temporary Police Office	46
77	Chislehurst Safer Neighbourhood Office	46
78	Farnborough Police Station	47
79	Hayes and Coney Hall Police Office	48
80	Knockholt Police Station 1895-1969	49
81	Orpington Police Station 1983 – present day	50
82	Penge Police Station 1872 –Present day	52
83	Rear Yard of Penge Police Station	53
84	St Mary Cray Police Station 1896-1988	54
85	Rear aspect of St Mary Cray Police Station	55
86	Cray Police Office 1994-Present day	56
87	West Wickham Police Office 1974-Present day	57

88	Warren Sports Club 2007	59
89	Warren Sports Club Grounds	60
90	Addington Police Office 1962-1977	65
91	Croydon Police Station 1843-1895	67
92	Croydon Police Station 1895-1980	68
93	Station Police Sergeant Harold Prewer 'Z' Division	70
94	'Z' Division Race Walking Team 1936	70
95	Kings Police and Fire Services Medal 1952	71
96	Police Constable Sislin Fay Allen	72
97	Croydon Police Station 1980-Present day	73
98	Kenley Police Station 1896-Present day	74
99	Kenley Police 1937	75
100	Norbury Police Station 1925-Present day	76
101	South Norwood Police Station 1873-1988	79
102	South Norwood Police Station 1988-Present day	80
103	'R' Division Officers 1912	85
104	Abbeywood Police Station 1906-1926	86
105	Eltham Police Station 1865	88
106	Eltham Police Station 1911	89
107	Sub-Divisional Police Inspector Hill 1903	90
108	Eltham Police Station 1939 – Present day	91
109	Map of Park Row 1888	92
110	East Greenwich Police Station 1873-1902	93
111	East Greenwich Police Station 1902-1962	94
112	Greenwich Map	95
113	East Greenwich Officers 1926	95
114	Bomb Damage 1941	96
115	Bomb Damage 1941	97
116	Blackheath Road Police Station 1836-1910	100
117	Blackheath Road Police Station Rear Yard	102
118	Greenwich Police Station 1910	105
119	Constable Dunn	106
120	Helmet Plate 1911-1936	106
121	Greenwich Police Station 1962-Present day	108
122	Plumstead Police Station	111
123	Plumstead Police Station Rear Yard	112
124	Plumstead Police Station 1991-Present day	113
125	Shooters Hill Police Station 1852-1915	115
126	Shooters Hill Police Station 1915-2001	116
127	Thamesmead Police Office 1973-1987	117
128	Thamesmead Police Office 1987	118
129	Westcombe Park Police Station 1885-Present day	119
130	Westcombe Park Police Station Rear Yard	120
131	Westcombe Park Police Station 1970's	120
132	Woolwich Police Station 1847-1910	122
133	Woolwich Police Station 1911	123

134	Woolwich Police Station 1910	126
135	Victoria Cross Lieutenant L. Robinson	127
136	Woman Police Constable Steere 1921	128
137	Christ Church Watch House 1819-1932	135
138	Brixton Police Station 1858-1909	137
139	Brixton Police Station 1909-1959	138
140	Police Constable George Applegate	139
141	Police Superintendent West MBE	140
142	Special Police Constables 'W' Division 1914	140
142a	Senior Officers of 'W' Division 1914	141
143	Brixton Police Station 1959-Present day	141
144	Clapham Police Station 1907-Present day	144
145	Kennington Lane Police Station 1871-1932	147
146	Kennington Road Police Station 1874-1939	149
147	Kennington Road Police Station 1955-Present day	150
148	Knights Hill Police Station 1886-1930	152
149	Gipsy Hill Police Station 1859-1940	153
150	Gipsy Hill Police Station 1940-Present day	154
151	Streatham Police Station 1868-1912	156
152	Streatham Police Station 1912 - Present day	157
153	Brockley Police Station 1883 - Present day	163
154	Catford Police Station 1892-1927	165
155	Catford Police Station 1940 - Present day	166
156	Deptford Police Station 1855-1912	167
157	Deptford Police Station 1912-Present day	169
157a	Deptford Police Station (showing extension)	170
158	Lee Road Police Station 1903-2003	171
159	Lewisham Police Station 1841	173
160	Lewisham Police Station 1899-2004	175
161	Lewisham Police Station and Court 2004-Present day	177
162	Sydenham Police Station 1848-1966	178
163	Police Constable Charles Henry Moore	179
164	Sydenham Police Station 1966-Present day	180
165	The Green, Mitcham	186
165a	The Causeway, Mitcham, Surrey around 1900.	189
165b	Mitcham Police Station 1965 – Present day	190
165c	Mitcham Police Station lamp	190
166	Morden Police Office	191
167	Wimbledon Police Station 1790-1844	193
168	Merton Police Station 1805-1931	193
169	Wimbledon Police Station 1860-1900	196
170	Map of Wimbledon 1888	199
171	'V' Division Despatch Van	200
172	McKenna Post Card	202
173	Wimbledon Special Constabulary rifle team 1916	203
174	Special Constabulary Long Service Medal	204
175	Women Police Service	204
176	Wimbledon Police circa 1920s	205

177	Wimbledon Police Station 1900-Present day	206
178	Wimbledon Police Station Lamp	208
179	Wimbledon Police Station 2010	209
180	Banstead Police Station 1906 - Present day	213
181	Carshalton Police Station 1848-1920	214
182	Epsom Old Watch House	215
183	Epsom Police Station 1857-1963	216
184	Funeral of Police Station Sergeant Green 1919	216
185	Epsom Police Station 1963 - Present day	218
186	Sutton Police Station 1854 - 1908	219
187	Sutton Police Station 1908-2004	220
188	Sutton Police Station 2003 - Present day	221
189	Wallington Police Station 1915-Present day	223
190	Worcester Park Police Office 1971-Present day	225
190a	Camberwell Police Station 1833-1898	229
191	Camberwell Police Station 1898-Present day	230
192	Retirement Group at Camberwell 1912	231
193	Group of Medals	231
194	Metropolitan Police Nursing Home	232
195	Police Superintendent Thomas Butt	234
196	Carter Street Police Station 1910-1993	235
197	Inspector Francis Odell and colleagues at Carter Street	236
198	HM The Queen Mother	237
199	Police Occurrence Book entry	238
200	HRH The Queen Mother etc	238
201	Bermondsey/Grange Road Police Station 1883-1940	240
202	'L' Division Special Police Constable	240
203	East Dulwich Police Station 1884-1977	242
204	East Dulwich Police Station 1977-Present day	243
205	West Dulwich Police Station 1887-1978	244
206	Peckham Police Station 1847-1893	245
207	Peckham Police Station 1893-Present day	247
208	Rodney Road Police Station 1873-1932	248
209	Old Watch House, St Marychurch Street	250
210	Rotherhithe Police Station 1836-1965	250
211	Rotherhithe Police Station 1965-Present day	251
212	Southwark Police Station 1870-1940	254
213	Sub-Divisional Police Inspector May	255
214	Southwark Police Station 1911	256
215	Southwark Police Station Outing 1910	257
216	'M' Division Football Team	257
217	Old Court Building, Borough	258
218	'M' Division Sports Day	258
219	Southwark Police Station 1940-Present day	259
220	Tower Bridge Police Station 1904-1999	260
221	Battersea Police Station 1861-1911	267

222	Map of Battersea	269
223	Battersea Police Station 1907-Present day	270
224	Rear of Battersea Police Station	271
225	Map of Earlsfield	272
226	Earlsfield Police Station 1914-Present day	273
227	Lavender Hill Police Station 1896-1962	274
228	Lavender Hill Police Station (Rear yard)	275
229	Lavender Hill Police Station 1963-Present day	276
230	Nine Elms Police Station 1925-Present day	277
231	Nine Elms Police Station Lamp	278
232	Police Constable Crawford	279
233	Putney Police Station 1903-2006	281
234	Rear Gardens	272
234a	Rear gardens view showing parade shed	273
235	Map of Roehampton	284
235a	West Putney Police Office	285
236	Roehampton Police Station	285
237	Tooting Map	286
238	Tooting Police Station 1864-1939	287
239	Tooting Police Station (Rear yard)	288
240	Tooting Police Station 1939-Present day	288
241	Wandsworth Police Station 1864-1883	291
242	Wandsworth Police Station 1883-Present day	292
243	Wandsworth Police Station (topographical)	293
244	Wandsworth Police Station Rear Yard (1)	294
245	Wandsworth Police Station Rear Yard (2)	294
246	Wandsworth Police Station Rear Yard (3)	295
247	Map of Wandsworth	298
248	Wandsworth Common Police Station 1883-Present day	299
249	Wandsworth Common Police Station Map	300
250	Wandsworth Common Police Station Rear Yard (1)	300
251	Wandsworth Common Police Station Rear Yard (2)	302
252	Metropolitan Police Dockyard Police Inspector 1860	307
253	Dockyard Police Constable	308
254	Dockyard Helmet Plate	309
255	Woolwich Royal Arsenal 1910	311
256	Royal Naval College Greenwich	315
257	The Water Police Royal Arsenal	316
258	Royal Arsenal female Workers	318
259	Royal Dockyard Gate Woolwich	319
260	Dockyard Bell	324
261	Dockyard Helmet Plate 1880-1902	324
262	Dockyard Police Constable 1870	325
263	Portsmouth Dockyard 1915	326
264	Portsmouth Dockyard Main Gate	327
265	Dockyard Fire Brigade	328

266	Hasler Naval Hospital	329
267	Unicorn Gates Portsmouth	330
268	Police Superintendent Carter	331
269	Portsmouth Dockyard Sergeants	331
270	The 1887 Jubilee Medal	332
271	Portsmouth and Gosport Dockyard Police	332
272	Royal Humane Society Medal	333
273	1916 Awards Ceremony	333
274	Portsmouth Dockyard Fire 1913 (1)	334
275	Portsmouth Dockyard Fire 1913 (2)	335
276	Dockyard Police Constable on Patrol	335
277	Dockyard Police Sergeant 1904	336
278	Dockyard Police Helmet Plate 1902-1935	336
279	Unicorn Dockyard Section House 1914	337
280	Portsmouth Championship Cup 1922	337
281	Devonport Dockyard Gate	338
282	Royal William Dockyard Gate	339
283	Devonport Police Shaving Mug	340
284	Police Superintendent Edwin Smith 1906	341
285	Sub-Divisional Police Inspector Alfred Sly 1911	342
286	Devonport Dockyard Fire Brigade	343
287	Devonport Dockyard Band 1912	343
288	Devonport Dockyard Rifle Team 1913	344
289	Devonport Dockyard Gas Training	345
290	The Gatehouse, Chatham 1865	348
291	Police Constable Rogers, Chatham Dockyard	349
292	Dockyard Helmet Plate 1863-1870	350
293	Police Constable 69 Collins 1865	351
294	Police Superintendent Josiah Hobbins	354
295	Sheerness Dockyard 1924	355
296	Senior Officers and men, Chatham 1896	356
297	Police Chief Inspector Kemp 1899	356
298	Pembroke Dockyard Gate	359
299	Pembroke Dockyard Fire Engine 1924	361
300	Police Constable Shepherd 1914	362
301	Rosyth Dockyard Police 1918	363
302	Rosyth Dockyard	364

More Behind the Blue Lamp

Index	i - iii
Introduction	iv - v
Ranks	vi - xx
Chapter One - London Borough of Bexley	pages 1 - 27
Belvedere	2
Bexleyheath	7
Erith	13
Sidcup	19
Slade Green	23
Welling	23
Chapter Two - London Borough of Bromley	pages 28 - 62
Beckenham	29
Biggin Hill	35
Bromley	37
Chislehurst	44
Farnborough	47
Hayes and Coney Hall	47
Knockholt	49
Orpington	50
Penge	51
St. Mary Cray	53
West Wickham	56
The Warren Sports Club	57
Chapter Three - London Borough of Croydon	pages 63 - 83
Addington/New Addington	64
Croydon	65
Kenley	74
Norbury	75
Sanderstead	77
South Norwood	78
Thornton Heath	80
Chapter Four - London Borough of Greenwich	pages 84 - 133
Abbey Wood	86
Eltham	87
East Greenwich	92
Greenwich	98
Plumstead	109
Shooters Hill	114

Thamesmead	117
Westcombe Park	119
Woolwich	122

Chapter Five - London Borough of Lambeth   pages 134 - 161

Brixton	136
Clapham	143
Kennington Lane	145
Kennington Road/Vauxhall	149
Knights Hill/Lower Norwood	151
Gipsy Hill/Norwood	153
Streatham	156

Chapter Six - London Borough of Lewisham   pages 162 - 183

Brockley	163
Catford/ Southend Village	165
Deptford	167
Lee Road	171
Lewisham	173
Sydenham	178

Chapter Seven - London Borough of Merton   pages 184 - 211

Mitcham	186
Morden	191
Wimbledon	191

Chapter Eight - London Borough of Sutton   pages 212 - 227

Banstead – now Surrey	212
Carshalton	214
Epsom – now Surrey	215
Sutton	218
Wallington	222
Worcester Park Police Office	224

Chapter Nine - London Borough of Southwark   pages 228 - 264

Camberwell	229
Carter Street/Walworth	233
Grange Road/Dunton Road	239
North Dulwich	241
East Dulwich	242
West Dulwich	243

Peckham	245
Rodney Road	248
Rotherhithe	249
Southwark/Stones End	252
Tower Bridge	260

Chapter Ten - London Borough of Wandsworth   pages 265 -305

Battersea	267
Earlsfield	272
Lavender Hill	274
Nine Elms	277
Putney/ Jubilee House	279
Roehampton	284
Tooting and South Tooting	286
Wandsworth/Arndale Centre	290
Wandsworth Common	298

Chapter Eleven - Dockyard Divisions   pages 306 - 369

1860 - 1934

Woolwich	310
Portsmouth	322
Devonport	338
Chatham	346
Pembroke	357

1914 – 1926

Rosyth	363

Appendices

1. List of Police Officers mentioned in this book	pages 370 - 384
2. Metropolitan Police Warrant Numbers - 1829 – 2010	385 - 389

MORE BEHIND THE BLUE LAMP

INTRODUCTION

'More behind the blue lamp' is the second book which continues the research of the police stations and officers in London since the Metropolitan Police was establishes in 1829. The first book covered North and North East London and this book looks at South and South east London and Dockyard Police.

In 1829 the Metropolitan Police were established in London to control the streets of the Metropolis. They were one of the largest employers, at the time, and later they became one of the largest landlords in the country. Today the Metropolitan Police is still the largest London employer. They had highly regulated and disciplined work practices, which led to distinct work patterns that changed the nature of employment. This had far reaching repercussions for society at large mainly because of daily contact between the police and public[1]. Since that time much has been written about the police in terms of enforcement, however little has been done to tackle the institutional [2] nature of policing and to show the social side of the police organisation. This book aims to fill that void.

A large number of local histories have been written and many forget to tell the story of the local police. Other more general histories have been written which tell the story of how the police evolved from early times, yet they omitted the day to day functions and duties of constables apart from riots, murders, and the strange or outrageous. The histories of the stations, section houses and other police buildings, which housed our police in London were also left out. We aim to put this right and tell the individual station histories.

A great deal of the recent comment on the police has been critical, but it is easily forgotten that the British police represent an admirable balance between liberal and authoritarian control. The increase in the pace of life, improvements in communication and advances in technology are all issues of the moment, and are matters which the police must consider in their daily tasks. Yet in many quarters we seem to expect more from our police than we do from any other profession. Many people, these days, only see the police when a uniformed police officer attends an incident out on the streets, or when a police vehicle passes them either on patrol or answering an emergency call. Lack of resources have always kept the police 'low on numbers' a fact which led to the old adage that 'you can never find a copper when you want one'. This, together with the fact that the majority of people never see the inside of a police station except perhaps when portrayed on television, attracts accusations from some quarters that the police are a secretive, covert and biased organisation. This book looks at the police culture from its very beginning through its organisation, buildings, equipment, work practices and social groups. It portrays the police at work and play.

Many of the older police stations have disappeared, and new ones have been built to keep pace with the increases in population and new technology. Police stations, like hospitals and schools, add to our sense of community, and it threatens our security when police decide to close them for ever and this also generates a sense of loss for those living nearby.

The gradual increase in manpower, changing work patterns and the implementation of new technology have all created demands for more space. Although many of today's police stations have been rebuilt on the same original sites, many details, photographs and plans of the original buildings have long since disappeared. Our research has involved collecting material from a variety of sources including the archives of the Metropolitan Police Historical Collection (formally the Metropolitan Police Museum), the National Archives (formerly the Public Records Office) and many Local Authority Libraries.

We have examined and documented details from existing records in the south and south east of London, and have included stations which have at some time either been within, or are no longer in, the Metropolitan Police District. We hope the book will be of interest to a wide variety of people, particularly those who enjoy police history and also those serving and retired police officers, special constables and civilian support staff, who want to remember some of the police stations where they once served or were posted to. This book may also be useful to those who have an interest in family history and want to add more detail to their family tree of ancestors who were, and may still be, police officers. A list of the named officers mentioned in this book is shown at pages 370 – 384.

This book is an opportunity to look behind the 'blue lamp' in a socio/historical way, and to tell the stories of the people who have lived and worked in these police stations. It reveals how police culture developed historically, socially and institutionally. The book is organised and set within each of the borough boundaries.

The next section deals with the little understood aspect of the police rank structure which the authors have revised.

POLICE RANKS

Since the formation of the Metropolitan Police there have been a number of different titles used for various ranks within the structure. As the size of the Force increased it was necessary to increase the number of supervisors. The Constable rank supports all those ranks above in the hierarchy. The history of the rank structure is as follows:-

Constables/ Detective Constable

This is the basic rank at the front line of policing within the police service. Before the establishment of the Metropolitan police in 1829, constables were appointed to keep the peace and detect offenders without any organisation directly supervising them. Local householders also served for a period of twelve months as the parish constable. In the early days they wore a re-enforced top hat which did not have any badge at all.

In 1829 the divisional numbers were stitched on to the collars however when the uniforms changed in 1863 the top hat gave way to the 'Prussian Helmet' and the plate attached to the helmet had the divisional letter and number in the centre. The stitched numbers on the collar were replaced also with silvered metal. There were a number of different classes of constable, each being paid extra money as they moved up through the grades. The constable can be recognised by a number and divisional letter (or two letters which show a station designation) which are shown on either shoulder. Oil skin and cloth

Metropolitan Police Constable 1865 - 1871

capes were introduced for wear by constables and sergeants and in 1882 a new pattern of the cape was issued with a wider skirt and lower neck.

In 1951 an open neck tunic was introduced that showed the divisional letter and numbers on epaulettes[3] however the ceremonial No. 1 dress uniform tunic was still in existence and showed the identification around the collar. Today constables wear their divisional numbers and letters on epaulettes on their shoulders.

Sergeant/ Detective Sergeant (2nd Class)

The next rank above that of Constable is Sergeant. It is the first supervisory level in the command structure. This was the only military title adopted in 1829. The badge of rank is that of triple chevrons on the sleeves. They are also known as Section Sergeants, as they supervised eight to ten Constables patrolling a section of the division. The badge of office was changed in 1864 and consisted of three chevrons made of silver lace (Russia Braid) together with worsted chevrons for greatcoats. At the start they were worn on the upper right arm only but after a few months they were worn on both arms. Within their one rank there have in the past been designated classes subdividing the rank. The rank of Acting Sergeant was introduced in 1864 to cope with the increasingly heavy work load of substantive sergeants. These constables who were considered responsible enough wore a pair of silver lace chevrons usually on one upper arm.

From 1872 until 1875 there existed the post of Schoolmaster Sergeant. The post was created due to the high rate of illiteracy in the Force. Whilst today sergeants perform a range of duties within their rank there have been divisions within the sergeant rank. Sergeants perform Custody Officer Duty when they are attached to charge rooms and Custody Suites. They can also be Section Sergeants, which requires them to perform duty out on the streets or section of the sub-division. Sergeants can also be attached to the Criminal Investigation Department (CID) but they wear no overt badge of rank because they operate mainly in plain clothes. Their identity and rank can be verified by disclosure of their warrant cards. The rank of acting sergeants still exists on a temporary basis and those nominated wear two stripes of the silver lace on each arm or cut down metal sergeant's stripes for attachment to the epaulette.

Station Sergeant /Detective Sergeant (1st Class)

In 1868, owing to a lack of Inspectors at that time, the senior Sergeant was known as the Station Sergeant/Clerk Sergeant and deputised for the Inspectors who were in charge of stations on the Division. The Chief Inspector rank was created in 1869, Inspectors on the Division became 1st Class and 2nd Class inspectors and then in 1878 Station Sergeants became 3rd class inspectors. The rank of Clerk Sergeant was created to be responsible for administrative work on a Division and was introduced in 1875. Originally the sergeants added an extra bar to the three chevrons making a four bar Sergeant however this was phased out in 1921 when a Tudor crown replaced the fourth bar. The picture above shows a Sergeant with four bars on each upper arm dated 1902. The picture below shows the badge of rank for Station Sergeant post 1921.

Station Sergeant pre 1921

From 1890 until 1973 the rank of Station Sergeant was unique to the Metropolitan Police and replaced the short-lived rank of Sub-Inspector. The badge of rank was three chevrons with a crown above the chevrons.

In 1950 a chromium-plated badge of four stripes was allowed on epaulettes for bush-type shirts (1961) and raincoats (1962)[4]. The rank was phased out in the 1970s when the last Station Sergeant retired.

Station Sergeant post 1921

Inspector/Detective Inspector/Junior Station Inspector/Station Inspector/Sub-Divisional Inspector

This rank was introduced in 1829 as the next supervisory level above that of a Sergeant[5]. At that time the next level above the Inspector was the Superintendent who was in charge of the Division. In 1838 Inspectors with Constables and Sergeants were permitted to wear suitable belts that were 2 and half inch wide with a brass buckle. In 1841 Inspectors had an embroidered double "'crow's toe' emblem" containing the divisional letter sewn onto the coat collar. The collar of the inspector's uniform showed silver oak leaves in the 1860's. The most able Inspector were promoted to Superintendent and the best Sergeants to Inspector. As can be seen from the 1864 picture below left there was very little elaboration on an inspector's uniform to denote the importance of the rank or set it apart from other ranks including that of superintendent. The Inspectors and Superintendents top hats were 1 inch taller than those worn by Constables and Sergeants.

By 1868 there were insufficient Inspectors so the rank of Station Sergeant was created between that of Sergeant and Inspector. In 1869 Inspectors were graded in classes from one to four with Inspectors on Division becoming 1st Class. In 1878 Station Sergeants were appointed for a short period of time as 3rd class Inspectors[6]. The picture at left shows an Inspector pre 1864 with Victorian top hat. By the 1880's Inspectors wore a helmet and plate similar to constables and sergeants except it showed a large divisional letter in the centre as shown in the illustration above.

Victorian Inspector pre 1864

Victorian Inspector's Helmet Plate for 'G' Division

The Inspector was responsible for the proper and efficient running of a police station. The picture at right shows an ordinary uniform Inspector with Kepi hat (introduced in 1865)[7] without badge or any indications of rank on the jacket collar, but with medals and ceremonial gloves. The medals are the 1887 Silver Jubilee, the 1897 bar, and the 1901 Coronation medal.

It appears that the picture was taken in a station yard outside the parade room.

The single star shown at left is the badge of rank for an Inspector. Inspectors had

Pre 1953 Inspectors silver star

Inspector circa 1906

ix

a better standard of uniform than Constables and Sergeants, with one inch black braid on the cap and four rows of black cord with drop loops on the shoulders on ceremonial uniforms[8]. The dark blue caps with ventilation holes shown below were introduced in 1906[9] and finally replaced the kepi in 1908.

From 1916 all Inspectors, Chief Inspectors and Sub-Divisional Inspectors wore a crown badge on the cap, although a simple metal crown had been unofficially worn prior to this date[10].

By 1919 the senior Inspector was known as the Station Inspector. Both Superintendents and Inspectors replaced their braid on their collars for two stars (sub-divisional Inspectors) and one star (Inspectors) in 1921. In 1922 all Inspectors were required to display their badge of rank on mackintosh epaulettes and greatcoats[11]. Lord Trenchard introduced the rank of Junior Station Inspector for the graduates from the newly formed Hendon College, but the rank was abolished in 1939. In the 1960s Temporary Inspectors wore only one star (shown above) during their probationary period. The picture at left shows an Inspector with ordinary plain flat cap without badge.

Inspector with flat hat without black braid peak

The picture at right shows a Sub-Divisional Inspector (SDI) in normal daily uniform plus spurs and a ceremonial sword. The SDI was first introduced in 1887 and a number of senior inspectors were re-designated. The picture shows the SDI with a star (introduced in 1904) located on each side of the collar and a hat badge on his cap issued in 1906 for use during the day and at night. The cap had a black patent leather chin strap secured by 2 silk buttons on the sides.

INSPECTOR

Sub-Divisional Inspector circa 1916

x

Inspectors would generally be accomplished horsemen because supervision at the turn of the century was often done on horseback especially in the outer Divisions. They therefore had riding equipment as shown in the photograph and would also have their chin straps down to secure their flat cap during riding. This Inspector is also displaying his service medals starting at left with the 1897 Jubilee, the 1901 Coronation and the 1911 Coronation medals. This meant that he took an active part in the celebrations and was on duty almost certainly as part of a serial of officers policing the event. It is hard to judge whether the picture was taken for ceremonial purposes, although this is doubtful otherwise he would have worn his more ornate ceremonial tunic with embellishments. The single star shown at right is the badge of rank for a temporary Inspector issued in the 1930s.

Two stars were introduced for SDIs in 1921 and all inspectors were now to wear one star on their collars of their tunics and on the shoulders of their greatcoats.

The current badge of rank for an Inspector is two stars and this is worn on the shoulders. The Inspector's kepis shows black braid on the peak (as shown on the cap of the Sub-Divisional Inspector above).

Chief Inspector/Detective Chief Inspector

The rank of Chief Inspector was introduced first in the CID in 1868 and in 1869 to Divisions. The Inspector's uniform, cap, kepis and other items of clothing remained the same for Chief Inspectors.

In Victorian times the rank was denoted with scrolled silver braid on both sleeves and silver oak leaves on the collar as shown at right. A silver Victorian crown for Chief Inspectors was introduced in 1871. Between 1875-6 the crown was displayed on each sleeve. The crown was again placed on the peaked hat in 1887 being replaced by a silver crown in 1896, an

Victorian Chief Inspector in ceremonial dress with sword

imperial crown in 1901 and a Tudor crown in 1911. In 1871 silver loops in bay leaf embroidery were introduced on the sleeves of the uniform as shown in the picture above.

Some confusion exists as both Chief Inspectors and superintendents wore crowns in their caps. The chief inspector had a smaller crown and a narrower peak. Superintendents were issued with these crowns which they hold to the present day.

Mackintoshes were issued to Chief Inspectors in outer divisions in 1904 and inner divisions in 1914[12]. The badge of rank was originally a crown but this later became three stars. In the picture at right the Chief Inspector is standing outside Buckingham Palace. The Chief Inspector is the last inspecting and federated rank before the Superintendent Ranks. Shirts, collars and ties were issued to Chief Inspectors in 1947. Open pattern jackets were also issued as was a new pattern cap with black braid peak.

Victorian Chief Inspectors' helmet plate

Chief Inspector circa 1916

Superintendent/ Detective Superintendent

The Superintendent rank in 1829 was the highest rank below the two Commissioners. The title used by them was seen as non-military and the same as used by orphanages, schools etc.

Between 1830 and 1843 a small piece of silver lace on the coat or the greatcoat collar denoted the badge of rank for Superintendent[13]. The tunic was single breasted having hook and eye fastening to enable them to done up. They had no shoulder straps and the

Superintendent Grade 1 - Pre 1953

xii

front was edged with two rows of plain black braid. There was an Austrian knot on the cuffs.

Later the badge of rank became a Tudor crown. When the Metropolitan Police District was extended in 1840 to cover an area of just under 700 square miles (about six times its former size) an Inspecting Superintendent was appointed. His job was to travel around the District and save the Commissioners a great deal of routine supervision[14].

In 1872 Superintendents wore kepi style caps, which differed from the Inspectors because it had a smaller peak. Whilst the peak for Inspector's was horizontal, for Superintendent's it was slashed to a 45° angle. The picture above right shows a

Victorian Superintendent's Helmet

Superintendents helmet with chain mail surround and Victorian Helmet plate badge bearing the letters VR. Superintendents were able to wear a Kepi of the standard pill box type with ventilation holes which had a crown at the front, knitted buttons and surrounded by black scroll embroidery. Kepis were replaced by caps in 1906.

The single crown shown at right shows the St. Edward's crown issued in 1953 until 1959 for grade 2 superintendents. Prior to 1953 there were three grades of Superintendent. Although designated by the Police Act 1964, which introduced two grades of Superintendent, these grades had been in force since 1953[15]. These were termed Class I and Class II and the same badge of rank was worn i.e. the crown. Class I Superintendent's in the Metropolitan Police were often called Chief Superintendents (see below). In 1959 grade 2 Superintendents were abolished. At the same time, Superintendents were required to remove the Imperial crown in favour of the St. Edward's crown pattern. The Metropolitan Police

SUPERINTENDENT

A Grade 2 Superintendent's crown pre 1953

Superintendents Class I wore a crown and Bath Star later known as Chief Superintendents[16].

Chief Superintendent/Detective Chief Superintendent

The first time the term Chief Superintendent was used in the Metropolitan Police was in January 1866 when the Superintendent on 'A' Division was recognised as the senior Superintendent and officially designated Chief Superintendent. The term only lasted until February 1869 when it was discontinued[17]. In 1949 the rank of Chief Superintendent was reintroduced initially to take charge of Divisions, which later became Districts. Divisions were divided into Sub-Divisions. It was phased out in 1995 as a formal rank although it is currently used as recognition of seniority. The badge of rank is a crown above a star.

This senior officer of the Metropolitan Police is wearing his ceremonial uniform together with a sabre. His helmet shows the 1911-1935 Senior Officer's ornate helmet plate together with a braided chin strap. His ornate ceremonial uniform befits the rank of Chief Superintendent. It was probably taken around 1935 for the Jubilee celebrations. Additionally he is wearing three medals, which from left to right are the Order of St. John of Jerusalem medal, the 1911 silver Coronation medal and the 1937 Coronation medal. One noteworthy point from this photograph is the fact that he does not have a moustache or beard which was common at the time for most police officers. The badge of rank to the left is the old style (1930s) Chief Superintendent's insignia.

Divisional Chief Superintendent Circa 1936

Chief Superintendent badge of rank - pre 1953

The Superintendent below is John Michael Mulvaney KPM. He joined 'H' Division of the Metropolitan Police as warrant number 54255 on 29th May 1871. He later rejoined 'H' Division as

Divisional Superintendent on 8th November 1895 and retired on 2nd September 1911 aged 61 years and with forty years service. He was awarded the King's Police Medal on 5th January 1912 after he retired for distinguished service. This picture of Mulvaney shows him wearing a flat cap introduced in 1906[18] with an embroidered crown at the front. He is shown wearing his ceremonial uniform although not with his sword or ceremonial helmet as shown in the illustration above.

John Michael Mulvaney
'H' Divisional Superintendent

CHIEF SUPERINTENDENT

In 1960 summer wear (lightweight) jackets were introduced for superintendents. Also in 1968 a lightweight light blue terylene cotton jacket was introduced for office duties.

Today, Borough Police Commanders hold the rank Superintendent Grade I but wear the crown and star attributed to the Chief Superintendent - a rank which was phased out in 1995. The additional star is to denote seniority over Superintendents (Grade II).

Chief Constable

Chief Constable, Deputy Commissioner and Assistant Commissioner

In the Metropolitan Police, this rank was created in 1886 (other Forces had Chief Constables before this) and in rank order is between Superintendent and Assistant Commissioner. It was given to the four District Superintendents placed in charge of groups of Divisions in 1869. In 1889 the first Chief Constable was appointed within the CID. The post holders were based at Scotland Yard until 1918 when they were required to work from an office within their own District[19]. The creation of the rank of Deputy Assistant Commissioner in 1928 was seen as more senior than the rank of Chief Constable, which was finally abolished within the Metropolitan Police in 1946.

xv

The picture at right shows Chief Constable P. V. Sprules MBE in 1939 who was attached to 4 District Headquarters. This is one of the only known pictures which feature a Chief Constable within the Metropolitan Police. It appears that his badge of rank shows cross tip staves in a bay leaf wreath – the same for Deputy Commander. He is shown wearing a collar and tie, open neck jacket with waist band and breast pockets. He is also wearing shoes rather than boots.

Chief Constable P.V. Sprules MBE 1939

Deputy Commander

Deputy Commander 1946 - 1972

The post was created in 1946 when the rank of Chief Constable was abolished, as a deputy to the new rank of Commander[20]. The badge of rank for Deputy Commander was crossed tip staves in a bay leaf wreath which were later used for Commanders. When the re-grading took place in the late 1960's most Deputy Commanders were re-graded as Commanders. The rank was abolished when those not re-graded retired.

Commander

The rank is between Chief Superintendent and Deputy Assistant Commissioner. It is the lowest rank of Chief Officer, conferring membership of the Association of Chief Police Officers (ACPO). It was introduced in 1946 to take charge of the four Districts of London. It is held to be the equivalent to Assistant Chief Constable rank. The rank of Commander today dropped the star leaving the crossed tip staves in a bay leaf reef.

Commander 1946 – 1969

When the rank was introduced the badge of office was similar to Deputy Commander but with the cloth star later used for Deputy Assistant Commissioners. In the late 1960s the Divisions were renamed Districts and the majority of the Chief Superintendents were promoted to Commander. The four original Districts were renamed Areas, and a Deputy Assistant Commissioner was placed in charge of each. The badge of rank for a Commander is crossed batons on a laurel wreath[21]. Two silver braid strips on an embroidered georgette are stitched onto the collar either side. The hat is embellished with laurel silvered braiding to the front of the cap.

COMMANDER

The uniform of Commander Baxter

Deputy Assistant Commissioner

The rank was introduced in 1919[22] and was used to head departments at New Scotland Yard. In 1925 the Bath star was added to the crossed batons[23]. In 1933 the four Chief Constables in charge of each of the four districts were replaced by four Deputy Assistant Commissioners (DACs). The DACs rank was seen as a grade senior to the Chief Constable rank it replaced. In March 1946 on each of the four Districts of the Metropolitan Police, the title of DAC was changed to Commander and that of Chief Constable to Deputy Commander[24]. The DACs replaced the Commanders in 1969 in each area and the DAC's deputy, a Commander, took over an inspectorial role over the Districts, which were themselves now commanded by Commanders.

In 1976 the DACs took over more of an operational and administrative role[25]. In 1995 it was considered that that it was not necessary for there to be the two ranks, DAC and Commander, to occupy the position between Superintendents and Assistant Commissioners. The

DEPUTY ASSISTANT COMMISSIONER

DAC title has been given to some Commanders to reflect higher responsibilities. The badge of rank is cross batons on a Laurel wreath and one Bath star. The collar georgette is also longer than those of Commanders.

Assistant Commissioners

The rank was first authorised in 1856[26]. The number of Assistant Commissioners was originally two but it was increased to three in 1884[27]. The number of Assistant Commissioner's were further increased to four in 1909[28] and to five in 1933[29].

The Assistant Commissioners were in charge of major head-quarter departments at New Scotland Yard. In recent years some of the Assistant Commissioners have been moved from New Scotland Yard and put into operational command positions. The badge of rank which has remained consistent (save for the crown) is the cross batons on a laurel leaf and a crown. The illustration at left is the current badge of rank introduced in 1953 and up until 2000 was also used for the Deputy Commissioner.

Deputy and Assistant Commissioners circa 1946

Assistant Commissioner

Deputy Commissioner

The fifth Assistant Commissioner post was created in 1933[30] and allowed the Force to use one of the Assistant Commissioners as a Deputy to the Commissioner. The rank was officially introduced in 1919 with a new pattern of uniform and marked the first time that the Commissioner and the Assistant Commissioner had a service uniform. Until 2000 the post holder wore the badge of rank of an Assistant Commissioner but now has Cross Batons on a laurel wreath, and small stars and a crown.

Deputy Commissioner

Commissioner

The Crown appoints the Commissioner, on the recommendation of the Home Secretary after recommendations made by the Metropolitan Police Authority and since 1999 and any recommendations made by the Mayor of London (Sec 9b Greater London Authority Act 1999). The Commissioner heads the Metropolitan Police Service. When the Metropolitan Police was first formed there were two Commissioners but only one from 1856[31]. The Commissioners badge of rank is Cross Batons on laurel wreath, one crown and a Bath star. To the left is the older commissioner's badge of rank which shows a Tudor crown rather than a St. Edwards Crown as worn today.

Pre 1953 badge of office

COMMISSIONER

There are two types of rank for Commissioner one having metal insignia whilst the other is of fabric construction. Furthermore the insert to the St. Edwards crown is now shown in blue rather than red. The metal embellished epaulette was for wear during inclement weather and for use on mackintoshes or operational jackets etc. The fabric epaulette is for normal day wear with a tunic and changed when Sir Ian Blair was Commissioner.

The picture at left shows the Metropolitan Police Commissioner Sir Joseph Simpson in his full ceremonial dress and medals taken in around 1960. Sir Joseph Simpson tragically died in 1967 whilst still serving. His death can be attributed to over work as he was a reforming Commissioner but at the same time

Sir Joseph Simpson Commissioner 1958 - 67

was a policeman having risen through the ranks. He was the third commissioner to die in service.

---

[1] Shpayer-Makopv, H. (2002) The making of a Policeman. Ashgate Press, Aldershot
[2] Ibid p7.
[3] Fido, M. and Skinner, K. (1999) The Official Encyclopaedia of Scotland Yard. Virgin, London
[4] Fairfax, N and Wilkinson, V. (1969) Uniforms of the Metropolitan Police (unpublished) Metropolitan Police Museum, Charlton
[5] Ibid
[6] ibid
[7] Fairfax, N and Wilkinson, V. (1969) Uniforms of the Metropolitan Police (unpublished) Metropolitan Police Museum, Charlton
[8] Ibid
[9] Ibid
[10] Ibid
[11] Ibid
[12] Ibid
[13] Ibid
[14] Heron F.E., (1970) A Brief history of the Metropolitan Police. p.17 (Unpublished)
[15] Fairfax, N and Wilkinson, V. (1969) Uniforms of the Metropolitan Police (unpublished) Metropolitan Police Museum, Charlton
[16] Devlin, J. D. (1966) Police Procedure, Organisation and Administration. Butterworths, London
[17] Ibid
[18] Fairfax, N and Wilkinson, V. (1969) Uniforms of the Metropolitan Police (unpublished) Metropolitan Police Museum, Charlton
[19] Metropolitan Police Orders dated 16th November 1918
[20] Metropolitan Police Orders dated 15th March 1946
[21] Fido, M. and Skinner, K. (1999) The Official Encyclopaedia of Scotland Yard. Virgin, London
[22] s11 Police Act 1919
[23] Fairfax, N and Wilkinson, V. (1969) Uniforms of the Metropolitan Police (unpublished) Metropolitan Police Museum, Charlton
[24] Heron F.E. (1970) A Brief history of the Metropolitan Police. P.17 (Unpublished)
[25] Metropolitan Police Orders dated 2nd July 1976
[26] s2 Metropolitan Police Act, 1856
[27] s2 Metropolitan Police Act, 1884
[28] s3 Police Act 1909
[29] Metropolitan Police Act, 1933
[30] Ibid
[31] s1 Metropolitan Police Act, 1856.

Chapter 1

London Borough of Bexley

Introduction

The village of Bexley (nowadays known as Old Bexley) has origins going back to the Domesday Book, and was included in an earlier Charter dating from 814 AD.[1] In the early 1820s the Bexley Vestry consulted with neighbouring parishes to set up a nightly foot and horse patrol because of an increase in crime, and in 1825 the presence of a Constable (a Mr Viner[2]) was recorded as being insufficient to stop indecent exposure and gambling on the heath. When the Metropolitan Police was formed in 1829, Bexley was unaffected, because it was outside the new police boundary which had originally been set at seven miles from Charing Cross. The nearest Police Division to Bexley was 'R' or Greenwich Division, formed in February 1830.

The area now covered by the London Borough of Bexley was then very clearly rural Kent in its nature. Although well outside the jurisdiction for the policing arrangements set up for the capital city, the London to Canterbury Roman Road, Watling Street, did pass nearby across uninhabited heath land where the only building was a coaching inn called The Golden Lion. The nature of this lonely road was the cause of some anxiety to travellers, not least because of the problems caused by highwaymen. One such highwayman, John Popham preyed on travellers, but in later life turned to the good, and apparently even became Lord Chief Justice from 1592 – 1607 [3].

For the new Metropolitan Police, London itself was the priority, but the problem of highwaymen in and around Bexley had already been part of the operations of the Bow Street horse patrols that were originally started in 1763 and re-instituted in 1806. The Bow Street men apparently had patrols based at Shooters Hill, Welling[4] and on Bexley Heath.[5] In 1836, Bow Street's operations were amalgamated with the new Police, and the need to carry on protecting travellers may have been part of the reason for a Parliamentary Act of 1839 extending the Metropolitan Police District to take in Welling, East Wickham, Bats Well, Erith, Crayford, Bexley and Blandon. The problem continued to some extent for some years: in 1877, for instance, Superintendent Baxter reported on a serious highway robbery on Blackheath where the two thieves had escaped at the time, but were afterwards arrested at

Portsmouth and given seven years' penal servitude at the Central Criminal Court.[6]

The new police arrangements also included Bexley New Town, now known as Bexleyheath. The heath land had been 'enclosed' through two Acts of Parliament in 1812 and 1814, and by 1837 there were 170 cottages and 100 houses in this 'new town'.[7] Expansion of housing was a feature in the Metropolitan Police District throughout the Victorian period. The Commissioner's annual reports set out the numbers of new houses built year by year as a reflection of increasing demands on the Service. By 1889, a total of 525,107 new houses were recorded as having been built in London in the period between 1849 and 1889, along with 11,202 new streets and 102 new squares that were 1,888 miles and 697 yards in length.[8] By 1889, the establishment of the Metropolitan Police had reached 14,725 officers (1829 – 3,341), more than double the equivalent number of 6,758 in 1860. In 1889 the population of the Metropolitan Police District was 5,707,061 compared with 1,468,442 when Sir Robert Peel established the new police force in 1829. It was the growth of what we now naturally call Greater London.

In 1866 the railway reached Bexleyheath, followed by other lines running to Dartford in due course. Main roads such as the A2 and A20 also had their impact on what is now a London Borough without an obvious historic, commercial 'hub', but containing large suburban areas of housing, including part of Thamesmead, Little Heath, Bostall, Picardy, Belvedere, Lessness, Erith, North End, Slade Green, Barnehurst, Sidcup, Foots Cray and North Cray.

The first police station in the area was a house in Bexleyheath, opened in 1840, followed by Erith in 1847.

Local Authority arrangements also evolved over the years for an area that was in Kent, but also part of an expanding London. Old Bexley was a local government urban district in North West Kent from 1894. It became a municipal borough in 1935 and then became a London Borough in 1965 when it was combined with Crayford Urban District Council, Erith Municipal Borough, and the Sidcup part of Chislehurst and Sidcup Urban District. At this point, Bexleyheath Police Sub Division, later Division, attained the same external boundaries as its Local Authority, and remained part of 'R' Division. Sidcup, Erith and Belvedere were sectional (or Sub Divisional) stations.[9]

Belvedere Police Station (RB)

In August 1878, R Division's Superintendent H Baynes submitted a report about a police station for Lessness Heath, and Police Orders of 8 October 1881 indicate that from that date the new premises were taken into Police use, the address being 33 Woolwich Road, Belvedere.[10] The cost of the land had been £275, and the station itself £3,386. The ground floor of the new station comprised a waiting room, charge room, three cells, a store and a lamp room, and there was also a mess room, kitchen, and a brushing room where officers could maintain their uniforms. A right of way was negotiated over a private road leading into Albert Road, one of the legal details that often had to be negotiated for developing such premises.

Belvedere Police Station
33 Woolwich Road, Belvedere, Kent.
1881 - 1968

An Inspector Meering was transferred to take charge of the new station, with two other Inspectors, 2 Sergeants and 1 Acting Sergeant. A Mounted Branch officer joined them on transfer from Blackheath Road, Greenwich.

Andrew Meering had himself been posted to Mounted Duty earlier in his career on 'M' (Southwark) Division as a Sergeant in 1869. Police Orders of 3 December 1879 announced that he had been given a reward of £1 in connection with a case he had worked on. At this time, such monetary rewards were frequent, sometimes originating from a grateful victim of crime after approval by the Commissioner. The rewards from the Police Fund appear to have been balanced by monetary punishments for poor discipline. Superintendent Meering finished his service as the officer in charge of 'J' Division (Bethnal Green) and retired on an annual pension of £266. 15s 4d (£266.77) on 1 March 1895. [11] He had finished as one of 32 Superintendents within the

Metropolitan Police, aged 49. The physical nature of the job in the lower ranks was reflected by the fact that only two constables and sergeants still serving at the end of 1895 had managed to serve more than thirty years, having joined before 1864.[12]

When Andrew Meering joined the Metropolitan Police with warrant number 45200 at Great Scotland Yard on 29 August 1864, London would have been pre-occupied with the search for Hans Müller. He had killed a chief bank clerk, Thomas Briggs, on 9 July 1864 on a Highbury-bound North London Railway train, the first murder in Britain to have been committed on a railway train. Müller had accidentally left his hat in the compartment, however, and, in an age when all men wore hats, had put on Mr Briggs' hat by mistake instead of his own. The hat left at the scene of the crime showed a distinctive style of stitching where it had been altered to make it lower. It transpired that Müller was a German tailor by trade. The murderer had also exchanged Mr Briggs' watch chain at a jeweller's shop, and had given the box from this shop to the child of his landlord. Müller was identified as the culprit from this evidence, but he had already left the country for America. One of the early detectives, Inspector Tanner from Scotland Yard, applied to the Chief Magistrate at Bow Street court to commence one of the first extradition proceedings. Tanner set off on a steam ship, overtook the sailing ship on which Müller was a passenger, and arrested him in New York. Müller was brought back to stand trial at the Old Bailey and was executed in November 1864.[13] Detectives like Tanner were introduced in 1842, 13 years after the Metropolitan Police itself, and were not employed on local Divisions until the Criminal Investigation Department was formed in 1877.

The living accommodation for officers who lived at the new Belvedere station was assessed for rent purposes as 3s 6d (18p) per week for Inspectors, 2s (10p) per week for Sergeants and 1s (5p) per week for Constables. These sums of money were in effect the rent charged to police officers for their accommodation. The Metropolitan Police accounts for the year 1884-5 indicate that a total of £10,159 was stopped from the pay of police officers for lodging, whilst the equivalent arrangement for officers employed in Her Majesty's dockyards amounted to £1,814. In that year, the expenditure of the Metropolitan Police totalled £1,378,407.

The pay of inspectors, sergeants and constables amounted to £987,947 that year, by far the largest item of expenditure (72% of the total). £760 (0.1%) was spent on rattles, truncheons, whistles, revolvers and belts etc; £66,110 (4.8%) on uniform and clothing; £13,839 (1%) on horses, stabling, saddles and carts; and £50,464 (3.7%) on the purchase, building, repairs and alteration of police stations.[14]

The rear of the Police Station, showing a garden where fruit and vegetables were cultivated for the families living in the Station accommodation.

In October 1921, Bexley became the Sub-Divisional headquarters in place of Belvedere, causing it to be re-named as Bexley Sub-Division. Sub Divisional Inspector Frederick Lummus took command there at the rate of pay of 96 shillings (£8) per week.[15] He had originally been a groom from Ampthill, Bedfordshire who had joined the Metropolitan Police on 20 November 1899 (warrant number 85747) at the age of 22, and had served initially on 'M' Division (Southwark). He had been promoted to sergeant in 1905, station sergeant in 1909, inspector in 1912, and Sub Divisional inspector in March 1919. When he retired in November 1924 after serving three years at Bexley, he was awarded a pension of £262. 11s (£262.55) per year[16]. By 1931 the station was located on 'R' or Greenwich Division and its address had varied to 15 Woolwich Road, Belvedere, Kent[17].

From April 1958 until 26 July 1965, Belvedere was a police station that closed at night[18]. In 1959 a site for a new police station was identified 200 yards away, opposite All Saints parish church at the corner of Nuxley Road with Woolwich Road, where an empty Church of England school had been due to be demolished and replaced by four houses. In

Belvedere Police Station
2 Nuxley Road, Belvedere Kent, DA17 5JF
1968 – Present day

due course the new police station opened on that site on 13 May 1968.[19]

The former school on the site and its church connections was ironic; the older Belvedere station was referred to by some as 'the chapel on the hill' because of prayer meetings held by officers posted there.[20] The new station contained police station offices, a CID suite, a charge room, two detention rooms, three cells, a writing room and a meal room with facilities for cooking meals. The cost of the new building was £70,000. The exterior was faced with dark brown bricks to blend in with surrounding buildings, and had an oil-fired central heating system. The architects were J Innes Elliott, with Mr S J Hanchet from the Chief Architect and Surveyor's Department in charge for the Metropolitan Police.

Belvedere remained under the command of an Inspector when a reorganisation in 1965 created Chief Inspector or Inspector units for police stations in the outer parts of the Metropolitan Police District[21]. In

1999 there were reduced opening hours for the station due to a shortage of civil staff.

Bexleyheath Police Station (RY)

The Bow Street horse patrol had established what could arguably be described as Bexleyheath's first police station, but the first Metropolitan Police building at Bexleyheath was opened in the year 1840. It was not purpose-built, but took the form of a new house rented from a John Franklin for £28 a year, located opposite the Twelfth Milestone[22] (by the current Civic Centre). A Sergeant was in charge, with nine Constables.

There had been proposals from December 1839 to erect a new police station complete with cells to accommodate prisoners from Bexley and North Cray, and eventually this station superseded the 1840 house and became the third police station, built on the new High Road into Kent. The cost of the land had been £330 in 1852, and the building itself cost £1,452. Some records indicate that it opened in 1855,[23] but the Surveyor's Property Register[24] states 'Erected in 1858'.

Bexleyheath Police Station
28 Broadway, Main Road, Bexleyheath, Kent
1855 (1858) - 1908

The building featured a charge room, reserve room, mess, kitchen, and two cells, whilst the first floor included a loft. The station's postal address became 28 Broadway, Main Road, Bexleyheath but was eventually sold in February 1908 after the police station had been replaced.

The Inspector in charge was based some miles away, at Shooters Hill. He was not designated for a particular station, but took overall charge of Shooters Hill, Bexley and Erith. In March 1865, the Sub Division was enlarged when it took in Eltham section from Lee Sub Division, and in 1881 the Sub Divisional headquarters was transferred to Belvedere. [25]

Bexleyheath Police Station
57 Broadway, Bexleyheath, Kent
1908 - 1994

After 50 years, Bexleyheath's 1855 station had become inadequate. In fact a survey in 1881 revealed the Inspector and his family to be living in a small wash-house or scullery, into which a water closet opened. There was much urgent work to be done to improve the sanitation and ventilation, including the need to cure a smoky chimney in the mess room. In due course a new site was found at the corner of the Broadway and Highland Road (also referred to as Dover Road) for Bexleyheath's fourth station. The land for the site was bought freehold

8

by the Receiver in 1904 for £1,200. The new station was built for £8,187 and taken into use on 7 October 1907.[26]

The new premises were much larger than its predecessor. There was an Inspector's office, and with the charge room were four cells, two of which were for women, a room for the matron who would supervise female prisoners, four cells and an association cell. A day room was provided for officers separate from the mess room, space for food lockers, a kitchen and a scullery. On the first floor was a library for the benefit of officers living at the station who needed somewhere for leisure pursuits. There were two sets of married quarters and accommodation for 11 unmarried men. It would another decade before women police officers were first recruited.

Bexleyheath Police Rifle Club Winners 1913 - 1914

The early twentieth century was marked by significant social and sporting activities on the part of police officers. Pictures from Bexley Central library show the Bexley Rifle Club in 1913-14 with their trophies. Senior officers encouraged competition especially with reference to accurate shooting especially in the run up to the 1st World War as by this time it was felt that war was inevitable.

Shown overleaf is the 'R' Division band playing, probably at a local sports day where officers took part in athletics, including tug of war.

In July 1912 a list of police boxes connected to the station by telephone featured locations at Wickham Lane (Welling), Mottingham Lane, Kidbrooke Green, Crayford and Bexley High Street by the railway station.

The 'R' Division Police Band with Superintendent shown without an instrument and with his hands on his hips.

By 1924, the Crayford area hosted a box at Slade Green as well as by Crayford Bridge. Police officers were given keys that would open the entrance door of these kiosks, and would use the telephone inside to send and receive messages from the police station, or as a convenient point for meeting the Sergeant or another Constable. A light on the top of the boxes would flash when the station needed to contact patrolling officers. There was a small desk on which officers could write reports, and it would be possible for a police officer to keep a prisoner detained there until transport arrived to take them to the station. A telephone link to the police station was also available for public use. The chain of boxes across the Metropolitan Police District was completed by 1937, supplemented in some central London locations by police posts that performed similar, but more limited functions. By the late 1960s, the increasing availability of domestic telephones, the introduction of personal radios and the greater use of motorised patrolling for police officers made these landmarks redundant. Despite their eventual removal, the image of the police box has been maintained in the public's imagination by the 'Tardis' time machine featured in the TV programme *Doctor Who*.   An experimental modern version, equipped with CCTV, was installed near Earls Court in 1997.

By 2009, Crayford had a Safer Neighbourhood Unit based at 15 Princess Parade, Waterside, Crayford.

The tendency to interchange the names of Bexley and Bexleyheath was resolved in Police Orders of 30 June 1961 when the name of the police station formally became Bexleyheath police station. The address was originally number 57, later 39, Broadway, Bexleyheath, Kent.

Safer Neighbourhoods Office
15 Princess Parade, Waterside, Crayford.
2009 – present day.

Finally, on 26 April 1994, the fifth police station for Bexleyheath opened at 2 Arnsberg Way, Bexleyheath DA7 4QS to replace the one opened in 1907.[27]

The new location is close to a pedestrian precinct and one-way streets surrounding the Broadway, an example of how modern schemes have attempted to separate road traffic from shopping areas.

The origins of traffic congestion in London are not new. In a report on London's traffic in 1903[28] it was found that the streets of London had suffered from;

> 'the manner of growth, which was, for centuries, totally unregulated by the control of any central authority. Hence there is an absence of plan in the construction and arrangement of streets; and, in addition, no adequate provision has been made to meet growing needs. Apart from a few exceptions, the streets in London are as narrow and irregular as they were a hundred years ago.'

Bexleyheath Police Office
2 Arnsberg Way, Bexleyheath DA7 4QS
1994 – present day

The Commissioner was given legal power under the 1839 Metropolitan Police Act to make regulations for preventing obstruction in the streets, and much as the police would have preferred to have concentrated on dealing with crime and disorder, dealing with traffic congestion, regulations, taxis and buses rapidly developed into a police responsibility because the Metropolitan Police was the only body with a jurisdiction that ran across the whole metropolis. In 1919, the four departments of Scotland Yard were reorganised so that B Department, under the command of Mr Frank Elliott, took responsibility for all traffic matters.

One of the stalwarts in the new department was Superintendent Arthur Bassom who was given, along with a Mr Suffield Mylius of the civil staff, the title of Traffic Advisor. Superintendent Bassom took charge of matters concerning summonses for traffic offences, an index for stolen motor vehicles, an index of motoring convictions, and the Public Carriage Office that regulated and licensed taxis, buses, and their drivers. Arthur Bassom became known as the 'father of traffic policing' and was only the third officer to be promoted to Chief Constable from the lower ranks of the Service. He had been transferred to the Public Carriage Office in 1887, and had taken an interest in the mechanics of the new motor omnibuses introduced a decade later. He had acquired an international reputation by the time of his retirement in 1925, and was the driving force behind the development of the rigorous test of London demanded as a condition of a licence for taxi drivers. He was awarded an OBE in recognition of his contribution to the management of traffic matters in a crucial period in London's development. [29]

Safer Neighbourhoods Unit
Old Bexley Primary School, Hurst Road, Bexley DA5 3JR
2009 – present day

The vehicle fleet of the Metropolitan Police in 1919 comprised 35 vehicles, including 11 two-seater Fords for the use of Superintendents on outer Divisions such as R (Greenwich). In 1940 there were 1,260 vehicles, and by 1995/6 4,500 vehicles travelled 83 million miles and used 14 million litres of fuel.[30]

By 2009, Bexley itself had a Safer Neighbourhood Unit based within the grounds of Old Bexley Primary School, Hurst Road, Bexley DA5 3JR, utilising the old caretaker's cottage:

Erith Police Station (RE)

In 1847 a new police station, including a section house for single officers, was built at Erith at a cost of £583 17s 2d (£583.86). The address was in Back Lane, later designated as 103 Bexley Road, Erith.[31] The land was leased for 99 years, the landlords being recorded as John Williams of Denbigh and Sir H.Wheatly of St James' Palace, and later as Frederick Arthur Kelsey of Park Hill, Bexley.[32]

Erith Police Station
Back Lane later
103 Bexleyheath Road, Erith, Kent
1847 - 1908

The police strength at Erith was shown in Police Orders of 11 January 1864 as 2 Sergeants, 10 Constables and one Mounted Sergeant. In 1870 Sergeants Henry Wilson and Joseph Bond were in charge, with 17 Constables [33]. There were six night beats and two days beats in Erith in 1861. The substantive sergeant was responsible for the night duty parading at published times along with 7 constables. The acting sergeant was responsible for two day duty constables[34]. The inspector from Shooters Hill would pay periodic visits to Erith on horseback and provide an additional level of supervision often during the day duty whilst the acting sergeant was present[35].

Superintendent Charles Digby of 'R' Division reported that in early 1871, a Volunteer Fire Brigade was established at Erith.

> 'It is composed principally of young gentlemen of the neighbourhood, and has already done good service by prompt attendance and energetic action at fires.'[36]

Later in his report he described how an explosion had occurred on the brig 'Ruth' lying at anchor in the Thames off Erith. The cargo of paraffin, oil and rosin caught fire, exploded, and burnt the ship to the water line, seriously damaging two other ships nearby, but nobody was killed, and only one of the seven crew on board at the time was injured. During 1871, the Commissioner reported that throughout the

A picture taken in Erith in 1865 with police officers either end of the group

Metropolitan Police District, 619 fires had occurred that had required the attendance of a total of 16,950 officers (165 Superintendents, 667 Inspectors, 1,760 Sergeants and 14,358 Constables).

The picture above was taken is 1865 when the new uniform changed. The most senior rank at the station was often a sergeant however in the picture the day duty sergeant shown extreme left was a responsible constable who was selected to become an acting sergeant and having two chevrons instead of the normal three for substantive sergeants. The acting sergeant has the new coxcomb helmet whilst his constable shown extreme right still has the old style top hat.

In a report dated 10 April 1900, the Sub Divisional Inspector complained that the administrative portion of Erith station consisted of only one room measuring 13 feet by 11 feet 6 inches. Although formally recorded as a charge room, this one space had to serve as a parade room, charge room, office, and place where members of the public would be attended to, as well as where the 30 Sergeants and Constables paraded for duty in inclement weather. There were also two cells, two water closets and two stalls for horses, no doubt all subject to being used for other purposes because of the lack of space.

The Commissioner's Annual reports contained individual accounts of the activity on each Division for a period, and for 1869, the Superintendent was able to report that:

> 'very few events of importance happened in this extensive district... no serious accidents, loss of life or riot occurred.... Only one murder was committed (in Rotherhithe)... there was only one serious burglary... and only three cases of highway robbery'   The report then continued, 'Only three sheep were stolen on the Division; detection did not follow in [any] case, owing to the exposed and unfrequented places whence they were taken; one, there is little doubt, was taken in a boat to a ship lying in the Thames. Great facilities are afforded for this kind of felony, as numbers of sheep are grazed in marshes and fields at a considerable distance from the public paths and roads, and to watch them, the Police have to cross fields and endeavour to count them, night and morning, a duty more properly belonging to a shepherd or watchman, but I find farmers prefer an occasional loss to paying a watchman.'[37]

This temptation for seafarers to acquire a source of fresh food as they passed down the river was part of the reason for Thames Division officers also being stationed in the area, using the cutter 'Spray' as their floating base. She had been purchased on 21 June 1878 for £110 and with repairs needed in the sum of £90, but by 1891 the cutter had become dilapidated, and was run aground in the August of that year to prevent her from sinking. In December, the lighthouse at the end of Ballast Wharf was rented at 24 shillings per month from John Parish & Co for storage of equipment, rather than as an office or station, and the 'Spray' was repaired and sold.

By 1891 therefore, both land-based and river-based officers had serious problems with accommodation. The Superintendent suggested that the Thames officers should be transferred to Hammersmith because there was no longer a problem with sheep stealing. This caused much controversy and objection by riverside businesses, who were then assured that river patrols from another police ship 'Royalist' would

Erith Police Station
22 High Street Erith Kent.
1908 - 2000

patrol their area. The real answer to the problem, however, was to give Thames Division officers accommodation within a new police station planned for the area.

Properties at 59-64 Crayford Road were purchased, but the site was considered too far from the Thames for the river-based officers to use it, and eventually the freehold of another site at 22 High Street, Erith, next to the river, was bought in 1905[38]. The new station also had a base for the Thames Division officers which had its own designated call sign in 1966 which was UE. The Crayford Road houses were eventually sold in August 1927 for £1,000, well below the £2,500 purchase price in 1902.

The plot of land at 22 High Street, Erith, Kent was on the site of a large house once owned by a John Snow who organised illegal gaming on the premises and forfeited his house for building it without planning permission. In 1872, the house was replaced by three homes, some shops and a slaughterhouse. These were demolished in order for the police station to be built,[39] and it was duly opened on 16 November 1908.[40] The old station building was eventually sold to a Mr F A Stone on 18 July 1921.

The riverside location was not without difficulty at times. In 1937 it was reported that members of the public were using the landing steps for gaining access to the river, from where boatmen were running river trips. The public had started to use the station toilets indiscriminately, so locks were fitted, and notices displayed banning unauthorised access.[41] Thames Division retained Erith as a river police base until 1978.

An Erith Special Constable in the station yard, demonstrating a mobile air raid warning system in World War 1.

In 1973, plans were drawn up for a new police station for Erith, but they were met with controversy at the Local Authority's planning committee, where some councillors were reported as having considered that the modern design was more in keeping with 'a power station or a factory'.[42]

This was a reflection of the fact that police stations have developed public expectations and images over the years. The style of red brick and stone of the 1908 Erith station, as also seen at Bexleyheath in 1908, and Sidcup in 1906, exuded a sense of solid warmth, conservative respectability and approachability, important factors in the relationship between the police and the public.

The proposed replacement police station was never built, and its predecessor was eventually sold for redevelopment. Erith was a sectional station of Bexleyheath sub division in the 1960's.

In 2009 at Safer Neighbourhood Team base was located at 70 Galleon Close, Erith DA8 1AP. A flat was rented to enable officers to patrol locally without the need to go to the nearest conventional police station, but it was not available for any form of front counter service for the public. Erith police station was shut in 2000.

Safer Neighbourhoods Unit located in this block of flats at
70 Galleon Close, Erith DA8 1AP
2009 – present day,

Sidcup Police Station (RS)

Located in the South East part of the London Borough of Bexley, Sidcup had been covered by the Bow Street horse patrols from as early as 1805, and when the Metropolitan Police took over these patrols in 1836, two horse patrol 'stations' were rented at Sidcup from a Mrs Mauney of Footscray. Sidcup officially became part of the Metropolitan Police District in January 1840, when R (Greenwich) Division was extended to cover approximately the same area covered by the London Borough of Bexley today.[43]

A police station was set up in the village of Footscray to cover the villages of the Crays (ie St Mary Cray, St Paul's Cray, North Cray and Footscray), Chislehurst and Sidcup, and their prisoners were sent to the magistrates at Locks Bottom (see London Borough of Bromley).

In 1842 the Receiver took out a 61-year lease from Thomas Norfolk Brewery of Deptford on a house in High Street Sidcup, adjoining the

Sidcup Police Station
High Street, Sidcup
1842 - 1902

'Black Horse' public house, to form a police station with two cells, a mess kitchen, a charge room, a wash house and a yard at the back with two stables and two water closets. In 1845 a survey found that the cleanliness was good, but the drainage was very bad. The cesspool needed emptying and the water was unfit for use because the cesspool was near to the well. It was also felt that a dust bin and water butt was required. By 1850, the opening of a police station in St Mary Cray had enabled the territory to be split, and by 1855 magistrates attended Sidcup police station itself on the second Monday of each month to hear charges.

Sergeant Robert Saunders was the officer in charge at Sidcup, with 7 Constables. A comprehensive survey of the condition of Metropolitan Police stations in 1881 found that one of the walls of the sleeping rooms was damp, that the mess accommodation was not sufficient, and that a significant amount of work was required to make the premises satisfactory.

In March 1865, Sidcup section, which had been part of Lee Sub Division, was placed under Bromley Sub-Division that also then took in Beckenham, Farnborough and the Crays. In 1873, Chislehurst was split from Sidcup to become a Section in its own right[44].

Sidcup Police Station
87 Main Road, Sidcup, Kent
1902 - present day

The present Sidcup police station originated from a decision on 24 January 1896 to purchase land on Main Road for the sum of £620, and a newly built station, at a cost of £8062 14s, was opened on 13 October 1902. There was accommodation for a married Inspector, assessed for rent at 5s 6d (28p) per week, for a married Constable at 3s (15p) and for 6 single officers at 1s (5p) per week. As times had moved on, provision was not only made for an Inspector's office, there was also a waiting room for the public, a telegraph room, a parade room, a day room, mess room and kitchen. It was before the days of the London Ambulance Service, and an ambulance shed was provided at the new station.

Front elevation of Sidcup Police Station in 1908

From 24 January 1906, Sidcup became the Sub Divisional headquarters, taking in Chislehurst and St Mary Cray stations, an arrangement that lasted until 1932 when St Mary Cray and Chislehurst were transferred to 'P' Division, with Sidcup remaining on 'R' Division as part of Eltham Sub Division.

There was the reorganisation of Local Authority and Police boundaries on 1 April 1965 that split Sidcup from Chislehurst & Sidcup Urban District Council and brought it into the new London Borough of Bexley for Local Authority purposes. Sidcup police remained on R Division as part of the Bexleyheath Sub Division (later Division).

Run as a Chief Inspector Unit from 1965, a further reorganisation on 30 March 1987 removed the Chief Inspector (the author being the last Chief Inspector serving there in that role) and brought the Sidcup Sergeants and Constables within the responsibility of the Chief Inspector (Operations) and Inspectors at Bexleyheath who then had teams of Sergeants and Constables parading for duty at each station within the Borough. Three Home Beat Officers did remain permanently at Sidcup, however.

North Cray Safer Neighbourhood Team Office
Davis Way, North Cray DA14 5JQ
2009 – Present day

By 2009, a Safer Neighbourhood Team had established an office in the North Cray Neighbourhood Centre, thereby providing a police service in the same building as Local Authority-related services. This was located at Davis Way, North Cray DA14 5JQ.

Slade Green

In 2009, the Colyers Safer Neighbourhood Team had established an office in The Howbury Centre, Slade Green Road, Erith DA8 2HX, where the Local Authority also based a pupil referral unit.

Colyers Safer Neighbourhood Team Office
The Howbury Centre, Slade Green Road, Erith DA8 2HX
2009 – Present day

Welling Police Station

Welling was originally one of the bases for the Bow Street horse patrol in 1827 [45] but proposals for a police office were put forward many years later in March 1965 because of the growth in the local population and the 2 mile distance from Bexleyheath police station. The office opened at 60-62 High Street, Welling in April 1967.[46]

Welling Police Office
60 – 62 High Street Welling, Kent
1967 - 2000

In the year 1870, Superintendent James Griffin reported that there were three sheep stolen on 'R' Division. Two of them were taken away by boat, and remained undetected. The third, however, was found to be missing at 6.30am on 4 December 1870 when one of the shepherds employed by Mr Bean of Danson's Park, Welling went with the gamekeeper, Mr William Robins, and knocked up PC 110 'R'Bromage, who had just finished night duty. In an incident that would later resemble part of the training of the Dog Section, they found the thief's tracks, and, after 300 yards, the sheep's entrails. 100 yards later they found the animal's head and part of the carcass. They lost the track at a road, but later picked it up again on a footpath towards Sidcup. Three miles away from the sheepfold, the scene of the crime, they found a labourer, James Gilbert, with 20 pounds of mutton in a canvas bag under his bed. Gilbert was not known to have a criminal record, and was sentenced to 12 months' imprisonment at his trial at Maidstone. The gamekeeper Mr Robins and PC Bromage were each rewarded by the Commissioner for their 'tact and vigilance'. The shepherd, Mr Bean, was not rewarded, perhaps because it had been his duty to look after the sheep in the first place. Nor was any mention made about any part played by a gamekeeper's dog.[47]

Later in the same report for 1870, Superintendent Griffin states;

> 'the men generally appear to be well satisfied with their present condition, and having received an increase of pay, they very willingly gave up the weekly leave, for the one day in a fortnight. Every man in the Division subscribes to, and I believe feels proud of, the Metropolitan Police Orphanage.'

Safer Neighbourhoods Office
Falconwood, the Harris Academy,
The Green, Welling DA16 7QS
2000 – 2009.

The Commissioner, Sir Edmund Henderson, had achieved a rise in pay for his officers, but instead of one day's leave per week, their rest days were reduced to one per fortnight. An increase of 400 officers had been approved, and the Commissioner calculated that by the increased recruitment, and the reduction of leave for serving officers, 1,231 officers could be provided towards the 1,442 that he had stated to be necessary to protect the public in 1869.[48] A system of fixed points where the public could expect to see a police officer, was introduced at this time, and was generally acknowledged to work well. These fixed points at strategic locations no doubt added considerably to the tradition of a beat officer invariably being available to the public. In the days before telephones, the public would rush to that point to call an officer when they required. Today's more mobile patrolling officers are not predictably at one point, but are invariably seen when responding to a call. By 2000, the Welling office had closed, but later a Safer Neighbourhood Team for the East Wickham ward had been established within the grounds of a local secondary school in Falconwood, the Harris Academy, The Green, Welling DA16 7QS. In premises that had seen better days perhaps because they were once portacabins containing class rooms, the location was good for a police presence within the school, and was equipped with the *Aware* internal Metropolitan Police computer system. It was scheduled to be replaced, by premises in Bellegrove Road, Welling.

The Metropolitan and City Police Orphanage arose from the harsh conditions of service for police officers of the time. If a Constable died from injuries he received in the course of duty, his widow would normally receive an annuity of £15 plus £2.10s.0d for each child. It was about 50 years later that widows' pensions were introduced, and the welfare system which later developed within the Service was unknown at the time. In January 1870, a committee of five Superintendents had considered the Commissioner's proposal for 'a widows and orphans fund and an orphanage of small size for children who have lost both parents'. The Orphanage was established at Strawberry Hill as a result of this, and a subscription of 1d, later 3d (about 1p) per week was levied on all officers to support the scheme. Within 10 years it had become clear that no building could adequately house all the orphans, and widows were then given direct grants to support children who remained living at home. The Orphanage closed its doors in 1937, by which time 2,807 boys and girls had been accommodated, and 5,194 widows supported by grants for 10,000 children. The Fund still operates from its base at 30 Hazlewell Road, Putney, London SW15. [49]

---

[1] A Brief History of Bexley by John Acworth http://www.bag.org.uk/Education/education.htm
[2] Bernard Brown
[3] A Brief History of Policing Bexleyheath, by George Palmer.
[4] A Short History of Bexleyheath Police, compiled by Acting Police Sergeant Bernard Brown
[5] National Archives ref: MEPO 2/25
[6] Report of the Commissioner of Police for the Metropolis for the year 1877 C 2129.
[7] The History of Bexleyheath by Father Michael Jones http://www.stjvianney.net/bexleyheath.html
[8] Report of the Commissioner of Police of the Metropolis 1889   C 6237.
[9] Metropolitan Police Orders dated 6th August 1964.
[10] National Archives ref: MEPO 5/51 (394)
[11] Pension certificate. National Archives ref: MEPO 21/24
[12] Commissioner's Annual report 1895   Table No 7.
[13] Alan Moss & Keith Skinner (2006) 'The Scotland Yard Files', That National Archives, London
[14] Metropolitan Police. Appropriation Account 1884-5
[15] Metropolitan Police Orders dated 10th March 1919
[16] National Archives refs: Pension Certificate - MEPO 21/55;

Certificate of service MEPO 4/418.
[17] Kirchner's Police Index 1931
[18] Metropolitan Police Orders dated 1st April 1958 and 23rd July 1965
[19] Correspondence LB 532/-/0 and LB 532/67/1
[20] Bernard Brown personal correspondence
[21] Metropolitan Police Orders dated 16th March and 23rd July 1965.
[22] Bernard Brown personal correspondence
[23] National Archives MEPO 2/76 and 5/26 (152); LB534/-/0
[24] Surveyor's Property Register 1858, Metropolitan Police Historic Collection.
[25] Metropolitan Police Orders dated 10th March 1865
[26] National Archives MEPO 2/649; LB 534/-/0 and Police Orders 5 October 1907.
[27] Police Notices 14/94 of 6 April 1994.
[28] Quoted in 'History of the Traffic Department of the Metropolitan Police' by Chief Inspector K. Rivers.
[29] Martin Fido and Keith Skinner (2000) The Official Encyclopaedia of Scotland Yard Virgin Books, London.
[30] Report of the Commissioner of the Metropolis 1995-6
[31] Metropolitan Police Orders dated 20th June 1884.
[32] Metropolitan Police Property Register, 1845, Metropolitan Police Historic Collection.
[33] George Palmer
[34] Metropolitan Police Special Orders 1861
[35] Ibid
[36] Report of the Commissioner of Police for the Metropolis 1871 C 652
[37] Report of the Commissioner of Police for the Metropolis 1869 C 150.
[38] John Back
[39] George Palmer
[40] Metropolitan Police Orders date 16th November 1908.
[41] John Back
[42] *Police Review* 22 February 1974, and Erith and Crayford Observer January 1974.
[43] 'The History of Sidcup Police Station', by Acting Sergeant Bernard Brown. (undated article)
[44] Metropolitan Police Orders dated 10th March 1865 and 15th October 1873.
[45] National Archives MEPO 2/25 and LB557.
[46] Metropolitan Police Orders date 28th April 1967.
[47] Report of the Commissioner of Police of the Metropolis 1870 C 358
[48] Report of the Commissioner of Police of the Metropolis 1870 C 358
[49] http://www.met-cityorphans.org.uk/history.php and Martin Fido and Keith Skinner (1999) The Official Encyclopedia of Scotland Yard by, Virgin Books, London.

Chapter 2

The London Borough of Bromley

Introduction

Now a large part of the South-Eastern suburban part of the Metropolitan Police District, the London Borough of Bromley was firmly part of rural Kent when the Metropolitan Police was formed in 1829. Gradually the rural Watch Houses were taken over by more formal Policing arrangements as London problems expanded, and the small villages grew to become part of the urban sprawl. Successive Police and Local Authority re-organisations have also complicated the story of Policing the London - Kent borders.

Before the advent of the Metropolitan Police in 1829, the Hundred of Bromley and Beckenham had a lock-up cage for prisoners in Widmore Lane (now Road) Bromley[1], and a brick-built structure at Church Hill, Beckenham that displayed an engraved notice *'Live and Repent'* above its door [2].

To the South, St Mary Cray and St Paul's Cray were part of the Hundred of Ruxley. There were stocks and a lock-up in the parish of St Nicholas Chislehurst, whilst Farnborough village used the local workhouse at Locks Bottom as a place of detention. West Wickham, Downe and Keston also had stocks. Even Bromley was a small place at that time with buildings clustered around what is now the Market Square, and no development apparent in what is now Bromley South. The surroundings were definitely rural. The boundaries of the Metropolitan Police District were determined by the isolated but strategic points along turnpike roads, which travellers passed on their journeys towards London itself.

On 13th January 1840 the Parish of Bromley came within the jurisdiction of the Metropolitan Police as part of Greenwich or 'R' Division[3]. The codes shown for each Station originated from the telegraph system but have been changed over time and were reorganised in the 1930s during the changes made by Lord Trenchard. From September 1867 they were a two-letter short form of the Station's name, but were revised in March 1936 so that the first of the two letters would always match the Division. The codes that are quoted therefore reflect the fact that Police Stations in the London Borough of Bromley came under 'P' Division for much of their lives.

The letter shown on a Police Officer's uniform, with a Divisional number (eg P 123), was the letter of the Division for many years, but after a 1985 Force Organisation and Management Review under Commissioner Sir Kenneth Newman, the two letters of the Divisional Code started to appear on uniforms.

Between 1870 and 1913 one may also see photographs of officers with two letters, the second being 'R'. This referred to a Reserve pool of Officers attached to each Division who had been specially selected for duties when required and for public order and ceremonial events. They received extra money for this responsibility. An Officer from 'P' Division with this status would therefore wear the letters 'PR' during this period.

Bromley is by far the largest of the new London Boroughs and in 1981 the population was just over 296,500 people[4]. The local district Headquarters have traditionally been located at Brixton Police Station[5] not only in the 1860s but also the present day.

Beckenham Police Station (PB)

In September 1833, Alderman Wilson applied for Beckenham to be covered by the Metropolitan Police because of the number of robberies that were occurring[6]. A diary in Bromley Central library referred to a loaded blunderbuss being recovered in a haystack near to Eden Cottage, perhaps indicating an intention to attack a Mr Oakley who used to travel home that way at 10pm at night[7]. One Sergeant and 7 Constables were duly posted there as the result of the Metropolitan Police Act 1839, and a Police Station was taken into use from Midsummer 1843. It was described as a 'common brick, tile and slate built house with a 2-stall stable, two cells and a wash house in the yard, with a garden behind occupied jointly by the Sergeant and men'. The landlord was a Mr C L Wilson of The Cedars, Beckenham[8].

Beckenham police station in 1875

In January 1864, Beckenham was part of 'R' (or Greenwich) Division with 10 Constables and two Sergeants who patrolled either on foot or on horseback. In October 1865, a reorganisation of boundaries transferred these Officers away from their 'R' Division Inspector at Lewisham to become part of 'P' Division (Camberwell). Instructions were given that the Lewisham Inspector was to patrol the areas of Beckenham, Sydenham, Bromley and Farnborough. He was not to perform station duty as his time would be spent moving between the stations where he would sign the Station's Occurrence Book for supervisory purposes on each visit. The station strength was 1 sergeant (who would patrol on the Station's only horse) and then on night duty for 9 hours out of each 24 hours where he would supervise the 12 night duty constables. There was an acting sergeant who would supervise the 4 Day duty constables and post them to their beats[9]. The supervision during the day duty involved meeting the sergeant at pre-arranged times and places on their beats. Failure to rendezvous would cause alarm especially in outlying district's where on occasions tragedy could befall police officers patrolling singly who encountered gangs committing crime and intervened.

In 1876 the Metropolitan Police Surveyor reported that the Station well had been contaminated by nearby cesspools, and recommended that it be connected to the nearby water mains[10]. By 1881, Beckenham was described as 'an old dilapidated cottage'. The bedrooms were 'damp and ill-ventilated'. The cells in the yard were also damp and the roof said to be dangerous. Beckenham and seven other buildings were found to be 'dilapidated, unsatisfactory and unsuitable for the purpose they have to serve'[11].

In September 1882 the freehold of a site at 27 (re-numbered in 1934 as 45) High Street, Beckenham, was purchased where a new Police Station was built for £4,200 and taken into use on 25 May 1885. The land had been bought for £950 and the building costs had amounted to £4,022 12s 1d. The new building incorporated an Inspector's office, charge room, waiting room and a store on the ground floor, along with 2 cells and a larger association cell. There was also a day room, mess room, kitchen, scullery, a clothes room and scullery.

A hay-loft was provided over the 2-stall stable in the yard, along with a parade shed, where Officers were inspected before going out on patrol[12].

Beckenham Police Station
27 High Street, Beckenham, Kent, BR3 1AW
1885 - 2010

In 1881, a comprehensive survey into the Metropolitan Police estate examined 176 buildings, 158 of which were Police Stations and 18 were Section Houses. 74 were owned freehold; the remainder were leased. At the time there were 99 purpose-built Police Stations, 50 houses that had been adapted for Police Station use and 27 houses that had not been altered at all. 95% of single Officer's, and 3.5% of married men lived in Police Stations or Section Houses at the time, so that Police Stations were a mixture of operational buildings, and private accommodation. This was not always a happy combination. Families often had to use the charge room and other parts of the Station to gain access to their quarters, or to reach washing facilities, and there were complaints from families whose daughters had to live in close proximity to single men. Of the 176 Police Stations, 13 (8%), mostly in central London, accommodated 50 or more Officers, 26 (16%) had 20 – 49 Officers, 29 (18%) had more than 10, whilst 80 Stations, just over half, had fewer than 10 Officers in residence.

The residential parts of the Police Station were assessed separately from the operational Police part of the building. In November 1878 for instance, the Inspector's accommodation at Beckenham was rated at 4s 9d

(24p) per week[13]. The Station code in 1893 was 'BC' and was not altered until the 1930s during general re-organisation by Lord Trenchard[14].

The Charge Room was where the Inspector, later the Station Officer, would investigate the evidence of Police and private witnesses and decide on the charge to be faced by the prisoner. The room was also used at the time for accident cases where a doctor would examine the injured person. In the case of 45 Stations, the residents of the Police Stations, men, women and children, needed to pass through the room to gain access to their living quarters. The 1881 survey found there was rarely any space for more than one case to be dealt with at any one time, and there was no waiting room for the public at all in 143 of the 158 Stations.

There was an innovation at Bethnal Green Station where the public could see the Inspector without having to use the Charge Room, and gradually Station Offices developed which separated prisoners from the public's access points. Later, when Station Officers, often Sergeants, were required to deal with prisoners, they would walk from the Station Office to the adjoining Charge Room, from where there would be direct access not only to the cells, but also to a Surgeon's room where the Police Doctor could examine any ill or injured prisoners or Police Officers[15].

After the Police and Criminal Evidence Act of 1984, the post of Custody Officer was created for Sergeants who dealt with prisoners. They acquired more formalised legal and procedural responsibilities, and it then became unrealistic to combine these duties with those of Station Officer. The Charge Room is now referred to as a Custody Suite. This will typically have interview rooms with tape-recording facilities for prisoners, interview rooms for prisoners with their legal representatives, closed-circuit TV systems, automated fingerprint equipment, and computerised custody record systems. All prosecutions are now subject to being recorded on files, statements and other paperwork that go through the Crown Prosecution Service. It is therefore hardly surprising that there needs to be much more office space to accommodate the additional staff to cope with these processes. Whereas a CID office would typically run with support staff consisting of a clerk and a typist in the 1960s, there will now be a fully-staffed Criminal Justice Unit responsible for supervising and processing court papers, the warning of Police Officers and private witnesses for court, liaison with the Crown Prosecution Service, and reporting court results.

When the Metropolitan Police was first formed in 1829, the Police Officers who arrested a suspect would often simply take them before a magistrate who, at that time, would have taken on the responsibility for much more investigation of the offence and the prisoner's culpability. In those early days the legal system was much simpler, but harsh by today's standards. It was not until 1836 that a barrister was allowed to address the jury on behalf of a prisoner accused of a felony, for instance. There was no Court of Appeal to review a judge and jury's decisions until 1907.

In legal terms, it was the Receiver for the Metropolitan Police District who bought and sold Police Stations rather than the Police Commissioners. From 1829 until June 2000, when the Metropolitan Police Authority started its life, the financial and support arrangements of the Police Authority were formally the responsibility of the Home Secretary, but arrangements were established by Sir Robert Peel so that there was a clear demarcation between the Commissioners, who took responsibility for the operations and discipline of the new Police Force, and the Receiver who organised the finance, buildings, equipment and ancillary support. So all Police Stations were in fact the property of the Receiver whose legal status was a *corporation sole,* andwho had the power to levy rates from the Local Authorities within London for the Metropolitan Police, for the Inner London Magistrates' Courts Service, and later for the Inner London Probation Service. This legal status for a public servant was a convenient and efficient method of operating at the time, and it is doubtful if any other method could have raised so many resources in the short time between the passage of the Metropolitan Police Act through Parliament in June 1829, and the first patrols of the new Force on 25 September of that year. The first Receiver, John Wray, was a barrister by profession and throughout his tenure as Receiver he also held the position of Resident Director of the University Life Assurance Society. He retired in 1860 at the age of 78 years. Never a man to become involved in detailed financial records, bureaucracy or written memoranda rather than oral communication, his departure caused some concern at the Home Office where they were unable to locate the personal bond for £9,000 Wray had been given when he took up his post.

In 1929 Beckenham Urban District Council increased the height of the wall at the back of Beckenham Station yard as part of a development to provide flats for firemen.[16] The watchmen who had operated before Peel's new Police were responsible for preventing crime, but also for raising the alarm for fires, and calling out the time. With the advent of formally constituted Police Forces, the responsibility for dealing with fires fell back on to the Fire Societies who provided fire fighting equipment on behalf of their subscribing members. In 1835 the London Fire Engine Establishment was formed. In October 1835 there was a call for the Police to be put in charge of fighting fires after a large conflagration at Millbank Penitentiary. The Metropolitan Police acted as firemen at the British Museum in 1860, and there were comprehensive instructions for Police Fire Brigades employed at Royal Navy dockyards, where the Metropolitan Police undertook policing responsibilities from 1860 until 1934. The Metropolitan Fire Brigade began life in 1866. Responsibility for the provision of a fire-fighting force later became a formal Local Authority responsibility. In some cases the Fire and Police Stations were located in adjoining premises, particularly outside London where there was a closer relationship of both Services with the Local Authority. The clear demarcation between the Police and Fire Services of today did therefore have origins in a much less straightforward situation.

Beckenham was part of Southend Village (Catford) Sub-Division in 1932, but from 1 April 1965 both Penge and Beckenham became part of Bromley Sub-Division when boundaries were changed to become aligned with the new London Borough boundaries[17].In 1964 Beckenham was shown as a Sectional Station with Penge and Bromley Sub-Divisions on 'P' Division[18]. Further re-organisation of internal boundaries took place in 1974[19].

Elmers End Safer Neighbourhoods Team Office

In 2001 Beckenham was shown as PB, situated at 45 High Street, Beckenham, Kent, BR3 1AW, and was not a nominated Station under the Police and Criminal Evidence Act 1984. It was therefore not a Station for the processing of prisoners and the taking of charges for court. In January 2010 the Station, which was said to be the oldest Police Station in London, was shut for operational purposes and put up for sale. A new Police Office was purchased nearby[20] for members of the public to make their enquiries.

Biggin Hill Police Station (PH)

The history and development of the farmland and countryside around the Aperfield Estate took on new impetus with the arrival of the Royal Air

Force at Biggin Hill, particularly in World War Two. The Local Authority was Orpington Urban District, which was otherwise policed by the Metropolitan Police, but Biggin Hill was policed by Kent Constabulary. The area was intended for transfer to the Metropolitan Police as early as 1932, but this was delayed by World War Two, the transfer of 17 square miles finally taking place on 1 April 1947. At this time Kent's Biggin Hill Police Station, probably a Police House, at Westerham Hill was closed [21]. In 1966 plans started to be made for a Police Office to serve the rapidly expanding housing developments in the area.

The Home Office approved the purchase of 195 Main Road, Biggin Hill as a Police Office, which duly opened on 29 June 1970 as part of the St Mary Cray Sub-Division[22], but closed around 1999. Biggin Hill was a Station located on 'P' Division. A Safer Neighbourhood Team was based in the area in 2007.

The Police Office was similar to many rural Police Stations that, outside London, were the home of the local Constable. The premises would have the outward appearance of a conventional house, but would sometimes be equipped with a small cell, a Police sign, notice board, communications equipment and a reception area for callers who would not infrequently be dealt with by the Constable's wife. This typical pattern of rural Policing could not be sustained for towns and cities, where the Police Stations needed to be larger, with more cells, bigger charge rooms, and offices for clerical staff.

Biggin Hill Police Station
195 Main Road, Biggin Hill
1970 – 2006

In central London early Police Stations provided accommodation for single Police Officers on the upper floors and sometimes a flat for the Superintendent or other senior Officers in charge. There was therefore a ready means for regular 24-hour supervision by the Officer in Charge, notwithstanding that a busy Station would mean that he would be kept permanently busy. In a disciplinary climate that would be regarded as harsh by today's standards, the Officer in charge of a Police Station would never be able to advance any argument with his senior Officers that he had been unable to fulfil a responsibility because he was 'off duty'. The expansion of office staff gradually took over the upstairs accommodation that had originally been intended for Officers living above the Station. Snooker rooms, once a common feature in Police Stations, have also become offices.

Biggin Hill Police Office
192 Main Road, Biggin Hill
2006- Present day.

By August 2006, the house at 195 Main Road was due to be sold, and had been replaced by alternative premises a few hundred yard away at 192 Main Road TN16 5DT, perhaps reflecting a trend towards placing Police Offices in former retail premises rather than residential property. In 2007, the Office was open Monday – Friday 10am – 12 noon, staffed by volunteers rather than Police staff.

In January 2008, Beckenham police station formally closed and it was auctioned in March 2008. Safer Neighbourhood Teams (SNTs) were by then firmly established as a means of providing local ward-based policing teams, normally 2 – 3 Constables and 2 – 3 Police Community Support Officers (PCSOs), headed by a Sergeant and

Albermarle Safer Neighbourhoods Team Base
Albermarle Road, Beckenham, Kent

concentrating on locally identified policing priorities. Some months before the sale of Beckenham police station, a SNT base had been put in place at Albemarle House, Albemarle Road, Beckenham, serving Shortlands and Copers Cope wards.

Bromley Police Station (PR)

Two Officers of the Bow Street Horse Patrols were stationed on Bromley Common in 1805 to protect travellers from highwaymen. Bromley parish had a population of 4,000 and its own Constable, and so tried to form its own Town Police in 1835[23]; the tithe map for December 1839 shows a cottage rented to Police by Robert Booth Latter on Bromley Common near the modern junction with Gravel Road, a location which would have been well-situated for protecting travellers from highwaymen. Nevertheless, Bromley was taken over by 'R' or Greenwich Division of the 'new' Metropolitan Police on 13 January 1840. The new arrangements brought in two Sergeants (one of them on horseback) who were responsible for 4 Constables in Bromley, two in the parish of Hayes, and two in West Wickham. Bromley's Police Station in 1845, and probably for a few years beforehand, was a brick-built house in Middle Row, Market Place on a yearly lease from Mr Marsden, a brewer from Lewisham[24]. The building had no yard or back entrance, but did have five rooms and a charge room, and acted as the Bromley Police Headquarters until about 1862, by which time the population had increased to over 5,000, partly assisted by the arrival of the new railway stations now known as Shortlands and Bromley South[25].

Bromley Police Station
The old Market Square, Bromley
1840 - 1865

In 1865 Bromley acquired the status of a Police Sub-Division, with responsibility for Beckenham, Farnborough, Sidcup and St Mary Cray,

Bromley Police Station
Market Square, Bromley
1865 - 1915

and new premises, part of a new site containing the Town Hall, were leased from Lady Day 1865 for 99 years from Mr. Coles Childs Esq. This was for the purpose of a Police Station and Section house and formed part of 'P' Division. It contained a charge room and library. There were also 2 cottages although the Inspector resided in the Station with his family for a rent of 5s per week or £13 per year.

A Constable paying rent of 3s per week was allowed one of the cottages whilst a Sergeant rented the other cottage for 3s. 6d. rent perweek[26].

James Linvell transferred from Lewisham to take charge and lived in the new Police Station, which contained a charge room, library, 3 cells and a store on the ground floor. The library was a feature of Police Stations of this period, and was provided as a means of recreation, education and somewhere to sit for Officers not on duty. A mess for Officers was also provided, often in the basement, and the 1881 report found that the men would frequently socialise in the rather unhealthy climate of the basement, rather than in the better ventilated libraries. Bromley's establishment of Constables was increased to 18 in 1869 when it was supervised by a substantive sergeant and an acting sergeant. The Lewisham Inspector would pay periodic visits to the station and patrol the area on horseback[27]. Ten years later, when the third railway station (now Bromley North) was built, the station strength was increased to 29[28]. Bromley's Station code in 1893 was BM[29].

By 1912 two extra rooms in the town hall were rented for Police purposes, and there were two Police Cottages known as Nos. 1 and 2 Market Square. The landlord was Mrs Coles Child, and her agent was E. Britten Holmes from Bromley Palace Estate Office.

During World War One, on 15 March 1915, the Police Station was given up, and two Police Cottages retained, the rent reducing from £150 to £30 pa. This was because the Widmore Road Station was then taken into use under the command of Sub-Divisional Inspector Vincent Coster, Inspector Clement Burton, a Station Sergeant, eight Sergeants and 70 Constables. The rank of Station Sergeant had been introduced in 1875,

Bromley Police Station
Widmore Road, Bromley
1915 - 2003

and was a position of some status within the Force. These Officers wore four stripes on their uniform, and three stripes and a crown from 1921. The rank, mid-way between Sergeant and Inspector, was only used in the Metropolitan Police, and occupied a point in national pay scales that arguably prevented the progression of senior Sergeants. In 1972 the Metropolitan Police started to phase out the rank, and this process was finally complete in January 1980 when the last serving Station Sergeant in the Metropolitan Police, William Palmer, retired from Highbury Corner Magistrates Court.

The freehold on Bromley had been purchased in 1910 and was described in the Property Records of 1924 as a 'Station, Section House and 2 sets of quarters'[30]. Bromley's no 2 Police Cottage, had a stable behind it for two horses, a harness room, store sheds and an ambulance shed. Hand ambulances were used by the Police from 1860; it was not until 1915 that the Fire Service was authorised to open a number of motor ambulance stations, and the Metropolitan Police had run a small horse ambulance service for the sick from 1884.

The hand ambulances were made by Bischoffsheim, and comprised a stretcher 2.7metres (9 feet) long mounted on an axle with two large wheels, and a smaller wheel at the front. Although sometimes used to transport sick people, their main purpose became the carriage of drunken and violent prisoners, and they eventually passed out of use in 1938.

A cluster of three medals with the Kings Police medal at left together with the 1911 Coronation medal centre and the 1935 Jubilee medal at right

The cottage itself was let for 3 years from 1916 to Bart Cooper and eventually sold in May 1935 to HG Dunn and Sons Ltd. The Army (Eastern Command) occupied the old Police Station next to the town hall for 6 months from January 1917. Then the Bromley detachment of the 7th battalion of the Kent Volunteer Regiment was allowed to use the premises until the end of the war.

In 1921, Bromley Police were involved in a serious incident when PCs Charles Hall and Jack Lewis were issued with revolvers to try to arrest four armed Sinn Fein fugitives. A short gunfight ensued between the

Officers and one of the terrorists as they decamped from a taxi in Bromley, and all four were arrested. The two Officers were awarded the King's Police medal for bravery (KPM), a medal that had been instituted twelve years earlier after the 1909 Tottenham Outrage, a running chase and gunfight with two anarchists who had undertaken an armed robbery. At the time there was no medal available for recognising Police Officers' bravery apart from the Albert Medal (replaced in 1940 by the George Cross). Of 226 KPMs awarded up until 1940 to Metropolitan Police officers, 33 (15%) were for saving, or attempting to save life from drowning, whilst 26 (12%) were for going into houses or other buildings that were on fire. A large group of 41 (18%) were for dealing with runaway horses, but the largest number, including PCs Hall and Lewis, were the 63 Officers (28%) recognised for their courage in incidents involving firearms.

The current Police practice is to maintain Armed Response Vehicles to attend the thousands of incidents each year that involve some threat of firearms. PCs Hall and Lewis would probably have booked out the Police revolvers under the watchful eye of the Station Officer, and then to have responded to the incident with the best courage and initiative they could muster. The training is much more sophisticated these days, partly because of the development of a specialist Firearms Branch within the Metropolitan Police who monitor each time a gun is used by Police. The first known recorded use of a firearm by the Metropolitan Police occurred on 18 February 1887 when PC Henry Owen, another Officer serving on 'P' Division, fired six shots from his revolver into the air in Keston Village to awaken the inhabitants of a house which was on fire, after the officer's shouting, hammering on the door, and blowing of his whistle had failed to rouse them from their slumber. Six months later, PC Owen (warrant number 52206) had left the Service, suffering from general debility at 42 years of age. He was awarded an annual pension of £29. 12s 10d[31].

On 1 January 1932 Bromley Sub-Division acquired St Mary Cray and Chislehurst Police Stations from 'R' Division. It lost Beckenham and Penge to Southend (Catford) Village Sub-Division, only to regain them in the later reorganisation of 1965[32]. Bromley was completely refurbished and repainted in 1937 on the instructions of the Surveyors Department after 17 years constant use 24 hours a day[33].

In 1958 a Bromley Officer, PC Henry Stevens, became the second of only five Officers from the Metropolitan Police ever to receive the highest possible civilian gallantry award, the George Cross. The Officer was covering the back door of a house in Bromley where a break-in was reported, and gave chase to an armed man who ran away through the garden. As PC Stevens gained on him and shouted that he was a Police Officer, the man pulled his gun and shot the Officer at very close range in the face, breaking his jaw. Despite this, the Officer caught up with him, seized and disarmed him. The prisoner broke free, but PC Stevens caught him again, and before collapsing, kept hold of the prisoner's jacket that gave clues leading to the man's arrest.

Bromley South Police Station,
High Street, Bromley BR1 1ER
2003- present day

Although still standing in 2007, and in the process of being converted into flats, the Widmore Road Station was closed when, under a £120m 25-year Private Finance Initiative contract, a new Police Station and Borough Headquarters were completed in 2003 at Bromley South. This included the provision of catering, reception, and maintenance staff for the building. This system of financing, encouraged by the government of the day, made a break from the previous trend to own the freehold of sites and to contract out the building work direct. The new Police Station, in High Street, Bromley BR1 1ER, is vastly bigger than its

Walpole Road Safer Neighbourhood Team Base
Walpole Road, BR2 9SF
2009 – present day

predecessors, reflecting the fact that more support staff and facilities are accommodated in such Police Stations in the 21st century. It is a Borough Police Headquarters and was opened in 2003.

Since 1965, London Boroughs have shared boundaries with Metropolitan Police Divisions. Sometimes, like Bexley, one Borough equated with one Division. 'P' Division itself comprised the Boroughs of Lewisham and Bromley; in some Boroughs, like Lambeth or Southwark, a Borough even comprised three or four Police Divisions. This was because the Police workload did not equate with the population and other criteria that defined a viable London Borough. In 1999 Police Divisions were re-organised to match Boroughs more precisely, partly because of the introduction of the Greater London Authority and the Mayor of London. Divisional command structures were then varied, according to the workload of each Borough, and were no longer consistent with each other across the Metropolitan Police as a whole. Police Divisions had been referred to as 'Operational Command Units' for several years before this, reflecting a national policing trend, and then became known as Borough Command Units, or simply 'Boroughs'.

Bickley Safer Neighbourhood Team Office
121 Widmore Road, Bickley BR1 2RH
2009 – present day

The job of a patrolling Police Officer has changed dramatically, particularly since the advent of motorised patrolling has removed the necessity for walking many miles each day.

The post of Chief Medical Officer was created in 1830, and in 1899 there was concern about the high rate of suicides among Officers. Some commentators blamed the harsh discipline and insensitive handling of junior Officers for this. Bromley's new Police Station is equipped with a gymnasium to assist Officers to keep physically fit. The modern Police Service has a significant Occupational Health Service

Burnt Ash Lane Safer Neighbourhood Office
121-3 Burnt Ash Lane, Bromley BR1 5AB

that concerns itself with the mental as well as physical health of the MPS staff.

By 2009, a Safer Neighbourhood Unit was based at Walpole Road, BR2 9SF off Bromley Common, renting a house adjacent to a builder's merchant business, and featuring bicycle storage containers. This base served Bromley Common & Keston, and Bromley Town wards.

Another base, utilising a former shop serving Bickley ward, was based at 212 Widmore Road, Bromley, BR1 2RH. To the north of Bromley, another shop was rented for the Plaistow and Sundridge wards at 121-3 Burnt Ash Lane, Bromley BR1 5AB.

These premises provided a local base for officers to patrol from without their needing to visit the main police station. They are often in fairly prominent positions, but provide only very limited access for dealing with public enquiries. In 2009, these typically might be a 2-hour period once per week, but in some parts of London, a front counter service has been extended by the use of trained volunteers.

Chislehurst Police Station (PC)

Policing the area prior to the introduction of the Metropolitan Police had taken the form of the Bow Street Horse Patrol in 1805 when Stations at Sidcup and Bromley Common had been brought into use[34]. The village of Chislehurst

Chislehurst Police Station
Chislehurst Hill, Chislehurst
1888- 1893

possessed a lock up and stocks near the Bulls Head for housing of prisoners prior to removal to the Station House at Foots Cray[35]. In October 1873 a new Chislehurst Section was formed from part of the former Sidcup territory, the Station comprising two cottages at the top of Chislehurst Hill (now Old Hill) that were converted to provide a cell, a magistrates' room and a lobby on the ground floor, and a day room on the first floor[36]. The cottages were leased from Mr Thomas Townsend of 9 Glenrose, Chislehurst Common, and living accommodation was provided for a married Inspector. The magistrates' room was not used as such after 1884. The local Police were particularly busy on January 1873 and July 1879 for two funeral processions marking the deaths of the Emperor Napoleon and the Prince Imperial Louis Napoleon who had lived at Camden House, Chislehurst.

In 1888 the freehold of premises in West Chislehurst High Street was bought for £800 from a Mr Owen Edwards, and the new Police Station, costing £3,453 16s 8d, started operations on 24 June 1893[37]. This year also saw Police Orders give the station telegraphic code as CT when it was confirmed as a Station on 'R' Division[38].

Fire fighting equipment was kept in a temporary shed from 1896, for which Chislehurst Urban District Council paid 5 shillings a year rent, and a more permanent structure, which effectively became a Fire Station, was built in 1910. When a motor fire tender was placed in the new structure, the Receiver for the Metropolitan Police District made new financial proposals and the Council withdrew their equipment from the shed[39]. Notification was received in 1927 that the address was 27 High Street as from the 19th May[40].

The premises included an Inspector's office, a charge room, waiting lobby, 2 cells, an association cell for more than one prisoner, an ambulance shed and a lamp room[41]. Simple oil lamps were issued to Officers from the inception of the Metropolitan Police, supplied initially by Thomas Joyce and Son who cleaned and trimmed their wicks daily for a charge of 5.5d (2p) per lantern. The oil of the lamps made them hot, smelly and dirty, and required a leather guard to protect the Officer's uniform. Eventually they were replaced in 1920 by an electric lamp

Chislehurst Police Station
Chislehurst Hill, Chislehurst
1888- 1893

powered by an accumulator and invented by George Wooton, who became the Metropolitan Police Chief Engineer from 1930 until 1935.

Mottingham Lane, once the local main route to London, was relieved of much of its traffic by the opening of the Sidcup by-pass in 1924, and the Police Station was able to concentrate on protecting the large houses in the area. Chislehurst became part of the Bromley Sub-Division of 'P' Division on 1 January 1932, and part of St Mary Cray Sub-Division from 1 April 1965. Inspector Sparrow became the Officer-in-charge of the Station that was intended normally to be self-sufficient in manpower on a 24-hour basis, and the 1961 arrangement for closing the Station at night was brought to an end.

Chislehurst Police Office
1A High Street, tucked discreetly behind a local bank.

A site was purchased for a new Police Station at 3 High Street, Chislehurst in 1964, but it was leased to the Local Authority for use as a car park and the new Police Station was not built. The Station had been the subject of night time closures since 1961 but under re-organisation in July 1974 24 hour policing was resumed[42]. With the introduction of personal radios in June 1970 'TARDIS' style Police Boxes were phased out[43]. Sector Policing was introduced in February 1993 when the area was re-named Chislehurst and Petts Wood Section[44]. The old Police Station was closed in 1999. The public were served by a temporary wooden building located in the car park until 2007.

Chislehurst Police Office
1999 - 2007

46

In 2007, new premises at 1A High Street were opened as a Safer Neighbourhood Unit for the Chislehurst, and North Chislehurst and Mottingham Sectors. The Safer Neighbourhood Policing Scheme is a variation of Neighbourhood policing, Sector Policing and other schemes which have aimed to create smaller self-sufficient patrolling bases linked to communities smaller than the Divisions. The aim of providing continuity of patrolling cover by Officers well-known to their communities had often been thwarted by the demands of responding to emergency calls on a 24-hour basis, the need to send reinforcements to other parts of London for public order and security operations, and the remorseless trend for creating specialist squads to deal with particular types of crime such as domestic violence. The new system largely employs Police Community Support Officers, auxiliaries who do not have the full powers of a Police or Special Constable, and who concentrate on providing visible patrolling to reassure the public and to respond to community problems. A Sergeant is typically in charge of each sector, and takes responsibility for liaising with Neighbourhood Watch and community working party meetings. The new base comprises a reception office, and accommodation for Officers who patrol by foot and cycle.

Farnborough Police Station (PF)

Originally part of 'R' Division, Farnborough was an area full of market gardens producing food for the local population and for sale in London. It is said that Sir Robert Peel had friends who lived at Farnborough Lodge who lobbied him to build a Police Station in the area because of problems with highwaymen, and the Metropolitan Police District was extended to nearby Green Street Green in 1840.

Farnborough Police Station
Farnborough Common, Farnborough, Orpington, Kent
1867 - 1987

Farnborough was policed in 1864 by a Sergeant and 2 Constables by day, and a Sergeant and 5 Constables by night. One of the Sergeants was mounted on horseback, and was required to patrol for nine hours daily and to take care of his horse[45]. In 1893 the station telegraphic code was FN and located on 'P' Division[46]. In October 1865 a major re-organisation of the outer parts of the Metropolitan Police resulted in Farnborough being transferred from 'R' (Greenwich) to 'P' (Camberwell) Division[47]. It became part of St Mary Cray Sub-Division on 'P' Division on 1 April 1965 [48].

In August 1867 two freehold properties at Locks Bottom were bought for £750 and then became the police Station that remained operational until its closure on 1 July 1987[49]. They were described in the 1881 survey as 'two country cottages in a healthy position', which had a charge room, 2 cells and a 2-stall stable. The walls were damp, however[50]. In the 1930s it was shown as a Sectional Station to Bromley Sub-Division.

Hayes and Coney Hall Police Offices

A shop Front Office was opened at 6 Coney Hall Parade, Kingsway, Coney Hall BR4 9JB as part of the 2006 Safer Neighbourhoods policy. A team, led by Sergeant David Black, operate from the Office. They communicate with the public as part of the Safer Neighbourhoods project.

They hold monthly surgeries at Hayes Railway Station for the benefit of commuters and attend other meetings with the public to hear concerns and relay information. The Office has three PCs, two Special Constables and six Police Community Support Officers (PCSO's). As part of their equipment they used cycles sponsored by a local company. The Office opening hours are from Monday to Saturday, 10am – 2pm.

Hayes and Coney Hall Safer Neighbourhood Team Office
6 Coney Hall Parade, Kingsway, Coney Hall BR4 9JB

Knockholt Police Station (PT)

In the eighteenth century, Knockholt village was on the main stagecoach road from London to Rye, with its fair share of problems from highwaymen, but in 1836 a new road between Pratts Bottom and Dunton Green by-passed the hills around Knockholt and removed through traffic from the village. Even the modern railway line, which still contains a small station called Knockholt, followed this trend by coming no closer than two miles away. Still within the M25 motorway, its relative quietness and position on the borders between Greater London and Kent has contributed to changes in jurisdiction for the village over the years. In 1857, the newly formed Kent County Constabulary policed the village as part of its Sevenoaks Division. On 27th May 1895 the Constabulary opened a new Police Station in Knockholt, from where responsibility was also taken for Chelsfield and Cudham. Sergeant Alfred Thompson was in charge, with the inappropriately named Constable A Fright. Within months, bicycles had been introduced for patrolling rural beats.

Knockholt Police Station
Main Road, Knockholt, Kent
From 1895

In 1929 the parishes of Knockholt, Cudham and Chelsfield passed from Bromley Rural District to Orpington Council, but remained, for policing purposes, part of Kent County Constabulary's jurisdiction. World War Two saw much activity, especially from the RAF at nearby Biggin Hill, and plans to amalgamate Knockholt and other parts of Orpington Rural District into the Metropolitan Police District were delayed by the war. Knockholt received more than its fair share of bombs, crashed aircraft and security scares during World War Two, with the Battle of Britain being played out in the sky overhead. Security was such that on one occasion a PC Kitney was on his cycle patrol at night near the RAF Station at Biggin Hill when even he was accidentally arrested on suspicion of being a German spy! The local population valued the service given by their Police and presented the occupants of 'The Bungalow', then the Police Station in Chevening Lane, with a brass coalscuttle engraved *'Presented to Knockholt Police. For Vigilance'.*

Eventually Knockholt changed Police Forces and became part of the Metropolitan Police District on 1 April 1947. Transfer of policing responsibility was one thing; Local Authority jurisdiction was much more emotive. When the London Borough of Bromley was created on 1 April 1965, Knockholt would remain under the eye of the Metropolitan Police but the inhabitants had no wish to become part of a London Borough. 72% of the inhabitants signed a petition against becoming part of the London Borough of Bromley, and Knockholt was transferred, along with its policing, back to Kent on 1 April 1969.

Orpington Police Station (PN)

The town of Orpington spent its early life as a village smaller than St Mary Cray, but the introduction of a railway station with a good service to London soon created a rapid expansion of housing development.

Orpington Police Station
The Walnuts
1983 – Present day

For many years the town was policed from St Mary Cray Police Station, which lived under the perpetual state of being intended for replacement by a new Station in Orpington. St Mary Cray was referred to as the 'temporary' Sub-Divisional Headquarters in the 1965 re-organisation, and

Orpington finally received its brand new Police Station in the then new The Walnuts shopping centre in December 1983.

The architecture of the Police Station reflects the times in which it was planned. Offices had become the largest use of space, particularly on the upper floors, and the constant changes of use made it worthwhile to have internal walls that could easily be moved. The Custody Suite was purpose-built for its time, and a trend to emphasise public service and community links meant that there was little taste for copying the more fortified appearance of some other London Police Stations that had been designed to withstand riots.

All Divisions at this time also had their own purpose-built Command and Control rooms, with computerised links from New Scotland Yard to transfer details of 999 emergency calls to a series of control monitors that could also deal with telephone calls, local radio traffic and other communications tasks. As the rise in telephone use has grown over the years, so the number of emergency and non-emergency call traffic has increased dramatically. The lone Station telephonist may have known the surrounding area well, but the modern trend is for more distant call centres, operated under contract, that can use large numbers of staff to aim for better standards of efficiency and flexible working to meet this particular form of demand.

Penge Police Station (PG)

It was in October 1867 that the overseers of the hamlet of Penge drew the attention of the Metropolitan Police Commissioner in strong but polite terms to the fact that they were contributing over £3,000 per annum to the Metropolitan Police rate, and had been begging for a Police Station for four years 'consequent on the growing poverty and want of employment of the lower classes in this locality.'[51]

The local Police had identified a site at the corner of Green Lane and Dulwich Road, Penge, and a year later Home Office approval came through to lease the premises. A temporary Police Station became operational on 2 May 1870, and was part of a new Sydenham Sub-Division where Inspector Ings took charge not only of the Police Station and the Officers, but the horse previously ridden by the Sergeant. The new Police Station at Penge was built for £788 10s 5d, and occupied on 17 May 1872, with its address clarified as 175 Beckenham Road, Penge in 1879 later re-named High street but keeping the same number[52].

The original lease belonged to Mr Cree Jew, Lower Tulse Hill, Brixton, from Sept 1868 – 29th Sept 1958 with an annual rental of £130. Later the lease passed to Mr Henry Chandless of Henrietta Street, Covent Garden, from whom the freehold was bought for £1,617 in January 1899[53].

Penge Police Station
175 High Street, Penge SE20
1872 – Present day

The building featured a Reserve Room (later the mainstay of the communications for Police Stations until the Command and Control project of the 1980s), an office and three cells. In the basement was a washing room, a cooking kitchen, a drying room, brushing room, a water closet and 5 cellars. Coal and coke were supplied throughout the Metropolitan Police District which was divided for contract purposes into eight Districts, South East London being supplied by Messrs Corrall& Co of Forest Hill in 1884[54].

Lockers were provided for food, but were found, in 1881, often also to contain a miscellany of boot polish and other equipment. Officers needed somewhere to dry their wet uniforms and to store their boots, and uniform lockers remain to this day a major accommodation issue in the basements of Police Stations[55]. Penge was a Station attached to 'P' Division and had been allocated a telegraphic code of PE[56].

The rear yard of Penge Police Station showing the stable with its hay loft.

Penge and Beckenham became part of Southend Village (ie Catford) Sub-Division on 1 January 1932, but were both transferred to Bromley Sub-Division on 1 April 1965 when Divisional boundaries were changed to match the new London Boroughs[57].

Penge Station was closed at night from October 1960 but re-opened in May 1966 to survive as one of the oldest Police Stations still to be operational[58].

St Mary Cray Police Station (PM)

The River Cray gave its name to a number of villages along its course towards the Medway, St Mary Cray being the most southerly of The Crays. As early as 1653, a parish Constable, George Burton, was put in custody for the manslaughter of a George Dixon who had been put in the stocks for being drunk. The problem of highwaymen caused the Bow Street Horse Patrols to visit the Crays, but in January 1840, the area became part of 'R' Division of the Metropolitan Police when three Constables patrolled St Mary Cray, then with a population of 470.

In October 1851, St Mary Cray received its first Police Station where Sergeant John Bovis was in charge of five Constables on a site in the High Street leased from Mr J Ayre, the proprietor of the adjacent 'Black Boy' inn. An old lock-up at Crayford was given up to a Mr Barne.

Kelly's 1855 Directory of Kent referred to the Crays as;

> 'four highly respectable villages..in beautiful countryside.. with paper mills.... interspersedwith numerous elegant seats and noble mansions".

St Mary Cray Police Station
79 High Street St Mary Cray
1896 - 1988

The area is today far more notable for its density of social housing.

Sidcup and St Mary Cray were initially part of Lee Sub-Division, but were transferred to 'P' Division's Bromley for a few months from March until October 1865. In 1873, an Inspector Samuel Higgins was in charge, and remained so until 1890. One of the most serious cases he would have dealt with was that of Joseph Waller, a former Constable, who was sent to the Maidstone Assizes charged with the murder of an elderly couple on St Paul's Cray Common in October 1880. Waller, like many prisoners, scratched a drawing on his cell wall: a picture of a cottage and a gallows was accompanied by a signed inscription:

'Joseph Waller, charged with the wilful murder of Edward and Elizabeth Ellis, shot down with a revolver by me'

The Police Station, with 6 rooms, a charge room, a kitchen and two cells was officially described as 'dilapidated' in 1887, and a new replacement building was finally completed on 14 September 1896, at a cost of £3,597 10s 2d, at a freehold site which became known as 79 High Street, St. Mary Cray, Kent. Allocated with a telegraphic code of SC in 1893 it was a station of 'R' Division[59].

A rare view of the rear of St Mary Cray Police Station showing to the left the original 4 cottages that formed the first police station there. Notice the washing hanging at left and the cultivated gardens

Ten years later, St Mary Cray became part of the Sidcup Sub-Division, and from 1 January 1932 was returned to 'P' Division as part of Bromley Sub-Division. The house next door, 81 High Street, once a shop, was purchased in 1939 with a view to the land providing the means to extend the Police Station. These plans never came to fruition, and despite the erection of a temporary wooden building, the accommodation became more and more cramped.

In April 1965, St Mary Cray became a Sub-Divisional headquarters within the new London Borough of Bromley, and, after Orpington Police Station was opened in December 1983, St Mary Cray's Station became a Police Office, finally closing in January 1988. The community felt the loss of the Police Station very keenly, and after a period of campaigning, a new Police Office was opened in September 1994.

It was on 15th August 1984 that a PC Martin Coxon was patrolling with his Police Dog Yerba in Petts Wood, part of Orpington Division, when they came by chance across a bank robbery in progress. PC Coxon immediately released Yerba, who like all Police Dogs, was trained to deal with armed men, but the robber, a 44-year-old man named Toni Baldessare, shot the dog with his revolver. Yerba continued, despite being wounded, and the man shot her again in the head, and for a third time in the back, which finally killed the courageous animal. A plaque was erected at the scene to commemorate the incident. Yerba was buried at the world-famous Metropolitan Police Dog Training Establishment at nearby Keston, where, as a minor part of their breeding programme, they have a practice of working systematically through the whole alphabet to name all dogs born in each litter with the same letter of the alphabet. Yerba's brothers and sisters would all have had names beginning with Y.

Cray Police Office
43-45 High Street St Mary Cray BR5 3NH
1994- Present day

Baldessare himself was traced by Police to a flat in Streatham that was placed under siege before he committed suicide by shooting himself, after burning a large quantity of stolen bank notes in his kitchen sink.

West Wickham Police Station

As long ago as 1606, the parish of St John the Baptist, West Wickham, had stocks installed at Norwood Cross, Wickham Street, outside 'The Swan' public house[60], where a large tree, known as the 'Stocks Tree' survived well into the twentieth century, and was blown down in 1968. In a document dated December 1839, a lock-up is mentioned as located in West Wickham, where Petty Sessions (the equivalent of magistrates' court hearings) were also held. Later, West Wickham's Police strength was shown as two Constables accommodated in private lodgings[61]. This was despite proposals for a local Police Station dating from 1887 when a vacant freehold site in Grosvenor Road was acquired for £480. The site was still in possession of the Metropolitan Police in 1924 and it was many years before Police premises finally arrived.

West Wickham Police Office
9 High Street, West Wickham , Kent BL4 0LP
1974 – Present day

In 1918 PC James Hardy was severely injured by an armed poacher in Ruffets Wood, West Wickham.   Despite his injuries, the Officer succeeded in arresting the man, and his bravery was recognised by an announcement that he would be awarded the King's Police Medal for gallantry. On the very day before the investiture ceremony, however, PC Hardy was killed in a cycling accident, and never saw the medal that he had been awarded.   PC Hardy's name appears amongst many other Officers who have died on duty on the National Roll of Honour that can be seen on the internet www.policememorial.co.uk The development of that Roll of Honour has been the fulfilment of many years' work by a Lancashire Police Sergeant, now retired, Anthony Rae, and the Police Roll of Honour Trust.

The Roll of Honour at Scotland Yard was introduced after discussions in 1935 between the Police Federation and the Commissioner, Lord Trenchard, as a means to recognise the heroic death of PC James Thomson KPM, who was killed by a cement lorry that was running uncontrolled down Barnet Hill.   PC Thomson remained in the road, clearing pedestrians from the danger, but was himself killed by the offending lorry. The Roll of Honour includes cases from 1924 and comprises an open book with ornately inscribed pages in a glass case, next to a permanent flame that burns in the entrance hall of New Scotland Yard. Over the years the entries have come to be restricted to cases where death has ensued as the result of an act of special gallantry or in connection with duty involving special risks.

On 27 July 1950 the Metropolitan Police War Memorial Book, also in the form of a Roll of Honour, was dedicated in Westminster Abbey in the presence of the King and Queen. The Roll contains 1,076 names of Metropolitan Police Officers and civil staff who lost their lives during the two world wars, either serving in His Majesty's Armed Forces, or as the result of enemy action at home.

In 1955 a Police Office for West Wickham was suggested for Glebe Way, and the matter was resurrected in 1963. Eventually negotiations commenced for the leasehold of 9 High Street, West Wickham, which, after conversion, was finally opened on 18 March 1974[62].

The Warren Sports Club

The house and lodge at what is now The Warren Police Sports Club was built in the Flemish style by Walter Maximilian de Zoete on land leased, in 1882, for 60 years from Dame Julia Lennard, the wife of Colonel Sir John Farnaby Lennard, a prominent landowner in the district. The de Zoete family, as their name suggests, came from Holland, and became prominent merchants, and then stockbrokers in the City of London. Walter's father Samuel was at one time Chairman of the Stock Exchange. Walter was a keen golfer, playing in the first Amateur Golf Championship at Hoylake in 1885, and was also interested in antiques and works of art[63].

The house was named Warren House after the wooded valley to the west of the house known locally as 'the warren' because of rabbits, which locals would catch with ferrets and polecats. A lane bordering the club is named *Polecat Alley* for similar reasons[64].

In 1885 Walter de Zoete gave up his interest in the property to a banker Martin R Smith, a great philanthropist and entertainer who extended the premises by adding a billiards room, a new wing, two cottages and a summer house. The main house had twelve bedrooms on the first floor, five staff bedrooms and provided employment for a butler, housekeeper, cook, two footmen, a hall boy, maids, governesses, coachmen and 18 gardeners[65].

The two cottages housed the head gardener and the watchman, a Mr Wilkins, whose duties had previously been carried out by Police Constables. In the North-East corner of the grounds is Julian's Wood. Julian, who died in the First World War, was the youngest of Mr Smith's four sons. Carnations began to be cultivated there in 1899, no doubt through the skill of the head gardener Charles Blick. Two of Martin Smith's daughters married into the Hambro banking family, Sir Edward Hambro living nearby in Hayes Place. The game of *bumplepuppy*, an early version of swingball, was played in the garden near the house.

The Warren Sports Club 2007

Martin Smith died in 1908, and his son Everard sold the house for £15,000 at auction by John Wood and Sons of Grosvenor Square London in 1909[66]. Sir Robert Laidlaw MP, a wealthy businessman whose company Whiteway& Laidlaw were known as the Selfridges of India. It was Sir Robert who planted the trees and rhododendrons that add so much beauty to the grounds.

During the First World War, Sir Robert gave the house to the British Red Cross Society for use as a 50-bed hospital, which continued until 1916, the year in which Orpington hospital was opened to treat wounded soldiers from the war. Sir Robert died in 1915, and in 1920 the house was sold to Edwin Preston of West Wickham for £19,500. Mr Preston was interested in growing flowering shrubs and rare plants, and changed the name from Warren House to The Warren[67].

Conditions were harsh for Police Officers in those days. Police pay had been 25 – 35 shillings per week in 1890, and started at 30 shillings per week in 1914. An increase of 13 shillings per week was given in 1918. In 1906 Officers had one rest day per fortnight, and received 10 days annual leave. The Desborough Committee, set up after Police Strikes of 1918 and 1919, started to improve pay and conditions, and recognised the need for welfare and sports facilities. In 1926 the Mayor of Bromley asked for gifts towards the purchase of a sports ground for the Police of 'P' Division, particularly as a sports ground at Thames Ditton was situated too far away to benefit local Officers. Mr Preston, whose home was later to become that sought-after sports ground, was himself a contributor to the fund.

In 1934 Mr Preston sold the house to Gordon Ralph Hall-Caine MP of Maidenhead, but he did not take up residence, and it was then bought by the Receiver for the Metropolitan Police District, with assistance from Lady Margetson, the wife of the then Deputy Commissioner Sir Philip Margetson. The Sports Club had previously been renting 18 acres at Monks Orchard, Beckenham[68]. Extensive work was needed to convert the house into a clubhouse with a playing field. The large ground floor rooms became dining rooms, one of which had a fine dance floor, and the Club was officially opened on 13 June 1935 by the Commissioner, Lord Trenchard[69].

During the Second World War the stables became a Home Guard base, and many pilots from Biggin Hill were entertained there[70].

Over the years a number of projects have improved the facilities. Six tennis courts were laid over the old sunken gardens, followed later by two squash courts to complement the football and cricket pitches, and picturesque bowling green. In 1974 the stables were refurbished to accommodate a unit of the Mounted Branch, who stayed until the stables were closed in 1997.

The rear of The Warren

The Hobbit sports pavilion and its facilities were opened in 1984, which released space in the main building for offices and a conference room. Then in 1989 the Coney Suite was opened as a popular functions room that can accommodate 300 people, or 200 for a formal dinner. The original drawing room became a members' bar[71].

This fine house and gardens continues to thrive as a recreational facility for serving and retired members of the Metropolitan Police Service and their families.

---

[1] Brown, B. (1997) Back to the Drawing Board – Law and Order in Bromley. Bygone Kent 2/97
[2] Brown, B (1997) Lock, Stock and Barrel. Bygone Kent
[3] Brown, B. (1997) Back to the Drawing Board – Law and Order in Bromley. Bygone Kent 2/97
[4] Cherry, B. and Pevsner, N. (1983) London 2: South. Penguin, Middlesex
[5] Metropolitan Police Orders dated 10th March 1869
[6] South London News (1970) A Police Stations History.11th October
[7] John Back (1975) Beckenham police station. The Metropolitan Police Collection, Charlton
[8] John Back (1975) Beckenham police station. The Metropolitan Police Collection, Charlton
[9] Metropolitan Police Special Police Orders 1869
[10] Metropolitan Police Surveyors Records 1878
[11] Metropolitan Police Surveyors Records 1881
[12] John Back (1975) Beckenham police station. The Metropolitan Police Collection, Charlton
[13] Metropolitan Police Surveyors Records 1881
[14] Metropolitan Police General Orders 1893
[15] Metropolitan Police Surveyors Records 1881
[16] John Back (1975) Beckenham police station. The Metropolitan Police Collection, Charlton
[17] John Back (1975) Beckenham police station. The Metropolitan Police Collection, Charlton
[18] Metropolitan Police Orders dated 6th August 1964
[19] Metropolitan Police Orders dated 12th July 1974
[20] London Evening Standard dated 21st January 2010.
[21] Brown, B. (undated) A new baby for Papa.
[22] John Back (1975) Biggin Hill Police Station. The Metropolitan Police Collection, Charlton
[23] Brown, B. (1997) Back to the Drawing Board – Law and Order in Bromley. Bygone Kent 2/97
[24] ibid
[25] Brown, B. (1997) Back to the Drawing Board – Law and Order in Bromley. Bygone Kent 2/97
[26] Metropolitan Police Surveyors Records
[27] Metropolitan Police Special Police Order 1869
[28] Brown, B. (1997) Back to the Drawing Board – Law and Order in Bromley. Bygone Kent 2/97
[29] Metropolitan Police General Orders 1893
[30] Metropolitan Police Property Records 1924
[31] Metropolitan Police Pension Records
[32] Brown, B. (1997) Back to the Drawing Board – Law and Order in Bromley. Bygone Kent 2/97
[33] Metropolitan Police Surveyors Records (Charlton)
[34] Metropolitan Police (1993) Chislehurst Centenary. A Celebration of the 100 years opening of Chislehurst. Police Station 1893 –1993.
[35] Metropolitan Police (1993) Chislehurst Centenary. A Celebration of the 100 years opening of Chislehurst. Police Station 1893 –1993.
[36] Metropolitan Police Orders dated 15th October 1873
[37] Back, J. (1975) Chislehurst Police Station. The Metropolitan Police Collection, Charlton
[38] Metropolitan Police General Orders 1893
[39] Back, J. (1975) Chislehurst Police Station. The Metropolitan Police Collection, Charlton

[40] Back, J. (1975) Chislehurst Police Station. The Metropolitan Police Collection, Charlton
[41] Metropolitan Police Surveyors records
[42] Metropolitan Police (1993) Chislehurst Centenary. A Celebration of the 100 years opening of Chislehurst. Police Station 1893 –1993.
[43] Metropolitan Police (1993) Chislehurst Centenary. A Celebration of the 100 years opening of Chislehurst. Police Station 1893 –1993.
[44] Metropolitan Police (1993) Chislehurst Centenary. A Celebration of the 100 years opening of Chislehurst. Police Station 1893 –1993.
[45] Back John, (1975) Farnborough Police Station. The Metropolitan Police Collection, Charlton
[46] Metropolitan Police General Orders 1893
[47] Back John, (1975) Farnborough Police Station. The Metropolitan Police Collection, Charlton
[48] Metropolitan Police Orders dated 6th August 1964
[49] Back John, (1975) Farnborough Police Station. The Metropolitan Police Collection, Charlton
[50] Metropolitan Police Surveyors 1881
[51] Letter dated 7th October 1869 signed by William Gibson. Metropolitan Police Collection.
[52] Kirchners Police Index 1931
[53] John Back (1975) Penge police station. The Metropolitan Police Collection, Charlton
[54] Metropolitan Police Surveyors Records 1881
[55] Metropolitan Police Surveyors Records 1881
[56] Metropolitan Police General Orders 1893
[57] John Back (1975) Penge police station. The Metropolitan Police Collection, Charlton
[58] Metropolitan Police Orders 13th May 1966
[59] Metropolitan Police General Orders 1893
[60] Brown, B (1997) Lock, Stock and Barrel. Bygone Kent
[61] Back, J. (1975) West Wickham Police Station. The Metropolitan Police Collection, Charlton
[62] Back, J. (1975) West Wickham Police Station. The Metropolitan Police Collection, Charlton
[63] Prowse, P and Simmons, J. (1998) The Story of our Club house 'The Warren'. (from the original by John Player and brought up to date by John Early.
[64] ibid
[65] ibid
[66] Wood, J. D. (Auctioneers) (1909) 'Warren House'. Particulars of sale for auction 9th June.
[67] Prowse, P and Simmons, J. (1998) The Story of our Club house 'The Warren'. (from the original by John Player and brought up to date by John Early.
[68] ibid
[69] ibid
[70] ibid
[71] Barr, S. (1988) We are open for business'. The Job 11th November.

Chapter 3

London Borough of Croydon

Introduction

The London Borough of Croydon is the southernmost and one of the largest of London's boroughs with a population of around 340,000 people. Much of the 34 square miles of the borough is urban and the town of Croydon itself is large with many tall buildings and business premises.

The main London to Brighton Road passes through the centre of Croydon and the town has its own tram service.

Policing

Croydon, and the area surrounding it, was originally policed by the first Division of Bow Street Horse Patrols in 1827[1]. Local policing for what was a small town had been in the hands of a beadle, who was responsible for being 'vigilant in clearing the streets of vagrants and beggars', since the end of the eighteenth century. Croydon Improvement Commissioners found that the parochial Police were somewhat inefficient and had established its own Police Force in the town as early as July 1829. The Metropolitan Police was not established until September of that year, and did not extend as far as Croydon until 1840.

The new Croydon Police consisted of three men appointed to patrol the town. These men were referred to as 'Patrols' or 'Privates' never as 'Policemen'. Their uniform was blue pantaloons, blue coat and red waistcoat which they had to provide themselves. Each was armed with a pistol and a cutlass - they also had a staff or truncheon bearing the King's Arms and the words 'Croydon Police'. This small Police Force was modelled on the Bow Street Runners who had withdrawn their services to Croydon once the new Police Force had been introduced[2].

In December 1829 Richard Colman, a former Bow Street Runner, was appointed Sergeant. The Privates were each paid one guinea (£1.05) a week and Colman received an extra nine shillings (45p) - two weeks later William Smith, the Assistant Overseer of the Poor, was appointed Superintendent. The Metropolitan Police took over the policing of Croydon January 1840[3].

The Police in London Borough of Croydon currently operate from two police stations, Croydon and South Norwood, which are open every day for 24 hours. Norbury, Kenley and New Addington areopen restricted hours. In addition there are nine Safer Neighbourhood bases spread throughout the Borough.

The current Borough Police Commander, based at Croydon Police station, is Chief Superintendent Adrian Roberts, assisted by Superintendent Dave Stringer and Detective Superintendent Jo Oakley[4].

Addington Police Office/New Addington Police Station

The village of Addington was separated from Croydon by woodland of the Ballards Plantation around Coombe Lane and the golf course, formerly the grounds of Addington Palace[5].

The Metropolitan Police District was extended in 1840 and records show that Addington was attached to Croydon Police Station, on 'P' Division:-it had the strength of one Constable who was privately lodged. The local Magistrates heard charges in their own homes[6]. In 1865 Croydon, including the Addington area, was transferred to 'W' Division.[7] In 1921, 'Z', or Croydon Division was formed sothe Addingtonarea was transferred to 'Z' Division

By 1957 consideration was being given for a small temporary building to be erected in the area of New Addington to enable Police on duty to take refreshment instead of having travel about 6 miles to Croydon Police Station. It was intimated that the building should be manned to deal with minor Police duties. When approached, the Town Planning Officer was not in favour of reserving a site for a temporary Police Station unless a permanent structure would be developed within 10 years[8].

The following year Police received a number of complaints about damage,hooliganism and the inadequate policing in the Area. In addition, the Council Estate had expanded andtherefore the workload had increased. Eventually, in 1960, a site in Overbury Crescent was selected for the erection of Police married quarters and a Police Office[9], designated (ZA), was opened on 23rd February 1962[10].

By 1966 the existing Police Office was inadequate to cope with the increased operational business and the cramped conditions in which the officers were obliged to workimpaired efficiency. It was suggested that a site be found for the erection of a new Police Station. The City Centre Service Station, Kent Gate Way, was closing down and the freehold land adjoining the petrol station was purchased in March 1976. In the meantime the Croydon Natural History and Scientific Society hadrequested permission to make archaeological investigations before the site was developed. It was believed that Addington had been a mediaeval village that had existed in Saxon Times. Permission was granted but unfortunately nothing of importance was found. It was suggested that any material might have been disturbed at the time that the Service Station, with its petrol tanks, was constructed[11].

Addington Police Office
OverburyCresent,
1962 - 1977

The old Police Office in Overbury Crescent closed in September 1977 when a new Police Station was opened in Addington Village Road, Croydon.[12] It is now sectional to Norbury[13], and currently the station is open Monday to Friday 8am - 7pm[14].

Croydon Police Station

The Metropolitan Police district was extended in 1840 and a distribution of the Force is shown in papers preserved in the Public Records Office. Croydon is shown not only as a Station where charges were taken, but also being responsible for policing the Outer District, which included Beddington, Carshalton, Sutton, Cheam, Banstead, Woodmarston, Coulsdon, Worlingham, Farley, Sanderstead, Addington, Chipstead and

Chelsham. It was designated "P" or Camberwell Division and had the strength of 1 Inspector, 3 Sergeants and 29 Constables - there were also three Mounted Sergeants. The officers stationed at Croydon were accommodated in a Section House, whilst elsewhere the officers were privately lodged. Petty Sessions were held every Saturday and a list of the names of the Magistrates is included in the documents[15].

A substantial brick and slate Station and Section house was rented in the High Street Croydon. Located on 'P', or Camberwell Division, it comprised a charge room, kitchen, magistrate's room and 3 cells. In the yard was a 5 stall stable. The premises, at 13 North End, Croydon[16] were leased from Mr Townley, of 3 Arlington Place, Kensington, for a period of 99 years from March 1841. Accommodation above the Station consisted of 2 rooms for 1 Inspector at a yearly rent of £15.12s[17]. The rent payable on the lease was quite high due to the fact that the owner, one James Townley, advanced the sum of £1719 to build the Police Station and needed repayment of the loan. The Station was opened in 1849 on a site where the Drummond Centre now stands. It consisted of four cells, a quiet/library room, four basement cellars and four stables. Almost immediately a letter from the Home Office, dated 22 June 1849, stated that consideration was being given for the enlargement of the Police Station[18]. A new site in Katherine Street was offered as a possible site for a Police Station but was declined. A sum of £950 was found for improvements to the existing Station.[19] The address in 1844 was shown as George Street, Croydon, with Inspector John Collier in charge (Collier had been promoted to Inspector in 1837)[20]. Superintendent Andrew McLean was in charge of the Division which was located at Park House, Walworth[21].

By 1851 Inspector W. H. Shaw was in charge of the Station and in command of over 100 men whose duties extend beyond Croydon. These included the Parishes of Addington, Beddington, Carshalton, Coulsdon, Mitcham, Merton, Mordon, Sutton, Streatham, Sandersteed, Warlingham, Wallington and Woodmansterne[22].

Croydon had a famous resident in the 1850sthis was none other than Captain (later Sir) Richard Maine, one of two Commissioners appointed in 1829, who resided in the Addiscombe area of the town. The local Inspector would have been aware of this and Maine without doubt would have paid visits to the Station[23]. Croydon Sergeant George Thoburn resided at 30 Adelaide Street, whilst another Sergeant, Thomas Prendergast, lived in Bell Yard.

In 1864 Croydon is shown as being on "P", or Camberwell Division, withstrength of 1 Inspector, 6 Sergeants and 50 Constables. There was stabling for 5 horses. One horse would beridden alternately by 2 Sergeants on Station Duty[24].

Croydon Police Station
North End Road, Croydon
1843 - 1895

CROYDON (circa 1890)
13 North End
Croydon
(In 1882 the address was 6 North End prior to re-numbering)

The following year the Force in that area created three new Divisions; "W", or Clapham; "X", or Paddington; and "Y", or Highgate. Croydon was transferred to "W" Division[25].

By 1869 Superintendent William Wiseman was in charge of 'W' Division. There were five Stations, each having an Inspector in charge; Brixton, Carshalton, Clapham. Croydon and Streatham. Sergeants were in charge of Banstead, Mitcham, Sutton and Tooting. At a meeting of the Croydon Local Board of Health held at the Town Hall on Tuesday 3rd January 1871 it was resolved;

"That in the opinion of this Board the Police arrangements in Croydon are of an inadequate nature and are not commensurate with the large amount contributed to the Police rate of the Parish, and that the Clerk be instructed to communicate with Colonel Henderson on the subject in the confident expectation that no time will be lost in providing a remedy for so unsatisfactory a position".

District Superintendent Baynes in a memo to the Commissioner, dated 10th January 1871, refutes the above motion.

In March 1871 Superintendent Wiseman of "W" Division requests an augmentation of 4 Constables for the Division for better protection of Croydon[26]. It was felt that Croydon was an important enough centre to require an officer of more senior rank and in 1878 Chief Inspector William Mason and Inspector Charles Hunt were shown to be in charge at 6 North

End[27]. This was probably because of the growing size of the town and the busy nature of the courts.

By 1881 an inspection of all Metropolitan Stations revealed that the Station was far too small for the amount of work carried out. There were also comments that the site was too small for expansion. In addition the quarters at the Station housed one married Inspector, one single Sergeant and 19 single Constables and the inspection made comment that living quarters ofthe single and married people were all mixed up[28].

By 1889 Superintendent Stephen T Lucas was in charge of 'W' Division and the strength of the Division was 38 Inspectors, 72 Sergeant and 584 Constables. A total establishment of 695 officers and men[29].

Although the Police Station was renovated in 1873/4 there was still a need for larger premises. In 1890 Croydon Corporation sold some of the land in central Croydon that it had purchased from the London, Brighton and South Eastern Railway to the Metropolitan Police Receiver[30]. As the new building was going to be next to the Municipal Buildings, Croydon Corporation insisted that the same stone was to be usedas that of other buildings in the vicinity[31].In 1891, just prior to the change, Chief Inspector Andrew Webb was shown in charge of the Station at 13 North End[32].

The freehold title to Fell Road, Katherine Street,was purchased in 1892and included a subway under Fell Road that was maintained by the Receiver of the Metropolitan Police[33]. In the meantime the North End Station was vacated and the premises sub-let. In fact, the Police were making profits from the oldStation which they had rented to Messrs Kennard Brothers in 1912 for £307 a yearwhile their ground rent and rent charges only came to £118 annually[34]. This carried on until at least 1924 at the same rental rate[35].

Croydon Police Station
Fell Road, Croydon.
1895 - 1980

The new Police Station, designed by John Butler at a cost of £12,000, opened in Fell Road, Croydon, in September 1895,[36] some 22years after the previous building was considered inadequate. The Station had an Inspector's Office, Charge Room, Parade Room, Matron's Room, Drying Room, Four Cells, Quiet Room, Library, Mess Room and Bathroom. In addition there were three stables and an Ambulance Shed. There was, in addition, accommodation for a married Inspector and 20 single Constables. The old Police Station continued serving the public, first as Wilsons Tea Rooms and Finally as Kennards[37]. Fredrick Bonner became the first Sub-Divisional Inspector (SDI) for Croydon followed by William Lemmey until 1898 when Samuel Parlett took over, and then Frank Chinn in 1902. By 1905 Chinn had transferred to Clapham as SDI.

Inspector William Lemmey retired from Croydon Police Station in September 1898 due to ill health. The Superintendent from 'W' Division, Mr Lucas, made a presentation to the Inspector of a 'handsome liquor stand' given as a mark of respect from the officers and colleagues in the Division[38].

In a letter from the Commissioner to the Home Office dated July 1920 there was to be the formation of a new Division on the south side of the Thames which would be known as the 'Z', or Croydon, Division. The Commissioner said,

> 'The question which was under discussion in the year 1913 was not proceeded with in consequence of the outbreak of the war, has now, owing to the ever increasing population and more exacting duties of Police, and from the point of view of efficiency become one of importance and urgency. It is proposed to vary the present boundaries and establishments of all the Division south of the Thames with a view, as far as possible, to equalising the area and personnel of each. The "W" Division in particular, will be considerably reduced, and the new Division, to a large extent, will embrace what is now part of the Division. The new 'Z' Division will be divided into three Sub-Divisions. Headquarters to be at Croydon.Croydon Sub–Division to be Croydon and Kenley Stations. Thornton Heath Sub-Division to be Thornton Heath and South Norwood Stations. Gipsy Hill Sub-Division to be Gipsy Hill and Knights Hill Stations.(Knights Hill closed in 1930)
>
> It will be within the knowledge of the Secretary of State that the residents of Croydon have agitated for many years past for a re-organisation of the Police arrangements within the Borough, and general satisfaction will doubtless be given by making Croydon the chief Station of the new Division".

The Home Office sanctioned the formation of 'Z' Division in a letter to the Commissioner dated 9th October 1920[39].

The new Division came into being on 28th February 1921[40] and with its introduction suitable Police Officers were transferred in from other divisions. For example, the picture at left shows Station Sergeant 84862 Harold Prewer (Ps 2Z) who was the most senior sergeant and who had been transferred from "W" Division on 24th February 1921. It was the same year that Station Sergeants were given a crown to wear above their stripes rather than a fourth stripe. Prewer remained on "Z" Division until he retired in February 1924.

Station Sergeant Harold Prewer 'Z' Division

By 1928 Superintendent Jas. Wilson was in charge of Croydon Division and under his command was Croydon Sub-Divisional Station and its Sectional Station at Kenley (Godstone Road), Norbury Sub-Divisional Station (London Road, Norbury) and two Sectional Stations, those of South Norwood (82 High Street) and Thornton Heath (Parchmore Road). Also included in the Division at that time was Gipsy Hill Sub-Division with Knights Hill as the Sectional Station[41]. By 1939, Superintendent H.C. Quincey was in charge of the Division in addition to the above Stations of Streatham, Gipsy Hill and Wallington[42].

The picture right shows a victorious "Z" Divisional Race Walking Team in 1936. The Barking to Southend Road Walk

'Z' Division Race Walking Team. 1936

70

commenced in 1921 and it was very prestigious to win the trophy and shield. Clearly the team won the highest number of points whilst also having a team member come first. The members of the newly formed Division were keen to show that they were as good physically as the much older divisions.

In 1944, towards the end of the Second World War, the town of Croydon was subjected to attacks by flying bombs. Some 20,000 women and children were evacuated, but still many people were killed or injured. One such incident in 1944 led Inspector William James Holloway to enter, at great risk, the debris of a house demolished by a Flying Bomb and rescue three people. For his "courage, perseverance and devotion to duty" he was awarded the British Empire Medal[43].

In 1952, Police Constable Sidney George Miles, was shot and killed on the roof of a warehouse near the Croydon Bus Station, while he and other officers were giving chase to two local youths who were suspected of being on the getaway from an armed robbery. Detective Constable Frederick Fairfax was shot in the shoulder[44]. Police Constable Miles was awarded the King's Police and Fire Services Medal (KPFSM).

This medal was only awarded posthumously for Gallantry from 1950 until 1954. Detective Constable Fairfax was awarded the George Cross which is the highest non-military gallantry ward, sometimes known as the civilians' Victoria Cross. Fairfax received his award because he walked unflinchingly towards the two youths who continued to fire the weapon until the gun was empty. It has only been awarded to five Metropolitan Police officers[45].

King's Police and Fire Services Medal (KPFSM)

The Kings Police Medal was one of the older awards, instituted in 1909 by King Edward VII but discontinued in 1954 when separate medals for Police and for Fire Service were substituted. It was originally titled the King's Police Medal, even though it could be awarded to members of theFire Service, and was awarded to Police or Fire personnel who perform 'acts of exceptional courage and skill, or who had exhibited conspicuous devotion to duty'[46].

In May 1968 Mrs Sislin Fay Allen, a nurse at Croydon's Queens Hospital, became Britain's first Black Policewoman. She started work at Croydon Police Station in a blaze of publicity. So much so that she remained on indoor duty throughout her first week to avoid being photographed or interviewed on the beat[47].

She said,"On the selection day there were so many people there, the hall was filled with the young men. There were ten women and I was the only Black person."

After taking a set of exams and a stringent medical, Sislin Allen was told she had passed and would start work at Croydon's Fell Road Police Station.

"I can remember one friend said, 'Oh they wouldn't accept you, they don't accept Black people in the force', and so I said 'Well my dear, I've got news for you' and I showed her the letter. The first day on the beat in Croydon was daunting, but it wasn't too bad because I went out with an officer. People were curious to see a Black woman there in uniform walking up and down, but I had no problem at all, not even from the public. On the day I joined I nearly broke a leg trying to run away from reporters. I realised then that I was a history maker. But I didn't set out to make history; I just wanted a change of direction."[48]

Constable Sislin Fay Allen

There were less than 600 Women Police Officers working in the Metropolitan Police at that time.

In 1969 the District Police Commander and his staff moved from the Station into the old Town Hall opposite and in 1977 they were joined by the Chief Superintendent of Croydon and the Juvenile Bureau[49].

A new Police Station had been proposed and discussed locally since at least 1967and was to be situated at 70 Park Lane in front of the law courts. Consultations were slow and a date in 1972 was discussed but theproposed construction was put back in time as building priorities changed. Originally it was proposed that the building would include an eleven storey Section House but that was abandoned because there was only a handful of unmarried men and women serving in the area[50]. There was also a view that the vast cost of building single persons' quarters was not cost-effective and that it would be better for single officers to make their own living provisions.

Croydon Police Station
71 Park Lane, Croydon Surrey.
1980 – present day

The building was designed by J. I. Elliot Metropolitan Police Chief Architect who had used a facade with horizontal brick bands[51]. Work on the new Police Station had begun in January 1974 when private houses on the site were demolished. The five storey building cost £2¼ million and at the time of opening would house 250 Police Officers, 100 Traffic Wardens and 35 civil staff. There is a 3-storey car park and recreational facilities at the Station together with a small arms firing range in the basement[52].

The old Croydon Police Station closed and was demolished 1980[53]. The vacant site was incorporated into the 'Queen's Gardens'. The new District Headquarters and Police Station at Croydon was opened by HRH Prince Charles on 6th March 1980 at 71 Park Lane, replacing the old Police Station in Fell Road[54]. This was the first time that His Royal Highness had performed the opening ceremony of a Metropolitan Police Station. Among the guests attending was the Home Secretary, Mr William Whitelaw Metropolitan Police Commissioner, Sir David McNee and the Mayor of Croydon, Councillor P Bowness.

The Station code was 'ZD'[55]. Currently, the Police Station is the Borough of Croydon Police Headquarters and is open 24 hours a day.[56]

Kenley Police Station

In May 1886 Home Office authorised the Receiver to purchase a freehold site at Kenley for the erection of a new Police Station for the sum of £419. The land was compulsorily purchased from a Mr William Taylor under a bill presented in the House of Commons on 25 March 1887 by one of Her Majesty's Principal Secretaries of State under the Metropolitan Police Act, 1886, relating to lands in the Parishes of Leyton (Essex) and Coulsdon (Surrey)[57]. The transaction for the land purchase was completed in July 1887[58].

Kenley Police Station
Godstone Road, Kenley.
1896 –present day

The new Station was erected and formed part of "W", or Clapham, Division. The building was designed by the Metropolitan Police Surveyor, John Butler, and completed by his son, John Dixon Butler, who followed his father into the Surveyor's post. The Architectural Plans at the National Archives are dated 1895[59]. The cost of the building was £3789[60] and consisted of a Station together with 3 sets of separate married quarters.

It was taken into occupation by the Police, and business commenced therein in July 1896[61].

At the formation of the new "Z" Division in 1921 Kenley was transferred from "W" To "Z" Division and designated a Section Station of Croydon Division[62].

The photograph opposite was taken in 1937 when the Officers received their coronation medals for being part of the ceremonies.

Kenley Police Officers 1937

With the new local authority boundaries created in 1965 Kenley (ZK) continued to be a Sectional Station to Croydon Sub-Division situated in the new London Borough of Croydon[63].

Currently Kenley Police Station at 94 – 96 Godstone Road, Kenley, is open Monday to Friday from 10am – 2pm [64].

Norbury Police Station

The area of Norbury was created around the railway station on the London Road which expanded in the 1930's and is now indistinguishable from Thornton Heath and the fringes of Streatham (Lambeth) and Mitcham (Merton)[65].

Superintendent West of 'W' Division submitted a report and plan dated 20th July 1910 for the consideration of the Commissioner for the purchase of a suitable site at Norbury; with a view to securing a piece of land while cheap and the erection of a new Station, at a later period, in this rapidly growing District.

The L.C.C. was erecting 800 workmen's houses on their Norbury Estate and a working class colony was springing up there; other areas surrounding the site were also available for building purposes. The Superintendent felt that it would in time be very necessary to have a Station at this spot to relieve Streatham and Thornton Heath Sections. The distance from Streatham was about 1½ miles, from Thornton Heath 1¼ miles, and about 2 miles from Mitcham Station[66].

The Commissioner in a memorandum to the Home Office dated 6 August 1910 suggested that a site be acquired in the Norbury area for the erection of a new Police Station[67].

On 30 December 1911 a freehold site at Norbury for the erection of the new Police Station was purchased for the sum of £900. The land, which was owned by the Master, Fellows and Scholars of Pembroke College, Cambridge, was on lease to the North Surrey Golf Club[68].

In September 1912 two local Officers, Police Constables 73 Preston and 186 Bevans, sought and were given permission to cultivate the new site on the understanding that they risk the loss of crops when building operations commenced; the Officers agreed to pay the Local Authority for any rates that were demanded.[69] Discussions on the erection of the new Police Station took place in June 1913 and plans and working drawings for the new station were approved in October 1915 by the then Commissioner, Sir Edward Henry.[70] It seems that the Officers enjoyed nearly three seasons on the site.

Norbury Police Station
1516, London Road, Norbury
1925 – present day

The new Police Station at Norbury was taken into occupation and business commenced on 17th August 1925. The Station included five sets of married quarters[71]. The Thornton Heath Sub-Division became known as the Norbury

Sub-Division and Sub-Divisional Inspector Pullen was transferred to Norbury[72]. On January 1928 the address for the Police Station was changed to 1516 London Road, Norbury[73].

In October 1931 Thornton Heath Police Station was closed to the public and the area, for policing purposes, was divided between Croydon, South Norwood and Norbury Stations[74].

A plot of land adjoining Norbury Police Station was purchased freehold for the sum of £575 from a Mr B Gilitting on 17 November 1938 with a view to further development of the Station[75].

It was recognised as long ago as 1938 that Norbury was totally inadequate for a Sub-Divisional Station and plans were made to bring it up to near Home Office standards. In the meantime the war intervened and it was not until 1962 that the building was finally ameliorated and alterations carried out[76].

In April 1965 with the creation of the new London Borough of Croydon, Norbury (ZN) remained a Sub-Divisional Station with South Norwood as its Sectional Station.[77] In 1968 Norbury Police Station became an 'Inspector Unit' with Inspector Derek Bainbridge in charge[78].

The address of the Station is shown as 1516 London Road, Norbury, and iscurrently open from11am – 2pm and 3pm – 7pm. The local residents are campaigning for their Police Station to remain openas notice has been served that the Station will close within the next three years.

Sanderstead (Hamsley Green) Police station

Sanderstead is an old village south of Croydon and its identity is preserved by the surrounding golf courses and open spaces[79].

In 1849 there was a Station on 'P', or Camberwell,Division situated here until 1865. It was a Sergeant Designated Station[80]. The Police rented a two-stall stable from Captain Wigzell at an annual rental of £10. Report dated May 1873 shows the stables[81]. In 1888 a Station at Sanderstead was shown as a Constable Station located on 'W', or Clapham, Division and no telegraphic communications had been linked to the main Station. By 1894 Sanderstead was shown as a Sectional station of Croydon.

Fredrick Bonner, the Croydon Sub-Divisional Inspector, would visit periodically to check that matters at the Station were in good order[82]. By 1898 the Station was no longer in existence with Kenley replacing it as the Sectional Station[83].

South Norwood Police Station

As the London population continued to grow in the early 1800's people started to feel that they needed their own Police Station. The population of the area tended to congregate around the railway station at Norwood junction[84].

In October 1871, Mr Haynes wrote on behalf of the residents of South Norwood to the District Police Superintendent, Captain Baynes. Haynes suggested that suitable premises in High Street, South Norwood, near the junction of Station Road, were available for conversion into a Police Station[85]. The property was obtained in 1872 on a 99 year lease from Charles Pawley of Kirkdale, Sydenham, at a ground rent of £19.10s.0d. Alterations to the property cost £1200. The freehold on the property was purchased in 1899 for the sum of £740[86].

A report in 1881 on the condition of Metropolitan Police Stations describes South Norwood as two adjoining ordinary dwelling-houses united as a Police Station. The quarters were occupied by one married Sergeant, one married Constable and eight single Constables but were notwell arranged, and the mess room was not being used[87].

The new Police Station opened in December 1873. The assessment for rent was one married Sergeant at 4 shillings a week, one married Constable at 3 shillings a week and eight single Constables at one shilling a week[88]. By 1884 the new address of the Police Station was 83, High Street, South Norwood[89]. South Norwood was a Sectional Station of Thornton Heath where Sub-Divisional Inspector William Lemmey was in charge[90].

In 1921 following the formation of the new "Z" Division South Norwood was transferred from "W" to "Z"[91].

In 1960 it was recommended that South Norwood Police Station should be rebuilt. The old building had outlived its usefulness. A new site near to the existing Police Station was sought. A possible site, 193/195 Selhurst Road, SE25, was earmarked for development, but the Planning Committee of the County Borough of Croydon turned down a planning application on the grounds that it was a residential site and it would be seriously detrimental to the area for a station to be built there. The Receiver then found an alternative site at Nos 1 – 11, Olive Road, SE25. The freehold-combined properties were purchased between the years 1964 – 1969 for the sum of £36,250. The site was later let to the London Borough of Croydon as a Public Car Park in September 1969[92].

South Norwood Police Station
83 High Street, South Norwood.
1873 - 1988

In 1961 the top floor of the Police Station ceased to be married quarters[93] and the space used for administrative matters. In 1968 South Norwood Police Station became an 'Inspector Unit' with Inspector George in charge[94].

In September 1985 Districts, formerly called Divisions, were abolished and the Metropolitan Police was re-organised into the new eight-area structures. South Norwood (ZN) became part of the new 4 Area South, with the following Divisions: - LD, LK, LM, VM, ZD, ZN and ZP[95]. This meant that police officers at South Norwood ceased to wear the single 'Z' letter and changed to having a two letter 'ZN' Divisional (Norbury) code on their shoulders[96].

The present new Police Station at 11 Olive Grove opened on the 21st November 1988 by Lord Lane and Chief Superintendent Sally Hubbard took possession of the new station. It then became the Divisional Headquarters (ZY) and all officers on the Division changed their shoulders letters to "ZY".

By 1994 the Metropolitan Police Service was restructured again from eight areas to five areas. South Norwood became part of 4 Area with Headquarters based in Sidcup. In April 2000 the Metropolitan Police restructured into Borough based policing within the local authority boundaries. South Norwood, New Addington, Kenley, Norbury and Croydon are all administrated under Croydon Borough Police[97].

South Norwood Police Station
Olive Road, South Norwood.
1988 – present day

Currently South Norwood Police Station is open 24hrs each day of the week[98].

Thornton Heath Police Station

The area of Thornton Heath developed in the late 19th Century and with the increase in population there was a need for a Police Station to be built in that area. The freehold title to a site located in Thornton Heath was purchased in 1885 and Thornton Heath Police Station, consisting of a Station and Section House designed by John Butler, was originally opened on 5th November 1887[99] at 80 Parchmore Road and the junction of Heath Road. The cost of the freehold in 1885 was £400 and the erection of the building was £2811. The architectural drawings held by National Archives are dated 1886[100]. The Station was closed in October 1931[101] when Norbury took responsibility for the area.

In 1933 an internal police report looked at what should be done with the old building. They described it as a fairly large building occupying a large site in a commanding corner position in a fairly good class neighbourhood. Part of the building was used as a Section House for 10 men and was still occupied. To convert the whole building into a Section House was considered but there was doubt that it would justify the cost, butit certainly wasn't viable to retain the building as a Section House for just 10 men. The sale of the building and land would have raised a substantial sum of money,however the building was retained. In July 1935 the then Metropolitan Police Architect and Surveyor, G.Mackenzie Trench, drew up plans to convert the building and land into a District Traffic Garage for 28 Police vehicles and suitable accommodation for Police staff and it was re-opened on 10th August 1936 as 4 Area District Garage (DG4). When the new traffic patrols took to the road a new batch of divisional numbers 767 to 834 "Z" were introduced.

After a period of closure again after the traffic officers moved out the premises were re-opened in April 1990 to house the Area Dog section and Territorial Support Group[102].

---

[1] MEPO 2/25
[2] Hobbs.D.C.H. The Croydon Police (1829-1840) Journal of the Police History Society. pp66-79
[3] Hobbs D.C.H
[4] http://met.police.uk accessed 10th October 2010
[5] Pevsner, N and Cherry, B. (1983) London 2. South. Penguin, Harmondsworth p203
[6] MEPO 2/76
[7] Metropolitan Police Order dated 28th October 1865
[8] J.Back Archive 1975
[9] LB 806
[10] PO23 March 1962
[11] LB 807
[12] PO26 August 1977
[13] Brown B. The Warren 1982
[14] http://met.police.uk accessed on 10th October 2010
[15] MEPO 2/76
[16] Metropolitan PoliceSurveyors Records 1912
[17] Metropolitan Police Surveyors Records 1912
[18] LB 800
[19] Croydon Police Station by PC 872 'A' Jephcote (1982)
[20] The Police and Constabulary List 1844 p3
[21] Ibid p2
[22] The Croydon Directory 1851 p156
[23] Ibid p54
[24] Police Order 11 January 1864
[25] Police Order 28 October 1865
[26] MEPO 2/139

[27] Kelly's Directory 1878 p2169
[28] Metropolitan Police Report 1881
[29] Police Almanac 1889
[30] Metropolitan Police Historical Collection
[31] Notes by Chief Inspector Delaney 1982?
[32] Kelly's Directory 1891 p1239
[33] Metropolitan Police Surveyors Records 1912
[34] Ibid p35
[35] Metropolitan Police Surveyors Records 1924
[36] Police Order 30 August 1895
[37] Croydon Police Station by PC 872 'A' Jephcote (1982)
[38] The Police Review and Parade Gossip 30th September 1898 p466
[39] MEPO 5/127
[40] Police Order 24 February 1921
[41] Post Office Directory 1928
[42] Post Office London Directory 1939
[43] Metropolitan Police Historical Collection
[44] Metropolitan Police Historical Collection
[45] The Official Encyclopedia of Scotland Yard 1999
[46] cfa.vic.gov.au accessed on 23rd March 2010
[47] Croydon Advertiser 17 May 1968
[48] http://www.blackhistorymonthuk.co.uk/uni/first_in_the_force.html accessed on 25th March 2010
[49] NSY Press Release dated 5 March 1980
[50] Croydon Advertiser 14 May 1971
[51] Pevsner, N and Cherry, B. (1983) London 2. South. Penguin, Harmondsworth
[52] NSY Press Release dated 5 March 1980
[53] Brown B. The Warren 1982
[54] Brown B. The Warren 1982
[55] MEPO14
[56] Metropolitan Police Asset Management Plan. November 2007
[57] LB 804
[58] Metropolitan Police surveyors records 1924
[59] MEPO 9/97
[60] Met Police Surveyors Book
[61] Metropolitan Police Orders dated 4th July 1896
[62] Metropolitan Police Orders dated 24th February 1921
[63] Metropolitan Police Orders dated 6th August 1964
[64] http://cms.met.police.uk October 2010
[65] Pevsner, N and Cherry, B. (1983) London 2. South. Penguin, Harmondsworth p225
[66] MEPO 2/1872
[67] MEPO 2/1872
[68] LB 808
[69] MEPO 2/1872
[70] MEPO 2/1872
[71] Metropolitan Police Surveyors Records 1924
[72] Metropolitan Police Orders dated 14th August 1925
[73] LB 808
[74] Metropolitan Police Orders dated 9th October 1931
[75] LB 808
[76] LB 808
[77] Metropolitan Police Orders dated 6th August 1964
[78] Croydon Midweek 22 October 1968
[79] Pevsner, N and Cherry, B. (1983) London 2. South. Penguin, Harmondsworth p227
[80] Kelly's directories 1849 - 1865

[81] MEPO 4/234
[82] Kelly's directories 1880 -1890
[83] ibid
[84] Pevsner, N and Cherry, B. (1983) London 2. South. Penguin, Harmondsworth p230
[85] www.met.police.uk/croydon/history.htm 11.08.2007
[86] Metropolitan Police Surveyors Book
[87] Metropolitan Police report 1881
[88] Metropolitan Police Orders dated 5th December 1873
[89] Metropolitan Police Orders dated 20th June 1884
[90] Kelly's Directory 1895
[91] Metropolitan Police Orders dated 24th February 1927
[92] Moore C. and Gerrard Derek A History of South Norwood Police Station Printed by the New Police Station Builders
[93] Moore C. and Gerrard Derek A History of South Norwood Police Station Printed by the New Police Station Builders.
[94] Croydon Midweek 22 October 1968
[95] Metropolitan Police Orders dated 29th August 1985
[96] Brown B. Policing Old Norwood 1998
[97] www.met.polce.uk/croydon/history.htm 11.8.2007
[98] http://met.police.uk October 2010
[99] Metropolitan Police Orders dated 4th November 1887
[100] MEPO 9/159
[101] Brown B. Policing Old Norwood 1998
[102] Brown .B. Policing Old Norwood 1998

Chapter 4

London Borough of Greenwich

Introduction

Greenwich is made up of the two old boroughs of Greenwich and Woolwich. Until 1965 Woolwich included a strip of land to the north of the Thames called North Woolwich, which now forms part of Newham (See Chapter 10). In 1981 the population of Greenwich was 211,840. Together with Deptford, the London Borough of Greenwich is bound up with Britain's naval and military past, and early development was concentrated along its northern boundary, the River Thames. To the west Greenwich is adjoined to Lewisham, Bromley lies to the south and Bexley to the east. Between 1800 and 1813 the villages of Deptford, New Cross, Blackheath, Greenwich and Woolwich saw considerable growth in populations, but it took longer for the villages of Plumstead, Charlton, Shooters Hill, Eltham, and Lee to expand. By 1851 Greenwich had seen a rise in Irish immigration totalling nearly 10%, whilst up to 1991 an influx of people from India amounted to nearly 5% of the population.

In 1738 the New Cross Turnpike Trust extended their improved road system from Blackheath to the notorious Shooters Hill and on to Dartford Town via Crayford. Further improvements in 1781 altered the route so that it would go through Nettlebed Bottom. This area had become relatively lawless, with Highwaymen, footpads, and housebreakers operating along the isolated roads and thoroughfares after dark, and inhabitants of the villages lived in constant fear of attack by the thieves and bandits. A plan was conceived in 1763 to introduce Horse Patrols to deal with the threat of highway robbery; however these patrols were not instituted until 1805. The Bow Street Horse Patrol or Foot Patrol was established along the main routes to Dover[1]. The original plan was for the Horse Patrol to be stationed at turnpikes, but this was rejected. These patrols were regarded as a success since there were a number of innovations introduced as well. The Horse Patrol was allowed to pass through all turnpikes free of charge, with the sole exception of Hyde Park Turnpike. Turnpike keepers were paid to hand out pamphlets about crime to travellers and horns were also issued to them, to help alert 'the Patrol' in the event of a traveller being robbed[2]. The Horse Patrol often stayed close to the turnpikes because the keepers would have information about people and suspects passing through the area. The turnpike keepers were occasionally paid for their information, especially when robbers or highwaymen were caught. John Fielding tried to get police offices established next to turnpikes but this also proved unsuccessful.

From the start of Sir Robert Peel's administration the new Police presence in 1829 Greenwich and Woolwich continued to grow in importance, which is shown by the rise in the number of naval and military establishments that spread out along the south side of the River Thames. The importance of making munitions and armaments for the wars and its close proximity to the centre of London made this also a rapidly growing residential area.

With the growth of populations and increased urbanisation came the expansion of the Police in London. The Metropolitan Police Service extended to 700 square miles with a complement of some 4500[3] officers and men radiating 15 miles from Charing Cross. Greenwich fell within the 6-mile-band from central London.

The allocation of divisional policing boundaries during Victorian times meant that Greenwich and Woolwich became part of a very large 'R' Division, stretching from Deptford to St. Mary Cray. Officers would have been required to patrol the parks of Greenwich and Southwark and man

Constables, sergeants and the Inspector of 'R' Division during the Dock Strike 1912

one of the three fixed points on the Division. These were located at the village centre of Blackheath, the Broadway, Greenwich, the High Street, Deptford and Lower Road, Deptford. Since 1829 many Police Stations within 'R' Division and the areas of Woolwich and Greenwich have both opened and closed. Today, under borough based policing, the London Borough of Greenwich has just four Stations, Greenwich (RD), Woolwich (RW), Plumstead (RP), and Thamesmead (RA).

During various times of unrest, including coal and dock strikes, 'R' Division sent serials of police officers to maintain law and order. The photograph on the previous page shows just such a serial sent in 1912 to police the Dock strike, with the Inspector seated in between his Sergeants. These are ordinary police officers from the division, probably drawn from all the Stations, whilst the Inspector is likely to have been the Reserve Inspector located at Blackheath Road. 'R' Division had also sent a contingent to police the Tonnypandy coal strike in South Wales in 1910.

In 2010 the Senior Officers on Greenwich Borough were Detective Chief Superintendent Richard Wood (Borough Commander), Superintendent Chris Hafford (Safer Neighbourhoods and Operations), Detective Superintendent Kate Halpin, Chief Inspector Dave Mann (Operations), Chief Inspector Andrew Johnstone (Safer Neighbourhoods), and Chief Inspector Neil Myers (Partnership and Olympics)[4].

Abbey Wood Police Station

In 1906 the Receiver of the Metropolitan Police purchased a freehold site and a Police Station was built there of brick and slate and, though small by normal standards, it also included a yard. It only existed as a Police Station for a short while and was probably used for other purposes while normal policing in the area seems to have been covered by Stations in Plumstead and Belvedere. The station was built with two sets of quarters with an address as Abbey Wood Road, SE2 in 1912[5].

Abbeywood Police Station
Abbeywood Road j/w Conference Road, Abbeywood.
1906-1926

In 1925 Abbey Wood was a police station attached to 'R' division and was located at the

86

Abbey Wood Road junction with Conference Road. It was a busy junction, with the Tram depot opposite and Abbey Wood Railway Station behind that in Harrow Manor Way. This road led to a powder magazine which was situated right next to the Thames for ease of transport. There were also police buildings further down that road as the general area was mostly set aside for munitions production. These police buildings would also have ensured greater security for the nearby gunpowder magazines and the rifle and artillery ranges on neighbouring Plumstead Marshes. By the mid 1920s it was felt that there was some duplication of policing responsibilities for the area so the station was closed in December 1926. The quarters and offices were retained for administrative purposes and for a time became a Traffic Warden centre.

In the 1950s, Abbey Wood became a boomtown with both industry and more housing arriving in the area which then became known as the Abbey Wood Estate. Little further building took place there until the 1960s, when the newly-formed Greater London Council, mindful of the need for more housing, took over the marshland which had recently been vacated by the Military and commenced a huge development which was later named Thamesmead, this name being chosen after a competition in the now defunct Evening News[6].

With the demise of the GLC in 1986, the town was handed over to a private company called Thamesmead Town Limited, which created concern amongst the local community by introducing higher rents whilst at the same time reducing services.

Eltham Police Station

The area of Eltham became part of the first Bow Street Horse Patrol Divisions in 1827[7], although the area had been patrolled since 1820 from their Station which was situated on Shooters Hill.

The Horse Patrols were introduced by Sir Richard Ford, Chief Magistrate at Bow Street in 1805, and were incorporated into the Metropolitan Police in 1836. These were armed horsemen in cavalry cloaks, blue coats and trousers, and red waistcoats. They patrolled the main highways and thoroughfares of the Metropolis giving confidence to the travellers, often with the cry 'Bow Street Patrol'[8]. A prisoner lock-up was situated in Eltham, and in 1827 the First Division of the Bow Street Horse Patrol began patrolling the area[9].

Watch Houses, which were built by and belonged to the parish, had been taken over by the Metropolitan Police under an Act of Parliament at the introduction of the new Police in 1829. These also included Watch Houses that fell into the Metropolitan Police area later as the boundary of the Metropolitan Police was extended, and this is what occurred in 1839 when Eltham was included.

Eltham was shown to have a Watch House called 'Blunts Cross', built by the Parish in 1745[10] not far from the present Blunts Road, and had an established strength of one Sergeant and seven Constables in 1839[11]. Eltham Watch House was built between Elm Terrace and Pound Place, including a Cage situated on the other side of the road that was used for stores, lost dogs and property. It had long been felt in the area that the old Watch House was worn out and no longer fit to be used. A new Station House was needed and correspondence passed between the Commissioner, Sir Richard Mayne, and the Chief Surveyor granting permission for a new Police Station to be created in Eltham. Final Home Office permission was granted on 2nd March 1863[12]. However, ownership of the Cage was in dispute between the Police and the original landlords, the 'Fifteen Penny Society', who insisted that 'since it had not been used since 1858 it should be returned'. The Police challenged their Trustees ownership claims but it was later proved, in meeting minutes taken in September 1745 that the Society was the Trustees of the land. The Police did not rush to return the property though, and this finally occurred in January 1875[13].

Because Eltham was a minor Station and only supervised by a Sergeant, instructions were given that further supervision would be undertaken by the Inspector at Lee (Road) who carried out patrols on

Eltham Police Station
172 High Street, Eltham, SE9
1865- 1939

horseback. The mounted Sergeant at Sidcup also provided supervision, patrolling on horse or foot for at least 9 of the 24 hours[14].

In 1870 Surveyors' records note that Eltham was a Station on 'R' Division built in 1865 at a cost of £1925. 7s., but the land on which the Station was built was leased from the Office of Woods and Forests at a ground rent of £15 3s 6d. p. a. The Station occupied a large corner plot

The rear yard of Eltham Police Station in 1911

situated on the southern side of the High Road at the junction with Victoria Road. The premises consisted of a basement, ground and first floor, and contained a charge room, 3 cells and a two-stall stable. There was also a drying closet, store, scullery and coal cellar. Accommodation for eleven single Constables was shown above the Station on the first floor where, in two rooms, the station Inspector also resided with his wife and family.

The resident Inspector was John Pryke, aged 31 years, who lived there with his family[15] paying the weekly sum of 3s 6d for rent. The address of the Station was recorded as 172 Eltham Street, Eltham,[16] although by 1898 this became 172 High Street, Eltham,[17] and changing again to 172 High Street, Eltham, SE9, before 1939[18].

To improve upon the cramped living conditions a re-assessment of space allocation took place in 1885 and the review decided to allocate five rooms for the married Inspector, but increased the rent to 5s. 6d. per week. The Section House still showed eleven Constables residing, each paying 1s per week rent[19]. The Sergeant paid the rent for the Station and was given an allowance for the cost of the charge room, which was a public room.

In the picture below Inspector 69265 Thomas Hill is shown on patrol when he was an Inspector on 'D', or Marylebone Division, in about 1903. Hill became the Sub Divisional Inspector on 'R' Division in 1905

Sub Divisional Inspector Thomas Hill in 1903

responsible for Lee Road and was a frequent visitor to Elham since this was one of his Sub-Divisional Stations. An accomplished rider, he shows that he is prepared for all weathers – note the riding cape, which is rolled at the front part of the saddle. Both he and his companion are in possession of sabres. The Station had a groom to keep the horses in top condition and, judging by the photograph above, he did an excellent job. Hill retired in 1909.

There was an expansion in the Eltham area where houses were built or found for munitions workers during the First World War and the growth of the workforce continued up to the Second World War and beyond. This increase in local population caused problems for policing, which meant that as new communities sprang up the needs of the police were reassessed and new Stations considered.

The address of the Station was 172 High Street, Eltham, SE9 in 1931 situated at the junction with Victoria Road later Foots Cray Road. The existing building was over 50 years old and not really suitable anymore as a Police Station, so efforts were made to find a new site. Land on which to build the new station[20], which was originally part of the Sherard Hall estate, was purchased in Well Hall Road in 1921 from Mr. Archibald Tarry. The old Station was closed at 6am on Sunday 12th March 1939 and business was moved to the 'new Station an art deco building' at Well Hall Road near the junction of High Street, SE9[21], Eltham. The new station, whilst not on the High Street was situated just inside Well Hall Road.

Eltham Police Station
Well Hall Road, Eltham,
1939 - Present day

During the 1930s Trenchard, as Commissioner, instigated considerable organisational change and improvements to the Metropolitan Police in a variety of ways. Improvements in communications commenced in June 1934 with the introduction of a wireless car scheme on each of the four Sub-Divisions, and the call signs allocated were 5R for Blackheath Road, 6R for Eltham, 7R for Woolwich and 8R for Bexleyheath. These communications are still in use today, using the phonic alphabet introduced in 1956. Following on from this, November 1934 saw the advent of the familiar blue 'Dr Who' style Police Boxes[22]. By November 1937 the famous '999' call system was also introduced. To improve railway communications and ease the growth of the travelling commuter, new railway stations were built at Albany Park (1935) and Falconwood (1936)[23].

Eltham Sub-Division was being broken up in 1959 when it became a Sectional Station and by the summer of 1968 Eltham (RM) was transferred to Greenwich Sub-Division. The Divisional Headquarters moved from Greenwich to Eltham, now (RD), although it remained as a Sub-Divisional Station in October 1984. Eltham also became a Traffic Headquarters for TDR and later the upper floors served 'R' District, 3 Area, 4 Area, SE Area and finally South Area before being transferred to Marlowe House, Sidcup, in 1996. The building is currently occupied by RM Sector, the Finance Unit, the Quality Performance Review Unit, the Training Department and a variety of business units including SO1(4) and SCG (South)[24].

East Greenwich Police Station

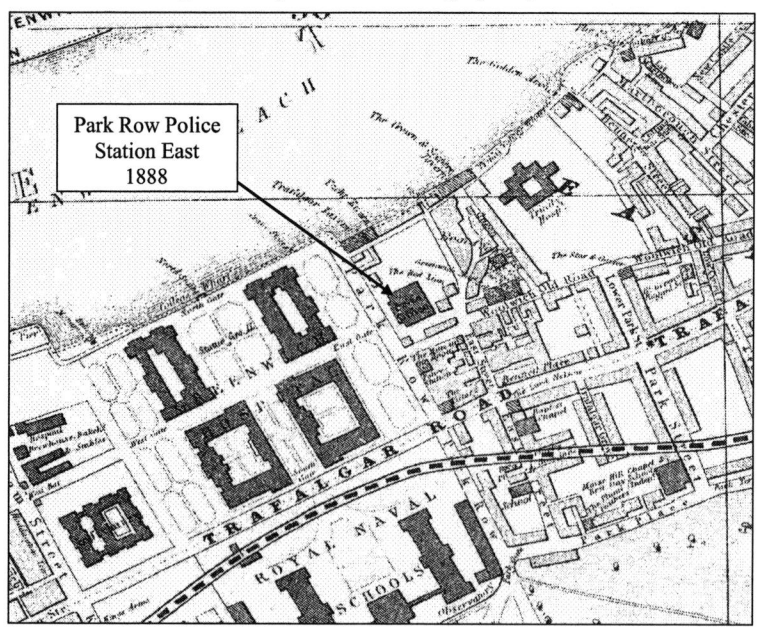

There was a Station House with a Sergeant in charge at East Greenwich, shown with an address of 2 Park Row, which was rented from Lewis Glenton of Pageot Cottage, Blackheath, for 21 yrs from 1849. The premises appeared to be not up to standard as there was a stipulation it should be occupied only when thoroughly repaired. The rent was reviewed yearly and cost the Receiver £63 per annum[25]. Later, in 1873, the Freehold was purchased for £1000. It was described as a substantial brick and slate built house having some 14 rooms over three floors which included a charge room, kitchen scullery, 3 cells and a 2 stall stable. It required maintenance, but had been kept clean and decorated. Surveyor's records show that it was redecorated and painted in 1853, and was then usually redecorated at 4 year intervals. The Station also provided accommodation at the time for 4 married Constables and 1 single Constable[26]. It was surveyed in 1850 to consider its suitability to remain a Police Station and was kept in service.

In 1867 the records show that a married Inspector occupied three rooms on the second floor at a cost of 3s per week. Rent generated at the time to defray the cost of the building amounted to £31. 4s per annum[27].

East Greenwich Police Station
2 Park Row
1873 - 1902

Police Orders, January 1864, referred to East Greenwich (Park Row) Police Station for the first time, when it was shown as a Station on 'R' or Greenwich Division with strength of 4 Sergeants and 19 Constables[28]. Two of the Sergeants, who were called Station Sergeants, did not leave the Station and had to work 12-hour shifts. Inspectors and Sergeants from Greenwich Police Station supervised the East Greenwich area.

By 1874 permission had been obtained from the Home Office by the Divisional Superintendent, James Griffin, for a freehold site to be purchased, since the old Station was no longer fit for its purpose. In 1881 substantial work was required to bring the existing Station up to a satisfactory level of health and cleanliness. It was reported that this was an old house with poor administrative accommodation and had a water supply that was insufficient for the Station's needs. It must have been very uncomfortable to live and work there, since the surveyors when commenting on the sewers, sinks, sewer pipes and gas mains[29] suggested work to be carried out urgently. In 1893 Park Row became a Sectional Station of Westcombe Park[30], but it would take a further 10 years before the Station was replaced.

Living there at the time under such conditions was the Superintendent of the Division, Christopher H. McHugo, a 44-year-old Irishman from Galway, with his wife and eleven children. There were not many Stations that could accommodate such a large family and he would have pressed for better conditions. McHugo had been well thought of by Senior Officers when he became the 'R' Divisional Superintendent in January 1879, after being promoted from being Chief Inspector at 'Y' or Hampstead Division. Promotion to Superintendent in 9 years was indeed

East Greenwich Police Station
Trafalgar Road SE 10.
1902 - 1962

rapid for McHugo, as he had been promoted to the rank of Reserve Inspector in 1870 when it was created for 'S' Division at a better rate of pay. McHugo was selected from all the Divisional Inspectors for this prestigious new position[31]. He remained in charge for 20 years until he resigned on pension in April 1899. Even in retirement his contribution was recognised when the Secretary of State granted McHugo an annual allowance of £25[32] in addition to his pension.

For communication purposes East Greenwich had call sign Papa Alpha (PA)[33]. Instructions were given to find land nearby on which to build a new station and in the meantime the Park Row site (now numbered 23)

Trafalgar Road Police Station

was sold to Mr J. P. Crosby for £450, some-what of a loss considering the Metropolitan Police had originally paid £1000 for the site in 1873. In 1881 a site premises in Lower Woolwich Road (now Bridge Terrace and Aldeburgh Street) was leased from Henry and Alfred Walker (Builders) of Greenwich for £41 per annum[34]. Plans were drawn up to build a Station, but the railway company purchased the land, which meant another site had to be found.

East Greenwich officers on duty during the 1926 General Strike

New premises were found at the junction of Park Row and Trafalgar Road and purchased on 22nd April 1902. The cost to the police was £8,250, the premises having been previously called 'The Good Duke Humphrey Hall and Coffee Tavern'[35]. The address was shown as Trafalgar Road, SE10, in 1931.

The picture above shows 'R' Division in the yard at East Greenwich during the 1926 General strike. The most senior officer, the Station Sergeant, is seated whilst the rest of the mobile unit parade at the rear of their van.

Instructions were given for the re-location of the Divisional Headquarters for 'R' Division to East Greenwich just three months before the outbreak of the Second World War [36]. As with the First World War, and because of their military significance, Greenwich, Woolwich, and the locality, became the focus of German bombers, flying bombs and rockets. Between June 1940 and July 1941 'The Blitz', as it was known, caused

East Greenwich Police Station Bomb damage in 1941

widespread damage in the area.

On the evening of 10th/11th May 1941 six 1000-pound bombs blew up most of Trafalgar Road, severely damaging the Police Station[37] and killing Reserve Police Inspector Arthur Wells, aged 51, and a War

Reserve Constable[38]. As a result of the damage to the Police Station the headquarters returned to Blackheath Road. Trafalgar Road was very unfortunate as a V2 rocket hit it on 8th July 1944 and five people were injured. However, after that only skeleton staffs were left behind to man the token Police Office, the remainder being transferred back to Blackheath Road. Some fourteen regular and auxiliary 'R' Division officers were killed during enemy air raids in the war[39] and between June 1944 and March 1945 no fewer than 241 Flying bombs, V1s also called 'Doodlebugs', and 92 V2s landed on 'R' Division[40].

East Greenwich Police Station showing War damage 1941

East Greenwich Police Station was shut for police purposes in 1962 at the same time as Blackheath Road. The new Station, and current Greenwich Police Station, situated on Royal Hill, opened in May 1962 and consolidated policing in Greenwich[41].

Greenwich Police Station

There have been at least four Police Stations which have been built in the Greenwich area over the past 200 years, namely in Greenwich Road, Blackheath Road, Parkway, and Trafalgar Road.

A Cage was erected to house prisoners in 1822 in Greenwich Road on the corner of Cut-throat Lane[42]. When the new Police were formed there in 1829, a Watch House called Rose Cottage, had been taken over in Greenwich Road. There was one other station on 'R' Division and this was located in Lucas Street, Rotherhithe[43] (now called Cathay Street), but its actual address was 23 Paradise Street[44].

Dominating the area is the Royal Naval College (formally the Royal Hospital, moved from Portsmouth in 1873) and the Royal Hospital School behind it. Premises at 2 Queen Elizabeth's Row, Greenwich, shown as a detached office of the 'R' Division[45] next door to the Alms Houses and opposite Greenwich Railway Station, were offered to the Police prior to 1832. In February 1834 the Home Office recommended that the premises, which were owned by a Mr Wright, were suitable as a Police Station and should be leased at £40 per annum[46].

Inspector Francis M. Mallalieu was promoted in 1835 to Superintendent, took command of 'R' Division, and had his Divisional Headquarters briefly at this Station prior to its move to Blackheath Road. The Greenwich Police Station address was shown as 1, Orchard Lane, Greenwich[47]. The Inspector in charge of the Sub-Division at the time was James Douglas and he had been promoted to Inspector in 1840[48].

In 1840 the boundary of Greenwich Division consisted of the parishes of Greenwich; St. Nicholas, Deptford; part of St. Paul's Deptford, in the county of Kent; Lewisham and Lee in Kent; Rotherhithe; that part of St Pauls, Deptford, in Surrey; and the hamlet of Hatcham[49]. Because the Division covered a large area with semi-rural villages, and to enable them to patrol and supervise the division, the Superintendent and Inspectors were trained in the art of horsemanship. As travelling by horse and cart was the normal mode of transport at that time, it was common for people to be experienced in riding horses.

In 1836 the Home Office approved another Police Station, called Greenwich - Blackheath Road, as they considered the old Station in Greenwich Road no longer suitable for the purpose. The new premises had been leased from Mr Thomas Pocknell for 50 years at an annual rent of £200 and there was a requirement to insure the premises for £4000. The Station was positioned along a busy thoroughfare running from New Cross Road, over Deptford Bridge and towards Blackheath Hill Railway Station. Located on the north side of the road, the Station was positioned between Greenwich Road and Egerton Road on the edge of Deptford New Town.

Before separate Dockyard Police were formed it was the responsibility of 'R' Division to provide security and post Police Officers there on duty. The Police and Constabulary List of 1844 shows that Inspector James Douglas, who had been promoted in 1840, was in charge of Blackheath Road Station, Greenwich. Improvements in communication in 1844 saw Blackheath Road Station linked to Scotland Yard by Telegraph. Supt. T. W. Baxter[50] was in charge of the Division at this time. A published list in 1898 shows Greenwich to have the code Romeo Delta (RD)[51].

Policing in Victorian times could be a dangerous occupation, with 'R' Division being a difficult area. For example, in 1852 Sergeant Joseph Rendall died of injuries, which he received during an accident while on duty on Greenwich Division[52], but a number of officers have been killed on the Division under mysterious circumstances. Sergeant Arthur Gaynor died of head injuries in 1879, Sergeant William Bacon drowned whilst on duty at Greenwich coal wharves in 1881, and Constable Edwin Cousins died of injuries received in 1886, Constable Fredrick Arnup died of a stroke whilst on duty in 1899 and Constable Richard Crabb died of spinal injuries in 1900[53].

A revision of boundaries in 1864 introduced a number of new Divisions, mirroring growth in the general population of London [54]. This led to the establishing of 'W' Division and meant that Greenwich Division was reduced in area to make it a more equal and manageable size.

In 1864 the Station strength was 2 Inspectors, 2 Sergeants, 1 Acting Sergeant, 11 day duty and 28 night duty Constables, and a number of 'A' Division Officers who were kept on reserve at the Station. These included 1 Inspector 2 Sergeants and 9 Constables. The Station had 10 beats and stables for 13 horses. There were two horses for supervision, one to be ridden by the Superintendent and the other for the use of the 2 Inspectors on day and night duty; each riding the horse alternately. Five horses were available for the van, which was used to transfer prisoners from court to prisons [55].

By 1869 land had been leased in Blackheath Road from the estate of Thomas Pocknell of Georges Place, Exeter, initially for five years but later extended until 1944. A building and stables were present and later re-furbished, with extensive work being done to the existing building and a new Section House, for the accommodation of 37 single Constables, was built. Firearms were issued to Stations, because occasionally criminals would take weapons with them to commit a crime. Adams breech-loading revolvers and ammunition were supplied to Metropolitan Police Divisions. Divisional Headquarters were issued with 10 revolvers in August 1868, later supplemented with a further eleven weapons in January 1869, bringing the total number held on 'R' Division to 39 firearms. Some ten rounds of ammunition were issued with each firearm[56].

As the area expanded it was necessary that security was required at vulnerable premises containing property so, as docks were being built to supply London's huge appetite, Police Officers were sent there on duty. In 1869 'R' Division supplied a total of 4 Constables to the Surrey Commercial Docks.

Blackheath Road Police Station
Greenwich
1836-1910

The Commissioner sanctioned recreation and games rooms in July 1869 and they were places where off duty officers could smoke. He paid for a billiard table, and games such as draughts, dominoes, backgammon, single sticks, and boxing gloves for their entertainment and exercise.

Billiard tables were generally reserved for Headquarters Stations like Blackheath Road, so the other 'R' Division Stations, Rotherhithe, Deptford, Woolwich, Shooters Hill, Bexley, Eltham, and Lee just received the games[57]. The introduction of these measures helped to ensure that single Officers remained in the Station during their off duty hours and stopped them from getting bored, frequenting public houses, drinking too much, incurring debts, or fraternising too much with the locals, who were perceived as villainous. Alcoholism was a problem at the time, since people often would drink beer rather than trust the water. The Divisional Superintendent commended the use of recreation rooms and in 1871 suggested to the Commissioner in his annual report that a billiard table ought to be introduced at all Stations where police reside[58].

Cattle plague was a problem in 1870 and farmers and drovers would herd their cattle to market by driving them along the main roads into the capital. Cattle drovers were required to stop at Police-manned posts on the boundary of any Division where the cattle would be inspected for signs of disease. Outer lying Divisions and other locations had checking points like railway stations, wharves or boundary points. 'R' Division had 8 boundary posts which were manned day and night by 24 Constables[59]. With the opening of the New Foreign Cattle Market at Deptford Dockyard (owned by the City of London Corporation) it meant a reduction in the numbers of Police Officers employed for Cattle plague duty on the boundary roads[60].

Later, in 1871 a new set of 6 stables were added to the 6 which were already present costing in total £890. 9s. In addition to the new stables a harness room, loft, 1 cart house and 1 van house were also added, all located in the grounds of the Station. The van was for the transfer of prisoners from the adjacent courthouse building to the prisons. Alterations to the Section House and Station in 1877 cost the sum of £1854. 11s. and a range of public and private rooms were shown located beneath the Section House. For example, downstairs on the ground floor there were two public rooms; one was the Superintendent's office and the Clerks to the Superintendent occupied the other. These were probably either the Clerk or the Station Sergeant and his staff. Also, shown as part of the Station House building were two further rooms, consisting of a charge room and the Sub-Divisional Inspectors Office.

The rear yard of Blackheath Road police station 1911

Somewhat strangely, the prisoners who were kept at the Station were taken upstairs to three cells, which were allocated on the first floor. This is odd since a determined prisoner could seek an escape by taking up floor boards, while it was usual for prisoners to be housed in cells on the ground floor since these were set in concrete foundations thus making escape more difficult. At some later stage the three cells were increased to five and a 'drunk-tank', called here an 'association cell', was added. The 'association cell' allowed for the retention of a number of prisoners together during raids or for drunken prisoners.

Greenwich continued to be the Divisional Station of 'R' Division in 1873, which covered a large area of south London and remained important enough to have an Inspector in charge. Other Inspector Stations included Woolwich (William Street) Lee Road, Shooters Hill, Rotherhithe (Paradise Street) and Prince Street, Deptford. Sergeants were placed in charge at East Greenwich (Park Row), Eltham, St Mary Cray, Sidcup, Bexleyheath, Erith and Deptford (Foreign Cattle market). Greenwich was one of the largest Stations on the Division and it was often the way that the most senior officer would also reside there, however the incumbent Superintendent resided at East Greenwich Station instead.

Trams were introduced in 1871 between East Greenwich and Canal Bridge and between Deptford Bridge and Blackheath Hill[61]. These changes in transport added to the general traffic travelling along the main roads of the Division making Police Road Traffic Duty more complex.

In 1881 Police Sergeant Donald Walters, a married man who came from Caithness in Scotland was shown resident at the Station. Records do not show if his wife resided with him. On the night of the census not only those on duty but also those who were resident at the Section House and prisoners in the cells were counted. This totalled some 31 Police Officers[62] although the allocation was 33 single Officers, which by 1883 had been revised down to 28 beds[63].

In 1882 a Criminal Investigation Office (CID) was created above on the first floor of the old stable block attached to the Station; originally this was part of the Section House that accommodated 4 single Constables. There were six rooms of various sizes used on the first floor to house single Police Officers in a Section House. The annual rent was £225; however this was defrayed as Section House charges amounted to £93. 12s p.a. Police Officers who were resident were allocated a certain square footage of space for themselves because it was recognised that more space improved conditions of health and hygiene. Because of this the allocation was increased to 600 sq. ft per Officer in February 1883[64].

A notification in Metropolitan Police Orders in 1884 indicated that the Station was allocated a postal address of 4 Blackheath Road, Greenwich[65]. By the start of the twentieth century the Division covered 60½ square miles from the Thames to Chislehurst and the Crays[66]. Extra cells had been added to the Station in February 1888 and at the same time the Section House allocation was revised down to 26 beds[67]. Increases in Station strengths and re-organisation of Station areas often took place and Deptford and Blackheath Road Sub-Divisions merged in January 1898. The new Sub-Division was called Blackheath Road and Police Orders showed that Deptford lost its Sub-Divisional Inspector whilst the Sub-Division gained an additional Inspector[68]. Freehold was purchased in 1899 for £9000 from Edward Pocknell and this was proportioned as £2,800 for the court and £6,200 for the station[69].

Permission to build a new Station in Blackheath Road was this was approved by the Home Office and completed in 1910 with new married quarters being brought into service a year later[70]. This also included a Court building. The cost of lodging was 11s. 6d per week (1 set of married quarters), 5s per week (1 set of married quarters, 1 unmarried

Sergeant's quarters 2s per week and 51 single Constables still paid only 1s per week each.

Sub-Divisional Inspectors (Greenwich)	Year
John Jackson	1893-5
Walter Lee	1895-1905
William Crostan	1905-08
Thomas Hill	1908-9
Arthur Pullen	1911-17

In 1914 'R' Division was described as "an area of London with closely packed towns, many villages and great stretches of smiling countryside"[71]. The outbreak of war saw the Special Constabulary quickly established under the leadership of Major Bradford Atkinson at Blackheath Road with units at Westcombe Park, Woolwich, Plumstead, Belvedere, Bexley, Erith, Sidcup, Lee Road, Chislehurst and St. Mary Cray[72]. There were 32 vulnerable points on the Division and it needed every man to cover these places. These included water works, railways, power stations, railway tunnels and telephone exchanges. Soon Major Atkinson was recalled to the Army and his place was taken over by Commander R. G. J. Rawlinson from Lee Road. He struck up a good relationship with Divisional Superintendent A. D. Smith who was often seen in the front passenger seat of his private motor-car visiting the vulnerable points, often at considerable speed[73].

The Divisional strength in 1915 was 985 regular men and by 1918 had reduced to 726 because many more men went to fight the enemy. One of the problems for the Commander was maintaining the strength of the Specials and 597 men left to join the forces. The death rate on the Division was fortunately low even though many of the Special Constables travelled long distances at great risk of bombing by Gotha bombers, bi-planes, and airships. Many Specials used their own transport like their Commander, and bought petrol even though it was in short supply[74].

The picture below on the next page shows Greenwich Police Court and Police Station in Blackheath Road in about 1907. The station is situated on the left and the Inspector is standing by the front entrance. Greenwich Police Court and station was designed and built by the Receiver and like the one illustrated was adjacent to the station. Operationally this made for ease of transport for prisoners and often when the courts shut for the day any remaining prisoners would be securely transferred next door.

Greenwich Police Station and Court (shown at right)
7 Blackheath Road SE10
1910 - 1962

Anti-German feeling spread with people breaking windows of shops and attacking likely suspects, the main troubles occurring in Deptford, Greenwich, Woolwich and Plumstead. The Specials supplemented the ranks of the regulars to stem the angry uprising and their contribution was recognised when the Commissioner issued a letter thanking those who took part. The Special Constabulary also played a significant part in mapping where the bombs fell each day and night and gathering evidence of injuries, death and damage. Each Division was required to complete a log of events and the information was recorded centrally. This was so that the Government could assess the death toll, aggregate the cost of the damage and set about the repair. Additionally the authorities would minimise the publicity by placing restrictions on the reporting on the death toll and damage thereby ensuring that the enemy would not capitalise on their attacks.

Bombing raids over London between 1914 and 1918 showed that 83 bombs fell in Greenwich and such was in the inaccuracy of it 7 fell in Greenwich Park and Blackheath[75]. Many bombs fell along main roadways and in towns where lights could be found. The Police strictly enforced the Blackout Regulations and people who failed to comply were initially warned and thereafter prosecuted. During the First World War, whilst on duty at Greenwich Station, Sergeant William James Wheller took his own life in 1917 as a result of injuries he had received earlier[76]. It was said that he was insane at the time, which was probably written on his death certificate to help relatives since it was at the time a criminal offence to commit suicide.

Blackheath Road Constable Leonard Dunn, shown left, has an interesting record. He joined the Police Service in January 1920 with warrant number 108747. Born in the East End of London he was a fitter's mate who had seen service in the Royal Navy during the war from September 1917 until May 1919.

He is wearing the Police Long Service Medal (instituted in 1951), and British War Medal for his service in the Royal Navy during the First World War.

On the 1st April 1929 he was posted as Pc 656 'R' Division to Blackheath Road where he remained for the rest of his service. He lived in Plumstead High Street SE18 with his wife and three children. The photograph was taken between 1936 and 1938 when the new helmet plate was introduced. A clearer example is shown above. He served over 33 years and retired in 1953 with a Certificate of Service that showed his conduct to have been exemplary. This is somewhat strange since Dunn had been disciplined four times during his service. His most serious violation occurred during the Second World War; one morning in May 1942 as he was trying to sleep after coming off night duty. A cat in a neighbouring garden was making a lot of noise, preventing him from sleeping. Dunn took his Police issue revolver, aimed at the cat, fired and killed it – making sure he got his sleep. The neighbour, unsurprisingly, complained to the Police Station. Dunn originally denied shooting the cat to his Sergeant, which

Constable Leonard DUNN circa 1953

Metropolitan Police Helmet Plate 1911-1936

got him into even more trouble. He was disciplined by the Divisional Superintendent for the offence of discreditable conduct for killing the cat and reprimanded, whilst lying to the Sergeant cost him one day's pay. Dishonesty was treated harshly whilst killing the cat deserved just a telling off! Dunn retired aged 55, living a further 6 years and died in August 1959. In the early days, because of the nature of the job, Police Officers did not live long in retirement[77].

In 1921 there were a number of divisional boundary changes with the formation of 'Z' or Croydon Division. Deptford Police Station was transferred from 'R' to 'M' or Southwark Division and the boundary of Blackheath Road was altered[78]. In 1928 the Superintendent in charge was Alfred J Barrett[79]. The address of the new Police Station was 7 Blackheath Road, Greenwich, SE10[80].

Such was the general condition of the Police those officers who were suffering from poor health or injuries could be pensioned off by the Chief Medical Officer if they could no longer perform the daily responsibilities of a Police Officer. This was the case in 1933 when Constable Albert Earnest Packer was pensioned from the Police and died shortly after from injuries received during an assault in 1932[81].

Police boxes introduced in 1934 were located on the Sub-Division at Tunnel Avenue, Box No. R2; Shooters Hill Road, at the junction with Dartmouth Terrace, Box No. R7; Tranquil Avenue, Blackheath, Box No. R19; together with two posts, one in the Blackwall tunnel, Box No R40 and Tunnel Approach, Box No. R40A[82].

During the early part of World War Two Greenwich and Woolwich became the front line for German air attacks where the dock areas and munitions works were the main targets. It was later in the war when the most damage was caused to the area as Hitler launched his vengeance weapons the V1's 'doodle bugs' and V2 rockets. This caused devastation and panic, killing 9,200 people and injuring a further 22,000 others in London. Some 82 'doodle bugs' fell in Woolwich alone whilst 73 hit Greenwich. In total Greenwich and Woolwich were hit by over 40 V2's[83]. Croydon suffered worst of all the boroughs with a total of 140 'doodle bugs' exploding in its area[84].

A bomb killed Special Constable Leonard Francis Clarke whilst guarding a disabled enemy aircraft downed at Woolwich in 1940 and Constable James Fredrick Tottey was also killed by a bomb as he left his home to assist during an air raid in 1941[85]. Also in 1940 the Police Station in

Greenwich was struck, killing Special Sub-Inspector Herbert Linkins, Special Constable Ronald Lewis, Special Sergeant George Martin and Constable William Locke[86].

The Station was still in service after the war and there were signs that it was no longer fit for its purpose. But that wasn't apparent until an inspection visit by Assistant Commissioner 'D' Department in 1951 to Greenwich Police Station left the Chief Officer disturbed, since many of the Section House rooms were being used for Police operational purposes. Clearly, the Station had outlived its purpose so he gave instructions for a new site to be found in the vicinity of the Town Hall as soon as possible. Later that year a new site was found for a Divisional Headquarters and Police Station in Greenwich but because of post war economics there was no rush to build the Station. It wasn't until May 1962 that the new Station was completed and opened for operational purposes at 31 Royal Hill, Greenwich, SE10, to replace East Greenwich and Blackheath Road Police Stations[87].

Greenwich Police Station
31 Royal Hill, Greenwich SE10
1962- Present day

With the Station were built eighteen sets of married quarters at Gloucester Circus, Greenwich[88]. Maurice Drummond Section House also closed at the same time for refurbishment.

There are a number of Officers attached to the Metropolitan Police who appear on the Roll of Honour and who died whilst stationed at Greenwich. In 1960 Pc Leslie Edwin Vincent Meehan was mortally wounded when he was run over by a vehicle he had stopped and which then had driven off with the Officer clinging to the side[89].

The Section House finally closed in July 1995 and was leased out, although the firing range in the basement was still in use[90]. This became a

Headquarters Station and housed the District Commander and staff who were responsible for 'M', 'P and 'R' Divisions, although the Divisional staff used to managing day to day operational policing of Greenwich were based at Eltham Police Station[91].

Blackheath Road was one of four Stations to pilot the 'Team Policing' system in what was an exercise in saturation policing. The 'Aberdeen scheme' as it was called (because it came from there) involved a Sergeant who had the use of a wireless car and who would ferry his Officers and flood each area at a time during every shift. This became the fore-runner to the Special Patrol Group introduced in 1965.

The London Government Act 1963 caused some boundary changes south of the Thames. Greenwich remained the Divisional Headquarters of 'R' Division and a Sub-Divisional Station (RD) with Westcombe Park (RK) as its sectional station[92]. By 1970 all the blue 'Tardis' Police Boxes were being removed, although a red one remained near to Blackwall Tunnel southern approach entrance for some years after[93]. Unit beat policing; the introduction of the Panda Car and the personal radio heralded the demise of the Police Box.

Changes occurred with the demise of the GLC in 1984 when 'R' District Office and Headquarters staff re-located to Eltham (RD) where it remained until 1999 when Borough based policing was introduced[94]. Eltham was to remain as a Sub-Divisional Station[95].

Since April 1999 policing in London has become borough based with boundaries for the Police following those of the local authority. Each Borough now has a Borough Commander in charge. From 2008 Greenwich has housed the Criminal Justice Unit and the Crime Management Unit as well as the South Area Telephone switching Centre. The old Married quarters, situated behind the Station, called Swanne House, is still used by a number of other administrative units[96].

Plumstead Police Station

Plumstead was not included into the Metropolitan Police area until 1839 when it became part of 'R' Division[97] and permission was given for the Police to take over from the local Parish Watch. In the 1840's Plumstead consisted of market gardens, brick-fields, chalk pits and tile kilns. A part of the Woolwich Arsenal was situated in the parish in the 1840's. By the

1850's the population in Plumstead had grown three-fold especially since the North Plumstead Railway was built in 1849[98].

Plumstead had its own Cage situated at Lakedale Road, as it was then known[99] and was later originally named Cage Road (now Lakedale Road), situated at the junctions with Brewery Road (so named because of the adjacent Park Brewery)[100]. Prisoners who were arrested and detained in the Cage overnight by the Police were taken the next morning to the local court proceedings which were undertaken by local Justices of the Peace at the Castle Public House in Powis Road, Woolwich Town.

Revisions to Police boundaries occurred in 1863 when R Division saw Eltham transferred from the Lee to the Shooters Hill Sub-Division which was also responsible for the sections east of the Plumstead parish at Erith and Bexley Heath[101]. Officers from Woolwich were used together with re-enforcements which were hastily drafted in to deal with the battle of Plumstead Common in 1878. Attempts to acquire the Common for the Metropolitan Board of Works caused major disturbances in the area. Police officers from Woolwich Watch House patrolled the environs of Plumstead until plans were approved in the late 1880's for a Station to be built there.

John Butler, Metropolitan Police Architect/Surveyor, designed Plumstead Police Station and the plans to build a Police Station there were approved by the Home Office in 1890, taking into consideration the substantial increase that had occurred of people moving into the area, and dwellings being erected. It was built by Lathey Bros who provided the lowest estimate from the 13 bids tendered[102]. A piece of land had been found in Plumstead High Street at the corner of Riverdale Road in 1891 belonging to Mr. Wilson and this was purchased for £1,140. The Station, which was built for £4,120 was opened in August 1893[103]. Pevsner described Plumstead Police Station being located in 1893:

> 'at the corner of Riverdale Road, are the only buildings which stand out in Plumstead, High Street'[104].

Taking charge of the new Station was Inspector Walshe, who had been transferred from Blackheath Road, and Sergeant Hudson[105]. The boundaries of the Woolwich and Belvedere Sub-Divisions were altered in August 1893 to coincide with the building of the new Sectional Station at Plumstead. Given the address 216 Plumstead High Street, SE18, it was accorded the status of Sectional Station of Woolwich Sub-Division[106].

Plumstead Police Station
216 High Street, Plumstead SE18
1893 - 1988

In 1897 Inspector Hocking was in charge of the Station where he stayed for at least two years. Sub-Divisional Inspector Goodhall at Woolwich was in overall charge of the Sectional Station until 1898 when his place was taken by Sub-Divisional Inspector Sara. By this time the Sub-Divisional strength stood at 4 Inspectors, 20 Sergeants and 98 Constables[107]. The telegraph was installed into the Station with the code sign Papa Sierra (PS)[108]. Space for the lodging of 8 Constables existed in the Section House above the Station and cost 1 shilling a week each[109]. There was for some years a Fixed Traffic Point in Plumstead High Street at the junction with Cage Lane (Lakedale Road) which was manned between 8am and 1am in all weathers. This Fixed Point was withdrawn when the new Station was built, however a new Point was established later outside Plumstead Railway Station.

Records show that in 1915 Sub-Divisional Inspector Gadd, and Inspectors Henry Jarvis and Charles Butt were resident at the Station together with their respective families.

The view to the rear of Plumstead Police Station with the garden in the foreground and the parade shed in the distance on the left

In 1965 under Local Government re-organisation Plumstead (RP) remained the Sectional Station of Woolwich (RW) that was situated in the new London Borough of Greenwich[110].

Major re-organisation in 1980 through the Metropolitan Police service saw 'R' Division re-named 'R' District.

The old Station was demolished in March 1988 and a temporary Police Office was opened at 295 Plumstead High Street, SE18, to cope with the routine day-to-day Police Station duties. The station remained in use until 1991 when the officers moved to the new station. In the meantime prisoners were taken to Woolwich for processing and detention for court. Other functions such as administration and support were distributed throughout the Division.

The Station at Plumstead was considered no longer suitable for Police purposes and it was decided to build a new modern Police Station. Plans were drawn up by the Metropolitan Police Property Services Department with designers Damond Lock Grabowski for a Police Station and Divisional Headquarters to be built on the site of the old Station. In 1988 work commenced on the new Plumstead Police Station and was completed in April 1991 at a cost of £2.5M. The Station was opened by the Princess Royal. Its three-storey building includes a charge room, 12 cells, two detention rooms, a restaurant, billiard room and space for 50 cars. Officers at the Station have since 1991 worn the two letter code RW on their shoulders. At roughly the same time a new maximum-security prison was opened on Plumstead Marshes and was named Belmarsh.

Plumstead Police Station
Plumstead High Street, SE18 1JY
1991 – Present day

The Station complement on occupation of the new building consisted of 1 Chief Superintendent, who is the Borough Commander, 1 Superintendent, 3 Chief Inspectors, 11 Inspectors, 17 Sergeants and 75 Constables. Supporting them were 54 members of the civil staff and 33 Traffic Wardens. The new address was 200 Plumstead High Street, SE18 1JY.

Shooters Hill Police Station

The 1st Division of the Bow Street Horse Patrol Station was situated on Shooters Hill near the present Brook Hospital[111] on the site of the Fox-on-the-Hill Inn. The Police established themselves on a very famous thoroughfare originally called Watling Street and built by the Romans. After some correspondence between the Commissioner and the Board of Ordnance, Woolwich (as both Lords of the Manor of Eltham and owners of the land), favourable consideration for a new Police Station was given in Old Dover Road, Shooters Hill. The Station was originally given the name Old Dover Road Police Station even though it was situated on Shooters Hill. Naming a Station like this often belies its real location.

Land was leased from the owners, on favourable terms amounting to 5s per year ground rent, on which to build a new Station and it was built in 1852 at a cost of £1513. 6s. 6d. It was a standard Station House, which consisted of a basement, ground and first floor. The Station was small by today's standards and consisted of a charge room, 2 cells, library, mess room, three-stall stable and hay loft.

A married Inspector was resident, occupying four rooms for which he paid 4s per week rent. There was room for 7 single Constables in the Section House, each paying a nominal 1s per week rent[112]. In the interests of hygiene, on the 1st floor was a bath and clothes room; a rare but necessary feature. The Police Station backed onto Eltham Common and by 1888 the Fire Station, also originally manned by Police Officers, was situated next door. In 1864 Shooters Hill within the Parish of Eltham was an important Station and had an Inspector in charge. There were two Sergeants and a further two Acting Sergeants who performed Station and patrol day and night duties[113].

There was also a total of 14 Constables. One Acting Sergeant also supervised the day duty of 4 Constables whilst the other was responsible for the night duty and 8 Constables. Two horses were available for supervision, one ridden by the Inspector in charge whilst the Sergeant, who would supervise not only his own Station area but also those of Bexley and Erith, took the other[114]. There were some boundary alterations in 1865 because of the creation of three new Divisions, 'W', 'X' and 'Y'.

Shooters Hill Police Station
Well Hall Road, Eltham SE9
1852 - 1915

In 1881 a further re-organisation saw Shooters Hill Sub-Division being absorbed into, and to be known as, Belvedere Sub-Division[115]. Inspector Meering was transferred from Shooters Hill to Belvedere to join three other Inspectors. There was an address change in 1884 to Shooters Hill Road, Shooters Hill[116], and their telegraph call sign in 1893 was Sierra Hotel (SH)[117]. Shooters Hill was occupied in 1893 on an annual tenancy of 7 shillings[118].

In 1908 there was a revision in the lodging assessment for the married quarters which rose to 5s per week[119]. As far back as 1905 the Receiver of the Metropolitan Police had decided to return the land leased (including the Station) back the original owners and move from the site. Some land to the west of the present Station owned by the War Office was strongly favoured and discussions commenced indicating that they were prepared to sell the freehold to the Police[120]. The Police initially agreed to rent the land at a nominal cost of 1s per annum but purchased the land for £629 in June 1912[121]. The old Station was given up once instructions had been received to move next door and take possession of the new Police Station on 12th May 1915[122].

The Station call sign was Romeo Hotel (RH) and the main building to the Station was built on the site of the Shooters Hill Gallows where a number of Highwaymen had been hung. The last ones were hung in public in 1805[123]. The Station had a large yard and also boasted a beautifully laid out garden with a palm tree, although Tooting often won the garden

Shooters Hill Police Station
Shooters Hill SE18
1915 - 2001

competition and Eltham only had window boxes.

In 1973 a Detective Constable had his finger blown off whilst opening a letter at the Station. Such was the public concern at the time, and given the positive image the local Police had, the Detective received many gifts and letters of sympathy. Many Officers were on duty and sent to assist during the bomb outrage at the Kings Arms Public House in Woolwich. All the Police Officers pitched in together.

The Station came up for sale in about 2001 and initially in the region of £340,000, but following outrage by the public who thought the premises were under-valued, the price was raised. The property later sold for over £1 Million and the site is now occupied by luxury flats[124].

In 2006 Shooters Hill Safer Neighbourhood Team was established with two Sergeants, two Constables and three Police Community Support Officers although they were stationed elsewhere. They are shown located at 31 Herbert Road, Woolwich, London, SE18[125]. This group of Police Officers etc. have been established to provide more community support.

Thamesmead Police Station

By the 1960's London's housing problem had become critical and long-term solutions were needed. Launched by Sir William Fiske as the Woolwich-Erith Project it was funded by the Greater London Council (GLC) in 1966. It had to overcome many obstacles like pollution from the nearby sewage works, drainage and building on peat land. The estate was built to house up to 60,000 residents, many taken from East end slum clearances and who had been housed in pre-fabricated buildings in nearby Belvedere. The Thamesmead Estate was built on Erith Marshes in the early 1960's and is situated between Abbeywood and the Thames. The estate is a riverside development of high- and low-rise blocks covering

Thamesmead Police Station
Tavybridge Centre
1973-1987

some 130 acres and which effectively became a new town. Its name soon became synonymous with crime, disorder and a variety of other social problems. Originally planned as a development of 100,000 people and dubbed "the town of the 21st Century", the initial stages were built of pre-formed concrete blocks, which proved to be hard to maintain and prone to cause damp and condensation.

The marsh was drained into a series of lakes that are interconnected by a number of canals. The fishing is excellent and provides some measure of relief to the starkness of the early development. By the 1970s Thamesmead should have been completed, but by 1974 just 12,000 people were resident and the project was shelved temporarily. Eventually, after a re-think, the use of concrete was dropped, the planners reverted to old 18th century brick and the building of high-rise blocks was halted. Today, Thamesmead is a town of more than 30,000 people and is still only half completed.

In 1973 a second Station or Police Office was established in South Thamesmead (RA) and shown as operating for Police purposes. This was located in the precinct at the Tavybridge Centre but closed in 1987.

Another Thamesmead Police Station was opened as a new Sub-Divisional Station with the designation RT in June 1987 and re-placed two smaller Stations in the area[126]. The Station is located at 90 Titmus Avenue, London, SE28 8BJ, and today is open 24 hours a day for Police business.

Thamesmead Police Station
90 Titmus Avenue, London SE28 8BJ
1987 – Present day

The Stations to close were Thamesmead (RA) and Titmuss Avenue (RT).These were a complex of porta-cabins as is shown. There was a transfer of staff from Plumstead Police Station to the new building and these consisted of the CID, Collator, Crime Desk, Scenes of Crime Officer and also the Metropolitan Police Special Constabulary (MSC). Thamesmead Police Station is located within the London Borough of Greenwich.

In 2008 the Station was still in use and housed the Safer Neighbourhood Teams. In the same year the Neighbourhood Policing Team in the area was designated the Thameside Moorings Team and consisted of 1 Sergeant, 2 Constables and 5 Police Community Support Officers. They still hold regular drop-in surgeries at the nearby Thamesmead Leisure Centre.

Westcombe Park Police Station

Local residents whose income exceeded £10 per annum paid for policing this part of Charlton in 1812. The 'Charlton Guard' as they were called were raised because of local concerns about criminals frequenting the area. The Guard were provided with a lantern, rattle and firearm and kept watch from 8pm – 5am. They were paid the sum of 4s per night but soon

Westcombe Park Police Station
11 and 13 Coomedale Road, London SE10
1885 – Present day

ceased to patrol. The Guard were again raised in 1827, paid only 2/6d per night but instructed to watch against resurrectionists and keeping guard in Charlton Churchyard during the night[127].

A new Station was considered to supplement those of Blackheath Road and East Greenwich because of the huge increase in population into the area. Accordingly, a new Station was built and occupied at 9 and 11 Coombedale Road, Westcombe Park in 1885[128] on land purchased from Mr.

The rear yard of the station showing the cell block on the left hand side in 1911

John Pound for £950. Rather than East Greenwich the new Station was called Westcombe Park instead and was occupied for Police purposes in December 1893[129]. The picture at left shows the rear yard of the new Station.

In 1891 the Inspector in charge of the Station was George Hocking who

A more modern picture of Westcombe Park Police Station taken in the 1970's

supervised six Sergeants and thirty-six Constables[130]. Hocking resided nearby with his family at 2 Farmdale Road[131]. The Station was renumbered in the street in 1925 so that the address changed slightly to 11-13 Combedale Road. Westcombe Park had a call sign Whiskey papa (WP)[132].

During World War One Charlton and Greenwich were bombed three times each, Blackheath seven times, and Woolwich with its military targets six times[133]. Westcombe Park Special Constables performed lookout duty to spot enemy bombers and Zeppelins. They would take turns to stand at the top of Severndroog Castle at the top of Shooters Hill and using binoculars would pass information via the telephone on top of the Central Observation Station at Spring Gardens[134]. Anti-German feeling was rife during the war and there were concerns that residents were passing information about targets to the enemy in Belgium and Germany. Police Orders dated 4th September 1914 instructed that Constables should visit every pigeon loft and release the birds so that they could be monitored by the Officers and see if they flew off in the direction of Holland and Belgium[135].

The Second War started with the issuing of Defence of the Realm Regulations that included blackout instructions and the Police prosecuted people if the blackout regulations were not properly adhered to. The Charlton Athletic Football Club were all enrolled as War Reservists and sent to the emergency Police Station in the basement of Charlton House. When SPS 20R Harold White arrived to take charge of the contingent he found the basement filled with coal, however the unit was posted to main Stations a year later when the air raids had stopped[136].

Westcombe Park survived the war, but often when Police Officers returned at the end of their shift they would find some of their numbers were not present and stayed behind to find their colleagues who had been injured or killed in bombing raids. Some fourteen 'R' Division Officers were killed in air raids during the war and a further twenty-three whilst serving in the RAF or Royal Navy. The cell area is believed to be haunted by a ghost ever since a prisoner hung himself there, however since an annex was added in 1990 there have been no further sightings[137].

Station Office counter facilities were withdrawn from Westcombe Park in June 1999. Later, in November the Millennium Policing Team moved into the Station to oversee the celebrations and taking responsibility for the Dome and the Greenwich Peninsula[138]. When the Millennium Team moved out it left the Station as the Greenwich Sector base.

Woolwich Police Station

The original Watch House and Cage used by the Parish Constable and his Watchmen were situated at the north end of Rope Yard Rails on the corner of the High street not far from Cannon Row[139]. Woolwich Parish petitioned the Home Secretary for an extension of the Metropolitan Police limits in February 1839 because of the lawlessness of the local area and being of the opinion that the local Watch could no longer cope with the situation. The Metropolitan Police arrived in Woolwich on 13th January 1840 not only taking over the duties of the Watch but also the Watch House. The Watch House was shown as a Station on 'R' Division of the Metropolitan Police and such was its importance that an Inspector was posted in charge. The areas of Woolwich, Wickham, Plumstead and part of Charlton were taken over by the Metropolitan Police.

The Police quickly realised the scale of the task when they arrived because they considered the resources inadequate and began looking for a suitable site on which to build a larger Police Station House. In 1841 the University Life Office leased land to the Metropolitan Police for 80 years

Woolwich Police Station
William Street SE
1847 - 1910

at an annual cost of £68. 14s. The new two storey Station House was built by the Receiver at a cost £1374 and was shown as a Station on 'R' Division in 1841[140]. In 1844 Inspector George Clifford, who had been promoted the year before, was shown in charge of the Station and Sub-division at High Street, Woolwich[141] a station which was retained until 1846 when a newer station at William street was occupied. There was another Inspector of 'R' Division by the name of Roger Howard, who had been promoted in 1839 and who was stationed not far away in charge at Woolwich Dockyard [142].

The dockyards had been taken over by 'R' Division in 1841 and possession of Woolwich Arsenal occurred in 1844 when it was removed from the responsibility of the Dockyard Police. A contingent of local Police Officers provided gate and perimeter security and also guarded the main magazine, which included the onerous task of guarding the magazine hulks moored off shore[143]. Occasionally there would be accidents when munitions exploded causing serious damage and loss of

Woolwich Police Station taken from Upper Market Street in 1911

life. In September 1845 an explosion killed 7 workers and another in December 1855 killed a further 4 more. Officers from Woolwich would be required to send assistance, help with first aid, and clear up the damage[144].

From time to time outside Police Forces would ask the Metropolitan Police for assistance in dealing with disorder or public unrest. In December 1843 an illegal prize-fight between Tass Parker and the Tipton Slasher was taking place at Greenhithe in Kent and disorder was expected. The Police at Woolwich were asked to supply assistance and sent 6 Officers immediately, however when disorder broke out amongst the 300 supporters they, with local Officers, were not enough to quell the trouble. A further 3 mounted Police and a Troop of Dragoons[145] augmented the numbers and soon established order[146].

The original Watch House was eventually surrendered back to the Parish Authorities in 1848[147], however in 1856 £260 was allocated in order to add 4 extra cells to those already present[148]. Such was the importance relating to the security of dockyards that a Senior Police Officer was placed in charge and those early Police Officers that had showed aptitude were quickly promoted. For example Charles F. Field was promoted from Constable or Sergeant to Inspector in 1833 (less than 5 years after the Police commenced) and posted in charge of Deptford Dockyard. Records show that in 1873 there was still an Inspector in charge of the Police Station at Woolwich, William Street, which was later re-named Calderwood Street[149]. William Street was situated between Powis Street and Brewer Street and the Police Station was next door to Woolwich Town Hall. The court building appears to have been owned by the Receiver for the Metropolitan Police [150].

The military authorities were anxious not to have Officers with local connections and put the Commissioners under great pressure to provide dockyard security outside London. It wasn't until 1860 that the Metropolitan Police took over responsibility for Woolwich, Portsmouth, Devonport, Chatham and Sheerness and Pembroke using a special detachment of Police from London[151]. The established strength of the Station rose in 1864 with numbers totalling 2 Inspectors, 5 Sergeants and 34 Constables. There were 8 day beats and 21 by night to cover[152].

The Special Constabulary has often augmented the Police during times of local disorder and riot. The forerunners of the IRA were causing mayhem on the mainland in 1867 so there was a recruitment drive which supplemented the Police with an additional 5000 men. Yet the finest hour for the Special Constabulary was during the First World War when large numbers of civilians supplemented their Police. Woolwich was issued with six Adams breech-loading revolvers in November 1868 together with 60 rounds of ammunition[153]. Woolwich Docks were a bigger operation than those of Greenwich in 1869, when records show that it had an establishment of 1 Superintendent, 14 Inspectors, 22 Sergeants and 136 Constables, making this by far the largest number in any of the dockyards in England and Wales[154].

One of the greatest tragedies to befall not only Woolwich but the country as a whole was the collision of two ships in the Thames off Tipcock Pier in September 1878. The 'Bywell Castle' collided with the 'Princess Alice', a paddle steamer, resulting in the deaths of 590 men women and children. Officers from Woolwich and the Thames Division worked tirelessly to identify bodies, ensure the safekeeping of a deceased's property, and notify the next of kin[155].

The Police rattle (cost to the Officer originally 2½d) was replaced in 1885 by the whistle which was used by all except those on night duty. They did not adopt the whistle until 1887.

The freehold to Woolwich (William Street) was purchased in December 1890 at a cost of £5000. This was a traditional 16 room Police Station House over three levels with basement, ground floor and first floor. On the ground floor there was a charge room, fodder room (for the horses) and Inspectors office that were all public rooms and therefore liable for rent to paid by the public. There were also five cells and a two-stall stable. There were two rooms on the ground floor, occupied by Inspector Elias Ford, his wife and five children[156] paying 5s and 6d per week rent. In addition there were twelve single Constables stationed in the Section House each paying 1s per week rent[157], their number being reduced to eleven in 1883. In 1879 the annual rent for the whole property was increased to £83. 14s. 2d [158].

The call sign for Woolwich Police Station was Whiskey Lima (WL)[159]. When the magistrates in 1893 instructed that a boy should receive a birching (a thrashing with a wooden birch) the offenders would have to return at the allotted time to Woolwich Magistrates Court and were introduced to Sergeant Gilham, the huge 22 stone Gaoler. Gilham was the 'official boy bircher' who would go easy on new offenders whilst regulars would be spared no mercy nor expect any[160]. The Refused Charge Book for the early part of the 20th century still survives and much space was devoted to the stealing of growing vegetables and fruit. Charges were declined in many circumstances, presumably at the instigation of a Station Officer with a sense of proportion.

There was a suggestion in 1903 that a new Police Station should be built next door to Woolwich Police Court but this was not to be. In July 1904 a site at 29 Market Street, Woolwich, SE 18 was compulsorily purchased from the Trustees of the Ogilby Estate on which to build a new Police Station, because the old one was no longer suitable.

In August 1910 the new Sub-Divisional Station of Greenwich of 'R' Division was opened for business with living accommodation comprising of 1 set of married quarters and a Section House with space for 25 single Constables[161]. Previously the Police were only entitled to one day off per fortnight but in 1910 this became one day off a week[162]. The new Station had all the amenities and services with piped flowing water, electricity and gas together with surface and foul water drains. The basement contained the parade room, billiard room, lost property store and male toilets. The first floor of the Station contained a large charge room, three cells, a detention room and the Inspector's office whose only door led into the charge room. The general front office could be entered through the lobby from Market Street, which took the visitor to the front counter. A substantial part of the ground floor Station was taken up with the canteen, senior officer's dining room, servery and kitchen. Originally the Mess Room was organised by a Constable who would take subscriptions from those who were part of the Mess Club. The weekly subscriptions paid for food that was cooked on the premises. Over time the canteen along with all other police station canteens, was taken over by the Metropolitan Police Catering Service.

Woolwich Police Station
29 Market Street, Woolwich, SE 18
1910- Present day

The first floor contained the Detective Inspector's Office, the CID Office, Collator's Office, Women Police Office and Women Sergeant's office. The offices of the Superintendent, Chief Inspector, Admin Inspector, Plan Drawer, the women staff rest room, and general administration were situated on the second floor. A variety of alterations were implemented in January 1969.

During the First World War German bombers, airships and Zeppelins targeted the areas of Charlton, Greenwich, and Woolwich, sometimes with great success. On the night of 2nd September 1916 Captain William Leefe Robinson, shot down at Cuffley the airship Schütte Lanz 11 piloted by Captain Wilhelm Schramm. The airship Captain had been born and had lived in London with his family at 9 Victoria Road (now Way), Charlton, and Wilhelm's father had worked in an executive position at the nearby German firm of Siemens. The searchlights at Woolwich had seen Schramm's airship hovering over East London and the Thames and when the heavy guns opened up the barrage forced it north to its fate. Schramm would have known the connection with Woolwich Arsenal and the Gunpowder factory at Waltham Abbey so it is likely that because of the barrage he went in search of the powder works instead.

Lieutenant Robinson together with his Victoria Cross and images of the battle above Enfield.

This was the first German airship to be shot down in the war and Captain Robinson was awarded the VC (shown at left) for his success.

The formation of the Women Police had its roots in Woolwich when the National Union of Women Workers of Great Britain and Ireland informed the Metropolitan Police Commissioner that it had raised a 'Women's Patrol Committee (Woolwich Branch)', a voluntary patrol to safeguard the morals of women munitions workers. The women would patrol in pairs, were dressed in black and wore red embroidered numbers on duty armlets. It was not until 1922 that an official Women Police were introduced into the Metropolitan Police and given powers of arrest. Those early volunteers laid the foundation for the modern day Women Police. Woolwich was called 'RW' and one of the famous Women Police Officers of her time was Winifred Gould who was born on 24th July 1905 and joined the Metropolitan Police on 24th August 1931. She retired eventually on 3rd December 1962 on a medical discharge, following a vehicle accident on duty. Her warrant number was 257 and her uniform collar number was 18. Winifred also had a strong family connection to Police work through her grandfather in Hampshire to her father who, by contrast, had joined the Metropolitan Police in 1887. Her father had retired after thirty-two and half years of service. George Gould was an 'R' Division Officer who drew his pension for twenty nine years and died in 1948. It is worth noting that Winifred would apparently be the first Policewoman at Woolwich to have the power of arrest; she also became a CID Officer. Winifred entered Peel House on 15th June 1931 and as previously stated joined the Force two months later[163].

Woman Police Constable 108 MP Steere taken in 1921

The picture at left shows the sort of uniform Winifred would have worn when she joined.

Her first posting was to Hyde Park Station under the tutorship of Women Patrol Annie Mathews, and later posted to Bow Street, Paddington and Hammersmith to gain wider experience. She was then transferred to Blackheath Road Police Station on 4th December 1934 where she worked with Women Patrol Emily Walsh. Winifred was transferred to Woolwich Police Station on 21st June 1937. Her further training included a short period at Vine Street to learn how to take 'sex offence statements'. Winifred also worked from time to time at Lewisham Garage, dealing with speeding against the new 30 mile per hour limit. This was a plain-clothes role for the two Officers, one male and one female. It appears Winifred was the first woman to issue a summons on Shooters Hill Road and take it before the court. She had been in company with Police Sergeant MacAndrew. She was referred to as the original 'Gertie the girl with the gong'[164]. A newspaper article from 8th December 1953 in the court report section the following is noted. On Monday, before Mr A. A. Pereira, WOMAN DETECTIVE COMMENDED.

> 'Woman Detective Winifred Gould attached to Blackheath Road Police Station for 'her plucky conduct in effecting the arrest of two men who were charged with being concerned in stealing a child's tricycle valued at £7 15s 2d from outside a shop in New Cross.'

It goes on to describe the struggle between Winifred, the two (one aged 29 the other 25) and the shop keeper. Both offenders had been drinking and were aggressive and threatening. The magistrate fined them £10[165].

Another such cutting, apparently from a paper in December 1948 refers to ARREST OF A 'PRAM THIEF', where Winifred and one other Woman Officer were deployed undercover to investigate the thefts from perambulators. The location was the Welfare Centre in Chevening Road, Greenwich. A woman from Spearman Street, Woolwich, was arrested as a result. Winifred gave the following evidence. The female suspect on being arrested said "please can't you forgive me this time? I promise not to do it again. Here is the purse". At the Police Station she confessed to stealing £2 from the perambulator the previous November. Winifred continued that the arrested woman "had three sons - boys of 16, 15 and 6 years of age. Her husband gave her £5 a week, out of which she paid 11s 9½d rent, and the two elder boys paid her £1 and 10s respectively"[166]. The woman was bound over at the Woolwich Court for seven offences of similar type, and fined £10 with 21 days to pay the magistrate, Mr L. A. Stevenson. Winifred, who certainly was a character, liked to refer to herself as 'Old Win the Rebel'[167]. She is certainly remembered with affection, as it is people who populate the space and time within the Police Stations – not the buildings.

In 1960 RW was a Sub-Divisional Station with Superintendent H. R. Abbott in charge[168]. By 2001 Woolwich had been relegated to office status and was located at 29 Market Street, London, SE18 6QS, but under the Police and Criminal Evidence Act it was no longer a charging Station[169]. In 2010 the opening Hours: Mon-Fri 0700-2000 and Sat-Sun 1000-18:00.

---

[1] Brown, B. (1997) 'Nothing to do with Reggie and Ronnie- Law and Order in the Crays' in Bygone Kent, Vol. 18. no. 9.
[2] Priggle, P. (unknown) Hue and Cry
[3] The Police and Constabulary list 1844, Parker, Furnival and Parker Whitehall, London.
[4] http://cms.met.police.uk/met/boroughs/greenwich/01whos_who accessed on 20th July 2010
[5] Metropolitan Police Surveyors Records 1912
[6] http//www.idealhomes.suberbiainfocus.org accessed on 4th March 2008
[7] MEPO 2/25
[8] Moylan, J. F. (1929) Scotland Yard. Puttnams, London p 210
[9] Greenwich-History of Greenwich http://intranet.aware.mps/BOCU_eh/Greenwich accessed on 5th March 2008
[10] Hadaway, D. (1985) 'Early Days of Policing'. Kentish Times July 4th
[11] John Back Archive 1975
[12] MEPO 5/36 (250)
[13] MEPO 5/23 (128)
[14] Metropolitan Police Special Order 1864
[15] Census Records 1881
[16] Metropolitan Police Orders dated 20th June 1884
[17] Premises in the occupation of the Metropolitan Police 1898, Surveyors' Department.
[18] John Back Archive 1975
[19] Metropolitan Police Surveyors' Records, Metropolitan Police Collection, Charlton.
[20] LB 544
[21] Metropolitan Police Orders dated 1st March 1939.
[22] Brown, B. (2001) 'Romeo- Law and Order in Old Greenwich' (part 2 1900-2000) in Bygone Kent Vol. 22 No 3.
[23] Brown, B. (2001) 'Romeo- Law and Order in Old Greenwich' (part 2 1900-2000) in Bygone Kent Vol. 22 No 3.
[24] Greenwich-History of Greenwich http://intranet.aware.mps/BOCU_eh/Greenwich accessed on 5th March 2008
[25] MEPO 5/53(425)
[26] Surveyors' Records, Metropolitan Police, Charlton.
[27] Metropolitan Police Surveyors' Records.
[28] Metropolitan Police Orders dated 11th January 1864
[29] Report on the conditions of the Metropolitan Police Stations 1881 p64
[30] Kelly's Directory 1893
[31] Metropolitan Police Orders dated 2nd July 1870
[32] The Police Review and Parade Gossip April 24th 1899
[33] Metropolitan Police General Orders 1893
[34] Metropolitan Police Surveyors' Records Metropolitan Police Collection, Charlton
[35] Metropolitan Police Surveyors' Records Metropolitan Police Collection, Charlton.
[36] Brown, B. (2001) 'Romeo- Law and Order in Old Greenwich' (part 2 1900-2000) in Bygone Kent Vol. 22 No 3.
[37] Brown, B. (2001) 'Romeo- Law and Order in Old Greenwich' (part 2 1900-2000) in Bygone Kent Vol. 22 No 3.
[38] Metropolitan Police Roll of Honour at www.policememorial.or.uk accessed 12th March 2002

[39] Brown, B. (2001) 'Romeo- Law and Order in Old Greenwich' (part 2 1900-2000) in Bygone Kent Vol. 22 No 3.
[40] Brown, B. (2001) 'Romeo- Law and Order in Old Greenwich' (part 2 1900-2000) in Bygone Kent Vol. 22 No 3.
[41] Greenwich-History of Greenwich http://intranet.aware.mps/BOCU_eh/Greenwich accessed on 5th March 2008
[19] John Back Archive (1975) Metropolitan Police Museum, Charlton.
[20] Register for the return of mops from cleaners dated 1st July 1832, Metropolitan Police Museum, Charlton.
[44] Chris Lordon (2008) History of Rotherhithe (forcoming)
[45] Metropolitan Cleaning records dated August 1832
[46] John Back Archive (1975) Metropolitan Police Museum, Charlton.
[47] Post Office London Directory 1838
[48] The Police and Constabulary List (1844) Parker, Furnival and Parker, Whitehall.
[49] Order of Greenwich Council 3rd October 1840, cited in The Police and Constabulary list 1844, Parker, Furnival and Parker Whitehall, London
[50] Post Office Directory 1879
[51] Metropolitan Police General Orders 1893
[52] Metropolitan Police Roll of Honour at www.policememorial.or.uk accessed 12th March 2002
[53] Metropolitan Police Roll of Honour at www.policememorial.or.uk accessed 12th March 2002
[54] Metropolitan Police Orders dated 28th October 1865
[55] Metropolitan Police Orders 11th January 1864
[56] Metropolitan Police Orders dated 28th January 1869
[57] Metropolitan Police Orders dated 15th July 1869
[58] Report of the Commissioner of the Metropolis 1871
[59] Report of the Commissioner of the Metropolis 1870
[60] Report of the Commissioner of the Metropolis 1871
[61] Report of the Commissioner of the Metropolis 1871
[62] Census records 1881
[63] Metropolitan Police Surveyors' Records. Metropolitan Police Collection, Charlton.
[64] Metropolitan Police Surveyors' Records, Metropolitan Police Collection, Charlton.
[65] Metropolitan Police Orders 20thth June 1884
[66] Brown, B. (2001) 'Romeo' – Law and Order in Old Greenwich (Part 2 1900-2000) in Bygone Kent Vol. 22 No 3 March edition.
[67] Metropolitan Police Surveyors' Records, Metropolitan Police Collection, Charlton.
[68] Metropolitan Police Orders dated 28th January 1898
[69] Metropolitan Police Surveyors' Records, Metropolitan Police Collection, Charlton.
[70] Metropolitan Police Orders dated 8th December 1911
[71] Reay, W. T. (1920) The Specials. Heineman, London. p79
[72] Reay, W. T. (1920) The Specials. Heineman, London
[73] Reay, W. T. (1920) The Specials. Heineman, London.
[74] Reay, W. T. (1920) The Specials. Heineman, London.
[75] Clout, H. (1997) The Times London History Atlas., Times Books, London
[76] Metropolitan Police Roll of Honour at www.policememorial.or.uk accessed 12th March 2002
[77] Metropolitan Police Records, Charlton.
[78] Metropolitan Police Orders dated 24th February 1921
[79] Post Office Directory 1928
[80] Police and Constabulary Almanac 1937
[81] Metropolitan Police Roll of Honour at www.policememorial.or.uk accessed 12th March 2002
[82] Brown, B. (2001) 'Romeo - Law and Order in Old Greenwich' (part 2 1900-2000) in Bygone Kent Vol. 22 No 3.
[83] Clout, H. (1997) The Times London History Atlas., Times Books, London.
[84] ibid
[85] Metropolitan Police Roll of Honour at www.policememorial.or.uk accessed 12th March 2002
[86] Metropolitan Police Roll of Honour at www.policememorial.or.uk accessed 12th March 2002
[87] John Back Archive (1975) Metropolitan Police Collection, Charlton..
[88] John Back Archive (1975) Metropolitan Police Collection, Charlton.
[89] Metropolitan Police Roll of Honour at www.policememorial.or.uk accessed 12th March 2002
[90] Section House Closure programme, Surveyors' Department (1997)

[91] Greenwich-History of Greenwich http://intranet.aware.mps/BOCU_eh/Greenwich accessed on 5th March 2008
[92] John Back Archive (1975) Metropolitan Police Collection, Charlton.
[93] Brown, B. (2001) 'Romeo - Law and Order in Old Greenwich' (part 2 1900-2000) in Bygone Kent Vol. 22 No 3.
[94] Greenwich-History of Greenwich http://intranet.aware.mps/BOCU_eh/Greenwich accessed on 5th March 2008
[95] Metropolitan Police Orders dated 15th October 1984
[96] Greenwich-History of Greenwich http://intranet.aware.mps/BOCU_eh/Greenwich accessed on 5th March 2008
[97] Greenwich-History of Greenwich http://intranet.aware.mps/BOCU_eh/Greenwich accessed on 5th March 2008
[98] Brown, B (undated) Not Quite a Century- The story of Plumstead Police Station.
[99] Hadaway, D. (1990) The Metropolitan Police in Woolwich.
[100] Hyde, R. (1987) The A-Z of Victorian London. London Topographical Society.
[101] Brown, B (undated) Not Quite a Century- The story of Plumstead Police Station.
[102] The Builder - 11th June 1892 p.467
[103] Metropolitan Police Orders dated 18th August 1893
[104] Buildings of England (South) Cherry and Pevsner. 1983.
[105] Brown, B (undated) Not Quite a Century- The story of Plumstead Police Station.
[106] Kirchners Police Index 1931
[107] Brown, B (undated) Not Quite a Century- The story of Plumstead Police Station.
[108] Brown, B (undated) Not Quite a Century- The story of Plumstead Police Station.
[109] Metropolitan Police Orders dated 18th March 1893
[110] Metropolitan Police Orders dated 6th August 1964
[111] Hadaway, D. (1990) The Metropolitan Police in Woolwich.
[112] Metropolitan Police Surveyors' Records, Metropolitan Police Collection, Charlton.
[113] Metropolitan Police Orders dated 11th January 1864
[114] Metropolitan Police Orders dated 11th January 1864
[115] Metropolitan Police Orders dated 8th October 1881
[116] Metropolitan Police Surveyors' Records, Metropolitan Police Collection, Charlton.
[117] Metropolitan Police General Orders 1893
[118] Metropolitan Police HC Document
[119] Metropolitan Police Surveyors' Records, Metropolitan Police Collection, Charlton.
[120] Metropolitan Police Surveyors' Records, Metropolitan Police Collection, Charlton.
[121] John Back Archive (1975) Metropolitan Police Museum, Charlton.
[122] Metropolitan Police Orders dated 13th April 1915.
[123] Jupp, E. (2006) Police Stations Past .The News Shopper
[124] Private correspondence
[125] http//www.met.police.uksaferneighbourhoods/boroughs/Greenwich/saferneighbourhoods.htm accessed 12th December 2006
[126] Metropolitan Police Orders dated 5th June 1987
[127] Hadaway, D. (1985) Westcombe Park Police Station Centenary 1885-1985,
[128] Metropolitan Police Orders dated 13th November 1885
[129] MEPO 5 no.55 – OS451
[130] Kellys directory 1891
[131] Hadaway, D. (1985) Westcombe Park Police Station Centenary 1885-1985,
[132] Metropolitan Police General Orders 1893
[133] Hadaway, D. (1985) Westcombe Park Police Station Centenary 1885-1985,
[134] Hadaway, D. (1985) Westcombe Park Police Station Centenary 1885-1985,
[135] Hadaway, D. (1985) Westcombe Park Police Station Centenary 1885-1985,
[136] Hadaway, D. (1985) Westcombe Park Police Station Centenary 1885-1985,
[137] Greenwich-History of Greenwich http://intranet.aware.mps/BOCU_eh/Greenwich accessed on 5th March 2008
[138] Brown, B. (2001) 'Romeo- Law and Order in Old Greenwich' (part 2 1900-2000) in Bygone Kent Vol. 22 No 3.
[139] Hadaway, D. (1990) The Metropolitan Police in Woolwich.
[140] Metropolitan Police Surveyors' Records, Metropolitan Police Collection, Charlton..
[141] The Police and Constabulary List (1844) Parker, Furnival and Parker, Whitehall.

[142] The Police and Constabulary List (1844) Parker, Furnival and Parker, Whitehall.
[143] Hadaway, D. (1985) Eltham Police Station; The First Hundred Years. Latter Books, Sussex
[144] Hadaway, D. (1990) The Metropolitan Police in Woolwich.
[145] The term "Troop" would have been used for a number of members of cavalry regiments at the time and would have consisted of approximately 40 men. Info from the 1st The Queen's Dragoon Guards Regimental Museum curator in Cardiff.
[146] Hadaway, D. (1990) The Metropolitan Police in Woolwich.
[147] MEPO 5/23 (128)
[148] Hadaway, D. (1990) The Metropolitan Police in Woolwich.
[149] Hadaway, D. (1990) The Metropolitan Police in Woolwich.
[150] Premises in the occupation of the Metropolitan Police (1898), Metropolitan Police Surveyors Department.
[151] Moylan, J. F. (1929) Scotland Yard. Puttnams, London p 217
[152] John Back Archive (1975) Metropolitan Police Museum, Charlton.
[153] Metropolitan Police Orders dated 28th January 1869
[154] Report to the Commissioner of the Police 1869.
[155] Hadaway, D. (1990) The Metropolitan Police in Woolwich.
[156] Census Records 1881
[157] Metropolitan Police Surveyors' Records, Metropolitan Police Collection, Charlton.
[158] Metropolitan Police Surveyors' Records, Metropolitan Police Collection, Charlton.
[159] Metropolitan Police General Orders 1893
[160] Hadaway, D. (1990) The Metropolitan Police in Woolwich.
[161] Metropolitan Police Surveyors' Records.
[162] Hadaway, D. (1990) The Metropolitan Police in Woolwich.
[163] Sculley, R., The Warren, Win the Rebel. Spring; 1977 pp31-37 (p32)
[164] Sculley, R. The Warren, Win the Rebel, Spring; 1977 pp31-37 (p35)
[165] Court report, paper unknown dated 8/12/1953
[166] Court report, paper unknown believed December 1948
[167] Sculley, R. The Warren, Win the Rebel, Spring; 1977 pp31-37 (p31)
[168] The Police and Constabulary Almanac 1960
[169] The Police and Constabulary Almanac 2001

Chapter 5

London Borough of Lambeth

Introduction

The London Borough Lambeth is a borough which forms part of what is known as Inner London. It measures seven miles north to south, and about two and a half miles east to west. It covers an area of around 10.5 square miles. It was created in 1965 by the merger of the Metropolitan Borough of Lambeth with parts of the Metropolitan Borough of Wandsworth, namely Clapham and Streatham[1]. It forms one of the most densely populated inner London Boroughs with a population of around 270,000[2].

At the northern end of the Borough are the Central London districts of the South Bank and Lambeth which have a developing tourist economy while at the very south of the borough are the leafy suburbs of Gipsy Hill, Tulse Hill, West Dulwich and West Norwood. In between the two are the built-up and inner-city districts of Brixton, Clapham, Herne Hill, Stockwell and Kennington which are each at different stages of gentrification and have elements of suburban and urban settlement while Vauxhall and South Lambeth are central districts being redeveloped with high density business and residential properties. Streatham is located between suburban London and inner-city Brixton with the partly suburban and partly built-up areas of Streatham Hill and Streatham Vale[3].

Policing

The Metropolitan Police first came to 'L' (Lambeth) Division in February 1830. The 10th Company took over the role of policing from the parishes of St George's Lambeth, St George's Southwark, Christchurch, Blackfriars and St. Mary Newington and also used three of the former parish Watch Houses at St Johns, Waterloo Bridge Road; Christchurch, Blackfriars; and High Street, Lambeth (eventually given up by police in 1858 when Kennington Lane Police Station was opened). The Watch House at Christchurch, situated in the grounds of the church of the same name by Collingwood Street just off Blackfriars Road, was passed into the ownership of the Receiver by Act of Parliament. This Station came with another adjoining building made of brick and slate and had two cells and a charge room. Shown as a Station on 'L' (Lambeth) Division it had a Constable in charge. It was retained as a Station until 1869 although it did not pass out of the ownership of the Police until at least 1871[4] as records show it was painted and ameliorated regularly until that date. The building appears to have been there still in 1888[5].

The parish Watch House, built in 1819, stood in the churchyard until its demolition in 1932. It was a plain brick building of two storeys divided by a slightly projecting stone string course and with a simple stone cornice. The building had three bays, the centre one being slightly recessed. The two end bays had flat stone pediments. A stone tablet inscribed "ChristChurch Watch-House. MDCCCXIX," formerly over the central doorway, was preserved and stood in the garden adjoining the present rectory.

Christchurch Watch House
1819 - 1932

Superintendent Maurice G Dowling was placed in charge of the Division by 1833[6]. As the accommodation at these Watch Houses was not fit for the Officers, two properties were acquired for the housing of Police Officers; one at 12 Walcott Place (now 149 Kennington Road) and the other at 9 Kennington Cross. The old Watch House in Waterloo Bridge Road was soon replaced in 1836 by one at 58 Tower Street (now Morley Street)[7]. The Tower Street address was leased from Miss Helen Orchard from Christmas 1836 to Michaelmas 1884 at an annual rent of £35. She charged an additional £30 per year for that part of the premises containing the cells[8].

Since 1830 there have been a number of different Police Stations at various locations in the Borough. This chapter will look at those which have operated in the current London Borough of Lambeth since that time, namely Brixton, Clapham, Kennington Lane, Kennington Road, Knights Hill, Norwood/Gipsy Hill, Streatham. In 1994 Kennington Police Station became the new headquarters of the Vauxhall Division.

Currently, there are six Police Stations policing the London Borough of Lambeth. There are Stations are at Brixton, Gipsy Hill, Kennington, Cavendish Road, Clapham and Streatham. The future of the last three

Stations is the subject of discussion. The Senior Management Team operates from the new office building called Frank O'Neill House, 43 – 59 Clapham Road, SW9 0JD. The building is named after Police Constable Frank O'Neill who was fatally stabbed whilst on duty in October 1980. It was opened by the Commissioner Sir John Stevens, QPM, DL, and Kathie O'Neill and family in October 2004[9]. Public can attend these premises by appointment only. There are Safer Neighbourhood Teams, each operating from the following locations, 411 Coldharbour Lane; 186 Norwood Road; Loughborough Junction and Frank O'Neill House; Gipsy Hill; together with teams working from Streatham and Cavendish Road Police Stations[10]. The current Borough commander is Chief Superintendent Nick Ephgrave, assisted by Detective Superintendent John Corrigan, Superintendent Andy Howe, Detective Superintendent Dave Palmer and Superintendent Paul Wilson[11]

Brixton Police Station

In April 1830 the new Metropolitan Police (13th Company – Camberwell Division) arrived to police the parishes of St. Giles Camberwell, St Mary Newington, St Mary Lambeth, St George-the-Martyr Clapham and the small hamlets of Penge and Hatcham[12]. The three Police Stations to cover this new area were Park House, East Lane, Walworth; Camberwell Green; and Brixton Washway[13]; so called due to the flooding by the local River Effra at high tide[14].

In December 1831 there was an early reference to Police in Brixton when the Brixton Wall Stables were leased from a Mr Elden on an annual lease of £9. The old Station in Brixton Road was the former old Watch House, located on 'P' Division[15]. It had some 16 rooms, a 5-stall stable, and 6 cells. In 1845 it was stated that the Station needed cleaning, had rain and damp coming through the roof, and was seriously in need of painting. The Watch House was vacated at Christmas 1858[16].

In the 1830s, with the arrival of gas for the lighting of lamps, parish authorities followed the lead given by the City of Westminster by asking the owners of public buildings to put a gas lamp on the outside of them. There was no proper street lighting at the time and Police Stations placed a gas lamp on the outside of their premises. The main gas pipe ran along the road named Brixton Hill and past the Police Station; gas was supplied at no cost to the Police Force. In 1851 a dispute arose as to who should pay for the gas when further gas pipes were being laid along Brixton

Road, The pipe to the gas lamp outside the Police Station was disconnected from the main supply pipe and attached to the paying meter that recorded gas burnt inside the Station[17].

The lamps outside the Police Stations were white glass until 1861 when each Superintendent was told to requisition for three pieces of blue glass to be placed in the front and sides of each lamp[18]. There were only two Police lamps outside Police Stations in the Metropolitan Police Districts which used white glass. The first was outside the old Bow Street Police Station which did originally display a blue lamp but when Queen Victoria was visiting the Royal Opera House she noticed the blue lamp opposite and objected to it. The reason for her decision appears to be related to the fact that Prince Albert had died in the Blue Room at Windsor Castle. The other Police Station was at Northwood where in 1911 a blue lamp was placed outside the new Police Station without planning permission. The local authority demanded that it be removed and a white lamp later replaced it.

In 1852 a freehold site was purchased in Brixton but it then took until September 1857 for the Home Office to approve the plans for a new Police Station to be built on that site. It was agreed that £3590 could be spent on the project[19]. The new Police Station was designed by Charles Reeves, the Metropolitan Police Surveyor, and opened in 1858[20]. The design of the building, which actually cost only £2974 to build, was very like other Police buildings at the time. It was built of stock brick and slate, was five bays wide, had a two-bay extension to the south, it was three storeys high on a semi-basement and formerly had a mansard roof. There were 16 rooms and 6 cells. It had an Engine house, dust and dung pits and a large drill ground. A Pound at the rear was also purchased for £400. It was painted outside in

Brixton Police Station
Brixton Road
1858- 1909

1861. Accommodation was provided for 1 married Inspector at a cost of £11. 1s. per year[21].

The doorway was altered later in the refurbishment in 1909[22]. The picture shows Officers appearing from the yard of the Station and marching out to their beats just prior to a shift change. They are marching in single file and will fall out when they reach their beats which they were not allowed to leave unless for a very good reason. The Officer had to make a note in his pocket book whenever he was absent from his beat. His pocket book was submitted to the Sergeant prior to going off duty and if it was judged by the supervisory Officer to have been a frivolous absence it may have made himself the subject to disciplinary proceedings. It was not uncommon for sergeants to disbelieve their constables.

By 1864 the total number of Officers at the Station was 2 Inspectors, 8 Sergeants and 77 Constables. There were also three horses stabled there. One to be ridden by either of the two Inspectors and one to be ridden by either of the two Sergeants when on duty alternately at Peckham and Brixton Police Stations'[23].

In 1865 there was a reorganisation of Police boundaries and Brixton was transferred to 'W' (Croydon) Division and became the Divisional Office where Inspector D Fraser took charge as an Acting Superintendent[24]. Four years later in 1869 'W' Division had 1 Superintendent, 9 Inspectors, 40 Sergeants and 343 Constables. In addition it also became the Headquarters of No. 4 District with District Superintendent Captain H. Baynes in charge[25]. By 1879 'W' Division, and its nine Stations, was under the command of Superintendent William Wiseman[26].

Brixton Police Station
Brixton Road
1909 -1959

A report in 1881 described Brixton Police Station as an important station on an ample site. It made comment that one of the sleeping rooms was very badly ventilated. At the time there were 24 single Constables living in the Station[27]. In 1884 the address of Brixton Police Station was shown as 367 Brixton Road, Brixton[28]. As time went on the accommodation at the station became very cramped and extensive alterations were necessary. Work started in 1905 and was completed by 1909[29]. The new refurbished Station and the Section House were taken into occupation in July 1909 and provided accommodation for 31 single men[30].

The picture above shows the Station with the new extension to the right of the main entrance built in keeping with the rest of the building and now spread over the four floors.

Constable 130 'O' Division (not 'W' Division) was George Applegate born 1st August 1855. In 1881 he was a single man residing in a Section House located at Plumstead Royal Arsenal (official quarters), Plumstead, Kent, and came from Standerwick in Somerset. George had retired on 1st April 1901 as 62 'WR' Division on a pension of £108 having joined the Metropolitan Police on 19th April 1875.

Constable George Applegate

Constable Applegate was originally PC 186 'W' but transferred to the Reserve with pay on 1.10.1890. He married Ann from Beauleigh in Hampshire in about 1883, was a Brixton Police Officer and all their three children (boys) were born there. In fact Applegate was the Groom responsible for the horses at Brixton and therefore a most trusted and respected Police Officer from the senior Officer's point of view. He was a retired pensioner who had been kept on reserve. Records show that he re-joined for 7 days on 10th June 1902 and 28 days on 5th August 1902. The latter was the Coronation of King George VII. Queen Victoria had died on 22nd January 1901 but the Coronation was not held until some 19 months later. Applegate joined for 7 days for rehearsals to the Coronation, carrying on with his role as Groom responsible for the horses.

'O' Division was not a recognised geographical division but was used by Scotland Yard (CO) and issued to supplement Force strengths for re-engaged pensioners. Re-engaged pensioners were used at both of the Jubilee celebrations in 1887 and 1897. In 1897 103 ex-Inspectors, 113 ex-Sergeants and 570 ex-Constables received clasps to their 1887 Jubilee Medal whilst 6 ex-Inspectors 2 ex-Sergeants and 38 ex-Constables were awarded the actual medal.

The picture at right is Superintendent West, MBE, of 'W' Division based at Brixton. The Superintendent, shown in full dress uniform, was awarded his honours in recognition of long and loyal service especially through the war years. He retired in 1921.

Below is the Brixton Section of the Metropolitan Police Special Constabulary who had paraded in the yard to show off the Transport Section. These are all part-time unpaid Police Officers who used their own vehicles to patrol the street and sound the alarm whenever Zeppelins or German bombers were on a raid.

During the war the Specials would watch from the top of the Station for lights in the sky. Brixton was badly hit

Superintendent West MBE

on a number of occasions because the German aircraft would follow either the road (main route into London) or the railway line. Special Constables would be despatched from the Station on motorised patrols, as shown in the picture below, to warn people to put their lights out or pull the blackout curtains. Failing to do so would render them liable to prosecution The 'All Clear' would be sounded by whistles and Special Constables would display a placard stating 'ALL CLEAR'.

Metropolitan Police Special Constabulary
Brixton Motorised Patrols

By 1928 Brixton Police Station was just one of eleven Police Stations under the command of Superintendent Charles H. Clark[31].

Once again, in 1932, Police boundaries changed and Brixton was transferred from 'W' Division to 'L' Division but continued to be the District Headquarters[32].

Senior Police Officers 'W' Division c1914

The picture left shows the Senior Officers of 'W' Division in 1914 just prior to the war. We see Superintendent West shown in the centre with his Chief Inspector on his left together with Detective Inspector Berrett, fourth from the left, who later went on to become a famous Scotland Yard Detective. He chronicled his experiences in a book published in the 1930s.

There was again a need to increase the size of Brixton Police Station due to lack of space, and in 1937 the freeholds of Nos. 2 and 4 Gresham Road were purchased. Later a small piece of freehold land was purchased in Canterbury Crescent[33]. With the commencement of World War II in September 1939 some work on Police buildings was suspended.

On the night of 8/9 October 1940, whilst Superintendent M Purbrick was in charge, a bomb fell on Nos. 6 and 8 Gresham Road and damaged the Police Station[34]. Later in April 1941 the Station was badly damaged by a parachute mine and incendiaries. The Fire Brigade were quickly on the scene but were unable to save the roof of the Station from being completely burnt. The siren on top of the Station was left hanging dangerously from a chimney stack and the basement of the building was flooded with water to the depth of about four feet[35], but there were no causalities[36]. The Station was closed and business was transferred to Nine Elms Police Station at 147 Battersea Park Road. SW8.

Subsequently a new Police Station, designed by J Innes Elliot, Metropolitan Police Surveyor, was erected on the same site, taken into use in 1959 and continued to be the No 4 District Headquarters, 'L'

Brixton Police Station
Brixton Road
1959 – present day

Division Headquarters and Brixton Sub-Divisional Station [37]. The new Police Station building won a Civic Trust Award in 1961[38]. When the new local authority boundaries were put in place in 1965, Brixton Police Station remained within the London Borough of Lambeth[39].

The District Headquarters eventually moved out of Brixton Police Station in 1977 to 173/183 Lordship Lane, SE22, the new East Dulwich Police Station[40]. The horses based at Brixton also moved to new stables at East Dulwich[41].

In April 1981 there occurred what is known as the 'Brixton Riots'. This incident ended with the injury of many Police Officers and civilians and a substantial amount of damaged property. At the time, there had been a large increase in street robbery and police started an operation which resulted in a significant number of black youths being stopped and searched on the streets of Brixton. There was strong resentment of police actions in the area and this led to civil unrest and violence on the streets. The riots led to 299 Police Officers and at 65 civilians being injured, 61 private vehicles and 56 police vehicles damaged or destroyed, 28 premises were burned, and another 117 damaged and looted. There were

82 arrests for various offences. Both the Police and the Community were to learn, from the experience, valuable lessons for the future[42].

In July 1987 Brixton Station was visited by the Prince and Princess of Wales. The royal couple were shown around by Chief Superintendent Richard Monk, and they unveiled a plaque to mark the major extension and modernisation of the Station, which has been on its present site for almost 130 years[43].

Currently the Front Counter of Brixton Police Station is opening all day and every day.

Clapham Police Station

In May 1830 the Metropolitan Police arrived in the parish of Clapham. The Station House was in the former parish Watch House in Old Town, Clapham Common[44].

In 1845 the Home Office gave authority to rent a plot of land near Lark Hall Lane on a 78 year lease to allow the building of a new Police Station, which opened in March 1846. The ground rent at the time was £16[45]. Records in 1847 mention that the old Watch House at Clapham Common, near the New Church, was no longer required for Police purposes[46]. This Police building was one of the three on the Wandsworth Division, the other two being The Plain, Wandsworth and 1 & 2 Millman's Row, Chelsea[47].

By 1865 'W' Division consisted of the following stations; Clapham, Brixton, Streatham, Croydon, Sanderstead, Carshalton, Mitcham, Sutton, Banstead and Tooting[48]. The total number of Police Officers on 'W' Division was 296 – all ranks[49]. In 1879 'W' Division was under the command of Superintendent William Wiseman and William Mason was his deputy.[50]

In 1881 a report stated that the accommodation had been originally built for two married men, but at this stage it was occupied by one single Sergeant and 21 single Constables. The report also made comment that the kitchen was too small and that the ablution room could only be reached by passing through the mess room.[51] Not much had changed by 1891 when the Census in April that year showed eighteen single Officers residing at the Police Station. This included Police Sergeant George Saich and seventeen Constables[52]. It is interesting to note that five of the Constables were born in Norfolk.

Clapham Police Station
27 Smedley Road, Clapham
1907 – present day

In 1884 records show the address of the Station as Smedley Street, Clapham[53]. By 1893 part of Norwood and Penge Sections had been transferred from 'P' to 'W' Division[54].

The freehold of the site was purchased in 1898 from the Reverend George Ferris Whidbourne for £434. Later, in 1903, extra land and buildings were purchased at 56 Union Grove, 27 Smedley Street and 49, 51 Union Grove, in order to enlarge the Station. This land was under Trust of the will of a Richard Allen. In March 1905 a letter was sent to the London County Council from John Dixon Butler, Metropolitan Police Surveyor, stating that he was intending to rebuild Clapham Police Station following the existing building lines[55].

The Receiver bought the freehold of these properties and offered to pay an annuity on 49 and 51Union Grove but in 1920 an agreement was reached for a payment of a lump sum of £200 instead[56]. The new enlarged Police Station, designed by Butler, reopened for business in 1907[57].

A further reorganisation of Police boundaries in 1921 meant that Clapham and Battersea Park Road (Nine Elms Police Station) were transferred to 'L' Division[58]. By 1930 'L', or Lambeth, Division consisted of five Stations; Clapham, Battersea, Kennington Road, Lavender Hill and Nine Elms. All the Officers were under the command of Superintendent Ernest Brind who was based at Kennington Road Police Station[59].

In 1994 Clapham Police Station was amalgamated with Kennington Road Police Station to form the new Vauxhall Division. Currently the Front Counter of the Station is open Monday to Friday from 10am – 6 pm and is the base for two of the Safer Neighbourhood Teams. The future use of the building by Police is the subject of current discussions.

Kennington Lane and Kennington Road Police Stations

Although Kennington Lane and Kennington Road are separate Police Stations they have been included in the same part of the chapter; this is due to their close inter-relationship.

Kennington Lane Police Station

In 1838 there were three Police Stations covering the area and prior to 1830 all were former parish Watch Houses. They were at 10 Tower Street, Waterloo Road, Lambeth; High Street, Old Lambeth; and Christchurch, Blackfriars Road[60]. The buildings were unsuitable to accommodate Police Officers.

The Tower Street Watch House, a Station on 'L' Division at 10 Tower Street, was handed over to the Police together with the lease which still had 50 years to run. The premises were owned by Mr William Hadnut of William Street, Westminster Road. The annual rent was £65 and the records show that this was:

> 'an old brick plaster and tile house with a covered yard with a parade ground. There is a small open yard at the back with three cells, water closet, coal store and dust hole. It contains 8 rooms including a scullery.'

The Metropolitan Police retained this old Watch House for some time and they maintained it well as in 1844 it was whitened, coloured and repaired. In 1853 it was cleansed and painted whilst the outside was painted in 1857, 1860, 1864 and 1871. The Police Surveyors were concerned about the cell floors which appeared to be deteriorating at the time of renting, whilst the drains were defective and had to be cleaned. The premises were generally clean, ventilation good and water in plentiful supply[61]. In 1844 it was important enough to be a Station designated for supervision by an Inspector[62]. Just behind the Watch House the Receiver purchased a house to use as a residence for Police Officers.

The Section House in Hertford Place, Webber Street adjoined the Police Station and was also owned by Mr Hadnut who leased the premises for 50 years from 1834. 23 Constables lived in the Station whilst one Sergeant and 5 Constables lived in the house. Both the house and Watch House were vacated in 1875[63].

In 1844 the estimated cost of erecting a new Police Station and Police Court at Kennington was £2,300. The Receiver was to be the copyholder and a tenant of the Duchy of Cornwall[64]. Prior to this, in 1842, it had been suggested that a Police Court be built for the Metropolitan Police District on a triangle of land bounded by Kennington Lane, Windmill Row and Kennington Road. This idea was abandoned after much public opposition[65].

In 1844 'L' Division was led by Police Superintendent Samuel Dicken Corbet Grinsell, who had been appointed a Superintendent in the Force in 1833 and was based at Tower Street, Waterloo Place.

Working with Grinsell were four Police Inspectors; D.Ferguson, J.Evans, William Stannard and William J Topp. The Inspectors operated from two Stations, one at Tower Street and the other at High Street, Lambeth[66]. All four Police Inspectors were recorded on 'L' Division in 1841 when Inspector Topp had recently replaced Inspector Joseph Wrangle who retired in May 1841 on an annual pension of £108 in consequence of being 'worn out'[67]. Many Police Officers were retired towards the end of their service and their cause for leaving shown as 'worn out', but this does not occur for the lower ranks in the present Police Service. However, the Superintending Ranks of the Metropolitan Police Service were not allowed to serve beyond the age of 55 years because of regulations laid down some time ago. It was stated that a Superintendent was 'worn out' by the time he or she reached 55 years. This regulation was certainly in place at least until the mid-1990.

The 1841 Census shows Superintendent Grinsell living in the Police accommodation at 9 Kennington Cross, with his family and eleven Police Constables[68]. Superintendent Grinsell is an interesting person. On leaving the Police Service he moved from Kennington Cross to Hillingdon Heath, Hillingdon, Middlesex, and became the Deputy Bailiff at Brentford County Court. He later moved to Camden Square, Camberwell, Surrey, and was occasionally employed in the Surrey Zoological Gardens. It is not certain how he was employed at the time but in July 1849 he found himself in debt and in Queen's Prison[69].

By 1849 there were four Police Stations on 'L', or Lambeth, Division under the command of Superintendent Anthony Rutt[70]. One was at Tower Street, Waterloo Road; one at Kennington Lane; one at High Street, Lambeth; and the other at Christchurch, near the old church[71]. However, by 1864 the Division had only two Stations: Tower Street (shown as No 58 in the National Census Return of 1841; the road was later renamed Morley Street in 1937) and Kennington Lane. The combined strength of the two Stations in 1864 was 4 Inspectors, 21 Sergeants and 178 Constables[72]. In addition, a Police Constable was on duty in charge of the lock up at Christ Church during the day; a stretcher was kept there, but no Station duty was performed there[73].

In April 1865, the Vestry of the Parish of Lambeth notified the Police that the address of Kennington Lane Police Station was changing from 4 York Row to 8 Kennington Park Road[74]. In 1868 the lease was extended for 63 years with an annual rent of £127 and a new Station was built on the site in 1870.

At various times in a Police Officer's career he may well find himself in a situation which could result in him being injured or, at worst, killed. This has been the reality since early times when Constables enforced the Law of the Land and many Officers have lost their lives whilst trying to uphold the Law. One such Officer, in May 1851, was Police Constable Henry James Chaplin who was

Kennington Lane Police Station
42 Lower Kennington Lane
1871 - 1932

attacked and struck with bricks by a disorderly crowd at Vauxhall Walk. The Officer is buried in St. Mark's Churchyard, Kennington[75].

In 1868 it was decided to erect a new Kennington Lane Station to be designed by Frederick Caiger, the Metropolitan Police Surveyor. The cost was calculated to be in the region of £8000, but actually cost only £7040. Three years later, in November 1871, the new Station opened for business[76].

A new detached Police Section House was built on the site of the Police Station rear yard, but facing onto Renfrew Road which ran down the side of the Police Station. There were originally objections by the local residents that the frontage line extended too far but planning permission was given regardless[77]. It was described as 'Home for Recruits'[78] and later as a 'Candidates Section House'.

This new Section House opened in October 1887 and was occupied by 1 Police Inspector, 30 Police Constables and 51 Recruits[79]. It ceased to house Recruits when, in 1907, Peel House was opened in Regency Street[80].

The Police Station at High Street, Lambeth was closed when the new Kennington Lane Police Station, whose address in 1880 was given as 42 Lower Kennington Lane (L) corner of Renfrew Road[81], was opened[82]. In 1933 it was often referred to as "Renfrew Road Section House"[83].

Detective Sergeant B. Leeson described how he joined the Metropolitan Police in December 1890 and was taken to Kennington Lane Section House, a Police barracks and school of instruction. The Courses there varied from three to five weeks in length and every morning after breakfast the Recruits were taken to Wellington Barracks for two hours of foot drill. Leeson also described his fellow Recruits as a mixed lot consisting of farm labourers, ploughmen and waggoner's from every County in the British Isles (See also end note[84]). At the end of the course they were marched from Kennington to New Scotland Yard to be 'sworn in'. They were issued with two complete uniforms, described as good but poorly made, and then posted to various Police Divisions[85].

In 1869 Superintendent Charles Webb was in charge of 'L', or Lambeth, Division and was based at Kennington Lane Police Station. An Inspector was in charge at 58 Tower Street, Waterloo.

In 1881 a report on Kennington Lane Police Station describes it as an important Station which had been recently built; it was a large site although on low lying land. The basement had been under water but steps were being taken to check the flooding[86] and some considerable alterations were made to the building in 1912. Inside there were two sets of married quarters and part of the main building was a Police Section House. The new Police Section House erected on the site of the old Kennington Lane Police Station became known as Gilmore House, Renfrew Street, SE11[87].

Kennington Road Police Station

A new Station was built, to the designs of Frederick Caiger, Metropolitan Police Surveyor, in Kennington Road and this Station was opened in August 1874[88]. In 1879 "L" Division comprised of just two Stations, Kennington Lane and Kennington Road with Superintendent Jas Brannan in charge[89].

Kennington Road Police Station
Kennington Road
1874 - 1939

A report in 1881 report described the Kennington Road Station as having the single men living in one block and married men living in the building containing the Administration. At the time of the report the accommodation housed two married Inspectors, two single Sergeants and forty eight Constables. This was a new Station which had been built for only six years but they criticized the same mess room and stressed the need for more cells to be built[90]. This was carried out and they were brought into use in 1890[91].

Superintendent Brannan was still in charge in 1891. At Kennington Lane he was assisted by Chief Inspector Chisholm and Inspectors T. Padgett, T. Green, J. Hill, W. Whatley, G. Bartle, J. Barrett, T. Neal and C. Easter. The following Inspectors were at Kennington Road, H. Garland, J.

Jackson, G. Lowe, G. Payne, G. M. Lennett and T. Martin[92]. The address of Kennington Road Police Station was 47 Kennington Road[93].

In 1893 Inspector H. Garland, who was mentioned above, retired. He had served at Kennington Road for twelve years and, as often happened when Officers retired, there was a presentation. The report was as follows:

> "A gratifying testimony to the appreciation in which Insp, Garland, of the L Division was held by the inhabitants of Lambeth has been supplied on his retirement, after holding the position for 12 years. His unvarying courtesy and integrity in discharging his duties had earned for him popularity and respect, and led the leading trade-men of the district to offer him a token of their esteem. The presentation took place at the horse and Groom, Westminster Bridge road, where, after a capital dinner, the host Mr Douglas Hart, who presided, handed Insp. Garland a purse containing 100 guineas and a gold albert chain............. The presentation was accompanied by a testimonial on vellum...[94]."

In June 1892 the Home Office approved the purchase of the freehold of the Police Station at 47 Kennington Road for £6000 from the freeholder, a Mr W. Stock, although the transaction was not completed until March 1893[95].

In 1928 Superintendent Thomas Abbott was in charge of 'L' Division and based at Kennington Lane Police Station. The Division also included Kennington Road, Battersea, Clapham, Lavender Hill and Nine Elms Police Stations[96]. By 1930 Superintendent Ernest Brind was in charge of 'L' Division[97].

During a reorganisation of Police boundaries of No. 4 District in 1932 Kennington Road Police Station was transferred from 'L' to 'M', or Southwark, Division[98]. Seven years later, in 1939, Kennington Road Police Station was closed for reconstruction and

Kennington Police Station
49-51 Kennington Road
1955 – present day

all business was transferred to a temporary Station at Gilmore House, Renfrew Street, SE11[99].

The Old Kennington Road Station was demolished and drawings prepared for the erection of a new Police Station, but the outbreak of World War II prevented further action. During the War the London Fire Brigade utilised the site to hold an emergency water supply for use during the air raids[100].

In 1949, after the War, the freehold of the adjoining properties, 49-51 Kennington Road, were purchased for £1,500 to increase the area for the new Station to be erected upon that site[101].

The New Sub-Divisional Police Station at Kennington Road, 'M' Division, designed by J. Innes Elliott, Metropolitan Police Chief Architect and Surveyor, was built and eventually opened for business in October 1955. The address of the Station was 49-51 Kennington Road, SE1. The temporary Police Station at Gilmore Section House was closed[102].

The reorganisation of local authority boundaries in 1965 moved Kennington Road Sub-Divisional Station (LK) back to 'L' Division within the London Borough of Lambeth[103].

In Lower Marsh in October 1980 Police Constable Frank O'Neill was fatally stabbed whilst attempting to arrest a suspect using a forged prescription. A plaque to his memory was placed in the foyer of Kennington Police Station and unveiled by the Commissioner, Sir David McNee, in May 1981.

The areas policed by Kennington Road and Clapham Police Stations were amalgamated in January 1994 to form the new Vauxhall Division.

Currently the Police Station Front Counter is open each and every day for the convenience of the public.

Knights Hill or Lower Norwood Police Station

In September 1870 the Police leased property in Knights Hill, Lower Norwood, until March 1879 from a Mrs Mary Buck for the sum of £1000. After adaptation and repair police took up occupation of the premises in March 1872. It became a Police Station on 'P' Division. The building was described in a report of 1881 as 'a cottage in a large garden, pleasantly situated. Two cells have been added'[104]. Knights Hill Police Station was often referred to as Lower Norwood.

In 1886 the Police service purchased a small cottage, built in 1854, at 59 Knights Hill, between Ernest Avenue and Knights Hill Square, and when renovated three cells were included in the building. The site on which the

Knights Hill Police Station
59 Knights Hill
1886 -1930

building stood was fairly large with a frontage of approximately 50 feet and a depth of 120 feet[105]. In June of that year the Police Station became operational and by 1891 Inspector Scantlebury was in charge[106]. It was part of the Norwood Sub-Division. The Station was very small and cramped. The ground floor, together with the upper floor, was Police married quarters. In fact, up until 1929 the one CID Officer at the Station had to use one of the cells as an office. The Station closed in June 1930 after exactly 44 years of service[107].

The staff included 1 Station Sergeant, 7 Sergeants, 21 Constables and 1 CID Officer and at the closure of the Station the work and all staff were transferred to Gipsy Hill Police Station as the Station had not been particularly busy during the preceding years. In 1927 there had been only eighteen arrests, in 1928 thirty two and in 1929 nineteen. However, most of their work was due to the close proximity of a tram station and omnibus depot. It became very convenient for their staff to hand in items of lost property to the Police Station. In 1929 some 4,000 items of lost property were handed in[108].

With the closure of the police Station one of the new Police telephone boxes was placed on the forecourt of the old Station. This provided a free direct line to Gipsy Hill Police Station where a garage had been built to house its first motor car – a Jowett – to be used when required for answering calls from Knights Hill and the district generally[109]. The site of the old Police Station was at one time considered as a possibility for a detached Police Section House for single Police Officers[110]. To mark the closure of Knights Hill Police Station the Crystal Palace District Advertiser printed the following words:

> 'West Norwood can pride itself on its good behaviour, surely, when a police station can be closed down' [111]

In 1938 the property came under the hammer at the London Auction Mart and was purchased for £1000 by 70 year old Mr Walter Booth who had lived in Norwood as a boy some 50 years previously when it was just a village. He bought the property as an investment and although he was not sure what he was going to do with the old Police Station he thought he would turn the cells into a garage[112]. Sadly, the old building was destroyed by a V1 flying bomb in 1941[113] and there are now modern commercial buildings on the site of the old Police Station.

Norwood/ Gipsy Hill Police Station

Gipsy Hill Police Station
Gipsy Hill, Norwood
1859 - 1940

In 1853 the Home Office gave authority for a search to be made for a site for new Police Station. The need for a new one was due to the start of transferring the Great Exhibition from Hyde Park to Crystal Palace in August 1852. By March 1854 a suitable site had been found in Gipsy Hill and leased for a period of 92 years from Mrs Mary Scott of Norfolk Terrace, Fulham Road,[114] with a ground rent of £26[115]. The new Police Station site was very near the Exhibition site, however, the building of the Station was delayed during the following months as the contractors had complained that the price of building materials had soared since tendering[116]. Queen Victoria formally opened the Exhibition in June 1854

A new Police Norwood Sub-Division was formed when the Station was opened for business. The building was designed by Charles Reeves, Metropolitan Police Surveyor, and erected at a cost of £2,461[117]. The Station was built of substantial brick and slate, had 16 rooms, a kitchen, offices, four cells, a three-stall stable, a loft, and two water closets. There were also Dung and Dust pits plus 5 coal vaults[118]. An Inspector was appointed for duty at the Station[119] and by 1864 the strength of Officers at the Station included 2 Inspectors, 8 Sergeants and 59 Constables. One horse was to be ridden by either of the two Inspectors alternately on duty[120].

In 1876 a Mrs E M Dowling requested permission to place a small window in the party wall adjoining Gipsy Hill Police Station and this was given. It will be noted that at this time the Station was being called Gipsy Hill rather that Norwood[121]. A later Police Order quoted the address of the Station as 6 Gipsy Hill, Norwood[122]. It was not until 1926 that the official name of the Station changed to Gipsy Hill[123].

In 1881 a report mentions the close proximity of the Station to Crystal Palace. The basement was occupied by the mess and the upper rooms were badly arranged into single men's sleeping rooms and a married quarter. It was at that time occupied by 1 married Inspector and 21 single Constables[124]. Policing at the Crystal Palace Exhibition caused additional work for the Police of

Gipsy Hill Police Station
66, Central Hill, SE19
1940 – present day

Gypsy Hill, so to ease the burden extra Officers were allocated to Police the Exhibition and Inspector John Fyfe was posted to the site with other Officers[125]. The Census data, ten years later in 1891, showed that there were still twenty single Officers living at the Station[126] and Inspector Ellams was the Officer in charge[127].

The formation of 'Z' (Croydon) Division in 1921 meant that Gipsy Hill was transferred from 'P' to 'Z' Division[128].

On the evening of 30th November 1936 at about 7.40pm a serious fire occurred at the Crystal Palace, Sydenham. The first Police Officer on the scene was Police Constable Parkins who called the Penge Fire Brigade; Inspector Hussey of 'Z' Division and Police Constable Wollard then arrived. The fire spread rapidly and within half an hour the whole Palace was in flames. Police estimated that a crowd of at least 100,000 people had gathered. The mass of people, and a large number of vehicles, caused the Inspector to request aid from other Police Stations. Eventually Superintendent White, two Chief Inspectors, seven Senior Divisional Inspectors, twenty one Inspectors, sixty two Sergeants, six hundred and fifty one Constables and five Mounted Police were in attendance[129].

In 1936 it was decided to rebuild Gipsy Hill Police Station on a different site as the existing site, which fronted on Gipsy Hill, was small and on the side of a steep hill. The freehold of that site had been compulsory purchased in the beginning and the Agent for the freeholders informed the Receiver that they would not sell any additional land voluntarily. In these circumstances another site called 'Highland House' was found, situated on the corner of Central Hill and Highland Road (now Vicars Oak Road). The property was not on the market at that time but the Ecclesiastical Commissioners were prepared to draw up a 999 year lease and sell for £3,750. Negotiations were concluded in 1937 and a new Police Station was erected[130].

The modern building was designed by G. Mackenzie Trench, Metropolitan Police Architect and Surveyor, and built by Gibson of Croydon. The design of the new Station had been exhibited at the Royal Academy in 1938. It was and still is an imposing structure in multi-coloured brick and stone with green Starreburg tiling on the roof. Because of World War II being in progress the Police Station was not officially opened[131], but it went into service at 16 Central Hill in April 1940[132]. The freehold of the property was bought later in 1953 for £1000[133]. During the Second World War the Station was badly damaged by a flying bomb, but there were no Police casualties and the Station remained operational.

Meanwhile the old Police Station was converted into Police flats in 1948; it is now owned by the local authority and called Gipsy Hill House.

The local authority boundaries changed in 1965 and this resulted in Gipsy Hill Police Station (LG) becoming the Sectional Station to Streatham Sub-Division (LS) on 'L' Division within the London Borough of Lambeth[134]. In 1975 the address of the Police Station is noted as being 66 Central Hill, SE19[135].

Currently the Police Station Front Counter is open Monday to Friday from 8am – 8pm. The Station is also the Borough Police Training Centre and the base for one of the Safer Neighbourhood Teams[136].

Streatham Police Station

In 1865 Streatham Police Station was show in records on 'W' (Clapham) Division[137].

In June 1866 Home Office authorised the acceptance of the tender submitted by a Mr Higgs in the sum of £3,117 for the erection of a new police station at Streatham[138]. The freehold of the site had been purchased for £1800 the previous year[139].

The new Station was opened in July 1868[140]. The Station was described as no more than 'a Policeman's cottage'[141] By 1879 Streatham had become an Inspectors Station under the overall command of Superintendent William Wiseman. 'W' Division at that time was comprised of Brixton, Clapham, Croydon, Streatham, Mitcham, Sutton, Banstead, Tooting and Charshalton[142]. In the animated picture you can clearly see the old Station at Streatham on the left hand side. It is a typical Victorian two storey

Streatham Police Station
High Road, Streatham
1868 - 1912

Police Station with two chimneys.

A report in 1881 stated that the men use the kitchen at Streatham Police Station as a mess room, the clothes room as a sitting room and the married and single quarters were mixed. The accommodation housed one married Inspector, one married Sergeant and eleven single Constables. All of these issues were unsatisfactory. In addition the report stated that the public could see into the cell passage and 'sometimes give trouble'[143].

In 1884 the address of Streatham Police Station was shown as High Road, Streatham,[144] and by 1891, whilst Clapham was still on 'W' Division, Superintendent S. T. Lucas was in charge, assisted by Sub-Divisional Inspector J. Janes and Inspector Worth[145].

Streatham's first Mounted Officer was Police Constable 759 'W' Edward Jeffrey who joined the Police in 1902 and then resigned through ill health in 1918 with 'traumatic arthritis of wrist'. He died in 1939[146].

Streatham Police Station
Streatham High Road, SW16
1912 – present day

In August 1908 the freehold of the Streatham Old Branch Post Office was purchased for £2000 with a view to rebuilding the Police Station situated at the corner of Streatham High Road and Shrubbery Road. In October 1909 the Commissioner, Sir Edward Henry, in a memorandum to the Receiver, informed him that the question of rebuilding the Police Station was a pressing one as the current building was no longer adequate for the important and growing district in which it was situated. The existing Station had been built 40 years before when Streatham was just a village. The population had grown from 33,000 in 1901 to 60,000 in 1909 and the Station was sited on the main London to Brighton Road. It received many callers and, as there was no waiting room, chaos often reigned in the

Front Office. In short, the present building was too small for present day requirements and the rebuilding could no longer be delayed. During the rebuilding, the day to day business was conducted in a temporary Police Station in the old Post Office at the rear of the premises[147].

The new Police Station designed by John Dixon Butler, the Metropolitan Police Surveyor, was completed in two stages. The administrative part was opened for business in July 1912[148] and the new Police Section House was ready for occupation in April 1913. Residential accommodation was provided for 30 single men at 1/- per week each. There were also two sets of married quarters. The building was designed as a cube over three storeys. At the third floor level the stone cornice is used to create a large stone pediment as a simple decorative device on the three visible sides of the building; the address was 101 High Road, Streatham, SW16. There was a commemorative foundation stone by the main door in Shrubbery Road[149].

In 1928 Superintendent Charles R. Clark was in charge of 'W' Division. Streatham Police Station and ten other Police Stations were under his command[150].

Following the revision of Police boundaries in 1931 Streatham was transferred from 'W' (Brixton) Division to 'Z' (Croydon) Division. Streatham was the Sub-Divisional Station with Gipsy Hill as its Sectional Station. Sub-Divisional Inspector Murrells was transferred from Gipsy Hill to Streatham[151].

In 1963 it was decided to acquire additional land at Streatham to provide a new site for the Station to be built between the years 1966-1970, so land to the rear of 103-113 Streatham High Road was purchased freehold for the sum of £5000 in January 1964[152].

The revision of local authority boundaries in 1965 moved Streatham and its Sectional Station from 'Z' to 'L' in the London Borough of Lambeth[153].

Currently the Police Station is open 24 hours a day and is the base for four of its Safer Neighbourhood Teams[154]. There has been much talk concerning the possible closure of Streatham Police Station[155].

[1] Lambeth Archives History
[2] www.lambeth.gov.uk 25.2.08
[3] www.lambeth.gov.uk accessed on 25th February 2008
[4] Metropolitan Police Surveyors Records, Charlton.
[5] Bacons Atlas 1888
[6] Robson London Directory. 1833
[7] Brown B. A Brief History of the Vauxhall Division. July 1997
[8] MEPO 4/234
[9] The Post 20.10.2004
[10] www.met.police.uk accessed on 10th October 2010
[11] www.met.police.uk accessed on 10th October 2010
[12] .Brown, B.. Police History Society Journal 1994.
[13] Post Office Directory 1838
[14] Brown, B. Police History Society Journal 1994
[15] MEPO 5/3 (10/8)
[16] Metropolitan Police Surveyors Records, Charlton
[17] MEPO 5/25 (142/1)
[18] Metropolitan Police Orders dated 4 February 1861
[19] MEPO 5/26 (156)
[20] LB440
[21] Metropolitan Police Surveyors Records Charlton.
[22] www.british-history.ac.uk accessed on 9th October 2007
[23] Metropolitan Police Orders dated 11th January 1864
[24] Metropolitan Police Orders dated 28th October 1865
[25] MEPO 2/37
[26] Post Office Directory 1879
[27] Metropolitan Police Surveyors Report 1881
[28] Metropolitan Police Orders dated 20 June 1884
[29] MEPO2/902
[30] Metropolitan Police Orders dated 17 July 1909
[31] Post Office Directory 1928
[32] Metropolitan Police Orders dated 1 Jan 1932
[33] LB 440
[34] LB 440
[35] Brown B. The Job Newspaper 5.2.1988
[36] The Metropolitan Police at War HMSO 1947.
[37] Metropolitan Police Orders dated 5 Jan 1959
[38] www.urban75.org/brixton/history/police. Accessed on 14th March 2008
[39] Metropolitan Police Orders dated 6th August 1964
[40] LB511
[41] South London Press 27th Sept 1977
[42] www.met.police.uk/history/brixton_riots. accessed on 9th April 2008
[43] The Job 10 July 1987
[44] Brown, B. A Brief History of the Vauxhall Division. July 1997
[45] MEPO 5/34 (214)
[46] John Back Archive (1975) Metropolitan Police Historical Collection
[47] Post Office London Directory 1838
[48] Metropolitan Police Orders dated 28th October 1865
[49] MEPO 2/26
[50] Post Office Directory 1879
[51] Metropolitan Police Surveyors Report 1881
[52] National Archives Census 1891
[53] Metropolitan Police Orders dated 20th June 1884
[54] Metropolitan Police Orders dated 13th February 1893
[55] London Metropolitan Archives - GLC/AR/BR/22/026347
[56] LB446
[57] Metropolitan Police Orders dated 10th August 1907
[58] Metropolitan Police Orders dated 24th February 1921

[59] Police almanac 1930
[60] Post Office. London Directory 1838
[61] Metropolitan Police Surveyors, Charlton
[62] Kelly's directory 1844
[63] Kelly's directory 1875
[64] John Back Archive (1975) Metropolitan Police Historical Collection.
[65] Surveyor of London Vol. XXVI St Mary Lambeth Part 2.
[66] Police and Constabulary List 1844
[67] Brown, B. Met Police Historical Collection. date unknown
[68] National Archives Census 1841
[69] London Gazette 20.7.1949 p.2324 and 24.7.1849 2347.
[70] Post Office Directory 1849
[71] Post Office London Directory 1849
[72] Metropolitan Police Orders dated 11th January 1864
[73] John Back Archive (1975) Metropolitan Police Historical Collection
[74] John Back Archive (1975) Metropolitan Police Historical Collection
[75] Fido, M. and Skinner, K. (1999) The Official Encyclopaedia of Scotland Yard. Virgin
[76] Metropolitan Police Orders dated 4th November 1871
[77] MBW/BA/36558
[78] The Builder 6 Nov 1886. p.686
[79] Metropolitan Police Orders dated 8th November 1887
[80] MEPO 2/2584
[81] John Back Archive (1975) Metropolitan Police Historical Collection
[82] Brown, B. Met Police Historical Collection. date unknown
[83] MEPO 2/2584
[84] In 1874 a survey of recruiting, over a two period, showed that those who had joined the Force, 31% came from land jobs, 12% from Military Service and 5% from other police jobs. The remainder mostly from manual jobs. The majority of recruits and serving officers at that time came from outside London. www.friendsofmethistory.co.uk/timeline accessed on 9th January 2008
[85] Leeson B. Lost London. Stanley Paul. Date unknown.
[86] Metropolitan Police Surveyors Report 1881
[87] Metropolitan Police Orders dated 24th.April 1939
[88] Metropolitan Police Orders dated 6th August 1874
[89] Post Office Directory 1879
[90] Report on the Condition of Police Stations 1881
[91] Metropolitan Police Orders dated 5th March 1890
[92] Kelly's Sydenham, Norwood & Streatham Directory 1891.
[93] John Back Archive (1975) Metropolitan Police Historical Collection
[94] Police Review Vol.1. 1893
[95] John Back Archive (1975) Metropolitan Police Historical Collection
[96] Post Office Directory 1928
[97] Police Almanac 1930
[98] Metropolitan Police Orders dated 1st January 1932
[99] Metropolitan Police Orders dated 24th April 1939
[100] John Back Archive (1975) Metropolitan Police Historical Collection
[101] John Back Archive (1975) Metropolitan Police Historical Collection
[102] Metropolitan Police Orders dated 25th October 1955
[103] Metropolitan Police Orders dated 6th August 1964
[104] Report on the Condition of Police Stations 1881
[105] MEPO 2/2584
[106] Kelly's Sydenham, Norwood and Streatham Directory 1891
[107] PC Roger Hickman The Beat. P.17
[108] PC Roger Hickman the Beat p.17
[109] PC Hickman
[110] MEPO 2/2584
[111] Crystal Palace District Advertiser 30 June 1930
[112] News Chronicle 11 April 1938
[113] PC Hickman

[114] Metropolitan Police Surveyors Records
[115] Surveyors Police Surveyors Records
[116] MEPO 5/28 (169)
[117] Survey of London. Volume 26. p.187
[118] Surveyors Police Surveyors Records
[119] PO 26 Jan 1859
[120] PO 11 Jan 1864
[121] MEPO 5/48 (342)
[122] PO 20 June 1884
[123] Metropolitan Police Orders dated 26th March 1926
[124] Report 1881
[125] Census Data 1881
[126] Census Data 1891
[127] Kelly's Sydenham, Norwood and Streatham Directory 1891
[128] Metropolitan Police Orders dated 24 February 1921
[129] Metropolitan Police Historical Collection
[130] LB 802
[131] West Norwood Times 19th April 1940
[132] Metropolitan Police Orders dated 5 April 1940
[133] LB 802
[134] Metropolitan Police Orders dated 6th August 1964
[135] Metropolitan Police Orders dated 1st August 1975
[136] Met Police Estate Asset Management Plan. November 2007
[137] Metropolitan Police Orders dated 28th October 1865
[138] John Back Archive (1975) Metropolitan Police Historical Collection
[139] Metropolitan Police Surveyors Records
[140] Metropolitan Police Orders dated 17 July 1868
[141] .Hickman, R. Police Constable in The Beat date unknown.
[142] Post Office London Directory 1879
[143] Report on the condition of Police Stations 1881
[144] Metropolitan Police Orders dated 20 June 1884
[145] Kelly's Sydenham, Norwood and Streatham Directory. 1891
[146] Material Police Museum Charlton.
[147] John Back Archive (1975) Metropolitan Police Historical Collection
[148] Metropolitan Police Orders dated 26 July 1912
[149] Planning Committee. Chief Executive Office, Lambeth. 7.12.1999
[150] Post Office London Directory 1928.
[151] Metropolitan Police Orders dated 9 Oct 1931
[152] John Back Archive (1975) Metropolitan Police Historical Collection
[153] Metropolitan Police Orders dated 6th August 1964
[154] Met. Police Estate Asset Management Plan November 2007
[155] Streatham Guardian 27th February 2008

Chapter 6

The London Borough of Lewisham

Introduction

The London Borough of Lewisham was created in 1965 and comprises the three old administrative parishes of St. Mary Lewisham, St. Margaret Lee, and St. Paul Deptford. In 1900 Lewisham and Lee were combined to form the Metropolitan Borough of Lewisham. Also in 1900 the parish of St. Paul became the Metropolitan Borough of Deptford. In 1996 the old Royal Dockyard at Greenwich was transferred to Lewisham[1].

The borough is bordered on the east by the London Borough of Greenwich; the London Borough of Bromley lies to the South and the London Borough of Southwark to the west. The River Thames runs along its northern boundary.

In 2001 the population of the borough was recorded as being almost 250,000.

Policing

In May 1830 the Metropolitan Police, known as the 14th Company ('R') of Greenwich Division, took over parts of Kent and the parishes of Bermondsey and Rotherhithe. Those Police Stations, which at one time or other were still in the London of Lewisham, are the ones which we will address in this chapter.

Currently, policing is located at seven key locations across the London Borough of Lewisham. Five of the Police Stations, Lewisham, Catford, Deptford, Sydenham and Brockley are open to the public, although the last two have restricted opening times. The future of Brockley Police Station is a subject of great discussion in the community. In addition to the five Police Stations there are eighteen Safer Neighbourhood Teams strategically placed across the Borough. The Borough Police Commander is Chief Superintendent Jeremy Burton assisted by Superintendent Lisa Crook, Detective Superintendent Si Cunneen and Superintendent Suzanne Wallace[2].

Brockley Police Station

In April 1880 the District Police Superintendent, Captain H Baynes, suggested that if a Police Station at Brockley was considered, the accommodation should consist of quarters for one married Officer (either an Inspector or a Sergeant), ten single men, three cells, an office and a charge room. He further suggested that it should be situated no more than 600 yards south of Brockley Lane Railway Station on the London, Chatham and Dover Railway[3].

After inspection a site at the corner of Howson and Kneller Roads was considered suitable. The freeholders were the Governors of Christ's Hospital and the lessee was Mr I W Webb. Home Office approval was given in February 1881 for the lease to be purchased and in May 1882 approval of a Tender for the work was accepted[4].

The new Police Station, designed by John Butler, Metropolitan Police Surveyor, was opened in December 1883 and Inspector Jewell was transferred from Lewisham to Brockley Police Station to take charge[5]. The address of the Station was shown as 4, Howson Road, Brockley[6]. In August 1899 the freehold of the property was obtained under the Compulsory Purchasing powers for the sum of £300[7].

Brockley Police Station
4, Howson Road, Brockley
1883 – present day.

In 1891 the England Census showed an Inspector Harry Croft living at the Station with his wife Elizabeth and four children. Also that night there were ten Constables 'lodging' there. The address was shown as 2 & 4 Howson Road. One of the Constables was named Charles Dickens, aged 25 years; was he named after the famous Charles Dickens who died in 1870? An interesting point to consider when looking at the census data is to see in which part of the country the Officers were born. Whilst the Inspector was born in Sussex the ten Constables came from Bedfordshire (2), Kent, Lincolnshire, Hampshire (2), Somerset, Surrey, Dorset and one from

Aberdeen, Scotland. This was an interesting mixture of people from different areas of Britain[8].

In 1960 it was decided to close the Station at night. This was to allow Officers who were normally employed there on the night shift to be posted to outside duties. A telephone connected to the Sub-Division Station was installed in a pillar by the front door of the Station for use by the public and Police[9]. The Station reopened at night from July 1965[10].

When police boundaries were aligned to the new local authority boundaries in 1965 then Brockley, as a Sectional Station together with Deptford, became part of the Lewisham Sub-Division on 'P' (Catford), Division[11].

In 2003 with the closure of Brockley Police Station and the staff being moved to the new Lewisham Police Station the local authority considered adding Brockley Police Station to the list of Locally Listed Buildings in Lewisham. The report included the following comments:

> " The station was built at the same time as the surrounding residential streets, which is contrast to later police stations, which were fitted into existing streetscapes. The building survives in its original layout with the sergeant's family quarters upstairs; offices on the round floor; the canteen in the Kneller Road wing and the cells in the opposite wing. Elements of the plain interior survive and include a small number of panelled doors and timber partitions. The station is surrounded by a yard with its original six foot wall and substantial gate posts. The two storey building is built of red brick in the neo-Georgian style with six-over-six pane sash windows. Portland stone rusticated door cases and stone lintels. The ground floor is in rusticated brick and the building is topped by a slate hipped roof and highly decorative chimney stacks and terracotta pots." [12]

Recently the Station has been open to the public from 1000 hrs to 1400 hrs Monday to Friday and closed on Saturday and Sunday. The area is policed by the neighbourhood team of one Police Sergeant, two Constables and six Police Community Support Officers.

The future of the Station is under threat. Many of the older Police Stations are in urgent need of repair and these Stations do not lend themselves easily to receiving new technology and increases in support staff. Some Stations do not comply with the disability discrimination rules because their structure does not easily convert to give proper access to disabled persons. The Metropolitan Police have indicated that Stations should be disposed with if they are not "fit for purpose". Brockley Police

Station is one of those buildings that could be sold for future development.

Catford and Southend Village Police Stations

The first Police Station in Catford was acquired as a freehold site on June 1888 from the Trustees of the late Major John Forster's estate. It was a few minutes walk from Catford Bridge Railway Station on the main Perry Hill Road leading to Lower Sydenham[13].

Catford Police Station
Catford Hill, SE6
1892-1927

The new Station, designed by John Butler, Metropolitan Police Surveyor, was built and opened March 1892.

Four Station Sergeants, one Section Sergeant and Four Constables (one Acting Sergeant) were posted to the new Police Station[14]. It slowly increased in importance and by 1899 Sub-Divisional Inspector George Smith and Inspectors Harry Knighton and John Cathcart were attached to the Station[15]. By 1903 Smith had been replaced as Sub-Divisional Inspector by William Phillips[16].

Mr Robert John Collie of St. George's Lodge, Catford, was appointed Divisional Surgeon to the Police of 'P' Division and covered Catford Police Station[17].

Catford was originally a Sub-Divisional Station but in 1905 lost that status when Lewisham became the Sub-Divisional Station. This meant that Sub-Divisional Inspector W. Fraser, Inspectors Charles Lane and William Austin, Section Sergeants Frederick Dyer and Ernest Coombs were all transferred from Catford to Lewisham[18].

In March 1913 the Town Clerk of the Borough of Lewisham informed Police that Catford Police Station, situated at the junction of Catford Hill and Rathfern Road, was to be known as 128 Catford Hill[19].

In due course of time a new Police Station was needed. Two houses were purchased, one known as "The Elms" and the other "The Limes"[20] and converted for Police purposes at 333 Bromley Road, Southend Village, SE. It was taken into occupation and business commenced in November 1927. It was to be known as Southend Village Police Station and situated some way away from the displaced old Catford Police Station. The old Catford Station later became the Metropolitan Police Engineer's Depot[21].

In 1932 Southend Village Police Station became a Sub-Divisional Station with Penge and Beckenham having Sectional Status[22].

In early 1936 it was found that, due to an increase workload, larger premises were needed, but the present site was considered too small for expansion. Messrs Wates had acquired land from the Forster Estate and offered the Police a corner site. The Police agreed to purchase the site but the London Council refused to approve the 'lay-out' of the estate as planned by Messrs. Wates. Eventually a revised site was offered and the freehold was purchased in November 1936 from the Forster Estate Development Company.[23] In January 1940 the new Catford Police Station opened at Bromley Road, Southend Village, SE6.[24] Superintendent W. Collins was placed in charge[25]. His command of 'P' Division now contained the following Police Stations - Catford, Lewisham, Brockley, East Dulwich, West Dulwich, Sydenham, Beckenham, Penge, Bromley, Farnborough, Chislehurst and St. Mary's Cray.

Catford Police Station
333, Bromley Road, SE6
1940- present day

By 1965 Catford (PD) Police Station was not only the 'P' Divisional Headquarters but also the Sub-Divisional Station with Section Stations at

Lee Road (PE) and Sydenham (PS)[26]. Currently, it is open all day Monday to Sunday and is the base for six Safer Neighbourhood Teams.

Deptford Police Station.

The town of Deptford, having derived its name from 'Depe-ford', a deep ford across the River Ravensbourne and situated at the mouth of what is now known as Deptford Creek, is located just 4 miles from London Bridge[27]. This area was at one time also known as West Greenwich and was situated in the Hamlet of Hatchem[28]. The ferry crossing was replaced with a bridge in 1805/6 and this allowed access to Greenwich and beyond. The Bow Street Horse Patrol operated in Deptford from 1805 from the Station at Rushey Green[29].

Records show that between 1830 and 1832 there was a Station at Lucas Street, Rotherhithe, which was one of two Police Stations or Watch Houses on "R" Division. The other Station was Rose Cottage in Greenwich Road[30].

In 1839 Police Constable William Aldridge died from a fractured skull after he was stoned by a mob during an arrest in Deptford. He was not the only Officer to die in the streets of Deptford during those early days. In 1846 PC James Hastie of 'R' Division died from extensive head injuries following a disturbance in the street in Deptford. He died in the execution of his duty having been beaten by several men[31].

Deptford Police Station
Prince Street, Deptford
c1855- 1912

It wasn't until the 1850s that the Home Office agreed to fund the purchase of a Police Station in Deptford, although the estimated cost was expected to be very high[32]. In about 1855 a Station was brought into service in Prince Street and although there was no indication from Police Orders when it opened[33] there is evidence from records that a delivery of coal was made there to Deptford Police Station[34]. Records show that it had an 80 year lease from the landlord, W.

J. Evelyn, from 1855 until 1935 at £12 per annum.[35] A Sergeant was in charge of the Station and it was a Sectional Station to Blackheath Road[36].

In fact the Station in Prince Street is shown in the Parish of St. Nicholas and had 13 Police Officers residing in the Section House in 1881. It was situated a short distance from the foreign cattle market and had the Cricket Ground and Racing Path to the north and Evelyn Street to the south. The 1881 census also shows that a number of Police Officers lived near the Station in Prince Street. Inspector Thomas Turk and his family had lived at the Station since his promotion in 1871 and remained there until 1888[37].

In 1867 Paradise Street, Rotherhithe became a Station on 'R' Division having been moved from 'M' (Southwark) but by 1881, following boundary changes, it was transferred back to 'M' Division. This was still a functioning Station in 1912 when its annual rent was £230. The lease had been taken out until 1982[38].

In 1855/6 Deptford became another suburb of the Metropolis and was absorbed into Greenwich District of the new Metropolitan Board of Works[39]. In 1864 Deptford Sub-Division was formed as part of 'R' Greenwich Division[40] and it would appear that the status of the Station was enhanced from that supervised by a Sergeant to an Inspector Station. The Station strength showed that it had a complement of 2 Inspectors, 4 Sergeants and 27 Constables[41]. The Police Officers at the Station could not have failed to notice the increased hardship amongst the local population, due in part because of the closure of Deptford dockyard in March 1869, although the opening of the Foreign Cattle Market in 1871 would have brought many jobs back to the area[42].

Deptford Police Station was located at 13 Prince Street and quite often a Station was situated near to toll gates. Deptford was no exception as there was one in Evelyn Street at the junction with Prince Street and just yards from the Station. Tolls were abolished in October 1865, much to the joy of the local population, although the bridge toll on the Creek swing bridge remained until March 1880[43]. Records also show that by 1873 Deptford had been connected by telegraph to Commissioners Office, 'CO' at Scotland Yard[44]. There were 6 cells located at the Station but in a review of accommodation in 1881 the Surveyor found that 4 more cells were required. He also found that the coal allocation per man was insufficient in 42 Stations he had visited[45].

In 1888 a Police Constable Thomas Dean drowned in the Surrey Canal at Deptford whilst patrolling his beat on a foggy night. Tragic deaths similar to this were not uncommon among those Officers Policing riparian Divisions and dockyards[46].

By 1889 Deptford ceased to be a part of Surrey or Kent and in April was administered by the London County Council (LCC)[47].

The old Station was no longer 'fit for purpose' so a new Station in the area was planned. A site was compulsorily purchased in July 1907 from Mr William Evelyn of Wotton near Dorking in Surrey. It was located at 114 and 116 Amersham Vale and 28 and 30 Napier Street and records show that the tenants and lease-holders were duly compensated by the Police[48]. Tenders were invited to build and equip the new Station and the bid originating from Messrs W. Lawrence and son was accepted[49].

The Station was built in a rough area consisting of bad housing, poverty, disease, and was rife with crime. The Divisional Superintendent at the time commented that;

Deptford Police Station
114 Amersham Vale, Deptford SE14 6LG
1912 – present day

'the conditions of the inhabitants round about was very poor, casual and in chronic want. It was a resort of bad characters, and many crime of a serious nature happened occasionally in the district and were to be expected' [50].

The Divisional Surgeon also added to the debate by commenting on the growth of diseases, especially tuberculosis and influenza, which were caused by bad air circulation, lack of sun light, below ground level rooms and over- crowding[51].

A new Police Station was designed by John Dixon Butler, son of the previous Metropolitan Police Surveyor, John Dixon, and opened in February 1912. It contained accommodation for 30 single Police Officers in the Section House and there was also one set of married quarters located there. These were usually kept for the Inspector in charge and his family[52]. The new Station was situated between New Cross Road and Edward Street, not far from New Cross railway station. The front of the Station was in Amersham Vale whilst the yard entrance was in Napier Street.

There had been moves before the war to re-organise Station boundary areas especially since Deptford Police Station was in the Borough of Greenwich whilst the opposite end of Princes Street was in the Borough of Deptford, but these revisions were delayed until the war ended. Accordingly boundary revisions in south London in 1921 transferred Deptford from 'R' (Greenwich) Division to 'M' (Lewisham) Division[53].

By 1931 Deptford was shown as a Sub-Divisional Station on 'M' (Southwark) Division and its address was listed as 116 Amersham Vale, Deptford, SE16, with Rotherhithe at 23 Paradise Street, being a Sectional Station[54]. Further re-organisations of the Force took place with Borough boundary changes in the mid 1960s and were introduced on 1st April 1965. Deptford was shown as a Sectional Station with Brockley on Lewisham, or "P", Division[55]. The Station telegraphic code was revised at the same time to PP from MF.

Deptford Police Station
114, Amersham Vale, SE14 6LG
present day (showing extension)

Internal boundaries were reviewed in the 1970s regarding 'P' Division, with some alterations being made to Deptford Section Station and Brockley being reduced to the status of a Police Office. With the demise of the GLC in April 1985 'P' District was abolished and Officers returned to having a single letter 'P' on their shoulders.

In 1994 further re-organisation of the MPD into 8 Areas placed Deptford under Three Area (South East), although not long after this it became, following the reduction to five areas, Four Area (South East) instead[56].

The New Deptford Police Station was built with public and private funding, is situated at 114-116 Amersham Vale, London, SE14 6LG, and is currently open 24 hours a day, 7 days a week.

Lee Road Police Station

The roads around London were divided into four Divisions and were patrolled by the Bow Street Horse Patrol. The first Division was responsible for that area of North West Kent which today is South East London and one of its Stations was situated at Lee Green. The Horse Patrol was embodied into the Metropolitan Police in 1836 and formed the nucleus of what is today the Mounted Branch.[57]

With the extension of the Metropolitan Police District under the Metropolitan Police Act, 1839, a new Police Station for Lee was proposed. This would cover part of Charlton, part of Lewisham, Kidbrooke, Mottingham and Eltham, all of which had been taken over by the Metropolitan Police[58] A new Station, designed by Charles Reeves, Metropolitan Police Surveyor, was erected in 1850 on land belonging to Lord Northbrook at 258A Lee Road, at a cost of £1265.12s.1d. It was leased at a ground rent of £7 14shillings per annum from Lady Day in 1850 to Lady Day in 1911[59].

By January 1864 the Station's address was shown as Lee Green, Lee[60] and had a complement of one Inspector, two Sergeants, two Acting Sergeants, 26 Constables and 2 horses.[61]

As the area around Lee was expanding in the late 1880s consideration was given to the building of a larger Station. With this in view the freehold of the existing Police Station site was purchased in May 1889 for the sum of £660. The freehold of the adjoining property, 258 High Road, Lee, known as 'Ivy Cottage', was purchased in October 1901 for £400 from the Board of Lewisham Guardians and the leasehold from a Mrs Mitchell for £800[62]. The stables to the rear of the site were used as a temporary Police Station during the rebuilding.

The new Police Station, also designed by John Dixon Butler, was erected on the combined sites and opened March 1903[63]. In 1909 the Station address was 418, High Road, Lee, as a result of renumbering premises in the High Road[64].

The new local authority and Police boundaries changed in April 1965 and Lee Road Police Station was transferred from 'R' to 'P' Division in the new London borough of Lewisham[65].

From time to time Police Stations needed to be fumigated after infestations of various vermin. One such occasion was in 1939 at Lee

Lee Road Police Station
Lee Green, SE12
1903 - 2003

Road Police Station when the CID office was infested with bugs. The Officers had seized some stolen bed linen from a local pawnbrokers shop. At the same Station in 1940 they had lice in one of the cells and in 1948 they were overrun with mice in the food store of the Police Canteen[66]. Lee Road Station was no different from other Police Stations in London when dealing with prisoners and property which was not always very clean.

In March 1980 Lee Road (PE) and Sydenham Police Stations were reduced in status and had a 24 hour counter service. All other matters were transferred to the Divisional Station at Catford[67].

In 1982 the Area Traffic Patrol Officers were using the premises[68]. The Police Station was later sold and the premises are now called the 'Met. Apartments'

Lewisham Police Station

Prior to the formation of the Metropolitan Police in 1839 there existed the Lewisham Cage. This was a small octagonal building that stood on Watch House Green (where the island between Lewis Grove and High Street is today), close to the stocks and whipping post and very likely on the spot now occupied by the post office. It was used for the temporary imprisonment of petty offenders, at least it was until the day when some unfortunates set fire to their straw bedding, and were burnt to death before the key could be found[69].

Lewisham Police Station (Shown as Catford)
Rushey Green
c1841

Lewisham's first Police Station was believed to have been located at Rushey Green close to the site of "Marks and Spencer's". The second Station was next to the Almshouses, also in Rushey Green and opposite George Lane[70]. The building was situated next door to John Thackeray's Almshouses and serving as the Police Station 1841. Prior to 1817 the building had almost certainly been the original parish workhouse[71]. The Police Surveyor reported that the lease on these premises expired at Michaelmas 1864. They were then retained on the basis of a yearly lease until disposed of[72].

In the early 1850s the Lewisham Police Station moved from its site opposite George Lane to a house just north of the Black Horse in Rushey Green, and again in the mid-1870s to one opposite Ladywell Road. All three were existing buildings that were converted so that they could be used as Stations. The first purpose built Police Station in the area was the one at Sydenham, on part of the present site and which opened in 1848[73].

In 1864 the Inspector at Lewisham was also responsible for patrolling the neighbouring Police Stations of Sydenham, Beckenham, Bromley and Farnborough. At that point Lewisham was part of 'R' Division, or Greenwich Division as it was known. There was one horse at Lewisham which was ridden alternately by two Sergeants on Station Duty[74].

In December 1864 the Commissioner directed that Superintendents (in communication with the Police Surveyor) of several Divisions should make immediate efforts to obtain sites whereon Police Stations may be erected. Lewisham was one of those Divisions in need of a new Police Station[75].

Meanwhile in 1865 Police boundaries changed and an Inspector residing at Lee Green Police Station was responsible not only for that Station but also Lewisham and Sydenham. Now known as the Lee Sub-Division, it was part of 'P' (Camberwell) Division[76]. The Superintendent of 'P' Division was Thomas Butt. He was assisted by Chief Inspector James Davis and Detective Inspector Daniel Hunt was in charge of the Criminal Investigation Department.

In October 1869 this all changed again when Sydenham, Lewisham and parts of Penge Police Section were formed into a new Sydenham Sub-Division[77].

In March 1870 a Mr Wiston of 45, Manor Road, Lewisham, SE, wrote to the Commissioner requesting that a Police Station should be built in the Lewisham area as the one at Blackheath Road (Greenwich) was too far away. In June that year a letter was received from a Mr Joshua Liddiard offering premises at 3 and 4 Vicarage Terrace, Lewisham for Police purposes on a long rental. At about the same time James C. Corbett of Lewisham Bridge wrote that the Police should purchase the site on the corner of Lady Well Park for a Police Station as one was needed in the neighbourhood. In September 1870 Home Office authority to lease 3 and 4 Vicarage Terrace for Police purposes from the trustees of the Morden College Estate was received[78]. The lease was for 30 years at £44 per annum[79].

In September 1871 the Metropolitan Police Surveyor, Frederick Caiger, reported that the old Station at Rushey Green would be surrendered and that the new Station at Vicarage Terrace, Lewisham, was to be taken into possession and duties to commence there forthwith[80]. The premises consisted of a brick and slate house with a charge room, basement (which housed the cooking kitchen and mess kitchen for the Section House) a ground day room, 2 cells and a two-stall stable[81].

A notice was received in August 1880 from the Lewisham Board of Works that the address of the Police Station would be 233 to 235 High Street, Lewisham, S.E.[82].

In 1881 there was a Report on the condition of Metropolitan Police Stations and it stated within it that the afore-mentioned two houses which served as the Police Station were of 'somewhat unstable construction' and that they were not well adapted to the purpose for which they are being used. These houses were occupied by a married Police Inspector, one married Constable and seven single Constables. The married Officers lived in one house with their families while the other was being used by the single men and administration. The report also went on to say that the kitchen and mess room were too small and unsatisfactory. It had also found that the two cells were very often insufficient for the number of prisoners detained. The Secretary of state had ordered that only one person should be confined in a cell at one time[83].

Lewisham Police Station
Ladywell Road, Lewisham.
1899 - 2004

By 1891 it appears that Superintendent T. Butt was still in charge of 'P' Division and Inspector Butcher was responsible for operations at Lewisham Police Station[84]. However, by 1899 Superintendent G.Carr had taken over the Division and there were two Station Sergeants, Albert Bright and Charles R Butler stationed at Lewisham[85].

The population of Lewisham expanded in the late 1880s and a larger Police Station was required. In November 1894 Home Office authorised the Receiver to commence negotiations for the purchase of a portion of the site of Lewisham House for the erection of a Police Station[86]. Lewisham House, which stood on the corner of Ladywell Road, was a large red brick mansion, built or rebuilt in 1680. The house was pulled down in 1894 and the area that it and its garden had covered became the site of the new Police Station, Fire Station (1898), some shops and the Coroner's Court[87]. The freehold site was purchased in March 1895 from Messrs Routh, Stacey and Castle of 14 Southampton Street, Bloomsbury, WC, for the sum of £1500. In October 1897 Home approved Messrs Hart's tender of £7,467 for the construction of the new Police Station[88].

The new Lewisham Police Station, designed by John Dixon Butler, was built in the 'Queen Anne' style[89] and was opened for business in January 1899[90]. Sub-Divisional Inspector Fraser and Inspectors Lane and Austin were transferred from Catford Police Station to Lewisham as a result of Lewisham being made the Sub-Divisional Station instead of Catford[91].

In April 1965 the new local authority boundaries, as defined in the London Government Act, 1963, meant that Lewisham (PL), designated the Sub-Divisional Station, with Deptford (PP) and Brockley (PK) were now within the new London Borough of Lewisham[92].

In July 1973 Lewisham Police Station was listed as a building with special architectural interest by the Department of the Environment[93].

Temporary closure of Lewisham Police Station took place in 1982 and an interim Station was established at Brockley[94]. Another temporary Police Station, was located at 300 Lewisham High Street (PL) and this closed on 26th September 1983[95].

In October 2002 the Metropolitan Police Authority authorised the sale of the old Lewisham Police Station, it having been made redundant by the building of the new one[96]. Currently the property is being turned into private apartments.

In 2001 the site of the new Police Station was the subject of an archaeological evaluation by Pre-Construct Archaeological Ltd., of Brockley, SE. The area examined was bounded in the north by St. Stephens Grove, to the east by Lockmead Road, to the west by Lewisham High Street and to the south by residential and retail buildings. No significant archaeological deposits had survived on the site[97].

The building of the new Lewisham Police Station was controversial. Lewisham Council objected to the site of the new Station, refused planning permission, but lost on appeal. The Council had felt that as this site was right in the centre of Lewisham it would have been better utilised for 'livelier retail or entertainment use'[98]. In addition, this is one of four Police Stations in the South-East of the Metropolitan Police area that was completed under the Private Finance Initiative (PFI). This is the Metropolitan Police's partnership with the private sector, formed to develop better equipped Police Stations and to replace some of the existing properties which are ageing and no longer suitable[99].

The private sector partner was 'Equion' which not only provides the building, services, and maintains it but also takes over some of the Metropolitan Police's civilian staff and employs them to provide back-up services. Equion, part of the Laing group, is contracted to do this for 25 years in return for rent (technically a "unity charge"). At the end of the

Lewisham Police Station and Court
43, Lewisham High Street, SE13 5JZ
2004 – present day

term the Police Station remains the property of Equion[100].

The new Lewisham Police Station was formally opened in April 2004 by the Metropolitan Police Commissioner, Sir John Stevens, and Toby Harris, Chair of the Metropolitan Police Authority[101]. The Station was built at the cost of £33.2 Million by Lang O'Rouke. The architect's for the project were Raymond Smith Partnership and Clifford Tewe & Gale[102].

Police Officers working at the Ladywell site and at Catford Police Station were transferred to the new 'state of the art' Police Station in November 2003 prior to the formal opening. The new Police Station will contain 36 Police cells, a new gym, a purpose built training suite, stables for 26 horses, a Scientific Support Unit and a Serious Crime Group[103]. Currently open 24 hours a day, it is the base of the Senior Management Team and three Safer Neighbourhood Teams.

Sydenham Police Station

A Police Station was erected at Sydenham in 1848 at a cost of £1231.3s.10d[104]. The Landlord at the time was Robert Harrild of Sydenham and the lease was from 1848 for a period of 75 years at £10 per annum.[105] The plans were drawn up and signed by Charles Reeves, Police Surveyor.[106]

In a letter dated 11 February 1853, Home Office authority was given to purchase a site for £350 if the Crystal Palace Co. would build a Station and the Receiver rent it, but this was not acceptable for the firm. Eventually a plot of land was leased near Crystal Palace from a Mr Nicholls on a 99 year lease at £16.10s per annum. Home Office authority was granted in January 1854 and there was an estimated outlay of £2080 for the building.[107]

Sydenham Police Station
Dartmouth Road
1848 - 1966

In June 1855, John Thomas Fox, aged 21 years, joined the Metropolitan Police as a Constable. His warrant number was 33705. The warrant numbers started at No 1 in 1829 so you can see just how many Officers had joined the Police Force since its inception (see pages 385 – 389 for the complete list). Fox had been recommended by submitting testimonials as a suitable candidate from a Mr John Scott of Limehouse and a Mr J. Harris. By 1861 Fox was living in Brockley Lane, Sydenham with his wife and four children.

In 1871 Fox, now a Police Sergeant, was living at the Sydenham Police Station, High Street, Sydenham, with his wife and three of their children. There were also ten Constables and one prisoner, a 67 year female named Mary Alden.

Writing his diary at about this time he recorded the following;

" 19.1.1877 – Apprehended a woman for highway robbery"

This was at a time when robbers on horseback terrorised the lanes and byways of Sydenham. Other entries in the diary showed monetary awards made to him from 1860 – 1878. One such reads:

" 2/6d Stopping a man with 15 fowls"

Fox was promoted to Inspector (3rd class) in August 1878 when Station Sergeants were upgraded. He then retired on a pension of £76 in 1881.

By 1864 there were 2 Sergeants and 17 Constables posted to Sydenham Police Station, which was then shown on 'R' Division. The Inspector at Lewisham Police Station had the responsibility for patrolling and supervising Sydenham, Beckenham, Bromley and Farnborough Police Stations. The mounted Sergeants at Sydenham, Beckenham, Bromley and Farnborough were each to patrol, either on horse or on foot, for at least 9 hours out of every 24 and care for the welfare of their horses. [108]

Sydenham then became part of 'P' Division in 1865[109] and later became the Sub-Division which was responsible for Sydenham, Lewisham and part of Penge. An Inspector Ings was placed in charge of the Station and directed to ride the horse of the Sergeant who became dismounted.[110]

In 1881 there was a Report which criticised the cramped condition of the station. It also drew attention to the unsanitary condition of the Inspector's quarters, himself and his family (six persons) having to sleep in one room. [111]

The address of the Station was 114, High Street, Sydenham,[112] and the freehold of the premises was purchased in February 1890. It was at about this time that Inspector J. Broadbridge was the Inspector in charge of the Station.[113] Inspector Swan was there in 1935[114] and by January 1937 the address of the

Constable Charles Henry Moore killed by parachute mine in 1941

Station had been changed to 179, Dartmouth Road, S.E.26.

In April 1941, during World War II, the shop next door to the Station was completely destroyed and the Station badly damaged by a parachute mine[115]. Police Constable 115732 Charles Henry Moore, formerly 463C and later to become 463P, was killed in this incident[116]. Moore lived at 4 Trilby Road, Forest Hill, London, SE23, and was pronounced dead at South East Hospital Mortuary, SE26. The picture above shows Constable Moore posing in his garden in full uniform (without duty armlet).

There were five other casualties as well[117]. The Police Station was then closed for business, and work was transferred to a temporary Station at 'The Towers', Sydenham Rise, 23[118]. The original Station reopened for business in October 1947[119]. In January 1948 the freehold was purchased for 181 Dartmouth Road so that the Police Station could be extended.[120]

In 1950 the Receiver purchased the freehold of sites in Willow Way in order to erect married quarters. On 31 March 1960 more freehold sites were purchased thus forming the nucleus of the Police Station, Section House and married quarters. Finally in June 1964 an exchange of lands was completed with the Church Authorities to adjust the boundary where it adjoined Holy Trinity Hall. [121]

In April 1965, under the new local authority boundaries, Sydenham and Lee Road became Sectional Stations to Catford Division. [122]

The new Sydenham Police Station at 179, Dartmouth Road, SE26, designed by J. Innes-Elliott, was taken into operational use on 7 March 1966 and the old Station was closed [123]

By 1980 the Station, together with Lee Road, had been reduced in status to Police Stations where a 24 hour public counter service only

Sydenham Police Station
179 Dartmouth Road SE26 4RN
1966 – present day

was provided. All administration and operational matters were then undertaken by the Divisional Station at Catford.[124]

The Station is currently open to the public from 10am – 6pm Monday to Friday.

---

[1] www.ideal-homes.org.uk/lewisham/main/index.html. 3.10.2007
[2] www.met.police.uk October 2010
[3] Back, J. (1975) The Metropolitan Police Historical Collection
[4] MEPO 5/52
[5] Metropolitan Police Orders dated 14th December 1883
[6] Metropolitan Police Orders dated 20th June 1884
[7] Back, J. (1975) The Metropolitan Police Historical Collection
[8] National Archives Census Records 1891
[9] Metropolitan Police Orders dated 8th July 1960
[10] Metropolitan Police Orders dated 6th July 1964
[11] Metropolitan Police Orders dated 6th August 1964
[12] www.2lewisham.gov.uk/161 accessed on 11th November 2005
[13] MEPO 5/502
[14] Metropolitan Police Orders dated 15th March 1892
[15] Kelly's Lewisham, Brockley & Catford Directory 1899
[16] Kelly's Directory 1903
[17] Metropolitan Police Orders dated 16th March 1892
[18] Metropolitan Police Orders dated 14th December 1905 and MEPO 2/905
[19] Back, J. (1975) The Metropolitan Police Historical Collection
[20] Covenants. Dated 24.1.1927 Lewisham Archives A93/4/12/55
[21] Metropolitan Police Orders dated 15th November 1927 and L.B.506
[22] Metropolitan Police Orders dated 1st January 1932
[23] LB 506
[24] Metropolitan Police Orders dated 1st January 1940
[25] Police and Constabulary Almanac 1940
[26] Metropolitan Police Orders dated 6th August 1964
[27] Brown, B. (1998) Up the Creek – Or Policing old Deptford.
[28] ibid
[29] ibid
[30] Metropolitan Police Return of Mops (1832) Charlton
[31] National Police Officers Roll of Honour 2002
[32] MEPO 5/29 (174)
[33] Back, J. (1975) The Metropolitan Police Historical Collection
[34] Metropolitan Police Orders dated 20th June 1884
[35] MEPO 4/234
[36] Brown, B. (unknown) Up the Creek – Or Policing old Deptford
[37] Kelly's directories 1871 - 1888
[38] Metropolitan Police Surveyors Records Charlton
[39] Brown, B. (1998) Up the Creek – Or Policing old Deptford
[40] Metropolitan Police Orders dated 18th April 1859
[41] Metropolitan Police Orders dated 11th January 1859
[42] Brown, B. (1998) Up the Creek – Or Policing old Deptford
[43] Brown, B. (1998) Up the Creek – Or Policing old Deptford
[44] Metropolitan Police General Orders 1873
[45] Metropolitan Police Surveyors Records 1881
[46] www.metcbb.co.uk accessed on 5th November 2009
[47] Brown, B. (1998) Up the Creek – Or Policing old Deptford
[48] LB460
[49] MEPO 2/686
[50] MEPO 2/686
[51] ibid

[52] Metropolitan Police Orders dated 3rd February 1912
[53] Metropolitan Police Orders dated 24th February 1924
[54] Kirchners Police Index 1931 p118
[55] Metropolitan Police Orders dated 12th July 1964
[56] Brown, B. (1998) Up the Creek – Or Policing old Deptford
[57] MEPO 5/25
[58] MEPO 2/76
[59] MEPO 2/26
[60] Metropolitan Police Orders dated 20th June 1864
[61] Back, J. (1975) The Metropolitan Police Historical Collection
[62] Back, J. (1975) The Metropolitan Police Historical Collection
[63] Metropolitan Police Orders dated March 1903
[64] Back, J. (1975) The Metropolitan Police Historical Collection
[65] Metropolitan Police Orders dated 6th August 1964
[66] MEPO 2/2619
[67] Metropolitan Police Orders dated 12th March 1980
[68] Metropolitan Police Orders dated 1st October 1982
[69] Coulter, J. (1994) Lewisham – History and Guide. Alan Sutton p.105
[70] Back, J. (1975) The Metropolitan Police Historical Collection
[71] Coulter, J. (1994). Lewisham – History and Guide. Alan Sutton p.30
[72] Back, J. (1975) The Metropolitan Police Historical Collection
[73] John Coulter. History and Guide, Allan Sutton 1994 p 52
[74] Metropolitan Police Orders dated 11th January 1864
[75] Metropolitan Police Orders dated 31st December 1864
[76] Metropolitan Police Orders dated 28th October 1865
[77] Metropolitan Police Orders dated 30th September 1869
[78] Back, J. (1975) The Metropolitan Police Historical Collection
[79] MEPO4/234
[80] Metropolitan Police Orders dated 29th September 1871
[81] Metropolitan Police Surveyors, Charlton
[82] Back, J. (1975) The Metropolitan Police Historical Collection
[83] Report 1881 – Report on the Condition of the Metropolitan Police Stations
[84] Kelly's Sydenham, Norwood and Streatham Directory 1891
[85] Kelly's Lewisham, Brockley & Catford Directory 1899
[86] Back, J. (1975) The Metropolitan Police Historical Collection
[87] Leland L Duncan. History of the Borough of Lewisham. Charles North The Blackheath /Press London SE 1908
[88] Back, J. (1975) The Metropolitan Police Historical Collection
[89] B.Cherry & N.Pevsner. Buildings of England. London 2 South Penguin Books 1983
[90] Metropolitan Police Orders dated 28th January 1899
[91] Metropolitan Police Orders dated 14th December 1905
[92] Metropolitan Police Orders dated 6th August 1964
[93] Back, J. (1975) The Metropolitan Police Historical Collection
[94] Metropolitan Police Orders dated July 1882
[95] B. Brown.
[96] www.mps.gov.uk/committees/f/2004/040923/14.htm accessed on 18th.November.2005
[97] Deeves, S. Archaeological Evaluation Report July 2001.
[98] Aldous, T. The Guide. November 2003
[99] www.met.police.uk/lewisham/new_station.htm 18.11.2005
[100] Aldous, T. The Guide. November 2003
[101] www.laing.com/equion_news_511.htm 9.3.2006
[102] Aldous, T. The Guide. November 2003
[103] Aldous, T. The Guide. November 2003
[104] MEPO 2/26
[105] MEPO 4/234
[106] London Metropolitan Archives MBO/Plans 140
[107] MEPO 5/3 (10)
[108] Metropolitan Police Orders dated 11th January 1864
[109] Metropolitan Police Orders dated 28th October 1865

[110] Metropolitan Police Orders dated 30th September 1869
[111] Report on the condition of the Metropolitan Police Stations dated 11 April1881
[112] Metropolitan Police Orders dated 20th June 1884
[113] Kelly's Sydenham, Norwood & Streatham Directory. 1891
[114] Kelly's Sydenham & Forest Hill Directory 1935
[115] Back, J. (1975) The Metropolitan Police Historical Collection
[116] www.policememorial.org.uk accessed on 19th August 2007
[117] Home Office (1947) Metropolitan Police at War
[118] Metropolitan Police Orders dated 7July 1941
[119] Metropolitan Police Orders dated 3 October 1947
[120] Back, J. (1975) The Metropolitan Police Historical Collection
[121] Back, J. (1975) The Metropolitan Police Historical Collection
[122] Metropolitan Police Orders dated 6 August 1964
[123] Metropolitan Police Orders dated 4 March 1966
[124] Metropolitan Police Orders dated March 1980

Chapter 7

The London Borough of Merton

Introduction

Located within the borough are the locations of Mitcham, Merton and Morden, the names of which originate from Anglo Saxon times meaning 'big home' or 'big place', 'the farm by the pool', and 'the hill by the marsh'. The area is of significant historical interest, since King Ethelred was killed at the Battle of Mereton in AD 871 during clashes with rival Saxon groups. Wimbledon village was first established by Wynnman a Saxon leader. During the Doomsday survey in 1086 the Arch Bishop of Canterbury owned the Manor of Mortlake which mentioned Merton and Morden although Wimbledon was excluded. By the 13th Century Wimbledon became the centre of the Manor, however, when the Estate passed into the hands of Arch Bishop Cranmer in 1536 Henry VIII ordered Cranmer to give the Estate to his Chief Minister, Thomas Cromwell, in exchange for land at Canterbury. Henry dissolved the Monastery which had been established in 1117 in the area and used the stone to build Nonsuch Palace at Ewell.

In 1553 the Manor passed out of Royal hands into the control of Richard Garth and over the next 200 years the Borough became the property of farmers, city merchants, and business men, who built fine houses throughout the district. The most influential of these families were the Cecils, with Sir William later becoming Lord Burghley, moving to Wimbledon in 1550 and setting up home in the Old Rectory (still located in Church Road). His son Thomas, Earl of Exeter, built the Manor House in 1588 and entertained Elizabeth I and James I there. The area became a fashionable place to live, especially as a country retreat. Although many famous people lived in the area in 1801 Admiral Lord Nelson purchased Merton Place, a house and 70 acres of ground, where he resided with Lady Hamilton and her husband, Sir William, who died in 1803.

Industries had strung up along the River Wandle and 1803 saw the arrival of the Surrey Iron Railway, which passed between Wandsworth and Croydon, to serve those industries. South of the railway new houses were being built in what was called New Wimbledon. In 1838 Wimbledon Station was opened on the London to Southampton Railway with the Wimbledon – Croydon Line opening in 1858 and Southampton Line in 1871. The Fire Brigade was established in Wimbledon in 1880. In 1867 John Innes (today of Potting Compost fame) brought land in the area, although it was not until 20 years after his death and with monies bequeathed that houses in the roads of Poplar,

Kenley, Erridge and Circles gardens were built. Later the John Innes Horticultural Institute was founded in 1910 moving to Hertfordshire in 1953 and later to Norwich.

The Victorian designer William Morris set up craft, fabrics, furniture, stained glass and tapestry industries in Merton in the 1880s. Morris's friend Arthur Liberty took over old premises along the River Wandle and developed hand printed fabrics which became world renowned. From a population of 4,387 in 1831 rising to 29, 606 in 1911 the area saw an explosion in numbers of people moving into the area.

A large number of houses both terraced and semi detached was being built in the area to accommodate the influx of people, although the Wimbledon Common area continued to attract the wealthy for which the larger mansions were built. In 1864 the 5th Earl Spencer, who was then Lord of the Manor, attempted to enclose the Common and convert the Windmill into six small cottages. This was not a popular move on his part and upset the locals who after a seven year fight saw the passing of both the Wimbledon and Putney Commons Act thereby protecting the commons for ever.

Lord Baden Powell penned 'Scouting for Boys' in 1907 at Mill House next to the windmill although earlier in 1868 the All England Croquet Club, later to become the All England Lawn Tennis and Croquet Club, was founded in Worple Road but later moved to a site in Church Road in 1922.

One of the largest manufacturers in the area situated on the Lombard Road Factory Estate was Lines Bros Ltd. Formed in 1919 by the three Lines Brothers under the Triang Trade-mark they employed 4000 people making toys. Large building works were being undertaken prior to the Second World War. For example the development of the St Hellier Estate between 1928 and 1936, part of which lies within the borough, saw 9,068 council houses being built for about 40,000 people at a cost of £4,000,000. Two hospitals in Mitcham were opened, the Wilson in 1928 and the Cumberland in 1937. Also at the time the Library, the Baths Hall and the Majestic Cinema were developed in Mitcham and the Odeon in Morden. The Royal (now the Odeon) cinema in Wimbledon Broadway was opened in 1933 and Wimbledon Stadium in 1928. The Town Hall was built in 1931.

In 2010 the records show that although Merton is one of the smaller London boroughs with a population of approximately 188,000, it has a surprisingly diverse community and has one of the fastest growing Black Minority Ethnic Communities in London. Merton, for example, is home to one of the largest Mosques in Western Europe. Merton is divided into three sectors that cover the areas of Wimbledon, Mitcham and Morden. These localities provide an interesting mix of communities with differing social, economic, educational and policing needs. Wimbledon Village has some of the most expensive residential properties in the whole of London whilst parts of Mitcham figure significantly in deprivation indices. There has been a positive history of Police/community working, which is being developed further through the advent of Safer Neighbourhood policing[1]. The Borough staff in 2010 were; Chief Superintendent Dick Wolfenden (Borough Commander), Superintendent David Paterson (Operations), Superintendent Pete Dobson (Community and Partnerships), Chief Inspector Jerry Peppin (Operations) and Chief Inspector Mark Lawrence (Safer Neighbourhoods and Partnerships)[2].

Mitcham Police Station

The London to Dorking Turnpike was established in 1755, passed through Mitcham and had a toll gate situated at Figges Marsh. In reports from 1738 it was considered that travel over Putney Heath was dangerous by both day and night and this did not change for some time. Even 60 years later Jerry Abershaw a local Highwayman was sentenced to death and hung for his deeds. The current Police Station overlooks Mitcham Cricket Green and is probably the most famous village cricket green in the world as the game has

The Green Mitcham with the Town Hall

been played there for more than 250 years. It was the cradle of cricket providing some of the most famous cricketers of their day. Lord Nelson and

Lady Hamilton would drive over to watch matches. Some matches used to attract 6,000 spectators and the famous W.G. Grace played on the green.

Records show that as early as 1841 there was a Police Station in Mitcham and under the control of Superintendent Andrew McLean of 'P' (Camberwell) Division[3]. Mr Simpson of Church Street, Mitcham, was the owner but Mr Pocock of 17 Lincolns Inn Fields handled the renting of the premises to the Metropolitan Police. The Station House was not purpose built and consisted of a brick and tile house containing 7 rooms with a stable at the rear. There were also 2 cells and the conveniences were located at the back in its long garden. In 1840 'P' Division (Camberwell) was enlarged to include the Parishes of Croydon, Streatham, Morden, Mitcham, Carshalton, Wallington, Beddington, Woodmansterne, Sutton, Cheam, Banstead, Farliegh, Addington, Coulsdon and Warlingham. New Police Stations were established at Steatham, Mitcham and Croydon[4].

Between 1844 and 1849 Henry Maude, the Brixton Road Inspector, was responsible for visiting Mitcham regularly for the purposes of supervision[5] and usually did so on his horse. The lock up or cells had been rented and were returned to the owner in December 1868, although no reason was given for this. The Police were responsible for good maintenance of the Station both inside and out, so to maintain a smart, white, Station exterior it was repainted in 1858, 1863 and 1868.

The rent for the Police Officers residing at the address was 2 shillings per week for the one married Constable whilst the 7 single Constables were charged 1 shilling per week rent. It would appear that the married Constable was in charge of the daily running of the Station up until 1864 when Mitcham Police Station, still a Station on 'P' (Walworth) Division, became a Sergeant designated Station. It had two Sergeants and 1 Acting Sergeant with 3 patrols covered by 3 Constables by day and 11 beats covered by 11 Constables during the hours of darkness. The Acting Sergeant was distinguishable by having two stripes (instead of 3) on each upper arm. The Inspector from Carshalton would also visit Mitcham on horseback to sign and check relevant books at the Station. The Inspector would record his visit in the occurrence book in order to show other senior Officers that visits had been made. This was a practice carried out by all senior Officers and at times with 'Royalty' visiting.

By 1867 Mitcham had been removed to 'W' (Clapham) Division under the charge of Divisional Superintendent William Hayes. In 1873 the Police leased property suitable for a Police Station from William Simpson of Church Street, Mitcham on a yearly tenancy of £25. This was a Sergeant's designated Station by 1873. In the same year general orders issued to all Superintendents instructed them to establish a Thieves Register at each station. This contained the name and antecedents of each convicted criminal or suspected person known to be residing in the Station area. The register was made available to all those Police Officers wishing to view it[6]. Other books held at Stations are called Felony Books and these were the equivalent to modern day Crime Books. Reports of crimes were entered into Felony Books.

Constables were earning £52 per annum in 1871 whilst their hours of duty were First Relief 6am – 9am, Second Relief 9am – 3pm and 7pm – 10pm and Night duty 10pm - 6am[7]. One day's leave was granted every 14 days and annual leave for a Constable was 7 days per annum. For Sergeants this was 10 days and Inspectors 14 days.

In 1877 the freehold for land situated at The Causeway, Lower Mitcham, was purchased by the Receiver at a cost of £650. The area was being developed and greater numbers of people were moving from the Home Counties, to Mitcham. This meant that the status of the Station was upgraded to an Inspector's Station.

A new Mitcham Station was built in the Victorian style on the purchased land with 2 sets of married quarters and a Section House situated at the rear. The Station also boasted a charge room, Inspector's office, cell, association cell. In the Station yard was a parade shed and an ambulance shelter for the hand ambulance. The Station had accommodation for 1 Sergeant and 6 Constables.

In 1878 this became a Station on 'W' or Clapham Division. In 1881 records show that during a review of cell space the two cells there were deemed inadequate for the number of prisoners being dealt with, so recommendations were made for a further cell to be added although the Station was considered to be very dilapidated[8]. In the same year the Station was linked by the telegraph via Streatham to its headquarters at Brixton. Any messages for the Commissioner's Office would be passed on from there. The telegraphic code used to identify the Station was Mike Charlie (MC), although this was changed later in the 1930s during the Trenchard re-organisation[9].

Elias Harris was the Sergeant in charge in 1878 and he supervised 19 Constables situated at the Causeway, Lower Mitcham[10]. The status of the Station remained that it was a Sergeant-supervised Station in 1879 with Superintendent William Wiseman being in overall charge[11]. Surveyors' records 1881 stated that;

'This Station is dilapidated and the construction of it has, been under consideration for years. It should now be taken in hand. The arrangement of the married and single men is bad. The Station is also occupied by One married Constable and six single Constables'[12].

Only minimum work was carried out as arrangements for a new Station had been made. By 1881 Mitcham had become an Inspector Station still on 'W' (Clapham) Division.

In 1889 the London County Council was formed and this caused the Police to reconsider its boundaries. Mitcham was a Station on 'P' Division and administered from Brixton Police Station where the Headquarters Station was situated. Inspector Robert Butters was in charge of the Station in 1891 and was assisted by 4 Sergeants and 22 Constables[13]. By 1894 Mitcham and Tooting had become a Sectional Station of Streatham[14]. The picture below shows the Causeway, Mitcham, around 1900 and the Police Station is the building just on the right beyond the cart. Only in 1912 were both Mitcham and Wimbledon Police Stations placed together on the same Division. Both were now under the charge of the Superintendent on 'V' (Wandsworth) Division[15].

The Causeway, Mitcham, Surrey around 1900. The station is just beyond the cart

In 1919 PC David Davies went down a sewer at Mitcham to investigate the whereabouts of two missing workmen. Davies knew that the fumes generated in the sewers could be lethal however he progressed with caution. After a short while he found both men collapsed, as they had become overcome by the fumes, and he with little regard for his own safety pulled both out of the sewer. For this brave action he was awarded the Kings Police Medal, a rare award.

After 1924 the address of the Station changed to 58 The Causeway, Lower East Street – later Lower Green East. The old style Station required modernisation and the influx of new residents of Mitcham meant that a new Station was needed. Adjacent to the Station some prime land became available and inquiries by MP Surveyors Department revealed five partly demolished cottages were up for sale. In 1936 48 – 56 Lower Green East, Mitcham were purchased from H. W. Harding of St Clements, Romsey, Hants, for £1,750[16].

In 1938 a telephone line was established between the Police Station and the Fire Brigade Station. The onset of deteriorating relations with Germany meant

Mitcham Police Station
58 Lower Green East, Mitcham
1965 – Present day

that war was a likelihood of war and other priorities meant that a new Station was not built immediately – in fact there was a wait of nearly thirty years before the new Station was built at all. In 1939 the address of the Station was shown as 58 Lower Green East and Superintendent M. Miller from Tooting Police Station[17] was in charge.

The lamp, right, was originally built as part of the Station in 1965 and as part of a re-vamp of Station lamps in 1978 the lamp was restored.

In 1954 PC 128776 John Richard Bailey was awarded the George Medal for bravery, courage and determination in

Mitcham Police Station lamp

effecting the arrest of a dangerous criminal in Mitcham who used a firearm to resist capture.

The current Police Station, shown above, was built in 1965 and located at 58 Cricket Green, Mitcham, Surrey CR0 5AQ. Built in the modern design over three floors this Station is similar to Albany street and Holloway Police Stations in north London.

Generally each Station has a different blue Police lamp situated at the front, a feature that originated in Victorian London and denotes a Police Station.

The Station is open 24 hours a day, 7days a week.

Morden Police Station.

Morden is situated at the end of the Northern Line and as an expanding area it was decided to locate a Police Office in Crown Parade.

It was shown in the records that this station was opened in 1995 and situated at 4 Crown Parade, Crown Lane, Morden, Surrey, SM5 5DA. It appears to have office status and in 2009 was open Mondays to Fridays 8am to 4pm[18].

On night duty in 1961 DC Peter George Bridgwood was killed driving the CID car between stations, when he lost control and collided with a lamp standard in the early hours of the morning at Morden[19]. This was a tragic story but sadly not an uncommon one.

Morden Police Office
4 Crown Parade, Crown Lane, Morden
Surrey SM5 5DA
1995 – present day

Wimbledon Police Station (and Merton)

In 1790 a new Watch House (Police Station) was taken over in Wimbledon Village. The stocks were situated next to it. There was also a Pillory near Wimbledon Common[20]. In 1804 'Chief Households and shopkeepers' agreed to pay for a Wimbledon Watch who would patrol the village streets and 'cry the hour'. This scheme was discontinued after two years when the Beadle

(Town Crier) was appointed Watchman and Constable of the Night[21]. Early records show that in 1840 Thomas Hunt Dann combined the work of Miller with that of the Parish Constable (even though a Metropolitan Police Horse Patrol existed in the village) and one day he ran from his mill having witnessed an illegal duel between Lord Cardigan and Earl Tuckett. Dann arrested them both although Cardigan had been the better shot having injured Tuckett. Cardigan was later brought before his peers in the House of Lords only to be acquitted. Illegal duelling on the Common was a regular pursuit, having over time involved some very famous people including the Duke of Wellington in 1829 and William Pitt in 1798.

In 1760 Sir John Fielding, the Bow Street Magistrate, had developed a plan for mounted patrols to deal with the plague of highwaymen infesting the metropolitan areas' Turnpike roads. The plan was so successful that the original Horse Patrol of 8 men was strengthened to more than 50 in 1805. The Bow Street Horse Patrol could then provide protection cover on all the main roads within 20 miles of Charing Cross. They were a regular sight in Merton. They carried a sword and a hand gun, wore scarlet waistcoats, blue greatcoats and trousers, with black leather hats and stocks. This was the first uniform ever issued to any Police Force in the world.

There was no immediate Wimbledon Police Station built in 1829 when the Metropolitan Police came into being although the 2nd Division of the Bow Street Horse Patrol (introduced in 1805) took responsibility for patrolling the area. Records show that a Station House existed just off Wimbledon Lane as early as 1844[22] although this had been the original Bow Street Horse patrol station.

Records held by the Metropolitan Police show that in 1845 they had taken control of a double cottage belonging to the Horse Patrol at 1 Brickfield Crescent on the Ridgeway, now 1 Oldfield Road and 3a The Ridgeway, Wimbledon village. This is directly opposite what is now known as Lingfield Road. Today Wimbledon Lane continues into Wimbledon Hill Road but in the 1860s the lane stretched from Wimbledon Village down the hill through the Broadway and into Merton Road continuing onto High Street Merton[23].

The Horse Patrol was under the supervision of Inspector William Richardson. Richardson was responsible for the Stations at Croydon, Sutton, Merton (Millers Mead), North Cheam, Wimbledon (village), Kingston, Robin Hood Hill and Ditton Marsh[24]. The Horse Patrol was incorporated into the Metropolitan Police in 1836 and the Magistrates at Bow Street relinquished control of them.

The Police Station House is shown above and the terraced house behind also acted as residential accommodation. The building was made of brick with

Wimbledon Police Station
The Ridgeway j/w Oldfield Road, Wimbledon Village
1790 - 1844

three bedrooms and had a slate roof with a small garden at the rear. It had a walled garden which can be seen at the front of the house. Also situated in the garden was a one stall stable for a horse. Access is from the Ridgeway where the single storey stable has now been converted into living accommodation and can clearly be seen from the main road. The Metropolitan Police Surveyors decided to renovate the building by converting several rooms to accommodate 7 single Constables. The first record of a professional Police Officer living in Wimbledon at Oldfield Road was Sergeant Pinegar who lived at the Station.

The local court records show they were kept busy dealing with men drunk and disorderly, costermongers, obstructing

Merton Police Station
2 and 3 Colliers Wood
1805 - 1831

the Broadway, owners of dangerous dogs and a man from Tooting driving a carriage without lights and trying to bribe a Policeman not to report him.

There was another Police Station used by the Bow Street Horse Patrol which was taken over by the Metropolitan Police. This was referred to as Merton Police Station and was situated at 2 and 3 Millers Mead, Colliers Wood at the end of Merton High Street. These were a pair of white - washed cottages at the front of Wandle Park just inside the Parish of Wimbledon. This ceased operation in 1831 when the cottages were sold to Moses Barton Legg[25]. Until then cottages with a stable were part of 'V' (Wandsworth) Division[26] and senior Officers came on horseback to supervise the area from the nearby Headquarters. It was also likely that the original occupant was retained by the Metropolitan Police and transferred to another Station to carry on his normal duties as part of the mounted patrol. The Horse Patrol was formed to combat the threat of Highwaymen and footpads especially crossing the wide commons, open spaces, and parks. The cottages were demolished in the 1970s[27].

In 1845 a double cottage was let for use as a Police Station and Section House in Merton Road and was originally the Horse Patrol Station. Leased from Mr F. Bower of Merton Park, it was in a sad state of repair when it was taken over by the Metropolitan Police. The building was in need of repair (as it is today) both inside and out and had not been painted inside for at least 5 years. The cottages had originally been painted outside with white and other colours which by now are indistinct. The buildings were vacated on 22nd June 1869 when notice was sent to the Superintendent that better premises had been secured[28] in the Broadway.

Police Stations would only be able to provide limited accommodation for a small number of Police Officers. Where none was provided the Police Officers needed to find lodgings near the Station. Further accommodation was needed and Surveyors needed to look for accommodation nearby. Premises were found in Larkhall Lane that offered room for 1 Sergeant and 8 Constables. Records show that in 1845 Mr Sankey offered the property on a yearly rental although these premises were in a very poor state of repair. Once renovated the Police Officers were able to move in.

In 1864 General Police Orders published a re-organisation of Police Stations, supervision and their strengths. It shows Merton, as it was then known, to have 4 day beats and 10 night beats. One Acting Sergeant supervised the 4 day beat Constables whilst the Substantive Sergeant was responsible for the 10 night duty Constables. The strength for the Station was 1 Sergeant and 15 Constables [29]. This was by comparison a small Station and accordingly there were no cells to house any prisoners there. No charges were taken there either, meaning that any prisoners would be arrested and taken to Merton to inform the Station Officer and then walked to Battersea where they would be charged and housed. Merton (together with Tooting) was a Sub-Divisional Station of Battersea. The mounted Inspector or Sergeant at Wandsworth would supervise generally and patrol Tooting, Merton and Battersea. The night and day Duty Sergeants would swap shifts every month. Because there was no additional space when the Commissioner informed Divisional Superintendents in July 1869 that they should install Recreation and Games Rooms with billiard tables at main Stations, none could be installed at Merton – a situation which changed in 1871 when they moved to a new bigger building[30].

In 1860 rifle ranges had been built by the National Rifle Association (whose patron was Queen Victoria) on Wimbledon Common for practice. Preparations were made for a Royal procession to Wimbledon when Queen Victoria opened the National Rifle Association ranges. Bunting and flags lined the route together with a great number of enthusiastic onlookers. Pc William Skinner stationed at Wandsworth was sent to Wimbledon as part of a serial[31] of Police to guard the Common, the ranges and important equipment. A sad incident soured the occasion when a man fell to his death from a ladder while putting up bunting[32]. Pc Skinner had another job which was to look after the rifle which the Queen used as the first person to fire a shot on the ranges. She scored a bull's-eye. Annual shooting meetings were held there until the increase in population made it too dangerous to stage the event and so it was transferred to Bisley in 1890. Police Officers were regularly seconded from 'V' Division to help with crowds and prevent crime.

One of the problems for Merton involved Cattle Plague. There were 6 Police Officers situated on the exterior boundary of the division at Wimbledon, Tooting, Kingston, Richmond and Barnes. One Officer during daylight hours was located at White Houses, Wimbledon Common to inspect cows being brought to market in London[33].

In March 1870 a piece of land was leased for £5 per year 1869 until 1919[34] and a newly leased building (later located in the Broadway) to act as a Police Station and Section House in South Wimbledon. In the 1881 census the address of the Station was 24 Merton Road although at 23 lived Constable David Cuthbert, his wife Mary and Ada his daughter[35]. This was described as a house adapted for Police purposes which had 1 married Inspector, 1 married Constable and 8 single Constable's resident there[36]. It was located just beyond the site of the future Victoria Crescent (made in 1887 to celebrate the Queens Golden Jubilee. It was staffed by one Sergeant (as it was designated a

Sergeant Station for supervision purposes) and 8 Constables who resided in the Section House above. The premises were leased for 50 years in 1869 on an annual rental of £120 from the owner Mr James Couch of Oakfield Lodge, South Wimbledon[37]. It is often the case that Police Stations took on the name of the road they were located in which has caused confusion as the Station was often quoted as Merton Road Police Station even though it was in the Parish of South Wimbledon. Superintendent Charles Digby had overall supervision of the division[38].

This was also a large brick and slate house which was repaired and adapted when it was occupied although Police Orders contradict this and state it was erected and purpose built. Alterations costing £566 were made to the building in order to ensure that it was suitably converted into a Station with appropriate accommodation for Police purposes. The Station had a charge room, living room, kitchen, scullery, reading room and two cells. In the yard was a two stall stable for horses. There was also an Inspector's office on the ground floor[39]. Merton was shown as a Station on 'V' (Wandsworth) Division in 1871 but by time the new Station was occupied in 1872 it had been renamed Wimbledon. The rooms upstairs were allocated to accommodate 1 Sergeant and 9 Constables. In 1878 Sergeant Benjamin Peake was in charge. Because of development in the town centre the address was changed showing that it was located at 21 Broadway, Wimbledon. Originally the Station was referred to as Merton or more probably Merton Road Police Station as this was its address in South Wimbledon.

Wimbledon Police Station 1860 – 1900 is the gabled building by the lamp post

In line with the general re-organisation in 1881 all the Stations on the Division were made Inspector Stations although there were not sufficient Inspectors to go round. A promise to increase the establishment of Inspectors was made by the Home Department and in the intervening period substantial numbers of Station or Clerk Sergeants were promoted to Inspector to cover all the Stations necessary.

By 1881 Inspector John Rogers resided at the Station with his wife and daughter. The Inspector was designated as attached to 'V' (Wandsworth) Division and probably did duty at the Station although he may also have been attached to another Station on the Division. The 37 year old Inspector and his family resided there until 1888. Another Inspector was attached to the Station by the name of John Fuller. The two Inspectors would cover both the day and night shift between them. Still living at the Station was Constable David Cuthbert and his family living in married quarters next door. Eight single Constables also resided in the Section House. Thomas Miles a 25 year old from Greenwich was designated Head Constable and he would have been charged with ensuring good order at the Section House[40]. When the Station was inspected in 1881 the surveyors were very concerned that the single Constables did not have sufficient washing arrangements. They said that 'the single men are washing in the cook's sink in the kitchen' seemingly concerned that washing and preparing food should not use the same sink. Clearly standards of hygiene were being established since disease amongst the Police Service often meant sick leave and absence from the Station or even death.

The Commissioner had issued instructions regarding feeding arrangements at Stations where Officers lived in Section Houses. Thomas Miles as the senior Constable at Wimbledon would have been made responsible for the Mess Room and the need to comply with the rules and regulations as laid down. The Commissioner issued instructions that where there was a Section House, arrangements should be made to establish a mess. This in effect created a canteen for Sergeants and Constables only. No senior Officer, in this case Inspector Rogers, was allowed to be a part of the scheme.

The mess would employ a caterer who would ensure that dinners, and often breakfasts, could be made for those who were members. Membership was to be paid for at a minimum of 1 penny per week or more if the members of the mess agreed. A suitable Mess Officer was appointed and he would arrange for the collection of monies (unusually each Monday) so that he could attend shops and markets on a Tuesday and collect the necessary provisions for the rest of the week. Bills from reputable tradesmen only were to be paid for on Tuesdays. The mess monies were collected also to buy plates, cutlery, pots, pans and table cloths. Such property belonged to the mess and when a member left he no longer retained any interest in any of the utensils. The ovens and cookers needed would be provided to the mess 'at cost' by the

Receiver. The meals would be arranged so that every member was able to sit down at the same hour. If a member was called out for something urgent his meal would be put in the oven and kept warm until he could get back. A printed scale of charges was put on display in the mess and to ensure good order the most senior Mess Officer had a duty to report to the Inspector if a Sergeant was absent at any time or if there was any bad language or behaviour by a Constable. Police officers were not to become cooks unless the Officer was still able to perform his normal duties.

Most Mess Officers managed matters extremely well however occasionally senior Officers learnt from some bitter experiences when Police Officers managed the financial affairs of messes badly. For example some Mess Officers found it difficult not to treat the mess account as their own and in effect embezzled monies from their colleagues. There was also the issue that some traders could be coerced into providing provisions for free. Some traders, especially at markets, found it difficult not to curry favour with the Police in giving away produce especially at the end of the day although the rules suggested that the lowest prices were to be obtained. Accounts had to be presented to the Inspector or Superintendent each week and he would sign as supervising. Vouchers for payment by tradesmen would be presented to the Inspector who would pay from the Petty cash account. Occasionally gratuities of food and drink were received in Stations and before these could be accepted a report was made to the Inspector.

A Police Surveyor's report dated 1881 described the accommodation as a house adapted for Police purposes. Its overall thoughts suggest that the situation was not at all satisfactory stating that the 'arrangements (were) inconvenient'.

> 'Single men wash in the cook's sink in the kitchen, a factor considered 8 years later which had not altered. Some of the rooms are said to be very cold and damp. It has a small mess room. The building is occupied by one married Inspector, one married Constable and 8 Single Constables'[41].

In 1885 this status was altered with the Station transferred to 'W' (Clapham) Division and placed in the charge of an Inspector. The Home Department's promise to increase supervisory strength of Inspectors had materialised by 1888 when 27 Inspectors had been posted to 'V' Division to provide cover for the 10 Police Stations. There were now sufficient Inspectors on the Division to have two per Station. By 1888 Wimbledon had been connected to the telegraph and had direct communication not only with Scotland Yard but to its surrounding Stations as well[42]. Wimbledon had a direct link to the

Superintendent at the Divisional Headquarters at Wandsworth. The Station code used to identify the station Whiskey Bravo (WB)[43].

Inspector Roger stayed until 1885 when he retired. The 1888 map below is of Merton and Wimbledon. It shows Merton Road junction with the Broadway and the Police Station is situated on the main highway. In 1893 the Sub-Divisional Inspector in charge was Edward Bonner although by 1894 a re-organisation saw the Station losing its Sub-Divisional status and becoming a Sectional Station of Wandsworth along with Wandsworth Common, Putney and Roehampton.

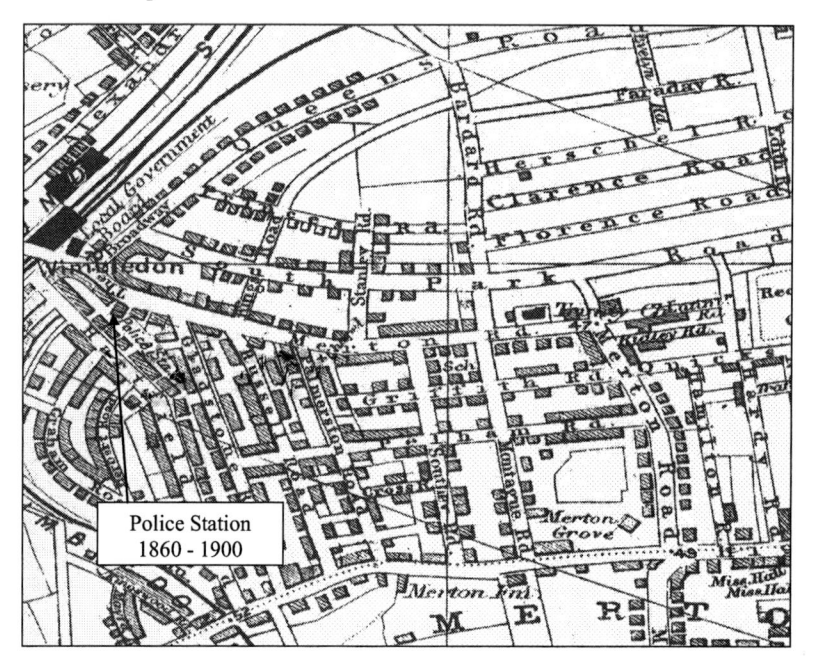

Police Station 1860 - 1900

After occupation surveyors reported that 'the men have a stove in the kitchen which is only fit for a bedroom, smokes and is very uncomfortable'. It has a coal box or dust hole and the water closet (toilet) was in a very bad state. The main concern was that the single men wash in the same sink used by the cooks in the kitchen[44].

In 1894 the Station was considered too small for Police purposes and a plot of land was found in Queens Road and in 1896 the freehold was purchased for £500. In the meantime the Metropolitan Police Surveyors designed a Police Station and contracted builders to build it. The Station cost £8,033 and was built with room for modern accoutrements like a telegraph room, charge room, Inspector's office, library, mess room, 3 cells and association cell. The yard also boasted a parade room, wash house and an ambulance shed. There was also a two-stall stable and room for 15 Constables to live[45].

The 'V' Division Despatch Van

In the photograph above is of the 'V' Divisional Despatch van is shown in the Station yard at Wandsworth. This was the Headquarters Station and formed the base from which the horses and men employed were allocated to either the prison van or despatch van. A groom at the Station was responsible for the welfare of all the horses kept at the Station. The Superintendent and Inspectors' horses needed to be available at a moment's notice and this was the groom's job. The Police Officer above would collect correspondence, papers and Police packages from and to Headquarters. The van would travel between all the Sub-Divisional Stations and park in the yard where he would take despatch bags into the front office and the Station Officer would ensure receipt of the bag coming and ensuring the outward bag was made up ready for onward transmission. The van was a secure internal system that ensured that only the correctly authorised people saw the sensitive nature of some of the correspondence. Even today the Police still run its own internal despatch network between Stations in London.

The United Kingdom became embroiled in a distant war with the Boers in South Africa and, in company with many other Police Officers (especially if they had served in the forces before joining the Police), a considerable number wanted to re-join their old units and fight the cause. A 20-year-old George William Draper was Pc 837 attached to Wimbledon Police Station and applied to join the Wiltshire Regiment as a private on short service for the duration of the conflict. A number of Police Officers were killed in the war however Draper survived the conflict and re-joined the Police at Queens Road in 1902 with his discharge papers saying that his conduct was very good.

Later in 1900 the Station was completed and fit for occupation[46] yet by 1905 its Sub-Divisional status had been lost again, returning it to where it had been before. There was a stable in the yard and accommodation above the Station for a Section House for single Constables. The old Station that had been given up in the Broadway, at the corner of Victoria Crescent, had become a jewellers shop in 1987.

In 1907 the Wimbledon Section showed the Station strength as 2 Inspectors, 9 Sergeants and 82 Constables. In February of the same year the Superintendent authorised two Constables from the station to be attached to the reserve and one Constable to be the Warrant Officer responsible for over seeing that all arrest warrants sent to the Station were carried out and the subjects brought before the court[47]. By 1908 'V' Division had established Wimbledon as a Sub-Divisional Station under Inspector William Hart. The address was shown as 15 Queens Road, South Park Road, Wimbledon SW19.

In 1912 a hand ambulance was stationed at the Grove Hotel in Wimbledon for drunks or injured members of the public. The old Station in the Broadway was retained until 1919. The re-organisation had attached two Sectional Stations to Wimbledon, these were Putney and Roehampton[48]. William Hart stayed until 1911 when his place was taken by William Barnham however by 1914 Race Hooper was the Sub-Divisional Inspector until 1917[49]. The duty of Sub-Divisional Inspectors was an important one and equal to that carried out by Superintendents today.

In World War one Wimbledon, still a station located on 'V' (Wandsworth) Division, formed part of No. 3 District that included 'L', 'M', 'P' and 'R' Divisions. Like all the other London Stations, Wimbledon Police Station displayed recruiting posters on bill boards at the front of the building. This helped to encourage ordinary working men to enlist in the Special Constables as volunteers in order to make up numbers of Police in the area. At each of the 180 Police Stations a unit of Special Constables were formed. A Group was 1 Sergeant and 9 men. A Squad was 1 Sub-Inspector and three Groups, and a Company was 1 inspector, 3 Squads and 1 Group[50].

The response to the campaign was overwhelming with large numbers of men doing their day job coming home, having their food and going out to their Stations for duty. But it appears that in the early days while the Home Office were trying to provision the Specials they left them short – understandable as they were fighting a war as-well. The indignant Specials resorted to their own means of obtaining funds and whilst this example of a post card relates to the Palmer Green Specials in North London many others produced their own means of raising funds.

> **In the House of Commons** recently, the Home Secretary Mr. McKenna, stated that in his opinion, the Special Constables were doing little or no work.
>
> **His Majesty the King,** a few days later, however, was graciously pleased to compliment that body, upon the excellent services they were rendering to their King and Country.
>
> *A few "Special" lines on the subject.*
>
> ## McKENNA!
>
> Who leaves our Germans free, to plot
> Their knavish tricks so very hot,
> Instead of locking up the lot?
>   McKenna!
>
> And yet who is it does not shirk
> The lie, that "Specials" do not work,
> But idly at their leisure lurk?
>   McKenna!
>
> Who thereby drags us from our cot
> At midnight, to the lonely spot,
> Where we fulfil our "Special's" lot?
>   McKenna!
>
> Who put the Suffragettes in gaol,
> And then released them without bail,
> When "forcing" proved of no avail?
>   McKenna!
>
> While we earn nought, as stands confessed,
> Who draws five thousand of the best,
> For chucking "piffle" off his chest?
>   McKenna!
>
> Till next Election sounds his knell,
> He is a chap he needs must tell,
> Emphatically to go to,—well,
>   Gehenna!
>
> When togs and clogs wear out and rot
> In Country's Cause, who pays the shot?
> You bet your bottom dollar, *not*—
>   McKenna!
>
> Comrades, meanwhile, let's work and sing
> With heart and voice, "God save the King,
> Who has, like us, to stick that thing—
>   McKenna!
>
> Printed and published by the Rhymster, Sergt. Imbrey (Special Constabulary), 90, Palmerston Crescent, Palmers Green, N., and sold by him at One Penny per copy, for the purpose of providing his Squad with needful accessories unprovided by the "Absent-minded Beggar" at the Home Office.
> (*Copyright Reserved.*)

Postcard produced to raise funds for the Special Constabulary

There was a very strong unit of Special Constables at Wimbledon. Lectures on Police subjects, ambulance training and rifle shooting were some of the tasks undertaken by the Wimbledon Special Constabulary. Apart from guarding vulnerable points Specials could be seen conducting people towards air raid shelters during bombing raids[51].

By 1915 Observation posts had been established on the Division and Wimbledon's Specials kept observation from the roof of the Station not only to give an early warning of Zeppelins and Gotha bombers but also to extinguish any suspicious lights during the blackout[52]. It was thought at the time that some of those sympathetic to the German cause deliberately left their lights on to provide an indication of a target.

The picture below shows Wimbledon's Sub-Divisional Special Constabulary Rifle shooting team in 1916. They had won the Divisional shooting contest

The Wimbledon Special Constabulary Rifle Team winners of 1916.

and proudly display their cup and team. The picture was taken in 1916 and shows 'V' Division on the collar of their greatcoats which had recently been issued. Notice also that the Sergeants have what appear to round strips rather than chevrons and then only on one arm. This was a distinction that was later changed but for the meantime it served to distinguish regular Police Officers to Special Constables who were temporary.

There was no official medal which was issued to commemorate the sterling work of the Special Constabulary. The medal on the right is the 1914 Special Constabulary medal issued to Metropolitan Specials after the war. It was a mark of their long and devoted service which was entirely voluntary. Only later was a medal struck and awarded to mark their contribution to the war effort.

Some of the very first Women Police came to do duty at Wimbledon during the war. The Superintendent of 'V' Division was presented with a letter of introduction written by the Commissioner of Police instructing that 2 Women Police from the Women Police Service (formally the Women Police Volunteers) should do duty at Wimbledon. The Women's Local Government Association had arranged for 6 Women Police to be paid for. Two were posted to Paddington, 2 to Wimbledon and 2 to Marylebone. The posts were purely unofficial however 'the Superintendent was glad to have their assistance'[53]. The picture at below left shows the uniform that the women wore. Notice they also wore the duty armlet denoting they were on duty. Times were changing for women especially since there was a drive in recognition for the good work of women who replaced men in factories during the war.

Police Officers were in a protected occupation, meaning that they did not need to apply to join the forces and fight in the First World War. However no obstruction was placed in the path of Police Officers wishing to apply to join the armed services. One such person who applied for a short service application was Enoch John Pierce from Wimbledon Police Station. In May 1915 he applied to join the Army Service Corps as a butcher, which had been his former trade and calling before joining the Metropolitan Police. Pierce was 25 years old, a single man and lived at the Station. The application together with the declaration was signed by Pierce and needed to be sworn in the presence of a magistrate. The magistrates in Wimbledon witnessed the oath and counter-signed the Army Form B 2505. Pierce notified his Sergeant in a report and this was passed to the Inspector and then to the Divisional Superintendent for information. A start date would be notified later where Pierce needed to report to Aldershot Barracks in Surrey.

Special Constabulary Long Service medal

A Women Police service Officer attached to the Metropolitan Police at Wimbledon

In 1928 there was a change of Sub-Divisional Inspector (today's Superintendent) who was responsible for the Sub-Division. This had been Sub-Divisional Inspector 86359 Albert Cavendish, who had represented the rank of Inspector on the Central committee of the Police Federation from 1922-23. As a Constable he had arrested Mrs Pankhurst – the suffragette who had presented him with a button badge bearing the words 'votes for women' and a sprig of heather as a keepsake in acknowledgement of his kindness and forbearance. He was retiring on ill health grounds after 28 years service and moving to the coast at Hove in Sussex. His place was being taken by Sub-Divisional Inspector Aylett on promotion from Peckham Police Station[54].

The picture at left was taken in the yard of Wimbledon (Queens Road) Police Station and shows the Inspector of Wimbledon Sub-Division with his Station Sergeant (to his left) and his men. This picture was taken about 1923 probably for a ceremonial event although no one is wearing the armlet denoting he was on duty. Only about one third of the Station strength of Constables is shown in the picture.

Wimbledon Police circa mid1920's

Harry Green was a Constable at the Station during the 1930s and he recorded his experiences whilst living there. He said;

> 'That a wooden partition separated each officer from its neighbour about 6 feet high. The beds were made of iron with pallet mattresses filled with straw. There were two gas lamps for illumination over the passage that separated the two lines of bunks. A man going on early turn would have to cook his breakfast, (prepare) his sandwich and make a flask of tea before Parade time at 5.45am. There were no traffic signals and no pedestrian crossings. Traffic was controlled by a Pc on Point Duty at Alexandra Road, The Grove, Hartfield Road Level Crossing and Skew Arches at Raynes Park. Trolley Buses went from Wimbledon to Kingston[55].

The Station address in 1928 was shown as 15 Queens Road, South Wimbledon SW19[56]. Because Stations were in operation 24 hours a day 365 days a week they need redecoration from time to time. They were generally re-painted every three or four years, however Surveyors planned ahead and in 1937 Wimbledon was re-fitted and the Station greatly improved. The Sub-Divisional Inspector was W. F. Kendall during 1937.

During World War Two Wimbledon town was bombed on a regular basis, possibly because bombs which were not dropped on London by German planes could be dropped on their way home on useful well-lit targets. Sand bags were placed around the front of the Station, usually to door height, and this acted as a protection barrier for those at work. At the front of the Station there was either a regular Officer, war reserve Constable or Special Constable on guard duty.

On 15th August 1939 Merton High Street and the Kingston Road area was bombed heavily killing 14 and injuring a further 59 people. Bombing continued until May 1941 however by far the worst night was the 6th November 1940 when 67 bombs fell on central Wimbledon within an hour. Remarkably, only 4 people were killed and thirteen injured. An incident occurred which was to seriously effect the supervision of the Sub-Division.

Wimbledon Police Station
15 Queens Road, South Wimbledon SW19
1900 – Present day

Wimbledon suffered from Flying bomb attacks in 1944 when on 19th June at 6.30am a V1 fell on Wimbledon Hill outside Emerson Court killing three people. Two of the deceased were Police Inspectors from Wimbledon, Reserve Inspector 0100478 Alfred John Giles and Inspector 114157 Bernard Sylvester[57]. This was a most unfortunate incident as one was driving the other home from the night shift when the flying bomb struck. The Police Station however escaped any damage during the war.

Contingency plans had been prepared by Scotland Yard to evacuate staff to less dangerous surroundings in the Wimbledon area. It was thought that even though it had been the subject of bombing attacks it may have been safer than central London, especially since the south turret of the Headquarters building had been struck and seriously damaged by German bombs on the 11th May 1941. A large school near Wimbledon common had become available and was later leased by the Metropolitan Police Receiver for this purpose[58] and staff from the Receivers' Office was relocated there. In fact many local people, particularly women, sought to work for the Receivers' Office.

After the war there was a recruiting drive to enlist more Special Constables and a figure of 9,000 more men were required to help combat very high levels of crime, including robberies, assaults and burglaries. However, because of the shortfall in numbers, applications were invited for the first time from women in 1950.

During the 1950s there was a recruitment drive and accommodation was sought and purchased to house Police Officers and their families in the Metropolitan Police area. This policy had a significant impact on Wimbledon since a number of premises or areas of land were purchased. For example Lantern House, The Downs Wimbledon, SW20, was purchased in 1951 for £15,000 where 18 married quarters were created. In 1953 a further 18 flats were created at Dunarden, 15 Inner Park Road, Wimbledon, SW19, when it was bought for £5,000[59].

In 1954 the Home Office suggested that Wimbledon Police Station needed refurbishment and extending because it was unfit for current purposes, however it took a further 32 years to achieve any sort of renovation. Between 1955 and 1978 plans were drawn up, and a number of properties surrounding the Station were purchased including 2 South Park Road (previously an Ambulance Station), and 17, 19, 21 and 23 Queens Road. These were also probably obtained by compulsory purchase.

The lamp on the next page is the one outside Wimbledon Police Station as can be seen from the picture of the Station below. The Wimbledon lamp, which is not unique, shares its design with Claybury, Gerald Road, Greenford and Lewisham.

Superintendents took over the supervision of important Stations from Sub-Divisional Inspectors when all those in the rank were promoted to Chief Inspector in the 1930's.

In 1957 Superintendent C. Rackham was in charge at Wimbledon also having responsibility for New Malden[60]. By 1960 Wimbledon (VM) had replaced Rackham and Superintendent W. H. Porter was in charge[61].

Claybury, GeraldRd, Greenford, Lewisham, Wimbledon.

Wimbledon station lamp

In 1965 Wimbledon, Mitcham, Merton and Morden were merged into the London Borough of Merton and simultaneously Wimbledon Sub-Division was re-organised. This meant that the administrative jurisdiction of the County of Surrey was removed with the formation of the London County Council. Consequentially this resulted in the re-alignment of the Police Sub-Divisions of Mitcham, Wimbledon and New Malden sections were reduced to conform to the new borough boundaries. New Malden was removed completely from the division.

In 1968 a tragic incident happened. PC George Arthur Dale was killed when his Police patrol car went out of control and crashed at Wimbledon[62]. A year later in 1969 PC Michael John Davies was off duty but, after identifying himself to warn a man on Wimbledon Common, he was attacked and stabbed to death[63]. Such events bring out the fact that policing is dangerous, risky and unpredictable.

In 1980 the Metropolitan Police Divisions in Surrey (AD, 'T', 'V' and 'Z' were all re-named Districts, however by 1984 the Metropolitan Police District was split into 8 Areas. There was somewhat of a confusion occurring on 'V' District since for a time it was being administered by both 'W' and 'Z' Divisions which were located on different areas. To resolve the problem Wimbledon Division was dissolved in completely in September 1985 and the responsibility split between the two Areas (4 Area South and 5 Area South West)[64]. Districts were dissolved in 1986 leaving the individual Stations as Divisions.

During 1984 the MP's own Surveyors Department sought contractors to complete the building works. This was not just building an extension but refurbishing the whole Station costing £1.5 Million, John Mowlems contractors were hired to complete the work in three stages, the extension, the alterations to the old building and finally the work in the Station yard.

In the 1980s the stables at the Queens Road Station were demolished to make way from additional car parking and an extension. The Section House was subsequently closed, converted into administrative offices and the residents re-housed.

After the introduction of the Police and Criminal Evidence Act 1984 certain Stations on Divisions were designated by the Commissioner as authorised to take charges and Wimbledon was a Charging Station for these purposes[65].

The extension of the existing Station shown in the picture below beside the old Station was opened in October 1987 by The Mayor of Merton, Councillor Harold Turner, with a state of the art spacious computerised Control Room, a good sized crime investigation office, more cells and charging facilities, more accommodation for the support and civil staff, and better canteen and recreation facilities. From the picture below one can see that the Station has been substantially enlarged with modern accommodation being built next to and attached to the old Station.

Wimbledon Police Station with new extension completed in 1987

Wimbledon became the Divisional OCU headquarters for the Borough of Merton in 1998[66].

In 1992 there was a change in name and Station codes for the Division. The 4 area Station that had been on 'Z' Division was now called Merton Division and Wimbledon became 'ZM', Mitcham 'ZC' and Morden Police Office 'ZE'[67].

Wimbledon itself is a busy and vibrant town centre with a thriving day- and night- time economy. The Borough is perhaps best known for the two weeks in summer when a large number of visitors and sports enthusiasts from around the world attend the famous Wimbledon Tennis Championships[68].

To deal with this and the usual wide range of policing challenges the borough has a total of 435 personnel including Police Officers, Police Community Support Officers and Police Staff.

---

[1] http://cms.met.police.uk/met/boroughs/merton/04how_are_we_doing/welcome_message accessed on 6th January 2010
[2] http://cms.met.police.uk/met/boroughs/merton/01whos_who accessed on 20th July 2010
[3] Kellys Directory 1843
[4] Brown, B. (date unknown) Metropolitan Police in the County of Surrey
[5] Kelly's Directory 1849
[6] Commissioners Annual Report 1972
[7] MEPO 2/135
[8] Metropolitan Police Surveyors Records 1888
[9] Metropolitan Police General Orders 1893
[10] Kellys directory 1878 p144
[11] Post office Directory 1879
[12] Metropolitan Police Surveyors Records 1881
[13] Kellys Directory 1891 p1373
[14] Kellys directory 1894
[15] Metropolitan Police Surveyors Records 1912
[16] Metropolitan Police Surveyors Records Charlton.
[17] Post Office Directory 1939
[18] MPA website accessed 15th Feb 2009
[19] http://www.met.police.uk/history/remembrance4.htm accessed on 4th January 2010
[20] Metropolitan Police Intranet doc
[21] Metropolitan Police Intranet doc accessed on......
[22] Police and Constabulary List 1844
[23] Bacons London Atlas 1862
[24] Brown, B. (date unknown) The Metropolitan Police in the County of Surrey.
[25] A. Montague 'Colliers Wood' A pictorial history
[26] Post Office directory 1841
[27] A. Montague 'Colliers Wood' A pictorial history
[28] Metropolitan Police Surveyors
[29] Metropolitan Police General Orders 1864
[30] Metropolitan Police Orders dated 15th July 1869
[31] A serial of police officer usually comprised of 1 Inspector 3 sergeants and 30 constables.
[32] Forrester, C (1996) 'Skinners Horse' in The Peeler Vol 1 pp7-11
[33] Commissioners Annual Report 1869
[34] MEPO 234
[35] Census records 1881
[36] Report on the condition of the Metropolitan Police Stations 1881
[37] Metropolitan Police Surveyors Records, Charlton
[38] MEPO 234
[39] Metropolitan Police Surveyors Records, Charlton

[40] Census records 1881
[41] Metropolitan Police Surveyors Report 1881
[42] Kellys directory 1888
[43] Metropolitan Police General Orders 1893
[44] Metropolitan Police Surveyors Report 1888
[45] Metropolitan Police Surveyors Records, Charlton
[46] Metropolitan Police Orders 27th September 1900
[47] Metropolitan Police Divisional Records for V or Wandsworth Division
[48] Kirchners Police Almanac 1907
[49] Kellys Law Directories 1908 -1917
[50] Reay, W. (1919) 'The specials'. Heinemann London p29
[51] Ibid p91
[52] Ibid p177
[53] Allen, M. S. (1925) The Pioneer Police Women p145
[54] The Police Review and Parade Gossip dated 27th April 1928
[55] Quoted from Pc Harry Green Constable at Wimbledon in the 1930's in the Chief Superintendents speech for the opening of the new station extension dated 1st October 1987
[56] Post Office Directory 1928
[57] Metropolitan Police Roll of Honour dated 2002
[58] Browne D. (1956) The rise of Scotland Yard. P359
[59] Metropolitan Police Surveyors Records, Charlton.
[60] Police and Constabulary Almanac 1957
[61] Police and Constabulary Almanac 1960
[62] http://www.met.police.uk/history/remembrance4.htm accessed on 4th January 2010
[63] http://www.met.police.uk/history/remembrance4.htm accessed on 4th January 2010
[64] Brown, B. 'The Metropolitan Police in the County of Surrey'.
[65] Police and Constabulary Almanac 1998
[66] Ibid
[67] Metropolitan Police Orders dated 12th February 1992
[68] ibid

Chapter 8

London Borough of Sutton

Introduction

The London Borough of Sutton covers nearly 17 square miles and borders the London Boroughs of Croydon to the east and Merton to the North. The remaining part of the Borough is bounded by the County of Surrey. The borough is largely a 20th century creation especially along the seemingly monotonous northern stretches, but is described as having, nonetheless, an area with a great deal of charm. The river Wandle runs through the northern part and attracted early industries and rural retreats. There are plenty of worthwhile buildings surviving in Cheam, Carshalton and Beddington[1].

The current Borough Police Commander, based at Sutton Police Station, is Detective Chief Superintendent Guy Ferguson together with Superintendent Chas Baily and Superintendent Phil Willis[2].

Banstead Police Station (now Surrey Constabulary)

Banstead is a village with a Police Station located about a mile and a half north of the Epsom Downs branch of the London to Brighton railway[3].

The first Police Station in Banstead was a building purchased in 1852 on the north side of High Street in front of Buff House. It was fitted out and opened in 1853.

In 1864 Banstead was shown as a Station on 'P' (Camberwell) Division. It was a Sectional Station and formed part of Carshalton Sub-Division along with Mitcham, Sutton and Carshalton Stations. The strength was 1 Sergeant, 11 Constables and one horse. The horse was ridden by the Sergeant who performed 12 hours duty daily from 9am to 9pm. The Station ground comprised of one Section divided into two beats by day and six at night. The Station was under the supervision of the Inspector from Carshalton[4].

In 1865 three new Divisions were formed, 'W', or Clapham, 'X', or Paddington, and 'Y', or Highgate. Banstead was one of several Stations transferred to form the new 'W' Division[5].

Discipline in the Police was harsh in those early days and many Officers were either dismissed or they retired early from the Force. In 1877 one young, 22 year old, Police Constable Joseph Stevens found himself before the Epsom Magistrates for being "unlawfully guilty of a violation of duty in his office of Constable in the parish of Banstead". Whatever he did cost him his job and 21 days imprisonment[6]

The address of the Station in 1884 was High Street, Banstead[7].

In 1891 the Census revealed that Police Constable James Childs, his wife Adelaide Elizabeth and their two daughters were living at the Station; there were also three single Constables living in the building[8]. Inspector Thomas Flynn was shown in charge of the Station in 1891 and he was responsible for ensuring that everything ran smoothly. He was also the supervisor in charge of three Sergeants and 14 Constables[9]. Flynn was replaced in 1893.

A communication was received on 4th October 1901 from the Secretary of State, Home Department, sanctioning the purchase from a Mr Lambert of a site proposed for the building of a new Police Station, almost opposite the old Police Station in Banstead, at a cost of £250. The freehold site was purchased on 2 May 1902[10].

The new Police Station in Banstead was opened for business in July 1906. There was accommodation for one married Sergeant, three married Constables and six unmarried men[11].

Banstead Police Station
168 High Street, Banstead
1906 - present day,

In 1960 Banstead Station was closed at night from 10pm for an experimental period. The Officers normally employed were posted to outside duties on the night relief. Incoming telephone calls to Banstead were diverted to Sutton Police Station[12]. In 1964 Banstead Police Station reopened at night[13].

In 1965 the local authority boundaries were changed in London and Banstead (ZB) was designated a Sectional Station of Epsom (ZP) Sub-Division situated in the local authority of Banstead (Surrey)[14].

In April 2000 Banstead Police Station was transferred to Surrey Police when the Metropolitan Police District Area was realigned. Banstead was one of the Metropolitan Police Stations transferred to County Authorities. There are currently plans being considered to close this Police Station[15].

Carshalton Police Station

The first Metropolitan Police Station built in Carshalton was at the junction of Pound Street and West Street next door to an old wooden slated house called "Wandle Lodge". It was built on the site of the "Cage for erring humans and a pound for straying animals"[16]. The Station was opened in 1848 and was the first one in the area to have a base for a horse patrol. Carshalton at the time was the largest and most important village between Croydon and Ewell.

In October 1870 Police Sergeant George Robins, aged 46, rode his Police horse from Carshalton to Wimbledon, stopped at an inn and spoke to someone in the stable about his horse. Suddenly the horse kicked the Officer in the chest and he died immediately. He was interred in Carshalton Church and over 100 Officers attended the funeral. Sergeant Robins left a wife and a number of children[17].

Carshalton Police Station
Pound Street, Carshalton.
1848 - 1920

In 1892 Inspectors Rowbottom and Holdaway (later, in 1891, he was the Inspector in charge of Sutton Police Station) were in charge of the Station.

It served the community until it was demolished in 1920 when Carshalton came under the new Police Station at Wallington. At the start of the 20th century

214

Carshalton had over 50 Constables and policed Wallington; when the new Station was built the staff moved over to Wallington.

When the Police Station was demolished the site was laid out with turf and flowers and enlarged later when "Wandle Lodge" was demolished.

Epsom Police Station (Now Surrey Constabulary)

The picture below shows the Watch House in the centre of Epsom before the Metropolitan Police arrived in the area. It shows the stocks situated outside the front of the watch House next to the pond.

The papers dealing with the extension of the Metropolitan Police District in 1839 showed Epsom forming part of the 'V', or Wandsworth, Division. It would seem that six Constables and one Sergeant (mounted) were responsible for policing Morden, North Cheam and Malden, Ewell and Epsom. At this time the population of Epsom was about 3,200[18].

Old Watch House, Stocks and Pond in Epsom

A Deed of Conveyance signed by the Secretary of State for a freehold site was received from the Home Office on 15 June 1852. Home Office approval was granted on 21 February 1855 for the building of a Police Station at Epsom at the cost of £917[19]. The Station was built at the corner of Ashley Road and Ashley Avenue[20].

In 1864 Epsom is shown still attached to 'V' Division with the strength of two Sergeants and eleven Constables. The Inspector at Kingston was not posted for duty at a Station but had to patrol and have supervision of Kingston, Ditton, Epsom, Hampton and Sunbury. The Patrol Sergeants were each to perform 9 hours out of every 24 on horse or foot and have care of his horse. The Stations, with the exception of Kingston, were closed when Sergeants or Acting Sergeants were patrolling[21].

In 1878 Henry Haynes was the Sergeant in charge of the station; it did not become an Inspector Designated Station until the following year. Haynes, who lived at the station, was supported by 1 other Sergeant and 17 Constables[22].

The Station at Epsom was a 'V' Division Station in 1891, shown as being located in Ashley Road. Inspector Charles Pearn was in charge with three Sergeants and 22 Constables attached to the Station. There were another five Inspectors posted there and their names were A. Wilson, W. Knights, J. Godden, A. Hill and W. Knott[23].

Epsom Police Station
6, Ashley Road, Epsom.
1857 - 1963

In June 1919 two Canadian soldiers were arrested for disorderly conduct and they were placed in the cells at Epsom. As a result of these arrests 400 soldiers marched on the Station from their Camp causing damage to property on the way. On arrival at the Station, intent on releasing the two detained soldiers, they created havoc by smashing windows, fittings and furniture. Inspector Pawley lived above the Station with his wife and children. During the riot a number of Police Officers suffered injuries including Station Sergeant 87V Thomas Green, Warrant No. 80417 who died from his wounds and is buried in Epsom Cemetery[24]. The picture (above) shows his funeral procession passing Epsom Railway Station on its way to the cemetery.

The Funeral of the Late Station Sergeant Green in 1919

216

The 'Z', or Croydon, Division was formed in 1921 and this caused a large revision of boundaries. The Stations of Earlsfield, Wandsworth Common, and Epsom were transferred from 'V' to 'W', or Brixton, Division[25].

In 1937 it was proposed to rebuild the Station on the existing site, and a private architect was instructed to prepare plans. These had reached an advanced stage by 1939 when the outbreak of World War II prevented any work being done. The architect, however, reported that in his opinion the site was too small and irregular for the type of Station required.

In July 1944 the first floor of the Station was demolished by enemy action, a V.1 flying bomb. The ground floor was so severely damaged that temporary accommodation was sought at "Worple Lodge", Ashley Road, Epsom,[26] until the ground floor was rebuilt, with indications that work would be completed by the end of 1946[27]. However by 1953 the first floor had still not been rebuilt[28].

In 1953 the Surrey County Council offered the Police a site for a new Police Station within the Civic amenities called "The Silver Birches". In this development it was hoped to incorporate the Welfare Clinic, Ambulance Station and Library.

In 1955 the owner decided not to sell the site and was not prepared to negotiate, so the question of compulsory purchase powers was discussed. Eventually the owner decided to sell part of the site to the Police for the purpose of building a Police Station. The price was agreed, authorised by the Home Office on 4th February 1960 and the freehold purchased on the 25 May 1960[29].

Epsom Police Station was built and became operational in July 1963[30].

The change in local authority boundaries meant that Epsom was transferred to 'Z', or Croydon, as a Sub-Divisional Station[31].

The Divisions of Epsom and Sutton were amalgamated into one Division called Epsom whilst Sutton, now designated a Sub-Division, retained its prisoner processing and charging facilities[32].

In April 2000 Epsom Police Station was transferred to Surrey County Constabulary when the Metropolitan Police District Area was realigned. Epsom was one of nineteen Metropolitan Police Stations transferred to County Authorities.[33]

Epsom Police Station
Church Street, Epsom
1963 – present day

Sutton Police Station

Sutton village, which lies between the Green and the north end of the High Street and the parish church, was transformed when the main Brighton Road passed through the High Street between 1775 and 1809. The coming of the railway in 1847 added to the expansion making it a town with a population of 1,304 in 1841 and which by 1881 had grown to 10,334[34].

In 1827 at Sutton there was a Station of the Second Division of the Bow Street Patrol. The Patrol was formed around the year 1777 and policed the main "Turnpike Roads" in and out of London. It came under the jurisdiction of the Bow Street Magistrates and complemented the famous "Bow Street Runners" and Foot Patrols which operated in the central area. The Patrols were the brainchild of the Fielding brothers. The novelist Henry Fielding was assisted by his blind half-brother John who was knighted in 1761 and succeeded him at Bow Street where he proceeded to put into effect some of the ideas expounded by

Henry. The Horse Patrol was transferred to the newly formed Metropolitan Police in October 1836 and formed the nucleus of the "Mounted Branch"[35].

The Receiver purchased a site at 84 High Street, Sutton, in 1852 for the erection a Police Station which was finally built and ready for occupation in 1854[36].

In 1864 Sutton Police Station formed part of 'P' or Camberwell, Division. It was a Sectional Station of Carshalton Sub-Division and was split into two beats.

Sutton Police Station
High Street, Sutton
1854 - 1908

The strength was two Sergeants, eleven Constables and one horse. The Mounted Sergeant had to perform 3 hours duty at the Station, and patrol on horse or foot for 9 hours out of 24; he also had to look after his horse[37].

On the formation of three new Divisions 'W' or Clapham, 'X' or Paddington, and 'Y' or Highgate, Sutton was one of several Stations transferred to form the new 'W' Division[38]. Between 1877 and 1882 Inspector Walter Goodall was posted in charge of the Station[39]. The address of Sutton Police Station in 1884 was High Street, Sutton[40]. By 1897 Inspector W. Northover was in charge of the Station[41].

In October 1886 the Superintendent of 'W' Division drew attention to the inconveniences and inadequate facilities at Sutton Police Station. The Superintendent reported in August 1887 that the Station was small and cramped and must, at no distant date, be reconstructed or rebuilt. In September 1894 certain modifications, especially to the drainage system at the Station, were carried out. By March 1905 the situation had become acute and the Home Office forwarded a letter to the Commissioner from the Receiver recommending that additional ground, space or a new site should be acquired with a view to the provision of a new Police Station for Sutton[42].

If the Police Station was small and cramped then the fact that Inspector William Holdaway, his wife Emily, their six children aged between 1 year and 20 years, one married Constable and five single Constables were all living at the Station must have caused the Superintendent to request larger premises[43]. Further staffing at the Station consisted of 5 Sergeants and 48 Constables in 1891[44].

On 29 June 1905 a letter was received from the Secretary of State at the Home Office approving the purchase of a freehold property known as "Sutton Court", at a price not exceeding £2,650, as a site for a new Police Station at Sutton. The purchase was completed on 10 October 1905. On 29 August 1906 the Home Office sanctioned the sale of a portion of this Police site at Sutton, facing Sutton Court Road, to the Surrey Standing Joint Committee for the sum of £800. This parcel of land was required for the provision of a Court House for the use of the Justices of the Epsom Division[45].

Sutton Police Station
Carshalton Road, Sutton. Surrey
1908 - 2004

The new Police Station at Sutton was open for business in December 1908. The lodging assessment at married quarters at the Station was one set of quarters at 10s per week and another set of quarters at 4s. 6d. a week. The 10 unmarried men were each charged 1shilling a week[46].

The old Police Station was sold in 1908 to Dendy Napper, miller and corn merchant, who had a shop next door to the old Station. In fact, behind the old Police Station stood a windmill, which later became Napper's steam flour mills. After purchasing the old Police Station he extended his shop across the front of the old building[47]

The boundaries of 'P', 'W' and 'Z' Divisions were revised in October 1931. Thornton Heath Station was closed and Streatham and Wallington Stations were transferred from 'W' to 'Z'. Sutton was designated a Sub-Divisional Station of 'W' Division with Epsom and Banstead as its Sectional Stations[48]. By 1931 Sub-Divisional Inspector S C Lawrence was in charge of the Station[49]

In October 1933 notification was received at Sutton Police Station from the Local Authority that in future the address of Sutton Police Station would change from No.1 to No. 6 Carshalton Road West[50].

By 1936 the Station was in need of refurbishment due to the wear and tear of the previous twenty-eight years; this was duly carried out.

With the reorganisation of local authority boundaries in 1965, Sutton (ZT) was designated a Sub-Divisional Station of 'Z' Division with Wallington (ZW) as its Sectional Station, both being situated in the new London Borough of Sutton[51].

In 1975 the United Reformed Church in Carshalton Road was bought by Police for £130,000 to be used for future extension to the Police Station next door. It was immediately demolished for short term use as a Police car park[52]

Between 1980 and 1983 the station call sign was Zulu Tango (ZT)[53].

With effect from January 1980, Epsom and Sutton Divisions were amalgamated. The new Division was known as Epsom Division with its headquarters at Epsom Police Station. Sutton Police Station was re-designated a Sub-Divisional but retained charging facilities[54].

Sutton Police Station
6, Carshalton Road, Sutton.
2004 – present day

In 1988 the Station was given a £650,000 facelift. An outbuilding was demolished and a new two storey extension built to accommodate staff[65].

It was decided that a new Police Station was necessary and planning permission was sought and given in 1996 but the finances were just not available to go ahead at this stage. It was two years later that tenders to build were invited[56]. Whilst all this was taken place a group of conservationists campaigned to save the old Sutton Police Station, a Grade II listed building. Their campaign, together the need for additional local authority building accommodation, saved to building and a new police Station was built next to the old one.

The new police station was built and officially opened in March 2004 by the Commissioner, Sir John Stevens, and the Borough Police Commander Joe Royle. The new Station has much better accommodation for staff and includes

30 cells and "state of the art" Custody Suite for dealing with prisoners. At the opening Sir John said:

> "The new police station will provide improved facilities for officers and also a more pleasant environment for members of the public who visit"[57]

The new Police Station building is dedicated to Police Constable Patrick Dunne. The Officer sadly died in 1993 having been shot and killed when responding to a report of gunfire in Clapham. His name on the front of the building is a fitting memorial to this brave Officer.

Sutton Police Station is currently open 24 hours a day[58].

Wallington Police Station

In a list of "Parishes and Places" the Hamlet of Wallington is mentioned; it was included when the Metropolitan Police District was extended in 1839. The Parish of Beddington is linked with the Hamlet and policed by three Police Constables from Croydon Police Station on 'P' Division.

Petty Sessions were held at Croydon and the Parishes of Addington, Beddington and Chaldon are aligned with the Hundreds of Wallington. The two Magistrates listed were Sir Henry Bridges of Beddington and Robert G. Loraine of Wallington[59].

Three new Divisions were formed 'W' or Clapham, 'X' or Paddington, and 'Y', or Highgate. Croydon was transferred from 'P' to 'W' Division[60].

There was an increase of strength for one Constable for Special Beat Patrol for the Wallington area authorised in 1904[61].

In 1905 the Wallington Parish Council requested the provision of a Police Station in the area of Beddington and Wallington. Authority was sought for a suitable site to be purchased for the purpose of erecting a pair of Police Cottages. In 1906 the Beddington Parish Council requested the provision of a Police Station in the area of South Beddington[62].

Wallington Police Station
84 Stafford Road.
1915 – present day

After protracted negotiations, a freehold site was purchased on 9th July 1912 in Stafford Road. It is quoted that "Stafford Road is an old highway leading from the South End of Sutton to Croydon"[63].

An extract from a letter dated 10th May 1913 said "Wallington is, and I should say must always remain, a fairly quiet neighbourhood. There is no Section House at the Carshalton Police Station, which the new Station at Wallington will replace......"[64].

The administrative portion of the new Police Station at Wallington ('W' Division) was staffed and business commenced on 24th May 1915[65].

On 7 June 1915 the two married quarters at Wallington Police Station were occupied. The lodging assessment of one was set at 9s 6d a week and the other at 9s. a week.[66]

The Police received a notice from the Beddington and Wallington Urban District council concerning the numbering of buildings in which it stated that the Police Station was numbered 84[67]. The boundaries of 'P', 'W' and 'Z' Divisions were revised in 1931 when Streatham and Wallington Sub-Divisional Stations were transferred from 'W' to 'Z' Division[68].

A reorganisation of the Force designed to relate Police boundaries to the new local authority boundaries meant that Wallington became a Sectional Station to Sutton Sub-Division on 'Z' or Croydon, Division[69].

Property at 16-18 Stanley Park Road was purchased in 1965 for the purpose of erecting a new Police Station however when the building Committee convened in 1971 it was recommended that on the completion of Sutton's new Station, Wallington should be removed from the building programme and reduced in status to that of a Police Office[70].

Like many old Police Stations where there is a possibility of either closure or restricted opening times, the local people feel that they will not receive the service and support previously given. When Wallington Police Station was in danger of complete closure in 1977 the local newspaper reported a strong feeling by the local people against the closure after its 62 years of service[71]. This was repeated in 1991 when it was proposed that the Station should be closed[72].

In 1987 the Station was visited by an elderly lady on the eve of her 100th birthday. She was Kate Blanche Gosling, one of Hertfordshire's first Police Women, with a warrant number of 303, and who had served in the Police nearly 80 years previously. She was given the opportunity to see how the Police Service had changed during the intervening years[73]. She died in 1994 aged 107 years.

The Station is open from 8am – 8pm Monday – Friday, and 10am – 6pm on Saturday and Sunday[74].

Worcester Park Police Office

When the Metropolitan Police District was extended in 1839 the Liberty of Worcester Park was one of the places mentioned. Being under the jurisdiction of Richmond Police Station 'V' Division, it had the strength of one Constable[75].

In November 1966 it was found that a number of areas near the outskirts of the Metropolitan Police District had no Police Station within easy reach, so it was decided that small neighbourhood Police Units should be formed. One of these areas consisted of parts of North Cheam and Worcester Park.

A site was found and Home Office authority was granted, but because of the protracted negotiations regarding a right of way the owner withdrew his offer. Other properties were sought, but it was not until 1970 that a suitable site came on the market. The lease was obtained for a vacant shop with living accommodation above which was tenanted[76].

On Tuesday 13th April 1971 a Police Office was opened at 154 Central Road, Worcester Park, Surrey, on Sutton Sub-Division.[77] It was opened by Chief Superintendent Frederick Jarvis from Sutton Police Station[78].

Inspector John Mower, the unit commander at Sutton, said "We hope local people will make full use of the Office and call in any time on any matter concerning the Police. It will save them a longish return journey to the Station at Sutton"[79].

The Police Office is open from 10am – 2pm on Monday to Friday[80].

Worcester Park Police Office
154 Central Road.
1971 – present day

---

[1] Pevsner, N and Cherry, B. (1983) London 2. South. Penguin, Harmondsworth p637
[2] Met.police.uk/met/borough/Sutton/index. Accessed on 26th October 2010
[3] Kelly's Directory 1891 p1164

[4] Police Order 11 Jan 1864
[5] Police Order 28 Oct 1865
[6] Old Banstead. 'Off Beat' April 2000
[7] Police Order 20 June 1884
[8] NA Census 1891
[9] Kelly's directory 1891 p1164
[10] LB682
[11] Metropolitan Police Orders dated 23rd July 1906
[12] Metropolitan Police Order dated 11 Nov 1960
[13] Metropolitan Police Order dated 28 Aug 1964
[14] Metropolitan Police Order dated 6 Aug 1964
[15] www.nork-residents.org.uk/banstead_police_station_to_close October 2010
[16] Jones A.E. An Illustrated Directory of Old Carshalton Published by the Author – date unknown.
[17] Sutton Journal 20th October 1870
[18] MEPO 2/76
[19] MEPO 5/26 (153 -155)
[20] LB 689
[21] Metropolitan Police Order dated 11 Jan 1864
[22] Kelly's Directory 1878 p2217
[23] Kelly's Directory 1891
[24] Metropolitan Police Orders dated 20 June 1919, 28th July 1919 and 5th June 1920 Also MEPO 2/1962 and MEPO 3/331
[25] Metropolitan Police Order dated 24 Feb 1921
[26] Metropolitan Police Order dated 17 Nov 1944
[27] Metropolitan Police Order dated 29 Jan 1946
[28] LB 689 and Met Police at War. HMSO
[29] LB 689
[30] Metropolitan Police Order dated 26 July 1963
[31] Metropolitan Police Order dated 6 Aug 1964
[32] Metropolitan Police Order dated 28 Dec 1979
[33] MPA Report 6 etc.
[34] Pevsner, N and Cherry, B. (1983) London 2. South. Penguin, Harmondsworth p654
[35] MEPO 2/25
[36] Letter to R.P.Smith from Metropolitan Police dated 24.12.58
[37] Metropolitan Police Order dated 11 Jan 1864
[38] Metropolitan Police Order dated 28 Oct 1865
[39] Kellys Directories 1877- 1882
[40] Metropolitan Police Order dated 20 June 1884
[41] Piles Sutton Streets Directory 1897
[42] MEPO 2/347
[43] NA Census 1891
[44] Kelly's Directory 1891
[45] LB 696
[46] Metropolitan Police Order dated 5 Dec 1908
[47] Berry P. Sutton in Old Photographs 1994
[48] Metropolitan Police Order dated 9 Oct 1931
[49] Piles Directory – Sutton and district 1931
[50] LB 696
[51] Metropolitan Police Order dated 6 Aug 1964
[52] Wallington & Carshalton Times 12th June 1975
[53] MEPO 14
[54] Metropolitan Police Order dated 28th Dec 1979
[55] Sutton Guardian 4.8.88
[56] Sutton & Banstead Independent 11.2.98
[57] Sutton Post 24.3.04
[58] www.met.police.uk accessed 10th October 2010
[59] MEPO 2/76
[60] Metropolitan Police Order dated 28th Oct 1865
[61] Metropolitan Police Order dated 16th June 1904

[62] MEPO 2/811
[63] LB 816
[64] MEPO 2/811
[65] Metropolitan Police Order dated 22 May 1915
[66] Metropolitan Police Order dated 5 June 1915
[67] LB 816
[68] Metropolitan Police Order dated 9 Oct 1931
[69] Metropolitan Police Order dated 6 Aug 1964
[70] LB 817
[71] Wallington and Carshalton Advertiser 4.8.77
[72] The Advertiser 29.3.91
[73] Sutton & Banstead News 12.11.87
[74] www.met.police.uk October 2010
[75] MEPO 2/76
[76] LB 844
[77] Metropolitan Police Order dated 8 April 1971
[78] Sutton and Cheam Herald 15.4.1971
[79] Sutton and Cheam Herald 8.4.1981
[80] www.met.police.uk accessed on 10th October 2010

Chapter 9

London Borough of Southwark

Introduction

The London Borough of Southwark was created in 1965 of the Metropolitan Boroughs of Southwark (which in turn was made from an amalgamation of the ancient parishes of Christ Church, St Saviour, St George the Martyr, and St Mary Newington), Bermondsey (which comprised the parishes of St Thomas, St John, Horselydown, St Mary Bermondsey and St Mary Rotherhithe) and Camberwell, which had the same boundaries of the parish of that name dedicated to St Giles. Camberwell parish was huge and also comprised of the districts of Peckham, Nunhead and Dulwich.

Today the borough is one of great contrasts: prosperity in its south; pockets of deprivation in Peckham and Walworth; ethnic diversity throughout; part of the cultural heart of London on its riverside and, in Tate Modern, its Jubilee Line stations and Peckham Library; modern buildings of international importance[1].

Policing

In February 1830 the 11th Company of the Metropolitan Police known as 'M' (Southwark) Division took over the parishes of St. Saviour, St Thomas, St Olaves, St John Horsleydown, part of the parishes of Christchurch, Blackfriars, St George-the-Martyr, St Mary Newington and St Mary Magdalene Bermondsey. There were two police Stations to cover this area, one at Guildford Street, a former Watch House, and the other at 4 (and 5) Southwark Bridge Road[2]. The latter Station had been built between 1814 and 1819 and was still in operation until 1845[3]. The parish watch-house, built in 1819, stood in the churchyard until its demolition in 1932.

Currently, policing is located at eight key locations across the London Borough of Southwark. Six Police Stations are open to the public. The Stations are Peckham, Southwark, Walworth, Camberwell, East Dulwich and Rotherhithe. The future of the last three is currently the subject of discussion within the community. These Stations are old and do not meet current Policing requirements. In addition to the six Police Stations there are additional Safer Neighbourhood Teams at the Chaplin Centre, Aylesbury Estate and at 121 Denmark Hill, London, SE5. At present the Metropolitan Police has 890 Police Officers, 156 Police staff and 100

Police Community Support Officers based in the London Borough of Southwark[4]. The Current Borough Police Commander is Chief Superintendent Wayne Chance assisted by Superintendent Richard Blanchard, Detective Superintendent Ian Smith and Superintendent Cheryl Burden.[5]

Camberwell Police Station

The old Watch House in Camberwell was used by Police and situated in Camberwell High Road near the 'Joiner's Arms' Public House[6]. It contained a small charge room with two cells leading off from it. In 1833 Camberwell Green was one of the Police Stations on 'P' Division and was under the command of Superintendent Alexander McLean. The Station was passed over from the Parish Authorities to the Metropolitan Police by Act of Parliament with the Surveyors noting that the Station was renovated in 1846[7]. The Station was one of those where Police Constables were in attendance at all times[8].

Camberwell Police Station
Camberwell Green
1833 - 1898

In April 1852 the Home Office considered the purchase of a freehold site for a Police Station and a County Court but the asking price of £4500 was thought exorbitant and so they looked elsewhere. In November 1857 an application was made to the Home Office to rent a house, owned by a Mr John Flower, next to Camberwell Police Station on a lease for 50 years for £100 per annum. Authority was given with the proviso that the proprietor constructed cells to plans approved by the Commissioner and Surveyor[9]. When the work was finished there was a reserve room, charge room, kitchen and reserve cell with accommodation for a Sergeant and two Constables[10].

In 1864 Camberwell Police Station is shown as being on 'P' Division and attached to Walworth Sub-Division (Carter Street). There were 2 Police Sergeants and 5 Constables attached to the Station[11].

With a revision of Police boundaries in 1865 'P' (Camberwell) Division consisted of the following Stations, Camberwell (sometimes known as Camberwell Green Police Station), Walworth, Peckham, Norwood, Sydenham, Lewisham, Beckenham, Bromley and Farnborough. Inspector D. Fraser was temporarily in charge as Acting Superintendent[12].

By 1879 the Camberwell Division was headed by Superintendent Thomas Butt assisted by Chief Inspector James Davis[13]. In fact Butt was still in post in 1889 although based at Peckham Police Station. By 1881 the Chief Inspector at the Station on the night of the National Census was James Perry Who was living at the Station with his son, also called James (14). One Sergeant and 28 Constables were also living in the accommodation[14]. The Division now had a total strength of 726 Officers made up of forty four Inspectors, sixty eight Sergeants and 613 Police Constables[15]. In 1889 the premises were enlarged at a cost of £579[16].

A report in 1881 described it as follows:

> "This is one of the old watch houses. The area is very cramped. It is occupied by some married people, who have all to pass through the charge room in coming and going. The accommodation was occupied by two married inspectors[17].

In 1884 the address of the Station was shown as Camberwell Green[18] and the freehold of the property was purchased in 1887[19]. During the National Census on 5th April 1891 one single Sergeant, Joseph Daniel and eighteen single Constables were residing at the Police Station. There was also one prisoner in custody – a local bricklayer/labourer[20].

In 1893 new premises were considered and the existing Police Station is quoted as being two old houses adapted for Police purposes at the corner where two roads intersect[21].

On 7th March 1894 a freehold site, 22 Church Street, Camberwell, was purchased for £4000 from Mr Humbert, the land having originally been owned by the Metropolitan Board of Works. The question arose about the Right of Way to the rear, and eventually the sum of £60 was paid in compensation

Camberwell Police Station
Church Street, Camberwell.
1898 - present day

to the Trustees of the Camberwell Green Congregation Chapel for a piece of land in Wren Road; the stipulation being that only the Police Authorities would have access to the Right of Way[22].

The new Police Station, designed by John Dixon Butler, Metropolitan Police Surveyor, was opened for business in June 1898 together with the married quarters and Section House at the Station. The lodging assessment was for one married Inspector at 5s 6d per week, one married Constable at 3s. per week and twenty four single Constables at 1s. per week each[23]. The building was described as follows:

> "The new building is a handsome edifice built of red brick and white granite. The base is of glazed brick" [24].

The picture at right shows a retirement at Camberwell of three Officers in 1912 who each received a nice carriage clock in appreciation for their long service.

Retirement Ceremony of Camberwell Officers in 1912

Apparently, the new station was opened without an imposing ceremony by Inspector Fox and his men. A few days later a dog, without a muzzle, ran into the Station through open door and claimed the honour of being the first 'run-in'. The old Station at Camberwell Green had been sold and was demolished to make way for a railway station on the proposed branch of the City and South London Electric Railway to Camberwell, Peckham and Dulwich[25].

Lt to Rt - Medals KPM, 1911 Coronation and 1935 Jubilee.

In October 1917 Police Constables Jesse Christmas and Robert Melton accompanied Police Inspector Frederick Wright into buildings that had been bombed in a Zeppelin raid in Camberwell. Ten people were killed and eighteen were trapped in the debris. The Officers cut a hole in the floor and dropped into the basement to search for survivors in spite of a fire raging above them and the risk of

231

wreckage collapsing on them. For their gallant efforts in rescuing thirteen people that night Inspector Wright was awarded the Albert Medal and Constables Christmas and Melton both received the King's Police Medal. The medals on the previous page show from, left to right, the KPM, the 1911 Coronation medal and lastly the 1935 Jubilee medal. The Albert Medal is awarded to those persons who endangered their own lives. The standard set for the award is that the chances of death are greater than the chance of survival, although some have said that the chances of survival had to be negligible[26].

In 1932 another police boundary reorganisation was made and Camberwell and Peckham Police Stations were transferred from 'P' to (L) Lambeth Division[27].

Behind the Station and just a short walk away was the Metropolitan Police Nursing Home, situated at 113 Grove Park Road, SE5. The picture at left shows Police Officers recuperating in the garden of the nursing home. The nursing home, originally called 'Inglewood', was bought in 1927 and was followed two years later by the purchase of 114 Grove Park Road for use of nursing staff.

Metropolitan Police Nursing Home

In 1933 the Metropolitan Police took over the responsibility for the licensing of drivers and conductors of trams, trolley vehicles and coaches, also cab drivers in the Metropolitan Police District and the new Metropolitan Traffic Area. This Branch was known as the Public Carriage Office. Camberwell was No.7 Passing Station but it is noted that it ceased to be one when the building (which was only a hut) was moved to Lambeth[28].

In 1934 it was proposed to reconstruct the Station elsewhere and extend the Section House to provide accommodation for 100 men; twenty years on it was still just a proposal, but it was decided that the Station was situated at a focal point and therefore it should remain where it was[29].

In 1954 the Dixon Committee proposed that Camberwell should remain a Sectional Station with a new Sub-Division of 'L' consisting of Peckham, Camberwell and East Dulwich. The question of the Section House was once more mooted and this was resolved by the purchase of a site at Clapham[30].

Another reorganisation of boundaries and Camberwell (MC) finds itself as a Sectional Station to Carter Street (MC) on 'M' Division[31].

In September 1970 Camberwell Police Station became a 24 hour Police Office[32]. In 1976 work on a £100,000 conversion of the former Section House behind Camberwell Police Station was completed[33]. In 2004 the Station had been closed three years and residents, businessmen and politicians were united in their desire to see the Station opened again. The Borough Commander, Chief Superintendent Ian Thomas, said that with the cost of staffing and arranging disabled access reaching an estimated £400,000, it would be difficult for it to be reopened. He would research this issue and submit detail to the Metropolitan Police Authority[34].

Currently Camberwell Police Station is the base for three Safer Neighbourhood Teams but the front counter is only open two days a week (Wednesdays & Fridays from 1pm – 5pm). However, this Station is one of those in the Borough currently the subject of discussion about closure[35].

Carter Street/ Walworth Police Station

In 'P' Division there was a Section House called Apollo Buildings situated in East Street, Walworth. This was a traditional brick and tile building which was rented from Mr. H. Davis on a yearly tenancy. The Section House also had a three-stall stable. This was given up in 1844.

The Receiver, John Wray, often travelled all over London on horseback looking for suitable premises in which he could house his Constables, and in May 1856 he leased a house and grounds in Carter Street, known as 'Walworth House', for a term of 26¼ years expiring in June 1882, for use as a Police Station[36]. The premises were owned by a Mr Gedge and had originally been occupied by him as his private residence. The rental was £80 per year. When the premises were taken, six cells were erected and other works carried out, including a three-stall stable/coach house[37], under the supervision of Charles Reeves, Metropolitan Police Surveyor, and involved an outlay of about £600. Accommodation was provided for 1 Inspector and 30 single Constables[38] and in March 1856 the Station was opened.

On 9th November 1860 at about 1 pm two persons called at Carter Street/Walworth Police Station. The Station Officer, Police Sergeant 18P, ascertained that the two gentlemen were from the London Chatham and Dover Railway and had called for the purpose of measuring a proposed line for the railway. They stated that the 'Station House' would have to come down. The Railway Company would require 13 perches of ground at the end of the Station Yard and the line would be open to traffic within the space of two years. In November 1861 the Receiver sold, for the sum of £300, his leasehold interest in the strip of land at the rear of the Police Station site to the Railway Company for the erection thereon of part of the viaduct to carry the railroad. A proviso in the agreement was that Police would have the use of the space under the arches[39].

In 1869 Carter Street Police Station was part of Camberwell Division of which Superintendent Edward Payne was in charge and who was based at Carter Street. The Division comprised of four Inspector Police Stations, Bromley; Clockhouse, Peckham; Gipsy Hill and Norwood. There were also five Sergeant designated Police Stations at Camberwell Green; Beckenham; Farnborough; Rushey Green, Lewisham and Sydenham[40].

In July 1869 the Secretary of State at the Home Office, on the recommendation of the Commissioner, agreed that a room at each Police Station be regarded as a Recreation Room in which smoking would be allowed. Expenditure was also agreed on the purchase of a miniature billiard table for each Division. Also games such as 'Draughts, Dominoes, Backgammon, Single-sticks, and Boxing Gloves for each principal Section House' Carter Street received the Billiard Table and other Stations on the Division just the games[41].

At an auction held on 26th June 1875 the Receiver's agent purchased the freehold of the residue of the lease of 1856 for £3,710[42].

In 1879 Carter Street was under the command of Superintendent Thomas Butt on 'P' (Camberwell) Division. The following Stations on that Division at this time were; Carter Street, Peckham, Gipsy Hill, Bromley, Sydenham, Camberwell Green, Rodney Road, Penge, Beckenham, Lewisham, Locksbottom, Lower Norwood and Dulwich. Superintendent Butt, Warrant No. 38649,

Police Superintendent Thomas Butt

joined the Police on 16 January 1860 and retired in 1892 after 32 years' service[43]

In 1881 a major report was prepared on the condition of Metropolitan Police Stations. Each station visited was in need of work to improve the sanitary conditions in which the policemen were working. Carter Street was described as:

> 'a fine open site. The buildings consist of an old residence with cells (5) &c, added to it. The basement is low and unhealthy. The bedrooms seem crowded, and the occupation not arranged for the comfort of the men' [44]

The accommodation was occupied by one single Sergeant and twenty nine single Constables. On the night of the 1881 census there were six prisoners detained at the Station – two unemployed females and four males. Two of those were unemployed; one was a bricklayer and the other a bookmaker[45]. The accommodation at the Station was unsatisfactory and major refurbishment took place but it was obvious that a new Station would have to be built.[46] It is interesting to note that the report referred to the Station as 'Walworth, Carter Street', as did the Post Office Directory of 1879.

In 1884 the address of the Station was recorded as 292 Walworth Road, SE.17[47] and was located on 'P' Division.

In 1886 Carter Street Police Station was transferred to 'L' Division. In 1891 Superintendent J. Brannan was in charge of 'L' Division together with six Police Inspectors; A. Waddell, J. Porter, G. Dunleavy, C, Branwhite, H. Powell and W. N. Race[48]. The telegraphic code or code

Carter Street Police Station
292 Walworth Road SE17
1910- 1993

signals for Carter Street was Charlie Whiskey (CW)[49].

In the early 1900's it was decided to re-build the Station to suit the growing requirements of the district and there was much discussion with the Home Office before they would approve the cost of a new Police Station at Carter Street. The Home Office was concerned about the increase in cost of new Police Stations. The Metropolitan Police Surveyor, John Dixon Butler, was required to make a detailed report tabulating the cost of materials necessary to build the Station, together with the costs, per cubic feet, of the thirteen Police Stations built between 1882 and 1903[50]. Eventually a new Police Station, designed by Butler, was built and opened in June 1910. Lodging assessment for Carter Street Police Station was established as 9s. 6d. per week for married quarters and 1s. per week each for 50 unmarried men.

Inspector Francis Odell and Colleagues
at Carter Street Police Station

James Ford became the Sub-Divisional Inspector in 1899 until 1903 when he was succeeded by Frederick Spencer, 1904; Francis Rolf, 1905-7; John Collins, 1908-11; Frederick Wright, 1911; and Francis Odell (77242), 1914-19. Odell is shown in the picture and was famous since he was the recipient of the RHS bronze award for saving life, a rare event for an Inspector. He is shown, together with his medals on both sides of his chest, seated second from the left together with his three Inspectors and five Sergeants.

236

In 1921, during an internal revision of Police Station boundaries the Division was transferred from Lambeth Division (L) to Southwark Division (M)[51]. Superintendent Henry M. Mann was in charge of Southwark Division which at the time consisted of the following Stations, Carter Street, Deptford, Grange Road, Rodney Road, Rotherhithe and Tower Bridge[52].

Nine years later, in 1932, Carter Street returned to Lambeth Division (L). This was when Kennington Lane (L) and Rodney Road (M) Police Stations were closed down[53].

A communication from the London County Council, dated 13th March 1950, was received at the Station informing the Metropolitan Police that as from 1 July that the portion of Carter Street in which the Police Station is situated would be renamed Carter Place. The Commissioner was approached to see if the Station name could be changed from Carter Street to Walworth Police Station but he felt that there should be no change[54].

The front of Carter Street Police Station shows a well-kept garden. The garden was tended by a group of Police Officers in their spare time.

HRH Queen Mother speaking to Constable Musto 1956

There was a Police Garden competition instituted that prompted a fierce rivalry amongst Police Officers, especially senior Officers, who would brag about their Divisional attainments in all sorts of sports etc. In 1956 Carter Street was visited by the HRH Queen Mother as part of her duties as patron for the London Gardens Society. The competition winner would receive the ultimate prize - the Lady Byng Trophy for the best Police Station garden. Police Constable Musto had tended the garden with a small group of other Police volunteers for some time and had told the HRH Queen Mother that he had done so for 31 years.

She added that;

> 'she was surprised to see such a nice garden in such a busy area; it's a little paradise'[55].

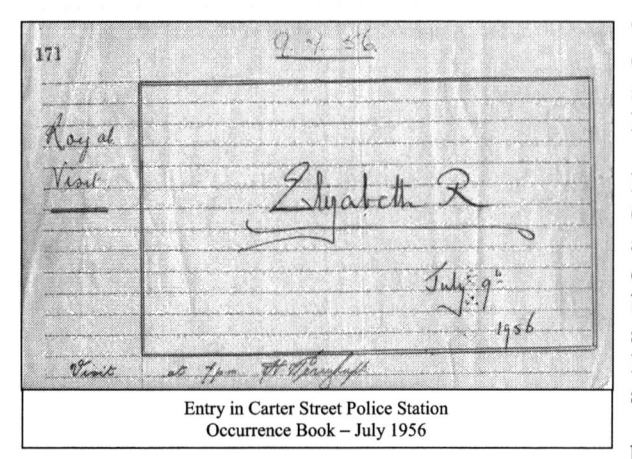

Entry in Carter Street Police Station Occurrence Book – July 1956

The HRH Queen Mother signed the Police Station's Occurrence Book in red ink (see copy left), a very rare event indeed, but this signature would lead, as we shall see, to an investigation because by the next day someone had torn the page from the book. This action caused a great deal of concern and consternation since this amounted to theft of Police property by an insider - a Police Officer or member of the civil staff. The local Complaints Department carried out a thorough investigation, although after many months of interviewing they got nowhere. The page could not be found and only re-surfaced in the 1980s along with other correspondence.

Another change of Police boundaries occurred in 1965 and Carter Street (MS) was designated a Sub-Divisional Station of (M) Division with Camberwell (MC) as its Sectional Station both situated on the new London Borough of Southwark[56].

By the 1990s the old Carter Street Police Station had become too small for the for Police purposes. The old buildings did not adapt well to the modern technology being used in the Police service and the increase of Police personnel meant that there was an urgent need to build a modern, and much larger, Police Station.

HRH Queen Mother, Commissioner Sir John Nott-Bower, Constable Musto

The author of many books on the

238

humorous side of Policing, the late Harry Cole, served as a Police Constable for 30 years at the old Carter Street Police Station. He said,

> "It always had a reputation as a violent station, which was nonsense really. It was a very happy station to work at" [57]

In November 1993 the new Police Station that replaced Carter Street was opened at 12 – 28 Manor Place, Walworth, SE17 3RL,[58] and was named Walworth Police Station. The £4.3 million new Station, took three years of planning and two years to build. The new red brick building is twice the size of the old Station with 4,200 square metres of floor space compared with 1,600 square metres. Before the new Walworth Police Station was built, the land had been occupied by a liquor warehouse which, had to be demolished to make way for the new Station[59]. An archaeological dig was made on the site before the go-head was given for development in an effort to trace historical artefacts from the Manor House which was originally situated near to the site, however nothing was found.

Walworth Police Station is one of the Police buildings in the Borough which is open 24 hours each day. It is the base also for four Safer Neighbourhood Teams[60].

Grange/Dunton Road Police Station (Bermondsey)

Bermondsey Parish Church Watch House at the junction of Abbey Street and Bermondsey Street was built in 1820. By 1850 the property was recorded as being owned by Mr J Greenwood of Arthur Street West, City, EC. The rental was £20 per annum for a period of 70 years[61]. Now a meeting place for local scouts[62].

1881 Report states that,

> "This station is not yet occupied, except by one married constable. It consists of two ordinary dwelling houses which it is proposed to adapt for police purposes. There appears to be vacant ground in rear of the houses, which it might be well to acquire as the freehold of the houses has been bought, and the yard space may be found too small" [63]

Bermondsey's second Police Station opened in October 1883 and although known as the Grange Road Sub-Division it was actually situated at 67- 69 Upper Grange Road (now Dunton Road).

The building had been adapted under the supervision of John Butler, Metropolitan Police Surveyor. The total cost was £4560 of which the

Bermondsey (Grange Road) Police Station
67 – 69 Upper Grange Road, Bermondsey.
1883 - 1940

freehold was £2200[64]. The new Station had 4 Inspectors, 6 Sergeants and 66 Constables. The 'L' Division Special Constable (shown below) is dressed in a 5 button tunic, traditional flat cap with water proof cover and duty armlet. The photograph was taken in about 1920.

In 1935 the Police Station at 67, Upper Grange Road, was renamed Dunton Road Police Station.

Dunton Road Police Station received a direct hit from a bomb during the Blitz, injuring seven people, and closed on 19th September 1940. All operations were transferred to Tower Bridge Police Station[65].

'L' Division Special Constable

North Dulwich, East Dulwich and West Dulwich Police Stations

North Dulwich

In the mid - 1700s a Watch House stood close to the junction of Calton Avenue and Dulwich Village and attached to it was a lock-up. During building works in the 1920s an inscribed stone dated 1760 was found bearing the following description,

> 'It is the sport of a fool to do mischief
> To thine own wickedness, shall correct thee'[66]

With the increase in crime local residents formed the 'Dulwich Patrol' to be armed with cutlasses and pistols and by 1812 had introduced horse patrols. Wooden Watch Boxes were set up near the 'Fox on the hill' and near Dulwich College[67].

The Police Station had been described previously in 1854 as a

> 'small brick message at the end of Boxall Row erected c.1810 by Charles Druce for the purposes of the Mounted Police on Patrol' [68]

The Station and Section House was rented by the Metropolitan Police in north Dulwich, on 'P' Division, and owned by Mr William Sawyer of Dulwich. This was a traditional brick and slate house which was rented from 29th September 1864 until 22nd September 1889 for an annual rent of £42, The Receiver was required to pay all other taxes[69].

In February 1868 a public meeting was held in Dulwich College to discuss the issue of the lack of policing in Dulwich. As a result North Dulwich Police Station was opened in March 1872 at 'Wellington House', again owned by William Sawyer, in Red Post Hill and almost next door to the North Dulwich Railway Station which had opened in 1866 on the London Brighton Railway.

A Metropolitan Police Report in 1881 described North Dulwich Police Station as,

> "A small cottage to which considerable additions have made. The lease expires in eight years. More space is required".

The building was occupied by one married Inspector and one married Constable[70].

East Dulwich

In the 1880s North Dulwich Police Station needed replacing as it had become too small for the number of Police Officers now needed to police the increasing population. In June 1881 Mrs Taite of 'Rose Bank', Crystal Palace Road, at the corner of Upland Road, East Dulwich, offered her house for use as a Police Station[71]. The premises were taken on an 85 year lease from 1883. The cost of adapting the property, under the supervision of John Butler, Metropolitan Police Surveyor, was £1800[72].

East Dulwich Police Station.
97 Crystal Palace Road.
1884 - 1977

The new Station at 97 Crystal Palace Road was ready for use in May 1884. At the same time Police Inspectors Pride and Pearn were transferred from North Dulwich to East Dulwich Police Station[73]. The freehold for the building was later purchased for £1550 plus costs in August 1899[74].

On the night of the National Census in 1891 a Police Inspector John Flanagan and his wife May and five of their children were recorded as living at the Police Station[75]. Flanagan had been a 'P' Division Inspector since 1885, having been promoted from Station Sergeant at the time when greater numbers of Inspectors were needed.

As early as 1959 it was realised that a new larger Police Station was needed. Accommodation was so cramped that in 1972 a two-storey prefabricated administrative building had to be crane-lifted into the yard behind the Station to give room for Constables to write their reports and to provide a separate interview room[76].

The site at 173/183 Lordship Lane, and 77/85 Whatley Road, East Dulwich, was purchased for the accumulative sum of £40,000 between the years 1962 and 1963[77]. It was still some time before the new Station was built.

In 1965 with the formation of the London Borough of Southwark, East Dulwich and West Dulwich became Section Stations to Peckham Division[78].

Work on the new East Dulwich Police Station eventually started in 1975[79] and was finally opened in September 1977. It was built with stables for twelve horses[80]. The new Station also served as the Area Four Headquarters (London at that time was divided into four areas each having a Deputy Assistant Commissioner in overall charge).

East Dulwich Police Station
Lordship Lane.
1977 – present day

Currently the Station is the base for three Safer Neighbourhood Teams and the Station is open daily between 6.0am and 10pm.

West Dulwich

The London Chatham & Dover Railway Company was extending the railway through Dulwich and acquired from the Governors of Alleyns College of Gods Gift, Dulwich, land which included that now known as 134 Thurlow Park Road. After building the Railway the land alongside West Dulwich Railway Station, which opened in 1863 (originally Lower Knights Hill Station) appears to have been surplus to requirements. In 1868 it was offered back to the Governors of Alleyns College who declined to accept it.

It was eventually sold by the Railway Company in July 1870 to Arthur Ashwell of Beresford Street, Camberwell, for £920. The house 'Fairfield' was built on the site. The buildings and grounds, which included a vinery, hot house, stable and a shop, which was let at 7 shillings a week, were sold by Ashwell to the Receiver of the Metropolitan Police in December 1885 for the sum of £2,400. To the east of the property, between the land bought by the Receiver and the Railway, was a public footpath to Crystal Palace.

Just over a year later the additional building work, under the supervision of John Butler, the Metropolitan Police Surveyor, was completed and the building opened as a Police Station. There were four floors. The basement contained the Stores, Parade room and WCs. The ground floor contained the public entrance, charge room, writing lobby, Inspector's Office, two cells, CID Office and Recreation Room. The two upper floors became Police accommodation later in 1924[81].

West Dulwich Police Station
134 Thurlow Park Road,
1887 - 1978

The large parcel of land beyond the Police Station was laid out into lawns and gardens. It also contained a water fountain[82].

In 1887 West Dulwich Police Station was opened[83]. These premises had been adapted as a Police Station at a total cost of £3067[84]; the bulk of the cost, £2400, was for the purchase of the freehold. The address was shown as 134 Thurlow Park Road, West Dulwich, next to West Dulwich Railway Station.

The National Census on 5th April 1891 shows thirteen Constable in residence that night[85].

In 1969 there was public disquiet over the proposed partial closure of West Dulwich Station. Local Police Senior Officers wanted the whole of Dulwich to be a composite Police Area when it introduced a new unit beat policing system[86]. When West Dulwich was closed telephone calls would be diverted to East Dulwich. The Station became a Police Office in September 1969[87].

In 1974 it was decided that the Police Station should be closed. Part of the building was then leased to the Metropolitan Police Trading Service (MPTS) who had vacated their premises at 222/224 Borough High Street,

SE. In September 1976 the large garden at the rear of the site was sold by the Receiver to the London Borough of Southwark for £2,250[88].

The Station was eventually closed on 28th April 1978[89]. In March 1980 the remaining land and old Police Station were sold to the MPTS for £18,900[90]. The premises are now known as 'Stephen Barrett House' after a Police Sergeant/ Federation member/Board member of the MPTS who died. Part of the property is rented to the British Transport Police Federation.

Peckham Police Station

Prior to the arrival of the Metropolitan Police the Watchmen worked from a Watch House at the corner of High Street and Hill Street[91].

Peckham Police Station
177 High Street, Peckham
1847 - 1893

In the year 1847 a property known as "The Clock House", situated at 177 High Street, Peckham was leased from a Mr Henry Thomas Perkins to be used for Police purposes[92]. The building had previously been occupied by the wealthy Dalton family, was formerly part of their fine mansion and was subsequently used a nunnery[93]. The lease ran from Michaelmas of that year to Michaelmas 1903 and the rental was £103.10.0d per annum. A year later, in 1848, the old Peckham Watch House was surrendered to the Parochial Authorities, as being no longer required[94].

In 1864 Peckham Police Station was on 'P' (Camberwell) Division. The Station strength was two Inspectors, seven Sergeants, sixty nine Constables and three horses. One horse was shared by the two Inspectors and another horse was shared by the two Sergeants when on duty; alternatively at either of the two Stations of Peckham or Brixton[95].

In 1880 the address of the Station was shown as 'The Clock House', High Street, Peckham[96]. In 1881 a report was made on the condition of all the Police Stations. Peckham was described as:

> "a fine property with large area. The principal building is an old Manor House, occupied as quarters for single men and one married man. The arrangement is inconvenient. There is another block, containing the administration and some sleeping rooms, not well arranged" [97]

During the 1880s it was decided to rebuild Peckham Police Station as the present one was considered unsuitable for the district which had grown up around it. With this in mind, the owner of the property, Mr Perkins, was approached to consider selling his freehold interest to the Receiver. He was not interested so the Receiver, using his powers under the Metropolitan Police Act 1886, was given approval by the Home Office on 11th September 1889 to acquire compulsorily the freehold of the Peckham Police premises. In May 1890 at the High Court of Justice, Mr Lumley Smith, QC, official referee, heard the case Perkins v The Receiver of Police to assess the amount of compensation to be paid to Mr Perkins for the compulsory purchase of the buildings and land at Peckham which had been rented for Police purposes. The sum award was £4000 and the purchase of the freehold was completed on 11th September 1890[98].

The National Census in 1891 recorded that there were nineteen single Officers living at the Police Station; Police Sergeant Joseph Daniel and eighteen Police Constables[99].

The new Station, designed by John Butler, Metropolitan Police Surveyor, was opened in November 1893[100] and cost £8,788 to build[101]. The new building was built on the same site as the old one at the corner of Peckham High Street and Meeting House Lane. Prior to the building of the new Station the Vestry indicated that they were unhappy that the new Police Station was not only replacing the old Station but that the boundary was too far out at the corner of the road. They had gained a road widening at this junction and the new Police Station, in spite of having a single storey front, was coming out over the building line. The Vestry was told that the Council were unable to alter the plans[102].

An interesting point to note is that on 3rd January, 1898, the parish of St. Giles, Camberwell granted permission for the display of a notice board outside the Police Station upon the nominal payment of 1s. 0d. per annum[103].

Charles Booth's *Inquiry into the Life and Labour of the People in London*, undertaken between 1886 and 1903, was one of several surveys of working class life carried out in the 19th century. Booth and his researchers walked with Police Officers in various parts of North and South London and in October 1899 records show that Police Constable Dolby of Peckham Police Station conducted the researchers around his beat. Dolby had been in the Police Force for about eight years and stationed at Peckham in all that time. He had been 'marked out' for promotion and was hoping to be promoted to Sergeant within the year. He was described as 'a good fellow, capable and honest'. He was one of the few 'cockneys' in the force having born in Fore Street, City[104].

In 1932 there was a reorganisation of Police boundaries and Peckham was transferred from 'P' Division to 'L'", or Lambeth, Division[105]. By 1939 the Division was under the command of Superintendent M. Purbrick[106].

With a view to the future and possible erection of another new Station for Peckham the derelict properties of 180 – 188 Meeting House Lane, which adjoined the Police Station site, were purchased on 1st September 1938 from a Miss Clayton for the sum of £1700 freehold. This project never got off the ground and in 1976 it was reported that it was no longer in the Building Programme.

Peckham Police Station
High Street, Peckham
1893 – present day

More boundary changes in 1964 moved Peckham (MM) as a Sub-Divisional Station on 'M' Division with East Dulwich (ME) and West Dulwich (MW) as its Sectional Stations, all situated in the new London Borough of Southwark[107].

In 1973 it was said that the Police Station would be demolished and a new one built at the cost of £500,000[108]. In 1985 Peckham Police Station was closed for major building work. Staff were relocated to Camberwell Police Station until March 1988

HRH Princess Alexandra reopened Peckham Station after it had been extended[109].

Peckham Police Station is open 24/7 and is the base for four Safer Neighbourhood Teams[110].

Rodney Road Police Station

A Brick and slate house was rented from Mr Golden, of Boyce House Whetstone as a Police Station and Section House at Lockfields, Walworth on 'P' Division. It had a small garden, a charge room and 3 cells for prisoners. It was painted in 1846, 1852, 1861, 1866, and 1869 at a total cost of £128. Its constant use meant that it became dilapidated and in need of repairs inside to the woodwork, cells, and drains into the common sewer. The surveyors reported that there was plenty of water leaking into the kitchen and the 3 cells. The cost of insurance was set at £25 per year[111].

A memorandum from the Commissioner dated August 1871 was enquiring about Lockfields, one of the chief Stations of 'P' Division. A further memo from the Commissioner in January 1872 stated that he proposed to have a Police Station at Lockfields Walworth. In June 1872 premises at Park House, Walworth, were leased from Mr Thomas H Golden at £105 per annum[112]. In May 1873 the building was ready for public business and was known as Rodney Road Police Station 'P' Division[113]. The Station strength on opening was two Station Sergeants and five Constables[114].

Rodney Road Police Station
1, Flint Street, Walworth
1873 - 1932

In August 1880 a notice was received from the Clerk to the Vestry, Vestry Hall, Walworth Road, that the address of the Police Station would be 1 Flint Street[115].

The Report of the Condition of Police Stations indicated that Rodney Road Police Station consisted of an administrative block that was currently occupied by one Inspector and four Constables and had three cells[116].

It was quite separate from another house occupied by married families in which the distribution of the accommodation among the various families was bad. Compulsory purchase powers relating to the premises were obtained in February 1889. The Station was rebuilt in 1892 at a cost £7648, of which the freehold was £2700[117]. The lowest tender by Garlick and Horton was accepted[118].

Inspector Philip McCarthy was a notable Officer whose service in the Police was merited by an article in the Police Review and Parade Gossip. He retired from Rodney Road in 1908 having been there for 6 years and during his service he specialised in cruelty cases against children and animals. He also concentrated on vagrancy patrols to ensure that only valid cases merited assistance and the professional vagrant was moved on. He left to become an Inspector for the Royal Society for the Prevention of Cruelty to Children[119].

By 1921 Rodney Road Police Station was on 'L' Division but was transferred to 'M' (Southwark) Division[120] where it remained until it was closed in January 1932[121].

In December 1933 consideration was given to selling the property. It was described as a substantial building occupying a corner site in a very poor neighbourhood. When in use there had been a Section House, which formed part of the Station, for 19 men, but it had not been occupied since the Station closed and it was suggested that the building be sold[122].

In 1991 it was noted that the old Police Station was now part of the English Martyrs Roman Catholic Infants School[123].

Rotherhithe Police Station

In the early 1800s there were two Watch Houses covering the Rotherhithe area; one had been built in Trinity Street (now Rotherhithe Street) and the other in Church Street (now St. Marychurch Street)[124]. The original Watch House was in Church Passage but it was moved to the entrance of the new burial ground on the opposite side of Church Street[125]. This was to keep watch over the new graves and prevent body snatchers from removing bodies after burial and selling them to hospitals for medical research. As early as 1839 Rotherhithe Parish became part of 'M' (Southwark) Division.

On 1 March 1836 the Home Office gave authority for taking over premises at Paradise Street, Rotherhithe, for Police purposes from a John Gaitskell at a rent of £75 per annum for 21 years. The building dates back to 1814 and the solid mahogany double doors had brass handles in the shape of a lion's head modelled, it is said, on those of Bermondsey Abbey[126]. The Watch House was closed when the new building was taken over by Police and further authority was given to renew the lease on 14 February 1857 for 50 years at £100 per annum. The building was insured for £2000[127].

Old Watch House, St Marychurch, Street.

In 1864 Rotherhithe Police Station was shown on 'M' Division together with Stones End (Southwark) and Bermondsey Police Stations. The total number of Officers at Rotherhithe was 117[128]. The following year Rotherhithe is shown on 'R' (Greenwich) Division[129].

The 1881 Report states that it was:

> " An old house with evidences of having been a first-class residence. The bedrooms are lofty, but the basement, in which is the mess, is very bad indeed, in a sanitary point of view. The outbuildings, including the cells, are dilapidated and unsatisfactory and require reconstruction"

The accommodation at that stage was occupied by one single Sergeant and thirty nine single Constables[130].

Rotherhithe Police Station. Paradise Street. 1836 - 1965

On an evening in 1881 the original two lion-head brass door knockers were removed, without authority, from the front doors of the Police Station. An investigation followed but the door furniture had disappeared. In 1952, nearly seventy years later, Police Constable Hynds was called to a house not far from the old Police Station where an elderly lady showed the Officer two lion head brass knockers. They had been carefully wrapped in tissue paper and had been found under the floorboards of the house. Apparently her father had removed the knockers from the Police Station door as a 'dare' whilst drinking with others in a local public house and had been too scared to return them. On his death bed he told his daughter what had happened and told her where he had hidden them[131]

Home Office authority was granted to surrender the old lease of the property on 11th April 1882 and take out a new one for a period of 99 years at a rental of £110 per annum when renovations were completed[132]. Rotherhithe moved back to 'M' Division in 1883 and joined the three other Sub-Divisions of Southwark, Bermondsey and the new Sub-Division of Grange Road. By then the number of Police Officers had reduced to 73[133]. The address of the Station was shown as 22 Paradise Street, Rotherhithe[134]. In 1905 the lodging assessment for each of the thirty one single Officers living at Rotherhithe was one shilling a week[135].

In March 1907 Police Constable Conrad Scott was given the Royal Humane Society Award for rescuing a woman who had been thrown into the Surrey Canal by her boyfriend[136]. This was one of the awards made by the Society to those persons who, at personal risk, save, or endeavour to save, life from drowning.

Rotherhithe Police Station
99, Lower Road.
1965 – present day

In 1924 the freehold of 99 Lower Road, was purchased for £5000 from the Port of London Authority. The property was a gentleman's residence called Landale Lodge, comprising of a very large house and grounds, and was leased to Mr George Blake. A local doctor, Alfred Salter, wanted the site to build a sanatorium for curing Tuberculosis (TB) that was rife in the area[137] but the Home Office wanted it for Police purposes. Evidence was placed before the Right Honourable Edward Shortt and the award was in favour of the Police[138]. The building was used for a time as living quarters for Police Officers, but was eventually demolished and flats erected. These were completed in 1953, are situated at the rear of the new Station, and are called 'Landale House'[139].

In 1965 Rotherhithe Police Station is shown as a sectional station to Tower Bridge Police Station[140].

A new Sectional Police station at Rotherhithe was opened at 99 Lower Road, SE16 in September 1965 and the old station at 23 Paradise Street was closed[141]. The old building was extensively refurbished by Dormer Builders Ltd., of Manor Mount, Forest Hill, SE, after buying the freehold, to provide 6000 sq. ft. of commercial office accommodation. The three storey building is a grade listed retained its railings and wrought iron archway from which use to hang the blue lamp[142].

In 1980 Robert Horne Computer Services paid almost £250,000 for the restored Victorian office building[143]. The Police Station is currently open (2010) from 7am until 9.30pm and is the base for five of the Safer Neighbourhood Teams. However, the future of the station is currently under review[144].

Southwark/Stones End Police Station

In February 1830 the 11th Company of the Metropolitan Police known as 'M' (Southwark) Division took over the policing of this area. There were two Police Stations, one at Guildford Street, a former Watch House, and the other at 4 & 5, Southwark Bridge Road (which had been built between 1814 and 1819)[145]. 'M' or Southwark Division consisted of one Superintendent, 4 Inspectors, 16 Sergeants and 163 Police Constables[146]. As a result of taking over the old system of policing the Metropolitan Police found that they had some 50 surplus Watch Boxes remaining in the area. These were later auctioned in six lots in 1830[147].

In 1832 a cholera epidemic killed two 'M' Division officers out of a total of thirteen metropolitan Police Officers who died that year; eleven of them dying between 20th July and 18th September 1832[148]. The return of a further epidemic in 1849 killed 10 Police Constables and one Sergeant[149]. A total of 27 Metropolitan Police Officers died, 26 of them between 5th July and September 1849[150].

The first purpose built Police Station for the Southwark area was designed by the newly appointed Metropolitan Police Surveyor, Charles Reeves, and erected in 1844 in Montague Street, Stones End at a cost of £4,435. The name of Stones End was chosen because it marked the end of the paved footway from the City. Montague Street became the name of the Station in 1856. Montague Street still exists but under another name, Stones End Street[151]. This new Police Station replaced the Southwark Bridge Road Station.

In 1840 Superintendent William Murray was shown in charge of 'M' Division. Murray was one of the first Police Superintendents appointed at the start of the Metropolitan Police in 1829[152]. He remained in charge until 1845.

Southwark Police Station was called Stones End and was the Divisional Station of 'M' (Southwark) Division. In 1849 the command of the Division was now in the hands of Superintendent Samuel Evans. There was one other Station on the Division at Paradise Street, Rotherhithe, near Mill Pond Bridge. There were four Inspectors, John Yates; George Hornsby; Philip Froud and John Richard Cowlin. There were fourteen Sergeants and one hundred and forty three Constables stationed there[153]. There was also one horse which was ridden by the Superintendent[154].

In December 1867 it was decided to look for a larger site for a new Police Station at Stones End and in January 1868 premises in Blackman Street, Borough, was obtained. The landlord was Alfred Cox of Somerset and the lease from 1868 for 90 years at £500 per annum[155]. This is the site of today's Station. It was estimated that the cost of the new building would be in the region of £10,000[156] and during the building of the new Station Superintendent Joseph Dunlop was in charge of the Division[157].

It was in 1889 that the County of London (L.C.C.) was created and 'M' Division Police Stations at Blackman Street (later renamed Borough High Street), Borough (new Station being built), Bermondsey Street, Rotherhithe and Grange Road, ceased to be within the County of Surrey[158].

The new Police Station was built to the design of Frederick Caiger, Metropolitan Police Surveyor, and Southwark Station was taken into use in July 1870[159]. The address of the Station in 1880 was shown as 50 Blackman Street, Borough.

Southwark Police Station
Blackman Street.
1870 - 1940

The 1881 Report states that:

"This establishment consists of two blocks; one is for married people only and is well designed. In the other there are married and single men's quarters kept separate, but not sufficiently distinct from the administrative portion. The bedrooms are not well planned. The water closets and urinals are in an underground cavity and deficient in light and air. The site lies low and the basement has been flooded; but steps have been taken to remedy this. More cells are required."

There were seven cells at the Station and during the 12 month period between October 1879 and October 1880 there was a total of 397 prisoners in excess of the number of cells[160]. To deal this problem 5 new cells were added a short time later at a cost of £951.00[161].

The Police strength in 1883 showed an increase as there were now eight Inspectors, 23 Sergeants and 187 Constables; Superintendent Harnett was in charge of the Division. This included not only Southwark but also Bermondsey, Grange Road and Rotherhithe[162]. In 1896 Grange Road and Southwark Sub-Divisions were amalgamated into one Sub-Division called Southwark[163].

In 1889 when the London County Council was formed the following 'M' (Southwark) Police Stations ceased to be in the County of Surrey: Bermondsey Street (replaced by Tower Bridge in 1904); Blackman Street, Borough; Paradise Street, Rotherhithe; and Upper Grange Road, Bermondsey[164].

Sub-Divisional Inspector May

The picture above is of Sub-Divisional Inspector May who took over the Borough Sub-Division, which included Upper Grange Road, Bermondsey Police Station, in 1911.

At Southwark Police Station in June 1893 a presentation took place to honour a retiring Police Officer. This was a normal occurrence at Police Stations throughout the country, particularly when the Officer had completed at least his 25 years-service. On this occasion ex-Inspector Henry Bealing, who retired on pension after 25 years-service, was presented with a handsome marble clock, and suitably engraved, by Superintendent Neylan on behalf of the Officers and men of the Division. Many officers and men were present including Chief Inspector Darling and Inspectors Robinson and Cleave[165].

To mark the occasion of the coronation of the King in 1911 the Police

Southwark Police Station 1911

Station was dressed up with flowers, bunting and floral decorations. Below shows the effort that a number of constables and their families put into dressing the outside of the station.

Charles Booth's Social History Project records that in March 1900 they visited Southwark Police Station in Borough High Street and interviewed Superintendent H. Wyborn who was described as a:

> ` strong, tall, rather portly man, between 50 and 60: vigorous with a short reddish beard turning grey. He is the only police superintendent who has Mr Booth's map (1887-9) hung up framed in his office'[166].

The fact that the map, which described the social conditions in London, was on display was of credit to Wyborn.

The picture on the left shows Southwark Station's Annual outing, circa 1910. When travelling outside the Metropolitan Police area the Officers had to be appropriately dressed and are wearing suits, ties, straw hats and even flowers in their lapels. Fifth from the left is Sub-Divisional Inspector Fredrick May.

Southwark Police Outing c1910

Notice that they are using a covered, open-sided charabanc, which was probably hired locally at very reasonable rates; these vehicles were open to the elements and very cold. This outing was only for the men; the married women stayed at home to look after the children. The two drivers, in white coats, are shown on the left.

Senior Officers encouraged the playing of sports to keep their Police Officers fit for duty, but sport was an ulterior motive for competition and

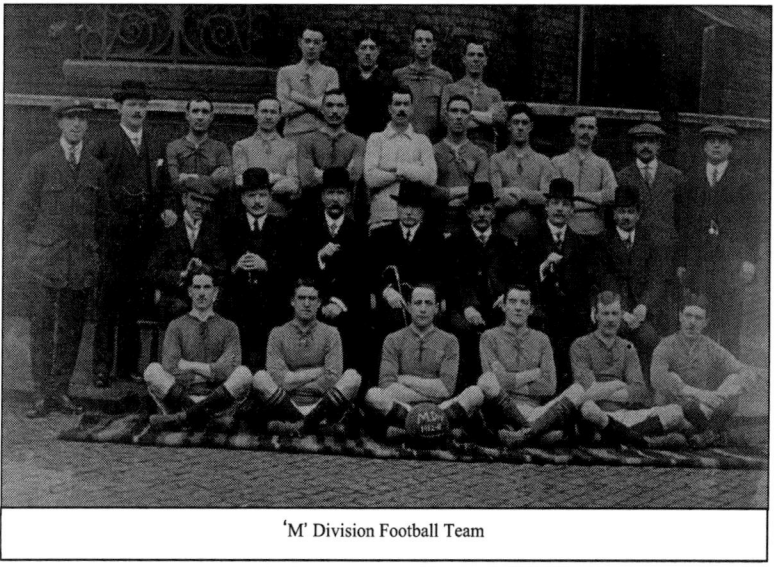

'M' Division Football Team

being the best. Right, 'M' Division won the Metropolitan Police Divisional Football Competition for 1912 -1913.

Old Court Building
Borough High Street

This was a prestigious trophy to win as the senior Officers could boast about their Divisional achievements to their compatriots. To mark the occasion the senior Officers would get together as seen above. The Superintendent, Donald Waters, is shown behind the player with the ball, whilst to his left is Sub-Divisional Inspector May. Waters had become the Divisional Superintendent in 1900, taking over from Superintendent Walter T. Wren who retired.

The Police had needed more space and had moved into the Old Court Building situated at 298 Borough High Street. In fact the premises were entirely used for Police purposes and had been converted to take the family of the Superintendent, the Divisional Offices, Stores and the Gymnasium[167].

On 21 July 1920 with an eye to future expansion of the Southwark Police Station site the freehold of the building at 323 Borough High Street plus those of the adjoining properties, Nos. 319 and 321, were purchased for the sum of £15,000[168].

'M' Division Sports Day

There were sports events which were held annually usually at the Police Sports Grounds. The picture above was taken at the 'M' Division Sports day and their particularly successful Tug of War team is shown in action.

In 1928 Superintendent William A. Ewart was in charge of 'M' Division[169] but by 1930 Superintendent Henry Mann had taken over. The Police Stations of the Division were Southwark, Carter Street, Deptford, Grange Road, Rodney Road, Rotherhithe and Tower Bridge Stations[170].

In 1938 plans were drawn up for a new Divisional Headquarters and Sub-Divisional Police Station for Southwark to be erected on the site of the existing building. In October 1938 Southwark Police Station was closed for re building and all business transferred to a temporary Station at 298 Borough High Street, SE1[171]. Some property was moved to other temporary premises in Montague Place opposite the old Police Station[172]. The new Station opened in September 1940 although the Divisional Headquarters temporarily remained in the old building[173].

Southwark Police Station
323 Borough High Street, Southwark.
1940 – present day

On 18th February 1957 the Borough of Southwark wrote to the Receiver requesting permission to erect an historical sign – a bronze plaque on the wall of Southwark Police Station facing Borough High Street. The wording to read:-

" Here was "Stones End" where "Town Street" met the old Turnpike Road. One of the parliamentary forts, erected to defend London during the Civil War, stood here".

Permission was readily granted and the sign was affixed to the wall of the Police Station in July 1958[174].

In 1974 the stables at Southwark Police Station were closed when new stabling accommodation for the Mounted Branch was opened at 'The Warren', the Police Sports' Club at Hayes, Kent[175]. Re-opening of the Station took place in October 1983[176].

Currently the Senior Management Team operate from Southwark Police Station which is open 24/7. Four Safer Neighbourhood Teams are also based there[177].

Tower Bridge Police Station

On 2 May 1898 the Home Office authorised the Receiver to acquire a site in Bermondsey for the erection of a new Police Station for that locality[178].

In March 1900 a freehold site was purchased for the sum of £10,000 from the Corporation of the City of London for a new Police Station. This was

Tower Bridge Police Station and Court,
Tooley Street
1904 – 1999

known as the Tooley Street and Queen Elizabeth Street site. A month later in April 1900 the Home Office sanctioned a proposal that a new Police Court for the Southwark District be erected in lieu of the existing Court. A parcel of land next to the Police Station site was purchased freehold on 30 September 1901 for £8,161[179].

Tenders were put out to various firms for the construction of a combined Police Station and Court at Bermondsey. The tender submitted by Messrs Grover and Sons for providing the foundations for the proposed buildings for the cost of £3874 was accepted. The main contract was awarded to Messrs John Mowlem & Co., of Grosvenor Wharf, Millbank, Westminster, SW, whose tender for the contract was £39,446[180]. The Police Architect/Surveyor, John Dixon Butler, was responsible for the design of the buildings.

Described by Pevsner as:

> "quite spectacular of its date, with a large broken pediment and an outward-curving balcony, and a doorway with a curved hood on elongated brackets". [181].

The new Police Station at 209 Tooley Street, Tower Bridge, shown on left of picture on the previous page, opened in December 1904[182]. In 1905 William Hopkins was appointed the first Sub-Divisional Inspector for Tower Bridge on 'M' (Southwark) Division. He remained there until 1910 when he was promoted to Chief Inspector on 'J' or Hackney Division[183]. Henry Nichols took over from Hopkins and remained until 1917.

The Police purchased the freehold to the Court in 1925[184]. On the creation of the London Borough of Southwark in 1965 Tower Bridge Police Station (MT) remained a Sub-Divisional Station with Rotherhithe as its Section Station[185]. During another revision of Police boundaries in 1980 Tower Bridge Division was amalgamated with Southwark Division[186].

The Station was reduced to Station Officer status in 1983[187]. Tower Bridge Police Station was closed in 1999. Tower Bridge Magistrates Court and the former police station building are currently Grade III listed. The Court could close in the light of recent (2010) proposals published by Government[188].

---

[1] www.idealhomes.org.uk 29.12.05
[2] Brown.B The Metropolitan Police in the County of Surrey. Police history Society Journal 1994
[3] Kelly's directory 1840 -46
[4] Asset Management Plan. Metropolitan Police Estate. November 2007
[5] www.met.police.uk October 2010
[6] MEPO 5/23 (128) (1)
[7] Metropolitan Police Surveyors Records Charlton
[8] Robson's London Directory 1833
[9] MEPO 5/26 (154)
[10] Metropolitan Police Surveyors Records, Charlton.
[11] Metropolitan Police Orders dated 11th January 1864
[12] Metropolitan Police Orders dated 28th October 1865
[13] Post Office Directory 1879
[14] Census data 1881
[15] Police Almanac 1889
[16] Ten Year Report 1884 - 1893
[17] 1881 Report
[18] Metropolitan Police Orders dated 20th June 1884
[19] John Back Archive (1975) Metropolitan Police Historical Collection
[20] Census Data 1891
[21] LB 442
[22] LB 442
[23] Metropolitan Police Orders dated 10th & 20th June 1898
[24] The Police Review and Parade Gossip 17th Jun 1898

[25] Local Press Report 1898 – Details of publisher unknown.
[26] www.historybytheyard.co.uk/gallantry accessed on 23rd March.2008
[27] Metropolitan Police Orders dated 1st Nov 1932
[28] MEPO 2/5359
[29] LB 442
[30] LB 442
[31] Metropolitan Police Orders dated 6th August 1964
[32] Metropolitan Police Orders dated 28th August 1970
[33] South London Press 27th January 1976
[34] Southwark News 5th February 2004
[35] Metropolitan Police Estate – Asset Management Plan – November 2007
[36] John Back Archive (1975) Metropolitan Police Historical Collection
[37] Surveyors Book
[38] John Back Archive (1975) Metropolitan Police Historical Collection
[39] John Back Archive (1975) Metropolitan Police Historical Collection
[40] Police Almanac 1869
[41] Metropolitan Police Orders dated 15th July 1889
[42] John Back Archive (1975) Metropolitan Police Historical Collection
[43] MEPO 4/339
[44] 1881 Report
[45] National Archives Census 1881
[46] Surveyors Report 1881.
[47] Metropolitan Police Orders dated 20th June 1884
[48] Kelly's Sydenham, Norwood and Streatham Directory 1891
[49] Metropolitan Police General Orders 1893
[50] HO 45/9999/A47675
[51] Metropolitan Police Orders dated 24th February 1921
[52] Police Almanac 1930
[53] Metropolitan Police Orders dated 1st January 1932
[54] John Back Archive (1975) Metropolitan Police Historical Collection
[55] The Daily Mail 10th July 1956
[56] Metropolitan Police Orders dated 6th August 1964
[57] Annette Butler The Job 7th January 1994
[58] Metropolitan Police Orders dated 24th November 1993
[59] The Job 7th January 1994
[60] Asset Management Plan – November 2007
[61] MEPO4/234
[62] South London Press 4th June 1974
[63] Surveyors Report 1881
[64] Ten Year Report Jan 1884 – Dec 1893
[65] Bernie Brown personal correspondence
[66] Green B. Dulwich – A History. College Press (2002) 2ed. p.32
[67] Green B. Dulwich – A History. College Press (2002) 2ed. p.32
[68] Estates Terrier (1854) in Darby William. Dulwich – A Place in History. William Darby, London. 1967 p.69
[69] Metropolitan Police Surveyors Records, Charlton
[70] Surveyors Report 1881
[71] MEPO5/53 (427)
[72] Ten Year Report.
[73] Metropolitan Police Orders dated 7 May 1884
[74] LB510
[75] Census data 1891
[76] South London Press 29th July 1975
[77] LB511
[78] Metropolitan Police Orders dated 6th August 1964
[79] South London Press 29th July 1975
[80] Metropolitan Police Orders dated 2nd September 1977
[81] MPTS Documents

[82] MPTS Documents
[83] Metropolitan Police Orders dated 24th December 1886
[84] Ten Year Report
[85] Census data 1891
[86] West London News 13th June 1969
[87] Lewisham Boro' News 11th Sept 1969.
[88] LB 522
[89] John Back Archive (1975) Metropolitan Police Historical Collection
[90] MPTS Documents
[91] The Story of Peckham. LB of Southwark. No 3 2nd Ed (1983) p.12
[92] John Back Archive (1975) Metropolitan Police Historical Collection
[93] John Beasley – Local historian
[94] John Back Archive (1975) Metropolitan Police Historical Collection
[95] Metropolitan Police Orders dated 11th January 1864
[96] John Back Archive (1975) Metropolitan Police Historical Collection and HO45/9675/A46779
[97] 1881 Report
[98] John Back Archive (1975) Metropolitan Police Historical Collection
[99] Census data 1891
[100] Metropolitan Police Orders dated 22nd . November 1893
[101] HBR/JD 5 Jan1959
[102] London Metropolitan Archives – GLC/AR/BR/22/004837
[103] HBR/JD 5th January 1959
[104] booth.lse.ac.uk accessed on 11th April 2008
[105] Metropolitan Police Orders dated 1st January 1932
[106] London Directory 1939
[107] Metropolitan Police Orders dated 6th August 1964
[108] South London Press 7th August 1973
[109] John Beasley – Local historian
[110] Metropolitan Police Estate. Asset Management Plan 2007
[111] Metropolitan Police Surveyors Records, Charlton.
[112] Met Police Surveyors Book
[113] MEPO 5/52
[114] Metropolitan Police Orders dated 12th June 1873
[115] MEPO 5/52
[116] 1881 Report
[117] Ten Year Report 1884 - 1893
[118] The Builder 1891
[119] The Police Review and Parade Gossip June 1908
[120] Metropolitan Police Orders dated 24th February 1921
[121] Metropolitan Police Orders dated 1st January 1932
[122] MEPO 2/2584
[123] Richard Sharp letter dated 15th February 1991
[124] Police Stations in Rotherhithe – A Short History- PC Chris Lorden
[125] A History of the Parish of St Mary Rotherhithe by E..W. Beck. Cambridge University 1907
[126] Guardian 30th July 1963
[127] MEPO 5/9
[128] Metropolitan Police Orders dated 11th January 1864
[129] Metropolitan Police Orders dated 28th October 1865
[130] Surveyors Report 1881
[131] Hynds Len – Letter to London Police Pensioner June 2009
[132] MEPO 5/9
[133] Metropolitan Police Orders dated 22th October 1883
[134] Metropolitan Police Orders dated 20th June 1884
[135] Metropolitan Police Orders dated 3th May 1905
[136] www.historybytheyard.co.uk accessed on 20th January 2008
[137] Police Stations in Rotherhithe – A Short History- PC Chris Lorden
[138] LB468
[139] Police Stations in Rotherhithe – A Short History- PC Chris Lorden

[140] Metropolitan Police Orders dated 6th August 1964
[141] Metropolitan Police Orders dated 3rd September 1965
[142] South London Press 15th April 1977
[143] Estates Gazette 11th October 1980.
[144] Met Police Estate. Asset Management Report. November 2007
[145] Brown .B. The Metropolitan Police in the County of Surrey. Police history Society Journal 1994
[146] Brown B. 'M' Division 1830-1899 December 1998
[147] Brown B. The Job March 1988
[148] Met Police Returns of Deaths Register 1829 - 1846
[149] Brown .B. The Job March 1988
[150] Metropolitan Police Returns of Death Register 1829-1860
[151] John Back Archive (1975) Metropolitan Police Historical Collection
[152] Police and Constabulary List 1844,
[153] Post Office 1849
[154] John Back Archive (1975) Metropolitan Police Historical Collection
[155] MEPO4/234
[156] John Back Archive (1975) Metropolitan Police Historical Collection
[157] Police Almanac 1869
[158] Brown B. Met Police in the County of Surrey Date unknown
[159] Metropolitan Police Orders dated 20th July 1870
[160] Surveyors Report 1881.
[161] Metropolitan Police Surveyors Records, Charlton
[162] Metropolitan Police Orders dated 22 nd October 1883
[163] Metropolitan Police Orders dated 15th October 1896
[164] Brown B. The Metropolitan Police in the County of Surrey. Police History Society Journal 1994
[165] The Police Review & Parade Gossip 26 June 1893 p.309
[166] www.booth.lse.ac.uk accessed in February 2010
[167] Metropolitan Police Surveyors Records 1924.
[168] John Back Archive (1975) Metropolitan Police Historical Collection
[169] Post Office London 1928
[170] Kirchners Police Almanac 1931
[171] Metropolitan Police Orders dated 20th October 1938
[172] Evening News 14th October 1938
[173] Metropolitan Police Orders dated 12th September 1940
[174] John Back Archive (1975) Metropolitan Police Historical Collection
[175] Metropolitan Police Orders dated 24th May 1974
[176] John Back Archive (1975) Metropolitan Police Historical Collection
[177] Metropolitan Police Estate Asset Management Plan November 2007
[178] John Back Archive (1975) Metropolitan Police Historical Collection
[179] John Back Archive (1975) Metropolitan Police Historical Collection
[180] John Back Archive (1975) Metropolitan Police Historical Collection
[181] Pevsner Buildings of England London South Penguin 1983 p. 602
[182] Metropolitan Police Orders dated 9th December 1904
[183] Kelly's Directories 1905-1911
[184] Metropolitan Police Surveyors Records, Charlton
[185] Metropolitan Police Orders dated 6th August 1964
[186] Metropolitan Police Orders dated 22nd January 1980
[187] Metropolitan Police Orders dated 25th October 1983
[188] www.london-sel.co.uk/news/view/4637 accessed on 10th October 2010

Chapter 10

The London Borough of Wandsworth

Introduction

The London Borough of Wandsworth extends from the industrial riverside of Battersea to as far west as some large open spaces like Wimbledon Common and Richmond Park. Battersea and Wandsworth had separate Parishes with their own churches and by the 18th century there were a number of villages situated close to the Thames. Prior to the 1965 Borough re-organisations Wandsworth was the Largest London County Council with a population in 1951 of 330, 000 people although by 1981 this was nearer 250,000[1]. Today Wandsworth Borough consists of Battersea, Wandsworth, Roehampton, Putney, Clapham, Balham, Tooting and Streatham.

Superintendent J. Bishop was the first officer in charge of 'V' or Wandsworth and he remained in post until March 1836[2]. Thomas Bicknell took over from Bishop and became Divisional Superintendent in 1836[3]. Bicknell took charge until January 1854 when he retired on pension having been succeeded by Septimus Fenn[4]. In 1851 Fenn who had been recommended by Bicknell was posted to the Division and the Commissioners were confident enough that he could carry out the appropriate superintending responsibilities for the Division.

By 1838 in addition to Wandsworth, located at The Plain, there were a further two Stations, one situated at Clapham Common near the church and the other at 1&2 Millmans Lane, Chelsea[5]. By 1841 the Division expanded to take in London Road, Kingston; Epson; Hampton; Sunbury; Princes Street, Richmond; and High Street, Mortlake[6]. By 1842 another three Stations at Salvador in Lower Tooting, Merton, and Priest Bridge, Barnes had been added[7]. Inspectors were put in charge of the Stations at Kingston; Millmans Row, Chelsea; The Plain, Wandsworth; Clapham Common; Princes Street, Richmond; whilst the remainder were designated Sergeant's Stations[8].

In 1844 there were 5 Police Stations shown on 'V' or (Wandsworth) Division. These were Kingston, Wandsworth, Richmond, Chelsea and Clapham. Wandsworth was the Divisional Headquarters with the address shown as The Plain, Wandsworth (later becoming Wandsworth Plain where there were a number of older properties originating from the Georgian period). Wandsworth Plain was located between Putney Bridge Road and Red Lion Street off Wandsworth High Street.

The Station House at New Street, Clapham, was added in 1851[9] as an Inspector Station and in 1860 Ditton Police Station was added with a Sergeant in charge[10]. Superintendent Fenn was pensioned in July 1861 when Edward Butt took over, transferring from 'A' or Whitehall Division. Butt died suddenly in harness in September 1874 and Charles Digby was quickly transferred from 'H' Division to take charge. Digby stayed until 1889 when he vacated his position to David Saines, his Chief Inspector.

Police records show the creation of three new Divisions in 1865, 'W' or Clapham Division, 'X' or Paddington Division and 'Y' or Highgate Division. The Police Order detailed the importance of Wandsworth as a Division by highlighting the established strength as 1 Superintendent, 8 Inspectors, 49 Sergeants and 385 Constables[11] however the Station establishment was much smaller and directed to be 2 Inspectors, 7 Sergeants and 52 Constables[12]. The Superintendent had allocated a Constable to be the Station Groom and attend to the 12 horses in the stable. A number of other Police Officers were directed away from street duty to other responsibilities. For example, there was a Divisional Clerk Sergeant to assist the Superintendent with the correspondence and administration, 1 Sergeant and three Constables for Court duty, 6 Constables for duty at Hampton Court Palace, 3 Constables to Kew Gardens, and one Constable each to Strawberry Hill House and Cremorne Gardens[13].

During the 1860s large numbers of beggars were frequenting London and in particular the Borough of Wandsworth where many complaints were being made by local residents. It was felt that the greater the number of vagrants, the higher the rate of crime. During 1869 there were 336 apprehensions under the Vagrancy Act 1824 although this was greatly reduced in 1870 to 181. Many vagrants would apply to the Borough of Wandsworth for support however the regulations in place involving compulsory labour and cleanliness gave many second thoughts and caused them to move to other neighbourhoods. With the reduction in vagrants the numbers of arrests also declined, from 2,736 in 1869 to 2,447 in 1870 and by a further 400 in 1871 as the crime rate continued to fall.

Against the background of political unrest in the 1880s, the renewed bombing attacks by the Fenians and the expansion in London's population the Commissioner was unable to raise further capital for urgent new buildings and Police Stations and to raise Police numbers. The government introduced the Police Acts of 1886 and 1887 that enabled the Police to raise much needed capital from the Police rate and to buy land and build Police Stations. Wandsworth like many other suburbs experienced massive expansion within population, building work and traffic and this was matched with the increase of the building of Police Stations in the borough.

Battersea Police station

The first records relating to situating a Police Station in Battersea occurs in 1858 when Superintendent Fenn of 'V' Division reported that a piece of land near the Castle Public House was available and suitable for erecting a Police Station. In February 1859 the Metropolitan Police Surveyor, Charles Reeves, recommended the purchase of the freehold land for £300. With the transaction completed a new Station was erected on the site.

BATTERSEA
118 Bridge Road
Battersea
1861 - 1911

Named Battersea Bridge Road Station it was taken into service by 'V' Division in January 1861[14] and was a Sergeant-designated Station. Situated at the corner of Battersea Bridge Road and Hyde Road (Later Hyde Lane) this was a standard two storey brick built Police Station that cost £2,911. 14s. to build including £700 worth of alterations. Upstairs was a Section House of five rooms for 13 single Constables and 1 Sergeant who resided with his family in separate rooms [15]. The basement contained a kitchen and a mess room where the Constables could relax or take their refreshments.

The Station strength in 1864 was 4 Sergeants and 20 Constables. Of the four Sergeants two supervised the day duty shift whilst the remaining two were responsible for the night duty. Two of the Sergeants (one by night and the other by day) were also required to ride one of the two horses stabled at the Station with the Inspector or Sergeant from Wandsworth patrolling Battersea, Merton and Tooting. The remaining Sergeant was to stay in the Station. Battersea was a Charging Station with cells and records show that Merton and Tooting did not have such facilities and prisoners would have to be taken to the main Station[16].

In 1868 it became a Sub-Divisional Station in its own right and Inspector Samuel Egerton was sent from Wandsworth (the Sub-Divisional Headquarters) to take charge of Battersea Bridge Road[17]. Egerton would have supervised his 4 Sergeants (in 1864) to ensure that all the beats were covered 24 hours a day by the 20 Constables. Duties would be planned in advance and Battersea was split into 2 sections and had 6 day and 14 night beats. More Police Officers were allocated to the night duty shift in order to man the beats and the times were determined by 'lighting up time' which was published in advance by Scotland Yard each year. There was little margin for error in terms of manning the beats since the beats matched exactly the numbers of Constables available so sickness meant sometimes that more than one beat would have been allocated to an individual Constable or even covered by the mounted Sergeant. Directions were given that Sergeant(s) on duty at Battersea were not to leave the Station[18].

Metropolitan Police Surveyors inspected the Station in 1881 and reported that it was occupied by one single Sergeant and 13 single Constables and that;

> 'This Station was originally designed for occupation by married officers. It is now wholly occupied by single men. The site is low, and subject to be flooded; the basement is damp, and it is therefore totally unfit for occupation'[19].

The Commissioner appointed Inspectors on Division to inspect local Common Lodging houses and report annually to him. In Battersea the poorer classes were mainly concentrated in Little Europa Place, Currie Street, Ponton Road, Southampton Street West and Latchmere Grove. The Inspector, after visiting the designated Common Lodging Houses, would supply a report to the Superintendent covering the conditions of the water supply, ventilation, privy accommodation (toilets) and over-crowding[20].

There were nine Stations on the Division, four covered by Inspectors and five by Sergeants. The Station address at Battersea was shown as 118 Bridge Road, Battersea,[21] and its call sign for the Telegraph which was connected to Scotland Yard was Bravo Sierra (BS) [22]. Above the Station lived Inspector

Albany J. Ollett, his wife and five children. Next to them was a Section House containing 5 single Constables[23].

Battersea Bridge Road was built with three cells however by 1888 these were considered insufficient due to the large numbers of prisoners being arrested and application was made for a further two cells[24]. A much larger association cell (drunk tank) and another cell were added. This showed that the numbers of prisoners were increasing and that insufficient space was available to house them. There were two Stations in Battersea itself, the other being located on 'W' Division and called Battersea Park Road.

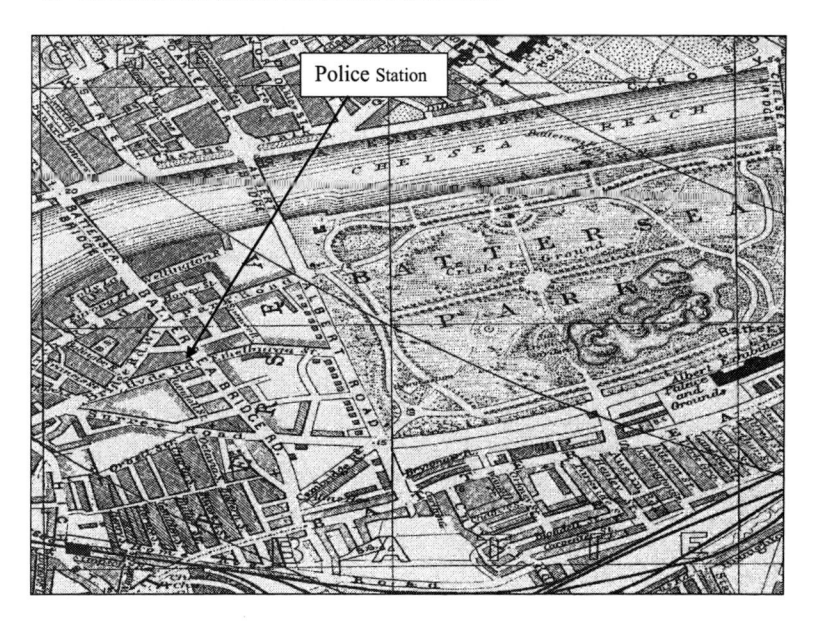

[Map showing Police Station location in Battersea]

By 1907 the address had changed to 112 - 118 Bridge Road, SW, with the purchase of some adjacent properties. Such was the state of the old Station that since 1901 the drains would over-flow and flood the basement whenever there was a down-pour, or if the Thames flooded, causing sewerage to seep in. This led to a number of Police Officers contracting diphtheria and typhoid fever. The gas lamps were also criticised as many were faulty and some were dangerous[25]. Battersea Police Station became a Passing Station for the Public Carriage Office which for a short period was responsible for the supervision of taxi drivers in London. Because the Taxi business was on the increase a more permanent site was selected so the Passing Station was moved from Battersea to another station.

In 1907 a new, much larger Station was built on the site by F. G. Minter, Contractors of Putney, together with a Section House and one set of married quarters.

Battersea Police Station
112 - 118 Battersea Bridge Road, Battersea, London, SW11 3A
1907 – Present day

In September 1914 Constable 78886 George Johnson (W) was on his patrol near a railway line when he was accidentally knocked down by a passing train and died from his injuries[26]. A service funeral was held and many of his friends and colleagues were there. The Divisional Superintendent and his deputy also attended as these events were paid for by the Police if the circumstances of the accident occurred on duty.

During the 1st World War aerial bombardment from German Zeppelins and Aircraft caused the anti-aircraft battery to respond, however one unexploded shell hit Grosvenor Road railway bridge at Queens Road [27] with devastating effect.

In 1921 Wandsworth Sub-Division was shown as a Station on 'L' Division although in 1932 it was transferred back to 'W' Division when the boundaries on 4 District were revised[28].

Records show that the Section House was closed for renovation between March 1926 and July 1929 and then opened again for a short period. The Section House was vacated again by residents in January 1932[29] and probably used as a temporary Station whilst the Station itself underwent improvement shortly afterwards in 1934. Because of its importance at the time Lavender Hill (WL) was the Sub Divisional Station with Battersea (WA) and Nine Elms (WN) as sectional stations. In charge at Lavender Hill was Sub Divisional Inspector F. Nichols[30]. But this was not to remain like this and whilst the station remained on 'W' or Clapham Division by 1966 Superintendent H. G. White was in charge with WL and WN now as sectional stations[31].

The picture at left shows the rear yard and back entrance to the Station lit by a gas lamp fashioned in the typical Police Station lamp style.

During the Second World War many Stations were kept open, surrounded with sand bags and guarded by War Reserve Constables. The duty shifts at most Stations were also augmented by War Reserve Constables who would help to replace those Officers who had left the Police to join the Colours. Many of the reserve were retired Police Officers who returned to duty until the end of the war. WRC Ernest Frank Hunt was killed by a flying bomb attack in 1944[32].

The rear entrance to the police station showing a station lamp with white glass

In 1965 Local Authority boundaries were revised and this meant changes in policing areas. Following these Battersea was shown as a Sub-Divisional Station with Putney and Tooting on 'W' or Tooting Division[33]. This had become a Sub Divisional station

In 2010 Battersea Police Station is still in the same place as it was when it was built, situated at 112 - 118 Battersea Bridge Road, Battersea, London, SW11 3A, and open 24 hours a day[34].

Earlsfield Police Station

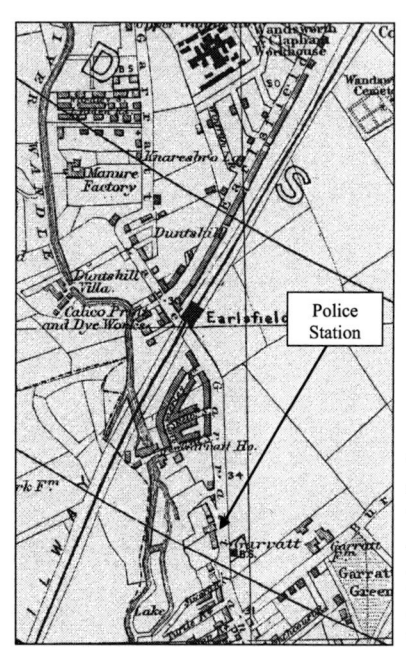

Sir Edward Henry, the Commissioner, had been lobbied by the residents of Earlsfield for a Police Station to be built. As a result the Receiver enquired into the possibility of purchasing a suitable site that was on the corner of Garrett Lane and Weybourne Street, Wandsworth. Negotiations commenced in 1912 to buy the freehold title from the present owners, Mrs E. E. Hardman and Mr. A. E. Boyce[35], which resulted in the Station being built in 1914. The address was shown as Garrett lane, Earlsfield, SW17, but later in 1931 it was shown as a Sub- Divisional Station with Wandsworth Common and Balham being Sectional Stations[36]. The Station was allocated to 'V' or Wandsworth Division. It was built with married quarters and a Section House attached. The development of the new Sub-Division caused a revision of the boundaries to Wandsworth, Battersea, Wimbledon and Kingston Sub-Divisions in 1914[37]. The Section House had been built to accommodate 33 single officers at a nominal weekly rent of 1s each. The married quarters were charged at 10s per week. The Station was refreshed in 1937 which meant that in addition to being completely re-painted, various building works and extensions would have been planned and carried out. In the same year Earlsfield was a sectional station to Balham (Cavendish Road) (WD) whilst Wandsworth Common (WC) was the other sectional station[38].

The London County Council informed the Metropolitan Police in 1945 that a change of street numbering was required and allocated No. 522 Garratt Lane to the Police Station and 520 to the married quarters[39]. In 1921 further revisions of boundaries and also the creation of the 'Z' or Croydon Division caused Earlsfield to be transferred to 'W' or Brixton Division[40].

Earlsfield Police Station
522 Garrett lane, Earlsfield, SW17
1914 – Present day

In 1960 Earlsfield was still located on 'W' Division with call sign Whiskey Foxtrot (WF) and being supervised from Balham where Superintendent F. C. Brown was in charge. Further Local authority boundary alignments in 1964 saw Earlsfield reduced in status to Sectional Station on Tooting Sub-Division[41]. By 1966 the station Tooting (Mitcham Road) continued as the sub Divisional station with Earlsfield retaining its status of sectional station[42].

The Station was closed in 1998 for operational purposes[43] although it remained in the possession of the police for use as offices.

In 1999 Earlsfield Police Station was used as a base by officers of the Area Major Investigation Pool (AMIP), and for local sector officers; for meetings of the local Sector Working Group; and, as necessary, for the storage of lost or stolen motor vehicles.

Earlsfield remained part of Wandsworth Police Division, and became part of Battersea Division as part of the Metropolitan Police's overall move to Borough based policing. This amalgamation led to a review of the use of Earlsfield as a sector base and for meetings of the Sector Working Group. It is envisaged that the AMIP officers will remain at Earlsfield and that it will continue to be used when necessary for the storage of lost or stolen vehicles[44]. By 2010 the Station was still in service but as a building used for administrative purposes housing the Earlsfield Safer Neighbourhood Team[45].

Lavender Hill Police Station

It was not until 1892 that there was a particular need for a Police Station to be built in the area. The Station that covered the area was located near the parish boundary and was considered too far away. The size of the local population had greatly increased and news had reached the Commissioner that a very influential petition was being prepared. A new Police Magistrate's Court had been built in the area (South Western Police Court at 176a Lavender Hill) and with this in mind a site next door was found and soon purchased for £3000; it was located at the corner of Latchmere Lane and Lavender Hill[46]. The new Station was designed by John Butler, the Metropolitan Police Surveyor, and built on the site. The Station was ready for occupation in March 1896 and there were boundary alterations as a result. As was usual, the Station was built with accommodation in mind for married and single Officers. The design allowed

Lavender Hill Police Station
176 Lavender Hill, SW11
1896 - 1962

for a married Inspector and his family in one set of rooms and also what was

> The rear yard view showing the boundary wall, coal store and the back gates in 1907

termed a Section House for 22 single Police Officers[47].

The Station was put under the supervision of Sub-Divisional Inspector John Concannon who was transferred from Battersea[48]. Concannon did not stay long at Lavender Hill but possibly of his own choice sought another posting elsewhere. By 1898 he was transferred to 'N' or Islington Division north of the River Thames[49]. Changes in Divisional and Sub- Divisional boundaries during re-organisations often meant that supervision would also change, occasionally quite frequently. For example, in 1924 the address was published as 176 Lavender Hill, SW11, and shown on 'L' Division although it was later transferred to 'W' or Clapham. Re-organisation of 4 District boundaries in 1931 saw the area transferred to 'W' or Clapham Division. Lavender Hill Station was renovated in 1936.

Between 1957 and 1960 Lavender Hill was a Station on 'W' or Tooting Division under the charge of Superintendent A. H. Jones[50]. The Station was also a Sub-Divisional Station where prisoners were housed and charges were taken and dealt with[51]. Within a few years the old Station was no longer suitable for its purpose and a temporary Station was brought into service at Theatre Street at the junction with Lavender Hill, SW11, whilst the old Station was demolished.

Before being demolished in February 1962[52] the Station had been gutted of all its equipment and removed to the temporary Station. Battersea Police Station became the Sub-Divisional Station following the closure however over a year later in December 1963 the new Station was opened for operational purposes[53] and the temporary station was closed. Its status was as sectional station to Battersea (WA)[54].

In 2001 Lavender Hill was a Station on Wandsworth Operational Command Unit (OCU) with charging facilitates and where prisoners were taken and dealt with under the Police and Criminal Evidence Act 1984. The OCU Commander was Superintendent Brian Wade, who was assisted by

Lavender Hill Police Station
176 Lavender Hill, SW76 1JX
1963 – Present day

Superintendent V. Marr, and the Sub-Divisional Superintendent was J. Long[55]. Restricted opening hours were in place in 2009 with the Station being closed at night and only open from 7am until 11pm daily[56]. By 2010 the Station was reduced to office status only and being open from 7am until 10pm daily[57].

Nine Elms Police Station or Battersea Park Road Police Station

Brought into service in 1878[58] it was rented for £38 per year from Mrs Amelia Bird of Kenley. Its address was 143 Battersea Park Road and the original contract was for 21 years. This was a conventional large Victorian house with basement, ground and first floor. The building required some conversion from an ordinary residential house and alterations costing £449 ensured the building was suitable for Police purposes. For example, there was room for two cells, a charge room, a reserve room and store on the ground floor whilst the basement contained a kitchen and two day rooms. There is evidence that 12 single Constables lived in somewhat cramped circumstances above the Station and a married Constable resided in the basement. At the time this cost the married constable £37. 16s per annum. Freehold to the premises was obtained in January 1888 and by August 1879 the premises were suitable for occupation[59].

Nine Elms Police Station
147 Battersea Park Road SW8
1925 – Present day

Police Orders reported that the building was to be occupied at once and that the lodging assessment was 3s per week for one married Constable whilst the 5 single Constables paid 1s per week each[60]. In the photograph above one can see part of the old Station situated to the left of the extension. In 1881

Constable Fredrick Petherick, his wife and daughter occupied married quarters at the Station in addition to 5 single Constables who occupied the Section House[61]. The Surveyor's report of 1881 showed that at the time of the inspection it was occupied by one married Constable and five single Constables and that the conditions were of some concern. They described the building as;

> 'An ordinary dwelling-house, to which some cells, &c. have been added. It is quite unsuited for its present occupation. The married woman has her washing boiler in the men's mess room'[62].

By 1887 the Home Office had decided to authorise the freehold purchase of the site and house together with an adjoining property. The cost of the Police Station came to £1550[63]. Police Orders in 1893 confirmed that the Station had been fitted with a telegraph and that its call sign was Papa Bravo (BP)[64]. Receiving and sending telegraphs was a responsible position and was carried out by an 'intelligent Constable' who would assist the Inspector in charge and had been carefully instructed in the use of the instrument. The Station was shown as a Sectional station of Clapham[65].

This was shown in 1912 as a Station on 'W' or Brixton Division with the address of 143 and 145 Battersea Park Road, SW,[66] and was not called Nine Elms until some time later.

Surveyor's records show that the Station was now called Nine Elms Police Station and consisted of a Station and Section House. The latter was replaced and 3 sets of married quarters were built in its place. Nine Elms was designated a Station on 'L' or Kennington Division in February 1921 when 'Z' Division was formed and there was a revision of boundaries[67]. The name change occurred in 1923 when notice was given that Battersea Park Road Station would in future be known as Nine Elms[68]. A new Station was built on the site and occupied for police purposes on 24th August 1925[69] although operational matters commenced in December 1925[70].

Nine Elms Station lamp

Re-alignment of borough boundaries under the Local Government Act 1963, introduced in April 1965, saw Nine Elms being transferred to 'W' or Tooting Division as a Sectional Station[71]. In 1972 the status of the Station was down-graded and Nine Elms became a Police Office[72]. Notice was given in 1977 that Nine Elms would cease to operate as a Police Station and that the premises would be taken over by other departments of the MPS[73].

Police search dog Jake and his handler PC Bob Crawford received the Blue Cross Medal for heroism, bravery, and dedication being displayed by the animal at a special award ceremony held by the Blue Cross Animal Hospital in Victoria.

The award, which was presented by actress Felicity Kendal in 2007, was in recognition for their work during the London bombings in July 2005. Jake, a cocker spaniel, and PC Bob Crawford, based at Nine Elms Police Station Wandsworth, were responsible for searching the bus at Tavistock Square and also the Underground tunnel at Russell Square for secondary devices in order that the injured could be evacuated[74]. The Station accommodates dog handlers and other Divisional units for operational purposes but is no longer open to the public.

Pc Crawford proudly showing off his dog Jake and the Blue Cross medal won

The country's oldest charitable animal hospital in London had reinstated the medal for one year only to mark the centenary of the Blue Cross Animal Hospital. Owners or handlers were requested to nominate animals that had come to the aid of another animal or a human and shown bravery, companionship, or loyalty[75].

Putney Police Station

Putney was part of the manor of Wimbledon, situated next to the river Thames and remaining quite rural, although by the 18th century it had become gentrified and remained so until the mid 20th century. The first Putney Bridge was built in 1725 and rebuilt in its current form in 1886.

Demand for a Police Station in Putney prompted a letter to be written by a Mr Hare that offered a site in Upper Richmond Road, Putney, on a 99 year lease from Christmas 1868[76]. It is not clear whether this option was taken up but the new Police Station was rented for 99 years at 9 shillings a week from James Dean, a builder of River Street Putney[77], and brought into service in August 1873. The Station, located on 'V' or Wandsworth Division, housed a married Sergeant, a married Constable and six single Constables[78]. The Sergeant was placed in charge and ensured that Police Officers were properly supervised[79].

Putney Police Station's address in 1880 was noted as Chestnut Cottage, Upper Richmond Road,[80] and numbered 191 a year later[81]. Constable 61607 Charles Edwards joined in 1877, resided there with his wife and three children and occupied the married quarters at the Station in 1881[82]; he retired in 1902. Whilst on duty at Putney, Constable William Silvey was on his patrol in 1883 when he stopped a passing wagon from which he could hear noises however whilst searching the wagon he lost his footing and fell, fatally injuring himself[83].

By 1881 the status of the Station was enhanced and an Inspector was placed in charge[84]. An Inspection by Metropolitan Police Surveyors in 1881 found that this was;

> 'A modern and substantial Station. The married and single men's quarters are not separated. Ablution room, inconveniently placed, can only be reached by passing through the mess rooms'[85].

It was occupied by 1 married Inspector, 1 married Constable and 6 single Constables[86].

By 1885 Putney had been relocated to the new 'W' or Clapham Division although a change back to 'V' Division occurred in 1893 when it became a Sectional Station of Wandsworth[87]. The Station was linked to a telegraph which made communication to Scotland Yard easy. The call sign for Putney in 1893 was Papa Yankee (PY). Standardisation of telegraph, telephone and later radio call signs relating to the Police Station areas along Divisional lines was not completed until the 1930's.

The increase in population during the latter part of the century placed extra demands on policing the area and so plans were made to enlarge the Station. Attempts were made to purchase the freehold title to the Station and this was purchased successfully from Mr John Temple Leader for £363 in 1899[88].

Between 1902 and 1904 the addresses adjacent to the Station were purchased at a cost of £1,600 and later renumbered 215-219 Upper Richmond Road in 1904[89]. There is evidence that the vendor reluctantly sold the buildings to the Police because an attachment was made to the deeds that the vendor was to be given 1st refusal if the premises were sold later. It was not uncommon for potential Police Station premises to be the subject of compulsory purchase at this time so a desired residence could be lost to an owner if the Police required it.

Yet the Police did not rush to design and build a new Station on the site to the obvious frustration of the previous owner. Instead, they sub-let 219 until 1909 to a Mr R. Waller for an annual rental of £40. The family continued to live at the address into the 1920s when the annual rental was increased to £48 by 1924[90].

There was a large contingent of Metropolitan Police Special Constabulary at Putney Police Station and during the 1st World War this was the Headquarters. The Division lost no fewer than 1,657 regular men to the Colours during the war. The Specials attached here knew that they would be kept active being assigned to man vulnerable points of which 'V' Division had a great number. These included the reservoirs, gas works, electric light works, power stations, the Sopwith Aviation Factory, an aqueduct and all had to be guarded. Unpleasant assignments also included the local sewage works, which saw Specials performing their 4 hours duty mostly without complaint. During air raids the Specials withdrew to air raid shelters which had become numerous in Wandsworth and ensured the good order and safety of the civilians seeking shelter. In June 1916 the local population were upset about foreigners living and trading amongst them and regularly the Police together with the Special Constabulary had to defend

Putney Police Station
215 Upper Richmond Road SW18
1903 - 2006

people's lives and protect their property in Putney. In December 1917 German air raids saw two bombs dropped on Putney in Lower Common Road and two people were killed. This was the furthest west of this night's attack[91]. The 'V' Division Special Constabulary also supervised food queues, national registration work and Election Stations where citizens recorded their votes. They involved themselves in Police Lectures, ambulance training, and rifle shooting within the Division. The Specials also had the most efficient drill instructor, Sergeant Major F. W. Eggleton, a champion ex-army swordsman of the army gymnastic staff. He regularly gathered the Division on Wimbledon Common for drill musters and to put them through their paces[92].

Percy Laurie Section House SQ 20 with accommodation for 101 single Police Officers was built in the 1930's at a cost of £90,000. Simultaneously a new Police Station was built which replaced Wandsworth as the Divisional Station

The rear gardens of the Police station in 1907

becoming fully operational in July 1935[93]. Wandsworth was relegated to Sectional Station with Putney as the Sub-Divisional Station.

The picture below shows the rear of Putney Police Station in 1908 with the parade shed on the right together with the Station's garden where potatoes and tomatoes seem to be growing. The rear of the Station is shown in the background.

The Police Station at Putney was struck by German bombs on the 9th September 1940 killing Stn/Sgt Wilfred John Chilcott, aged 46, who was on duty at the time[94].

During the Local Government re-organisations of the 1960s Putney, designated call sign (VD), was transferred (with Wandsworth) to W Division and re-designated (WP). Both Stations were located within the London Borough of Wandsworth.

The rear of the station showing parade shed to the right

In 1981 the orientation between Putney and Wandsworth changed. Both Station areas were amalgamated and Putney Division of 'W' Division was now called Wandsworth Division with the main headquarters function being established back at Wandsworth. The Chief Superintendent, Superintendent and part of the admin were located at Wandsworth whilst the Chief Inspector (Admin) and the Process Section retained at Putney[95].

A Police Office was opened at Jubilee House, 230-232 Putney Bridge Road, Putney, SW15, on Wandsworth Sub-Division in May 1978. Known as Putney Bridge Office it was given the telegraph designation (WB). The opening hours were Mondays to Saturdays between 10am – 12 noon and 3pm to 5pm. Designated a Sectional Station it was opened when needed, such as for the Oxford and Cambridge Boat Races or the Head of River Boat Race[96]. This office was not open for long and was closed in 1983[97].

Percy Laurie Section House was sold to developers during the 1990s as part of the Section House closure programme. The scheme to reduce bed spaces for single Officers also ended any automatic obligation by the Police to provide any single accommodation.

In 2010 Putney Police Station had the status of an office and was located in Putney High Street adjacent to the Odeon Cinema. The front counter is open Monday to Friday 11am – 2pm and Saturday 10am –2pm. A Police Officer is present during these times for taking crime reports; property marking; and giving crime prevention advice. The office is unable to deal with the production of driving documents or changes to immigration papers; these matters are dealt with at Wandsworth Police Station.

Roehampton Police Station

In 1871 a cottage was leased for 7 years from Miss Snow of Wimbledon for the sum of £22 per annum[98]. By 1881 a small cottage acted as the Station in Roehampton and housed two married Constables and their families[99].

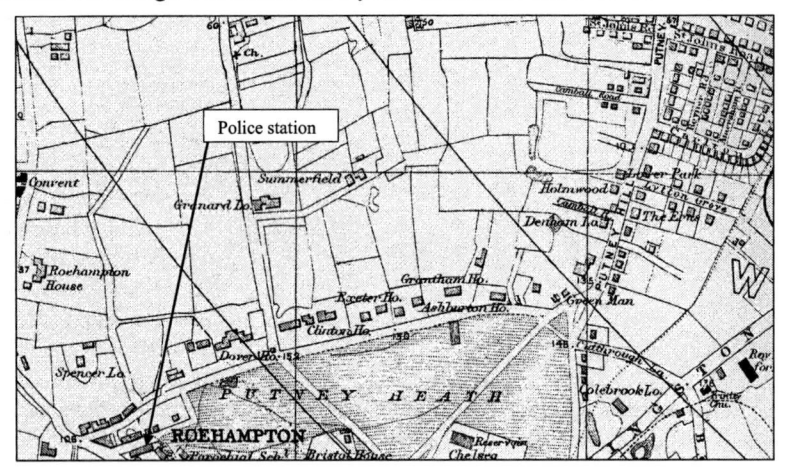

A Station in Roehampton was brought into service in 1894 to cope with demand and the increased density in population. Expansion in the Roehampton area particularly necessitated the Divisional Superintendent to reconsider the boundaries within his Division. A suitable site with three cottages was found and although originally rented they were purchased later in 1908.

The address of these was 6, 8, and 10 Medfield Street, Roehampton Lane, SW15. Roehampton became a Station in a loose sense of the word, on 'V' or

Wandsworth Division[100] because as records show each cottage comprised of just accommodation with three sets of quarters but not necessarily having other features like cells, charge room or Station Office for visitors. Although originally called a Station, this was one of low status and it became a Sectional Station (with Wandsworth Common, Wimbledon, and Putney) to Wandsworth, which of course was not only a Sub-Divisional Station but also the Divisional Headquarters as well. The postal address to which correspondence and inquiries were directed was no.8[101].

Roehampton Police Office (side entrance)
117 Danebury Avenue, London, SW15 4DH.
1967 – present day

In 1871 Widows and Orphans boxes were sanctioned to be place d at the front of Police Stations in order to support orphaned children but to help towards the cost of the Metropolitan Police and City Orphanage in Strawberry Hill.

The Station was still in Roehampton in the 1930s but today Roehampton Police Station is little more than an office and is situated at 117 Danebury Avenue, London, SW15 4DH. This is between Putney Heath and Richmond Park Golf Club. The office was formally a flat on the ground floor however it has wheel-chair access, a feature built into the office

West Putney Police Office
117 Danebury Avenue, London
SW15 4DH

285

when it was constructed in the 1960's. In 2010 the office now called West Putney Police Office is still in use although it has the police blue façade. A new police office is also located at 325 Tildesley Road, Roehampton, London, SW15 3BB in 2010.

Tooting (and South Tooting) Police Station

The earliest records for Tooting Police Station are shown in 1842 when a station located at Lower Tooting, Salvador, is recorded as having a Sergeant in charge and located on 'V' or Wandsworth Division[102]. The station was located at the Broadway, Lower Tooting and the turning where the station was located was called Salvador. Both this Station and the Station in the Broadway at Amen Corner have in the past been referred to as South Tooting Police Station.

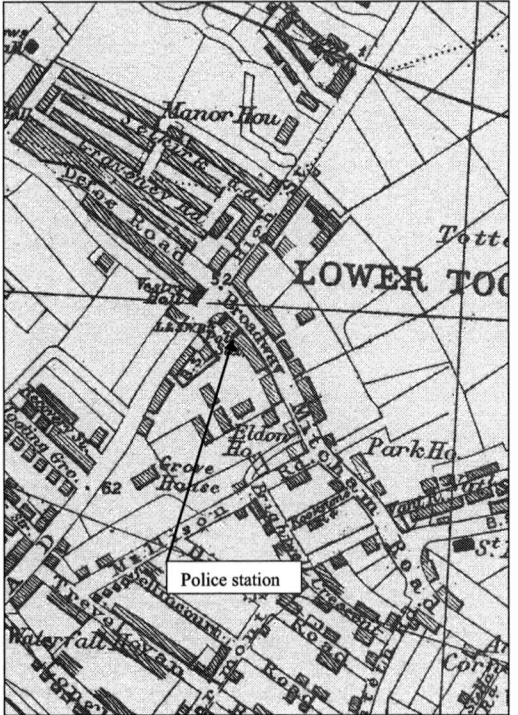

In 1864 the Station strength was shown as 1 Sergeant and fourteen Constables. Two horses were stabled at the Station with one being ridden alternately by the two Station Sergeants and the remaining horse, in the charge of either the mounted Inspector or the Sergeant, patrolled the neighbourhoods of Battersea, Merton and Tooting from Wandsworth[103]. The shift system was different at Merton and Tooting with both the Acting Sergeants and Sergeants on Section Duties changing from night to day duties monthly.

In 1865 three new Divisions were formed and Tooting moved to 'W' or Clapham Division[104]. The new landlord was George Houghton, of 40, St. Johns Park Villas, Haverstock Hill, who leased them a building for 21 years from Michaelmas, 1870 at £45 per annum. The status of the Station was raised in 1881 when an Inspector was placed in charge replacing the Sergeants. Inspector Joseph Ashley his wife, and four children occupied the married quarters above the Station and three single Constables lived in rooms nearby[105]. Metropolitan Police Surveyors reported in the same year that it was occupied by one married Inspector and three single Constables. Additionally they made the comment that this was;

> 'a poor class of dwelling. Two cells have been built in the back yard. The arrangements of the occupation are very bad indeed. The men's ablution room is the women's wash-house. The men's bedroom door is opposite that of the Inspector's daughter'[106].

Tooting Police Station
204 Mitcham Road SW17
1889 - 1939

The address of the Station was published as 'The Broadway, Lower Tooting'[107]. In 1889 Superintendents of Division were asked about any problems with cell space and the two cells at Tooting were considered sufficient for current prisoner numbers[108].

Between 1881 and 1885 there was a significant push by the Commissioner to replace the Sergeant-designated Stations with those of Inspectors and whilst not completely successful the majority of Stations had an Inspector in charge. All the stations on 'W' or Clapham Division were now Inspector-designated Stations with the exception of Sanderstead which was too small for even a

Sergeant to be in charge therefore a responsible Constable was selected to take over. Tooting's call sign for the telegraph was Tango Golf or (TG); then the call signs did not correspond to the Division it was on.

A new venue was being sought for a Station because the old one was no longer suitable. A site a short distance away in Mitcham Road was found and purchased by the Receiver at a cost of £480 in 1886. Plans were drawn up for a Station to be built and tenders were put out

The rear of the station showing the back gate and boundary wall

Tooting Police station
251 Micham Road, Tooting SW17 9QJ
1939 – Present day

for a builder. The Station was built at a cost of £3,149 and came into service in May 1889[109]. It was relatively small and designed to accommodate about a dozen Police Officers. No longer called Lower Tooting, the name became Tooting Police Station and later the address was shown as 204 Mitcham

Road, S.W[110]. With the building of the new Station there was a change in status. Tooting became a Sectional Station of Streatham and remained one until the 1920s.

Tragic events occur from time to time and the dangers of policing can become much more noticeable when a Police Officer is killed in the line of duty. In 1930 Tooting Constable Arthur Laws, who was on night duty, attempted to stop a stolen car that was being driven without lights when he was knocked down and killed[111]. In 1937 Sub Divisional Inspector A. Robertson DCM was the officer in charge of the sub division with Mitcham being a sectional station[112].

Changes in Divisional Station boundaries 1930s caused the Police to re-think the importance of the area and plans were made to create a new much larger Police Station and Divisional Headquarters in Tooting built on a substantial piece of land. A site 150 yards away was purchased in 1931 although a Station and adjoining Section House was not built and completed until 1939[113]. Designed by G. Mackenzie Trench, Police Chief Architect and Surveyor, the new Station was built to front two streets, Mitcham Road and Ascot Road. Almost immediately the old Station was put up for sale by local estate agents. The new Station was built with a Section House to accommodate 80 single Officers plus stables, which were located in the basement, garages and administrative offices. Built with three canteens (Senior Officers', Sergeants' and Constables' dining rooms) to be served by one kitchen provided the architect with the problem of service and inter-communication. The problem was solved by placing the canteens in a row and providing a continuous counter through each room. The new Station was designed to provide the six Police Stations of the Borough of Wandsworth that make up 'W' Division with Headquarters support. The Station was also built with 12 flats for married Officers and their families.

In 1957 Chief Superintendent W. E Davis was in charge of the whole Division assisted by Superintendent T. Evans as Staff Officer. The functions of the CID were also localised with Detective Superintendent F. Close also being located within the Headquarters Station at Tooting. Normal day to day policing of Tooting Sub-Division was supervised by Superintendent J. Lawlor who also took responsibility for Mitcham Police Section as well[114].

In 2002 the station was open from 8am until 8pm however by 2009 the hours had been extended and Tooting closed during the night but open from 8am until 11pm daily[115]. Since 2002 the station address has been 251 Mitcham Road, Tooting, SW17 9JQ

Wandsworth Police Station

This station is not to be confused with Wandsworth Common Police Station situated in Trinity Road, Tooting which is dealt with later.

Records show that from 2nd May 1830 provision was made for Police premises to be leased for 3 years in Bridge Field, Wandsworth, on an annual rent of £52[116]. It is uncertain whether this was for use as a Police Station, detached office or for accommodation however further references give an address as 10 Love Lane[117]. Documentation relating to the cleaning of Metropolitan Police Stations in 1832 shows a Station located at The Plain, Wandsworth, being a station on 'V' Division[118] where the Superintendent had his offices. In those earlier days there was only a Wandsworth designation and a divisional letter had not yet been brought into use. However by 1840 Wandsworth was shown as part of 'V' or Wandsworth Division.

Later references also show that Wandsworth had a Watch House and that as of 25th June 1850 it was no longer used for Police purposes[119]. This was probably the one in The Plain. Wandsworth was not apparently under Metropolitan Police jurisdiction until 1839, disputing the claim made earlier that the boundary extended to cover the Parishes of Battersea, Wandsworth, Barnes, Mortlake, Wimbledon, Merton and Tooting[120]. Prior to this policing was carried out locally by the Parish Constable and aided by paid constables from the watch house premises and they were said to be very efficient in their duties. Wandsworth was also the place where Petty court sessions were introduced at the same time and a list of magistrates together with their addresses were published[121]. Another building was used as a also located in Love Lane and was brought into service in 1864. The property was leased from Mr Joseph Langton for duration of 21 years at an annual cost of £85[122].

Wandsworth Police Station was referred to as Wandsworth, Love Lane and it retained its Divisional Headquarters status as well being an operational Station. It had three cells, a recreation room and large stables accommodating up to 15 horses. In the yard were a van house and a coal shed. The Station strength in 1864 was 2 Inspectors, 7 Sergeants and 52 Constables. The Station had a Superintendents Office, a Divisional Office occupied by the Divisional Clerk. Instructions were issued that the mounted Inspector or Sergeant was also to patrol Battersea, Merton, and Tooting[123].

The prisoner transport van was stationed at Love lane as well as a hand cart for the removal of drunken prisoners from the street. The Divisional Criminal Investigation Department (CID) occupied the whole of the second floor after those single Constables were moved out in 1878 to live at Bay cottage next door[124]. In 1881 the cottage was still occupied but arrangements were being made move the occupants out. This was given up in March 1884[125].

The Section House, called Bay Cottage, that was situated in Love Lane

Wandsworth Police Station
Love Lane
1864-1883

housed ten single Constables with the head Constable being George Dowty, aged 34, from Wiltshire[126].

The Metropolitan Police Surveyors concern with regard to the poor state of the Station was evident in their report in which it said that;

> 'This station has for years been abandoned as a police dwelling on account of its dilapidated condition and because it was infested with vermin. A site for a new station was purchased about 1874, and the constables have been located in a small cottage not far off as a temporary expedient, but the erection of the new station is not begun'[127].

The Police Station and Court House stood where Armoury Way now stands and was demolished in 1892. The old Station remained occupied until 1883 when it was vacated[128].

The Station also had a recreation room where there was a billiard table for the use of off duty Officers. The Commissioner instructed that Wandsworth should receive a new billiard table in 1870 and Battersea was allocated a variety of games for its recreation room[129]. Ten revolvers were issued to Wandsworth on 19th November 1868; these firearms were kept in a secure cabinet in the Station[130].

Often Police Officers would be assaulted in the execution of their duty, a risk

Wandsworth Police Station
146 High Street, Wandsworth SW18 4JJ
1883 – Present day

at that of which Officers were most aware.

Whistles were issued (from 1881 onwards) to each Police Officer to summon help; three short blasts and a Constable on a neighbouring beat would hurry to render assistance.

Drunken males were often a problem as they could be violent and Constable Joseph Eite was kicked and died whilst trying to arrest a person for drunkenness in 1868[131].

292

Rank	Name	Date appointed	Address
Inspector	John Bussain	Promoted 1830	The Plain Police Station at Wandsworth
Inspector	Richard Turner	Promoted 1830	Princes Street Police Station at Richmond
Inspector	Richard Dowset	Appointed Inspector in 1814	London Road Police Station at Kingston
Inspector	James Shepherd	Promoted in 1837	Milman Road, Chelsea
Inspector	Henry Creed	Promoted 1842	Clapham Common, Clapham

What is clear from the listing above was that the most experienced and longest serving Inspector was Richard Dowsett who had been transferred

A topographical aspect showing the location of the police station in Wandsworth

from the Bow Street Horse Patrol in 1837 prior to being posted to Kingston, a Thames-side posting. He retired on pension in September 1849 after 35 years service.

Boundary revisions between Wandsworth and Clapham were included in the changes in borders between 'B', 'L' and 'V' Divisions in 1863[132]. From 1864 Wandsworth was designated as a Station on 'V' Division and that it was a place where Police duties were to be carried out including the parading of Police Officers, charges taken and prisoners detained in cells[133]. The Station must have been important as it was shown as having a strength of 2 Inspectors, 7 Sergeants and 52 Constables. It contained stables to house the horses which were used by Sergeants and Inspectors for supervision purposes.

Two Sergeants at the Station would take it in turns to ride one horse on the Sub-Division whilst either the Inspector or the remaining Sergeant was to use the other to patrol further afield including visiting Battersea, Merton and Tooting[134].

Superintendent Butt reported the problems of policing in Wandsworth in his annual report to the Commissioner but indicated that crime had dropped by 20% between 1869 and 1871, that vagrancy offences had also fallen by 70% and that there were far fewer complaints of begging. Other issues related to leaving washing out during the night and the control of public houses and beer houses[135].

The photograph left shows the large rear yard of the Station; a separate Section House was later built further away.

In 1868 Wandsworth Sub Division was divided in two and a separate Sub-Division of Battersea was created; Inspector Egerton from Wandsworth was transferred to Battersea to take charge of this newly-created area. Some 22 horses were stabled at the Station including 6 horses which were used for Prisoner van transport from the Court to prison. The Division had expanded to include Wandsworth, Battersea, Merton, Barnes, Richmond, Kingston, Ditton and Epsom.[136] Firearms were stored at the Station and Wandsworth is shown to have had 10 2nd issue revolvers which were distributed on 19th November 1868. Ten rounds of ammunition were issued for each weapon[137]

The huge rear yard of the station

A rear view of the station with access to the main building

The pictures on the previous page shows the rear aspect of the station and the access to the main building.

By the mid 1870s the old Station House was considered no longer suitable for carrying out the duties of policing and suggestions were offered about finding a larger site on which to build a bigger and more up-to-date Police Station. Some available land located on higher ground seemed perfect for the job as it would offer better access for the prison van to facilitate the transport of prisoners and on 6th April 1875 the freehold was purchased for £2,000.

The picture below shows another aspect with the parade shed where the constables would form up prior to coming on duty and be inspected by the sergeant. During the parade the constables would produce their appointments, their note book, handcuffs, truncheon and whistle for inspection. Any Constable unable or who produced defective appointments would may become the subject of a disciplinary charge. Also any important local intelligence would be disclosed and noted down such as stolen cars or details of persons wanted.

Interestingly part of the premises had formerly belonged to the Lord of the Manor [138]. Building started on the new Police Station in 1882 and by Christmas Eve, 1883, the administration section of the building was suitable for occupation. The address was recorded as West Hill, Wandsworth,[139] and the Police Station was duly built on the site of 'Sword House'.

The lack of a sufficient number of Police was often the cause of increased assaults on Officers and 1881 saw the sad death of Inspector John Pearman, who had been at Wandsworth since 1877, who perished from wounds which he received following an arrest[140].

Wandsworth Police Stations Parade shed in the yard at rear

A substantial Station was built on the site at a cost of £10,738 3shillings and contained accommodation for the 'V' Division's Headquarters.

Superintendent Charles Digby took charge of the Station and as married quarters of five rooms had been built on the 1st floor these were occupied by him and his family.

In addition, thirty-four single Constables resided on both the first and second floors and with the constant comings and goings of the Divisional Superintendent and his family the Constables needed to behave themselves at all times otherwise serious disciplinary issues would have arisen. Later, in 1881, Digby and his wife and daughter moved from the Station to Thurnhill Villa, Rose Hill Road, Wandsworth[141]; special Police dwellings for senior Officers. In 1888 Digby was assisted by David Saines as Chief Inspector and George Earwaker as Reserve (mounted) Inspector.

Wandsworth Sub-Divisional Inspectors	Years
William Gillies	1893 - 1895
Edward McKenna	1895 - 1905
James Andrews	1905 - 1906
Walter Cleave	1906 - 1908
William Brice	1908 - 1910
Charles Hodges	1910 - 1914
William Barham	1914 - 1917

Premises were still being retained in Love Lane, (later re-named Putney Bridge Road[142]), Wandsworth, as a Section House for single Officers however in 1878 they were relocated to Bay Cottage, Love Lane, which was to be a temporary Section House[143]. The common lodging fee for the 10 single Police Officers residing in Bay Cottage was set at 1s per week[144]. Freehold to the land had been purchased in 1875 [145] and the Station also had a Section House located at the rear of the Station.

By 1893 because of the appointment of large numbers of Inspectors the Commissioner decided that there should be a more senior Inspector between the Chief Inspector and the ordinary Station Inspector so he appointed Sub-Divisional Inspectors on promotion. These were usually responsible, trusted and experienced Inspectors and they were easily distinguishable by having 2 stars on either side of their tunic collar. Whilst all Stations on Wandsworth Division had Inspectors Sub- Divisional Inspector William Gillies took charge of Wandsworth, Wandsworth Common, Wimbledon, Putney and Roehampton.

Sometimes when an Officer takes action in the line of duty unfortunate circumstances which could lead to tragic events may occur. In 1896 Constable Edwin Stone died of a heart attack whilst arresting a violent prisoner at Wandsworth[146].

By 1907 the address of the Station was shown as High Street Wandsworth. It was a Station on 'V' Division and was also the Divisional Headquarters. A

Sectional Station was also shown at Wandsworth Common. The Division, together with 'L', 'M', 'P', 'R', and 'W', formed the Southern District which was under the supervision of a Chief Constable stationed at New Scotland Yard, S. W. [147].

The ranks of the Police at Wandsworth were swelled by large numbers of the Special Constabulary who as citizens held down essential jobs but also volunteered their services free to supplement dwindling Police numbers. In June 1916 for example the Wandsworth men joined the regular Officers in saving the lives of enemy aliens (usually people of German or European extraction) and protecting their property from public wrath.

A revision of boundaries between Wandsworth and Richmond Sub- Divisions resulted in a new Station at Kew being opened[148]. Further revisions established the Sub-Division of Earlsfield, which meant that there were boundary alterations at Wandsworth, Battersea, Wimbledon and Kingston. A new Division was formed in 1921 called 'Z' or Croydon Division which led to further alterations to 'W' or Wandsworth Divisional boundaries[149]. In 1937 Wandsworth was a Sectional Station of Putney (VD)[150].

A review of Police buildings took place in 1959 and it was recommended that even though Wandsworth was built in 1883 and was old, it was not recommended for rebuilding until at least 1974[151]. In line with the creation of Local Authority Boundary changes taking place in London under the London Government Act 1963 the status of Wandsworth as a Station was reduced to that of Sectional Station to Putney Sub-Division. The Station was shown as being located on 'W' or Tooting Division at this time[152] and this was still the case in 1966[153].

In 1931 the details of V or Wandsworth were shown as;

V or Wandsworth	Wandsworth	146 High St, Wandsworth, SW18
	Putney	215 Upper Richmond Rd. SW15
	Roehampton	8 Medfield St. SW15

In 1981 Putney Division was re-designated as a Sub-Divisional Station and absorbed into 'W' Division. Its Divisional administration of Chief Superintendent, Superintendent and a portion of the general administrative staff was transferred to Wandsworth Police Station. Chief Inspector Admin together with the Process Section remained at Putney[154].

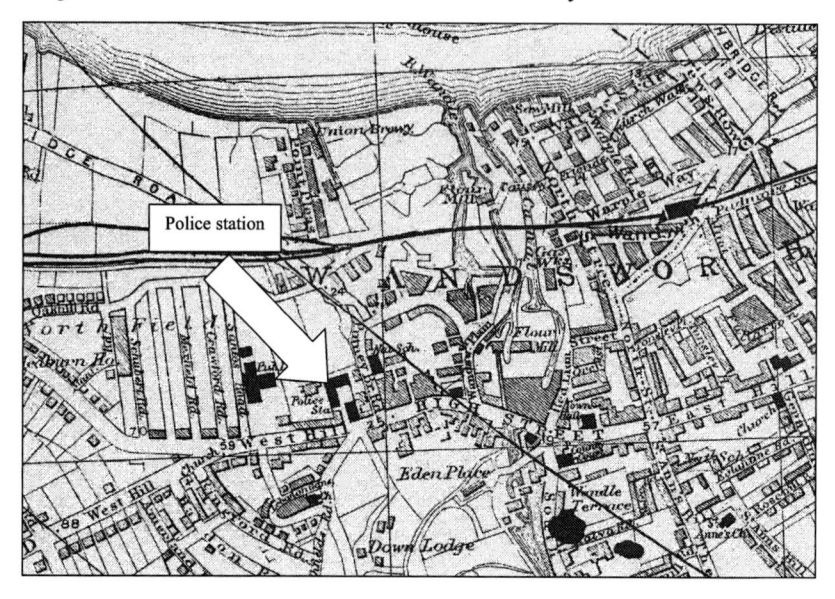

In 2009 records show that a Police Office had been established in the Arndale shopping Centre, Wandsworth, and that it is open Mondays to Saturdays. Although fixed opening hours are not available these appear to be the same as the Shopping centre itself[155].

Wandsworth Common (Trinity Road) Police Station.

This Station was shown on the corner of Trinity Road, Upper Tooting, SW17, and situated at the junction with St. Nicholas Road. Often the Station has been referred to as Trinity Road Police Station; this was a road that stretched from East Hill, Wandsworth, straight through Wandsworth Common to Balham. The Station was situated at the Balham end of the road. In 1873 Wandsworth Common was shown as a Station of 'V' or Wandsworth Division and had a Sergeant in charge.

In 1878 additional premises were leased until 1886 from Mr H. P. Rainbow of Broderick Road, These were to be used as a Section House and living accommodation for an Inspector, a Sergeant and five Constables. The two-storey premises in Broderick Road, Wandsworth Common, cost £50 per year to rent and there were stipulations in the contract that the premises were not to

Wandsworth Common Police Station
76 Trinity Road, Upper Tooting SW17
1883 - Present day

be used for cells or a lock up and that no other buildings were to be erected on the site[156]. This meant that this was not a Police Station and that prisoners were transferred to Wandsworth for charging etc.

Metropolitan Police Surveyors reported in 1881 that the premises for use as a Police Station at Trinity Road were occupied by one married Inspector and five single Constables and that the Station was:

> 'an ordinary dwelling house in a suburban road, ill-adapted to the requirements. The men wash in the inspector's scullery and a proper station would be a great advantage'[157].

Freehold to the site was purchased in 1882 and a Police Station built and occupied in 1886. It also contained a Section House which was built at the location. The Station was built in about 1890 and (was constructed using a plum brick, had egg and dart mouldings to string courses and a stone stair case.

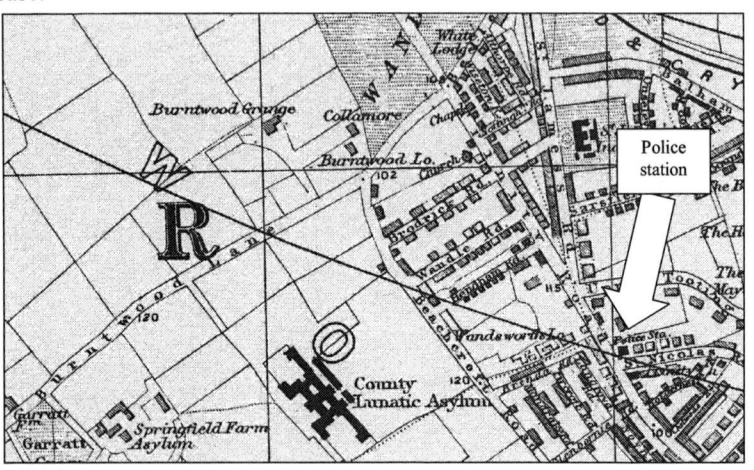

Records show that in 1893 the Station was situated on 'V' or Wandsworth Division and was connected to the telegraph system. In fact both Wandsworth and Wandsworth Common Police Stations had been connected to the telegraph system on September 23rd 1886 and having the code Whiskey Charlie (WC)[158].

During Trenchard's reforms of the 1930s the oddity for this Station was that it retained the same telegraph code and was probably the only Station in the Metropolitan Police to do so.

Rear yard of the police station

The picture above left shows the rear yard aspect.

During 1885 the Sub-Inspector at Wandsworth Common was Nathan Thompson Lee, born 1824 at Strelton in Cumberland, who had joined the Police in 1868. He had come to note as a self-taught amateur wood worker, winning 23 prizes for his exhibited works at various industrial schools in London. His distinguished Police career was marked with a full page tribute in the Police Review and Parade Gossip 1895. Amongst his many commendations were the 'clever capture' of two house breakers at Hampton Wick and the arrest of a local notorious ruffian, Patsy Ryan. The article reports that he was promoted to Sergeant on the strength of these arrests and transferred to Arbour Square on 'H' Division in London's East End. What was unique in Mr Lee's service was the fact that he did not miss one hour's duty through sickness. He received substantial gifts for his loyal service together with an oil painting of himself in uniform painted by a local artist. After two years at Wandsworth Common Inspector Lee was transferred to Battersea where he saw out his service[159].

In 1924 Wandsworth Common was a Station on 'W' or Brixton Division and not 'V' Division. In 1925 a strip of surplus land with a frontage was sold to Messrs Frost for £230. Its address was shown as 76 Trinity Road in 1931.

A fixed point box was located in Alma Terrace but in June 1932 it was removed to Wandsworth Police Station and replaced with Telephone Box No. 37[160]. The Station was given a substantial re-build in 1937 it was shown as a Sectional Station to Balham (Cavendish Road) in the same year.

During the 1960s the status of the Station was shown as Sectional to the Sub-Divisional Station situated at Balham[161]. In May 1971 application was received by Wandsworth Council from the Surveyor of the Metropolitan Police for a re-building of the Station. Plans submitted requested that a bigger Station was required for Policing purposes and re-building was to include the adjoining site in Upper Tooting Park[162].

Wandsworth Common Police Station amalgamated with Earlsfield Police Station in January 1974 and adopted the status of Police Office, being open from 8.30am until 11.30pm when the Station would close. Outside of opening hours a telephone link to Tooting Police Station was available free of charge to provide immediate contact for callers[163].

A rear view of the main building in 1907

In 2007 the Station was still in use as a Police Office and houses the newly introduced Safer Neighbourhood Teams which consist of 1 Sergeant, two Constables and five Police Community Support Officers[164].

---

[1] Cherry, B and Pevsner, N. (1983) The Buildings of England – London 2: South. Penguin Books, Middlesex
[2] Metropolitan Police Orders dated 4th March 1836
[3] The Police and Constabulary List 1844 , Parker, Furnivall and Parker, Military Library Whitehall.
[4] Law Directory 1854.
[5] Kelly's London Directory 1838 p1012
[6] Kelly's 1841 London Directory p877
[7] Kelly's 1842 London Directory p1042
[8] Kelly's 1844 London Directory p1373
[9] Kelly's 1851 London Directory p1482
[10] Kelly's 1860 London Directory p1023
[11] Metropolitan Police Orders dated 11th January 1864
[12] ibid
[13] ibid

[14] Metropolitan Police Orders dated 5th January 1861
[15] Metropolitan Police Surveyors Records 1860
[16] Metropolitan Police Special Order dated 1864
[17] Metropolitan Police Orders dated 13th July 1868
[18] Metropolitan Police Orders dated 11th January 1864
[19] Metropolitan Police Surveyors Report 1881 MEPO 2/234
[20] Metropolitan Police Annual report 1874
[21] Metropolitan Police Orders dated 20th June 1884
[22] Metropolitan Police General Orders 1893
[23] Census date 1881
[24] Receivers List 1888
[25] LB 684 and MEPO2/578 Public Record Office, Kew
[26] Metropolitan Police Roll of Honour dated 2002
[27] Reay, W. T. (1919) The Specials. Heineman, London
[28] Metropolitan Police Orders dated 1st January 1932
[29] Metropolitan Police Surveyors Records 1924
[30] Districts and Divisions 1937
[31] Metropolitan Police List 1966
[32] The Metropolitan Police Roll of Honour dated 2002
[33] Metropolitan Police Orders dated 6th August 1964
[34] http://cms.met.police.uk/met/boroughs/wandsworth/09contact_us/index accessed on 27th january 2010
[35] LB686
[36] Kirchners Police Index 1931
[37] Metropolitan Police Orders dated 27th August 1914
[38] Districts and Divisions 1937
[39] LB686
[40] Metropolitan Police Orders dated 24th February 1921
[41] Metropolitan Police Orders dated 6th August 1964
[42] Metropolitan Police List 1966
[43] Metropolitan Police Authority (MPA) Committee reports accessed on 15th February 2009 http://cms.met.police.uk/boroughs/wandsworth/09contact_us/index
[44] Hansard HC Deb 29 March 1999 vol 328 c532W
[45] http://www.earlsfieldhub.co.uk/viewtopic.php?f=7&t=90 accessed on 29th January 2010
[46] LB690/1/1
[47] Metropolitan Police Orders dated 29th February 1896
[48] ibid
[49] post office directory 1898
[50] Police and Constabulary Almanac 1957 and 1960
[51] Police and Constabulary Almanac 1960
[52] Metropolitan Police Orders dated 16th February 1962
[53] Metropolitan Police Orders dated 13th December 1963
[54] Metropolitan Police List 1966
[55] Police and Constabulary Almanac 2001
[56] Metropolitan Police Authority (MPA) Committee reports accessed on 15th February 2009 http://cms.met.police.uk/boroughs/wandsworth/09contact_us/index
[57] http://cms.met.police.uk/met/boroughs/wandsworth/index accessed on 29th January 2010
[58] Metropolitan Police Orders dated 13th August 1879
[59] MEPO 5/50 (376) Public Record Office, Kew
[60] Metropolitan Police Orders dated 13th August 1879
[61] Census records 1881
[62] Metropolitan Police Surveyors Records 1881
[63] LB450
[64] Metropolitan Police General Orders 1893
[65] Kirchners Almanac 1907
[66] Metropolitan Surveyors Records 1912
[67] Metropolitan Police Orders dated 24th February 1921
[68] Metropolitan Police Orders dated 21st September 1923
[69] Metropolitan Surveyors Records 1924

[70] Metropolitan Police Orders dated 7th December 1925
[71] Metropolitan Police Orders dated 6th August 1965
[72] Metropolitan Police Orders dated 29th December 1972
[73] Metropolitan Police Orders dated 29th November 1977
[74] ibid
[75] http://cms.met.police.uk/news/policy_organisational_news_and_general_information/police_dog_jake_is_awarded accessed on 30th January 2010
[76] MEPO 5/53 (419)
[77] MEPO 03/234
[78] Metropolitan Police Orders dated 30th August 1873
[79] Kelly's Directory 1875 p1989
[80] MEPO 5/54 (441)
[81] MEPO 5/53 (419)
[82] census records 1881
[83] National Roll of Honour dated 2002
[84] Post Office directory 1881 p1970
[85] Metropolitan Police Surveyors Records 1881 MEPO 02/234
[86] ibid
[87] Police Office Directory 1894 p2203
[88] LB664/-/0
[89] LB664/-/0
[90] Metropolitan Police Surveyors Records 1924
[91] Reay, W. T. (1919) The Specials. Heineman, London
[92] ibid
[93] Metropolitan Police Orders dated 27th June 1935
[94] http://www.policememorial.org.uk/Forces/Metropolitan/Metropolitan_Roll_1940-1945.htm accessed on 3rd Februray 2010
[95] Metropolitan Police Orders dated 4th August 1981
[96] Metropolitan Police Orders dated 28th April 1978
[97] Metropolitan Police Orders dated 15th February 1983
[98] Metropolitan Police Surveyors Report 1881 MEPO 04/234
[99] Metropolitan Police Surveyors Report 1881 MEPO 04/234
[100] Metropolitan Police Surveyors Records 1912
[101] Metropolitan Police Surveyors Records 1924
[102] Post Office Directory 1842
[103] Metropolitan Police Orders dated 11th January 1864
[104] Metropolitan Police Orders dated 28th October 1865
[105] Census records 1881
[106] Metropolitan police Surveyors Report 1881 MEPO2/234
[107] Metropolitan Police Orders dated 20th June 1884
[108] Receivers List 1888
[109] Metropolitan Police Orders dated 25th May 1889
[110] Metropolitan Police Surveyors Records 1912
[111] The National Police Roll of Honour dated March 2002
[112] Map of Districts and Divisions dated 1937
[113] Metropolitan Police Orders dated 21st June 1939
[114] Police and Constabulary Almanac 1957
[115] Metropolitan Police Authority (MPA) Committee reports accessed on 15th February 2009 http://cms.met.police.uk/boroughs/wandsworth/09contact_us/index
[116] MEPO 5/3 Public Record Office, Kew
[117] MEPO 5/54(441) Public Record Office, Kew
[118] Distribution and return of Wool mops for cleaning stations on each division dated 1st July 1832
[119] MEPO 5/7 Public Record Office, Kew
[120] MEPO 2/76 Public Record Office, Kew
[121] ibid
[122] Metropolitan Police Surveyors Records, Charlton
[123] Metropolitan Police Orders dated 11th January 1864
[124] Metropolitan Police Surveyors records, Charlton.

[125] Metropolitan Police Surveyors Report 1881 MEPO 04/234
[126] Census Records 1881
[127] Metropolitan Police Surveyors Report 1881 MEPO 4/234
[128] Metropolitan Police Surveyors Records 1864
[129] Metropolitan Police Orders dated 15th July 1869
[130] Metropolitan Police Orders dated 10th March 1869
[131] National Police Roll of Honour dated 2002
[132] Metropolitan Police Orders dated 21st October 1863
[133] Metropolitan Police Orders dated 11th January 1864
[134] ibid
[135] Commissioners Annual Report 1971 p68
[136] Metropolitan Police Orders dated 13th July 1868
[137] Metropolitan Police Orders dated 10th March 1869
[138] John Back Archive (1975) Metropolitan Police Historical Collection, Charlton and LB 670.
[139] Metropolitan Police Orders dated 20th June 1884
[140] ibid
[141] Census records 1881
[142] Shaw, R. (1981) Battersea District Library. Correspondence held by MPS.
[143] Metropolitan Police Orders dated 18th June 1878
[144] Metropolitan Police Orders dated 20th June 1878
[145] Metropolitan Police Surveyors Records
[146] The National Police Roll of Honour dated 2002
[147] Kirchners Almanac 1907
[148] Metropolitan Police Orders dated 29th January 1914
[149] Metropolitan Police Orders dated 24th February 1921
[150] Districts and Divisions Map 1937
[151] John Back Archive (1975) Metropolitan Police Historical Collection, Charlton and LB 670.
[152] Metropolitan Police Orders dated 6th August 1964
[153] Metropolitan Police List 1966
[154] Metropolitan Police Orders dated 4th August 1981
[155] Metropolitan Police Authority (MPA) Committee reports accessed on 15th February 2009 http://cms.met.police.uk/boroughs/wandsworth/09contact_us/index
[156] Metropolitan Police Surveyors Records 1878
[157] Metropolitan Police Surveyors Report 1881 MEPO 4/234
[158] Metropolitan Police General Orders 1893
[159] Police Review and Parade Gossip March 1st 1895
[160] Metropolitan Police Surveyors Records 1924.
[161] Police and Constabulary Almanac 1960.
[162] Balham and Tooting News (1971) Police Station rebuilding? 14th May
[163] Wandsworth Borough News (1974) Police Stations combine. 4th January
[164] http//www.met.police.uk/wandsworth/saferneighbourhoods.htm accessed on 3rd September 2007

Chapter 11

The Royal Dockyard Divisions

Introduction

The Naval Dockyards have had a long history with Chatham dating back to the 1570's. The London area boasted the most prestigious engineering and ship building industries in the land. There were four Royal Docks and 160 private yards in London, most of which were located between London Bridge and the Woolwich Ferry. Since the 16th Century this stretch of river equipped England with most of its Battleships, merchant ships, fishing boats and barges[1].

A dedicated Dockyard Police Force had been introduced in 1831 and by 1834 they had taken over control of all Royal Naval Dockyards[2], however they were not to last very long in London. The key posts and authority for the Police of the dockyards had traditionally rested with ex naval officers who perhaps did not understand the function of security as it was common knowledge that vast quantities of stores were being regularly misappropriated. The Admiralty had noticed the success of the new Police which had been introduced in the metropolis in 1829 and the former was concerned that the law enforcers employed in dockyards had not been totally satisfactory. Using members of the workforce as Watchmen or having Porters, Rounder's, Warders, Watchmen and later Wardens was obviously a problem[3]. The Admiralty decided to consider a better system and following considerable discussions decided to introduce a more efficient force based on the Metropolitan Police model.

Unlike the force they replaced the full powers of a Constable were granted to the Police of the new Dockyard Force but this was found to be unworkable. Powers extending beyond the dockyards were more appropriate since it was often necessary to search the houses of suspected workers for stolen property. Search warrants were easily obtained as the Naval Superintendents were also ex Officio Magistrates by virtue of their appointment[4].

The Metropolitan Police had for some time been responsible for patrolling the Royal Naval dockyards at Greenwich and Woolwich on 'R' Division and this gave them a special expertise which had helped to make them successful. Because of this experience, especially during strikes and industrial unrest, including in wartime, meant that Police were later seconded under special arrangements that ensured the security of all the royal dockyards. Many of these dockyards had no outer walls and these yards provided an open invitation for thieves to steal timber and other supplies meant for HM ships.

Woolwich Dockyard, because it was located in London, was policed from 1841 until 1916 by the Metropolitan Police. Other dockyards were gradually taken over by the London Force and policed from 1860 onwards. These included Devonport (until 1934), Chatham (until 1932), Portsmouth (until 1933), Rosyth (from 1914 to 1926), and Pembroke Docks (until 1926).

Metropolitan Police Dockyard Inspector at Portsmouth 1860 - 1865

The picture at left shows a Metropolitan Police Inspector in the uniform of the time at Portsmouth Dockyard and included a top hat. This style of uniform was replaced by a different one in 1865 that included a helmet with a reef helmet plate.

Superintendent Mallalieu from 'R' Division (Woolwich) had experience in the supervision of London Dockyards. He was asked to review the old dockyard system and make recommendations to the Admiralty on the efficiency of the Dockyard Force. He concluded that the Dockyard Force 'gained much from giving little' so they were inefficient and ineffective. This led to the disbanding of the dedicated Dockyard Police and replacing them with Metropolitan Police Officers in December 1860[5]. This move saw the spread of Metropolitan Police Officers extend beyond the Metropolis to other Royal Dockyards and War Department premises throughout the UK. There were other advantages which were seen by Mallalieu relating to the interchange ability of the workforce. It was a distinct advantage to have a mobile force where individuals could be transferred to other Dockyard Divisions at a moment's notice.

Following a force-wide re-organisation in operations and supervision of the Metropolitan Police in 1859, five new exclusive Dockyard Divisions were established detaching them from supervision of Land Divisions. They were given a one year trial. Each was set up with a Superintendent in charge and consisted of Woolwich, Portsmouth, Devonport, Chatham and Pembroke. Rosyth joined this group in 1914.

Recruits who joined the Police and were then subsequently posted to the dockyards or military stations were required to swear a separate oath to the Queen. This was different to the oath sworn by Police Officers appointed to the Town Divisions located in London. The oath for the dockyards etc. varied to include duty outside London at any War Department establishment, which included an area some 15 miles outside their place of duty. In other words an Officer could swear two separate oaths during his service.

The uniform of a dockyard constable showing rolled cape, lamp and spring loaded truncheon case

Superintendent Mallalieu made periodic and unannounced visits for supervisory purposes. He became the founding father of all the Dockyard Divisions by introducing new methods and differing working conditions. He was an extremely thorough man who neglected nothing[6] and soon made a number of changes by establishing a new system of Stations, beats and patrols. He improved the shift pattern system and based his style of policing on making Stations of the docks, hospitals or buildings located within. He placed an Inspector in charge of each and added support staff to equal that in a Police Station. He also established Woolwich as the Divisional Headquarters and introduced training for Police Officers as firemen; all unmarried Constables had to live in the dockyard and to receive educational instruction[7]. This group of officers were often kept on reserve to be used when needed. In January 1871 instructions were given to ensure not only the security of dockyards but also that under no circumstances was information about naval dockyards to be given to persons connected with the press[8].

There is a general perception that Police of dockyards wore different uniforms, helmets and accoutrements to their Town based counterparts in the Metropolis. They wore the distinctive garter helmet plate showing the fouled anchor and divisional number.

The picture on the previous page also shows the Police Officer/Fireman dressed in a double breasted coat and long boots. He also has a bull's eye lamp attached to his belt, a rolled cape under his left arm and a truncheon in a leather case. The only difference from Town based Divisions was in the badge detail. The badge shown at right that was issued in about 1870 shows the Queen's crown whilst underneath the 'fouled anchor' indicates his membership of a Dockyard Division. Below this is shown the Divisional number, which was allocated on arrival at Divisional Dockyard Headquarters once the Officer was posted. The only difference to the Town based Divisions was that the anchor would be replaced by the Divisional letter.

Dockyard helmet plate circa 1870

In 1863 a new Instruction book with a cream cover was published and issued to 7,254 Constables in the Force. Additional copies were supplied to Inspectors, Sergeants and for placing in reading rooms[9]. A special, smaller, black-covered instruction book for Police Officers posted to dockyards and war department Stations was introduced in 1873. This contained the instructions to all ranks on the efficient running of the royal dockyards and in 1890 was reprinted with a blue cover and containing other details. Since the Police had been given extra powers at dockyards information on duties performed there were also included and copies were issued to the 203 Constables at Woolwich, 182 Constables at Portsmouth, 154 Constables at Devonport, 116 Constables at Chatham and 32 Constables at Pembroke.

Generally when the Metropolitan Police took over any dockyard they occupied existing buildings or ships for duty and accommodation. It was the responsibility of the Admiralty to make the necessary arrangements for Police accommodation although the Metropolitan Police surveyors attended from time to time to see if the Police Officers were housed in adequate accommodation. If not they would render any repairs or alterations with the permission of the Dockyard Captain Superintendent.

Police Officers and their families paid a reduced rent if they lived within the docks.

Woolwich Dockyard or 1st Division

Superintendents	Chief Inspectors	Sub div inspectors
Alexander Thompson 1842 – 63	Colin Forbes 1863 Deptford Dockyard Philip Brine Royal Arsenal 1863- 65	
Kingston Mark (Jnd1835) 62 -64	Thomas Carnelly Royal Arsenal (1843) 1865 – 1877 John Pethers -1867 Deptford (on promotion from Chatham) Philip Beare (1844) 1867-1869 (rtd) (Deptford) Dockyard	Michael Money 43163 (j1862) 1869-1888
Robert Bray 1862 (From 'N' temporary during the suspension and supervision of Supt Mark)	Clement Gosby 1885 Daniel Collins 1869 William Capon 1878 Robert. W. Congdon (j1863) 1883 –89	
Alexander Thompson (From Pembroke 1865 -71	Charles Woonton 44275 (j1863) 1888 –92 (rtd)	Alfred Chatterley 70947 (j1885) 1908-17(rtd) Adam Llewellyn 65822 (1881-1906) Joseph Spry 62359 (j1878) -1902-03 (to Chief Inspector Woolwich)
Thomas E. Hindes (j1853) 1871-89 (rtd)	George Harding (j1860) – 1897 (Rtd) John Willmott (40960) (j1861) 1885- 1894 (rtd) George Cavell 43696 (j1863) 1891-1894 (to Chatham) James Tait 54915 (j1871) 1898-1903(rtd)	Thomas Evans 1903-06 James Haynes 64246 (j1880) 1903-04 (to Chief Inspector Woolwich) Francis Shorthouse 70825 (j1886) 1910-1912 (rtd) Elias Thomas 78684 (j1893) 1917-1923 (rtd)

Robert. W. Congdon (44172) (j 1863) 1889 – 1894 (rtd)	Thomas Rogers 1902-1904 (Trans to Chatham)	James Shorthouse 74225 (1885- 1923 rtd)
	James Haynes 64246 (j1880) 1904 -09 (rtd)	SDI Walter Mcintyre (80525) 1926 (Royal Arsenal)
Josiah C. Hobbins 44292 (j1863) 1895-1903 (rtd)	Joseph Spry 62359 (j1878) 1903-04 (rtd)	Charles Ferrier 79438 (1894-1920 rtd)
	Owen Webb 78058 (j1892) 1915 – 1917	
John Devine OBE 64460 (j1880) 1903-1924 (rtd)	Fredrick Spencer 1914 -1915	Willie Smith 80236 (j1895) 1917-1923 (rtd)
	Henry Morgan 1914 Fredrick Wright 74225 (1889 - 1920)	
	Albert Saunders 80946 (1896 – 1923(rtd)	

Woolwich Dockyard was protected by the Metropolitan Police from 1841 until 1926. In the early days of the Metropolitan Police it was the responsibility of the Division on which the dockyard was located to provide the manpower and supervision for dockyards. This meant that Woolwich Dockyard became the responsibility of 'R' Division which policed the Thameside area of Greenwich, Woolwich, Plumstead and Blackheath. Regular supervisory visits were made by the Divisional Superintendent who would sign the visitors' book as a mark of his supervision. The dockyard was a designated Inspector Station and therefore an Inspector was in overall charge of day to day operations.

Woolwich Royal Arsenal about 1910

Responsibility for the policing of Woolwich Arsenal passed to the dockyards in 1844 and from this date the old style Dockyard Police were replaced. The picture on the previous page shows the front gate of the Royal Arsenal. A contingent of local Police Officers, provided gate and perimeter security; they also guarded the main magazine which included the onerous task of guarding the magazine hulks moored off shore[10]. Records show that an Inspector of 'R' Division stationed in charge at Woolwich Dockyard by the name of Roger Howard was stationed there in 1844. Howard had been promoted to Inspector in 1839[11] and was an early recruit.

The stations located within the dockyard between 1860 and 1907 consisted of Woolwich Royal Arsenal, Woolwich Dockyard, Deptford Victualing Yard, Naval Store Depot, West India Dock, Powder and Cordite Magazines and Railway depot, Plumstead Marshes, Floating magazine 'Thalia', and the Royal Military Repository Woolwich Common[12].

Living conditions for Police Officers of all ranks and their families was interesting. Woolwich Dockyard for example provided married quarters in the factory gate for Police Officers and their families. However, the gate would have been locked after bell ringing and the key to be let in was kept at the main gate[13]. Only the Main gate had sufficient space for a Section House for use by the twenty single Officers. This was to ensure proper supervision of daily activities by the Superintendent who resided in the Main Gate House at Woolwich. Two days would be set aside during the week when washing and drying clothes could take place[14]. Married men, even when off duty, needed to be in their quarters by 10pm, in order that they became a reserve should a fire or other emergency take place[15]. All reports of missing persons, or property lost or stolen would have been forwarded to 'R' Division or sent direct to the Commissioner's Office (CO)[16]. The Dockyard Police were responsible for receiving, housing in police cells and escorting naval prisoners from ships at Sheerness, Woolwich and Chatham for onward conveyance to Lewes gaol. Records showing the expiry of sentence details were kept by police so that they were aware of the release date[17]. Policing in the dockyards was different from policing in the Town Divisions. For this reason it was difficult to get serious incentives for deserving 2nd class Constables to transfer to The Royal Arsenal, Woolwich. The Commissioner made offers in Police Orders to entice extra committed Constables for duty at the dockyard[18].

One of the less attractive features of policing in the Dockyard Division were the many dangers that existed. Occasionally there would be serious accidents when munitions exploded causing serious damage, fire and loss of life. In September 1845 an explosion killed 7 workers and another in December 1855 killed 4 more. Police Officers from Woolwich would have been required to send assistance, help with first aid, and clear up the damage[19]. This meant that not only were Police required for security purposes but they were also employed as fire watchers and were at all times required to remain vigilant over the threat of fire. They later became part of the Dockyard Fire Brigade which was often a mix of all professions within the dockyards. In the very first year there was a Fire Brigade established and such was the professionalism and efficiency that they were able to put out some 26 small fires[20].

Woolwich Dockyard was used as a training base to teach Divisional Police Officers on transfer their dockyard duties and responsibilities. Once competent and if confirmation of the transfer was agreed, those who passed would be transferred to other Dockyard Divisions at the expense of Commissioner. Regular notices for volunteers were posted in Police Orders to get volunteers to sign up to dockyard duties[21].

It was in Police Officers' interest to ensure that provisions were not stolen or removed from the yards without authority. It was the responsibility of the Police to detect crime and, on occasions, failure to prevent a crime on their beat rendered them liable to discipline. A large quantity of sugar had been stolen from a naval store at Woolwich in April 1863 and suspicion fell on Constable 89 Wright and Constable 88 West who were both in the vicinity at the time. The subsequent and very rigorous inquiry by the Dockyard Superintendent produced evidence to Sir Richard Mayne, the Commissioner, which exonerated both officers[22]. It was not uncommon at this time to suspend Police Constables from duty without pay during their suspension, or even make them pay a fine if they failed to discover a crime committed on their beat while they were on duty. Any suspended Officer was required to hand in his appointments, truncheon, note book, whistle, and handcuffs, etc.

Instructions were regularly issued alerting all Police of the names of Officers of ships moored in the docks or harbour so they would be able to give visitors reliable information when they were visiting those officers, ships, etc[23]. Alexander Thompson was the first Police Superintendent of the dockyard from 1842 until 1863 and was an experienced and respected Officer. He was transferred to Pembroke Dockyard, but he was not there for long as he was recalled back to Woolwich following concerns that the new Superintendent was not up to the job. In charge of the dockyard in 1863 was Superintendent Kingston Mark [24] although at times his name was frequently reversed in Police Orders. The Superintendent's residence was in the main gate and he lived there with his wife and 5 children. Superintendent Mark had been the subject of Police discipline the year before when he was suspended from duty and his command taken over by Ex-Dockyard Superintendent Mott of 'N' Division. This must have been a huge embarrassment to Mark because he still resided at the dockyard and while he was suspended he received no pay. He appeared at Scotland Yard following an inquiry where he was found at fault and the Commissioner fined him 1 weeks pay and reprimanded him for a failure in supervision[25]. Mark was re-instated and advised by the Commissioner that any further infractions would mean loosing his command. Kingston Mark had joined the Metropolitan Police in 1835 and became a Dockyard Police Officer as an Inspector in 1858 when he joined Woolwich. He had been highly regarded as he only spent 4 years as an Inspector and was then promoted straight to Superintendent. Mark retired in 1864 when Thompson returned for a short while before he retired.

Inspector James Gill, his wife and child lived in the Factor Gate where two Sergeants and their families also resided. The Superintendent had been aware that Inspector Kell had been unwell for some time. The Police Physician had asked the Dockyard Superintendent for his views on the continued employment of his Inspector. Inspector Kell, who had joined the Metropolitan police in 1836, had been stationed at the Royal Arsenal for some time and had become unwell and unable to do duty. This meant that another Officer had to take responsibility for the Inspector's duties. Kell was later retired and the reason was stated was that he was 'worn out'[26]. There were a number of general health problems which came with working in the Dockyards Divisions. These mostly seem to have been rheumatism, and for those working as Water Police the constant rolling had led to a number of cases of vertigo. Considering the openness and location of dockyards with their equally damp atmospheres and windy conditions it would have been hardly surprising that many Police Officers resorted to these as reasons for retiring early.

The photograph on the next page shows the main gate at the Royal Naval College which had to be manned by Police for security purposes, as can be seen. Police were required to check the passes of people entering and leaving the establishments and to detain any goods or persons who were responsible for illegal removal.

Police wives often worked for the Metropolitan Police in the dockyards in a number of capacities since they did not have to travel far, could earn

The main entrance the Royal Naval College, Greenwich

some pin money and raise their children at the same time. The senior officers realised that this relationship was beneficial to both sides, especially since Police Officers' wives were generally not allowed to work. For example the wife of Constable 140 Archer was employed to clean the single Constables' bedrooms and the family occupied apartments in the Main Gate[27]. It appears also that employing Police wives in the Mess[28] was a condition of occupation of some of the married quarters rather than a voluntary matter[29].

The Superintendent would have been aware of tragic events taking place in his dockyard, especially for example the death of a police officer. Such was the case for Superintendent Thomson who by this time had been transferred from Pembroke Dockyard to Woolwich. In 1865 Constable George Sykes died from his injuries whilst attempting to release a brig that had become stuck in the mud at Woolwich Dockyard[30]. In the same year Inspector Brine also died although the details are not available.

By 1866 the dockyard was replenishing its stock of fire engines and new steam engines were being issued to replace manual ones. The steam engine replaced three manual engines and these were returned to the store keeper as instructed[31]. Steam driven fire engines were far more powerful and efficient compared to the hand pumped versions.

During 1868 the War Department Stores called back the firearms which it had issued to the Metropolitan Police Dockyards, however it allowed 12 guns per Division to be kept[32]. Also cutlasses which had been issued to Sergeants and Constables were withdrawn and returned to Stores[33]. In

1869 Woolwich Dockyard had by far the largest complement of men with a total of 173. Apart from 1 Superintendent there were 14 Inspectors, 22 Sergeants and 136 Constables[34]. The War Department owned houses in Czar Street, Deptford, which was near the dock gates and where Police Officers were housed at a nominal rent. Instructions were issued that these houses were to be vacated should the War Department require their use for the public service at any time[35].

The Royal Dockyard at Deptford had been a responsibility for 'R' Division to police but in 1871 it was sold off to become the Foreign Cattle Market. Police deployed there were withdrawn and posted to other dockyard duties elsewhere. In the same year Woolwich Dockyard extended its security to take in the Army service Corps barracks, also known as the Grand Depot Stores, where 1 Sergeant and three Constables were added to the Sub-Divisional strength[36]. Other duties for the Constables consisted of escorting railway wagons across the rifle range to the gate leading to the Magazines. This was a precarious and dangerous undertaking. There was an elaborate system of crossing the ranges which involved a Constable hoisting a small red flag and sounding a bugle which would then be acknowledged at the shooting point in the same manner. Once the trucks and escorts had arrived the Constable would sound the bugle once more to announce the successful crossing[37]. One of the greatest fears in the dockyards was fire, especially with some highly flammable material being stored and which included immensely volatile munitions and explosives.

The Dockyard strength at Woolwich in 1873 consisted of 1 Superintendent, 12 Inspectors, 21 Sergeants and 125 Constables[38].

The Water Police the Royal Arsenal with Superintendent shown at centre

Special Fire Brigade training sessions were introduced and these were attended not only by Metropolitan Police Officers but also suitably trained dockyard workers who had particular skills. All Police Officers were members of the Brigade and the equipment was issued into their control and supervision. All Police at the yards were trained in fire drills, and the use of engines, ladders and pumps. The picture on the previous page shows the Royal Arsenal Dockyard Police with their Superintendent, Chief Inspector and Inspector.

There was no reserve of men waiting on standby at the dockyards for a fire, like the Fire Brigades of today, however there was a person who was allocated the task of keeping the steam engine fire stoked up and ready to go just in case. In the event of a fire all trained officers would make their way as quickly as possible to the scene and operate under the instructions of the Superintendent or his deputy. There was constant vigilance regarding fires and inspections of buildings would take place to see if any fires had been left on when the work force had gone home[39]. The Fire Brigade at the Woolwich Dockyard was tested early in 1864 when a powder magazine on Erith Marshes, which was adjacent to the Thames, exploded. The devastation resulted in a breach of the Thames wall and the Police who responded to the call 'worked tirelessly in relays to shore up the breach and prevent serious flooding'[40]. Furthermore, a serious fire broke out at Plumstead several years later and such was the level of professionalism displayed that a Letter of Commendation was sent to the Commissioner of Police from The Inspector of Works, Royal Arsenal, Woolwich, which bore testimony to the job well done in extinguishing the fire[41].

In the same year, during the introduction of the Dockyard Divisions, the Royal Arsenal Sub-Divisional New Stores Depot was also established. This was the land based Police Section who were supported by their own Marine Police as shown in the picture on the previous page. Very often their duties were very dangerous and not without accident. They included having to escort gunpowder barges from Waltham Abbey Gunpowder works through the various canals to the River Thames. The gunpowder was for delivery to the various munitions depots in Plumstead, Woolwich, and beyond.

Uniform security was considered important enough for a Chief Inspector to be placed in charge at the Arsenal together with 1 Sergeant and 4 Constables. The Sergeant resided at No 1 Cottage, a short distance away, and his tour of duty was from 7am until 7 pm each day. No 2 cottage was occupied by a Constable who took over duty for the remaining 12 hour tour. The Constables were split into 1 for day duty, 2pm until 10pm, and the remaining 2 Constables, from 10pm until 6am, to guard the entrance gates. The gates were visited by the Chief Inspector at least once during the day or night and by an ordinary Inspector during each tour of duty[42].

The picture below shows a group of women involved in the manufacture of munitions at Woolwich. They wore a sort of uniform made of a lint based product that reduced any friction that might cause an explosion.

A group of women who worked at the Royal Arsenal

Checking passes both in and out of the dockyards, apprehending people illegally on the premises, stopping and recording the details of visitors, preventing loitering, and the controlling of prostitutes in or near dockyards, were some of the duties of the gate Constables. Many females worked in the Royal Arsenal and they could only enter with the necessary authority.

In 1865 the Commissioners attention was drawn to the fact that 'a number of Police residences at Woolwich Dockyard were occupied illegally by unauthorised personnel'. The system of monitoring the occupation of Police premises in Dockyard Divisions at Woolwich had become rather lax and when a number of Sergeants and Constables moved away the premises granted for Police occupation were handed over to relatives or members of their family who were not wives or children. Other Police rooms were taken over illegally by some Police Officers whose families had grown too large. Those who had taken charge of these premises were given three months notice to vacate their own premises or comply with the regulations[43].

Officers were reminded that they should also immediately report any damaged lamps or leaking gas pipes in order to prevent fire and explosion. In 1870 George Potts a dockyard Constable went missing on duty and a search was made of his beat at Woolwich Dockyard. Tragically he was found floating in the dock having drowned. The reason for this was uncertain although foul play was not ruled out. Sadly the death of a serving Police Officer was not uncommon during these times and he was one of 42 Metropolitan Police Officers who died in service that year[44]. The duties and responsibilities of the Dockyard Police were many and varied.

The picture below shows the Royal Dock gate at Woolwich and as can be seen there was a constant movement of supplies through the gate. Passes and supply papers would need to be checked by the Constables on gate duty before any visitors would be allowed in.

The Royal Dockyard, Woolwich

A glimpse of life can be found when looking at reports from Superintendents. In 1875 the report to the Commissioners by Superintendent Hindes states that there had been 38,171 persons who had visited the Royal Arsenal, some 5,572 admission passes had been handed out and eleven small fires had been found and put out without loss or injury. Another of the obligations of night duty Constables stationed at dockyards was the daily lighting and extinguishing of gas lamps situated within the yards[45]. Hindes further comments on the newly formed Fire Brigade when he confirms that it had been a great success with the men being efficient, 'maintaining their drills and keeping their fire plants in excellent order'[46].

One of the problems which beset the Police in Dockyard Divisions were the numbers of common women loitering nearing the vicinity since it was necessary for them to have a medical examination under the Contagious Diseases Acts, but the Superintendent reported that 54 fewer women were proceeded against than in the previous year[47].

Records show that in 1877 Thomas Hindes was still the Superintendent in charge and he was assisted by Thomas J. Carnelly as the Chief Inspector. The Inspectors were Robert Congton, John Cronk, James Tunbridge, John Willmott, George Godfrey, William Payne, Edward Coffey, Donald Taylor, Henry Parker, James McElliott and Michael Money[48].

The Metropolitan Police Surveyors inspected the premises to which Police Officers were posted or in which they resided. The same was true even if they did not own the buildings as it appears that they were responsible for comfort and safety. In 1881 they inspected the Woolwich Division Victualling Yard at Deptford and reported that 1 married Inspector, 3 single Sergeants and 12 single Constables resided there. Many of the buildings occupied by dockyard Police Officers were very old and suffered from neglect. An inspection took place of the Inspector's quarters in Greenwich Naval College and it was noticed that damp had penetrated the walls, ventilation was poor and sunlight did not reach the basement rooms[49].

It occasionally transpired that army deserters, once identified, were returned under escort by soldiers to their various regiments although often these duties were delegated to the dockyard Police Officers. In October 1893 the non police escort party from the Royal Horse Artillery collected a prisoner from Holloway Gaol and escorted him back to Woolwich Dockyard. They travelled by train to Woolwich Arsenal Station and on arrival, and taking their prisoner with them, decided to refresh themselves in the Bull public house, but a short while later a problem arose when the escorted prisoner escaped. When Gunner Pennant realised this he came rushing out from the public house, aimed his rifle and fired at the fleeing escapee but fortunately missed hitting him. Discharging a firearm in a public place is not only against the law but allowing a prisoner to escape as well are both offences in breach of army discipline. They were Court Martialled and punished heavily[50] although they were not discharged from the army.

Some Police Officers attached to the dockyards had complained that such work was boring and monotonous for most of the time and for this reason they did not want to stay so there was a need to offer incentives for Police Constables to remain. Promotion in dockyards was also a bone of contention since it appears to have been very slow[51]. There was also less chance of arresting people for crimes than would be the case if stationed on Division as crime arrests might be rewarded with extra pay or expenses. The work was at times difficult and dangerous. In 1893 two brothers Richard and John Crawley were part of a team of labourers engaged in discharging grain into a barge when a dispute arose over the size of grain sacks. There was a dispute between the supervisors and labourers who said that they were too large to be carried by them. A crowd assembled and two Metropolitan Police dockyard Constables, PCs Gundrey and Butcher, attempted to resolve the dispute only for the two bothers and the crowd to attack both Constables. Amidst calls from the crowd for them to be thrown into the river a boat was sent across just in case the crowd carried out its chant. Later when the brothers were arrested they were charged with assaulting the two Constables and taken before the court. Richard was sent to prison for four months with hard labour whilst his brother was imprisoned for two months[52].

During the 1st World War a number of bombs were dropped by Zeppelins and Aircraft on the Royal Dockyard. Four bombs landed in the Royal Arsenal causing minimal damage, three others fell in the dockyard itself while one struck the hospital and a further two hit the Artillery barracks[53]. There was a considerable amount of traffic both in and out of the dockyard and in 1918 Constable Edward William Swan was killed when he was run over by an army lorry whilst on point duty[54] there. Superintendent J. Devine was in charge of the dockyard and supervising 170 Police Officers in 1924[55], an increase in strength of 11 since 1873.

Many Police Officers, in true tradition over the years, have been involved in some acts of outstanding bravery. None more so than in 1919 when extreme danger occurred as a munitions train caught fire at Woolwich Arsenal. PC 92939 Percy Carr, PC 93291 William Mewton and PC 78028 William Monnery, all stationed at the Royal Arsenal, managed to extinguish fires in two adjacent trucks of a 26-truck ammunition train standing beside a magazine at Woolwich Arsenal. Carr had ran immediately to the nearest fire hydrant, connected the hose and then ran it down to the train. Two trucks were by then alight and both Mewton and Monnery (the older officer who took charge) played the hose on the flaming trucks until the flames went out. Hot ammunition and fuses continued to be discharged, even after the fire was put out. The Officers could have been killed at any time as they had to reach the fires by approaching through a hail of exploding bullets and fuses. For extinguishing the fire and preventing a far greater tragedy all three were awarded the well deserved Kings Police Medal[56].

Police pay rises in the early 1920s and the creation of the Police Federation made the Metropolitan Police Dockyard contingents very expensive and the Admiralty and the War Department tried to consider ways of minimising the cost. It was decided that with effect from the 1st January 1927 the security of Woolwich should be transferred to the Marine Police. This was a special force drawn from Military backgrounds. Sub-Divisional Inspector (80525) MacIntyre and his deputy Inspector (86374) Michael Lofus together with 3 Station Sergeants, 8 Sergeants' and 55 Constables were transferred to other Divisions within London[57].

Portsmouth Dockyard or 2nd Division

Superintendents	Chief Inspectors
James Mott 1861-3 Customs	
Henry Guy (1836)1863-69 (rtd) From Woolwich	Joseph King 1867 -1869
Archibald Macdonald 1869-82 (died in service of Cancerous tumour)	William Rivers Willson 1868 – 71
George Godfrey Acting Supt 1882 -1883	Robert Martin 1877-83 (to Supt Portsmouth)
Robert Martin 1883 - 1885	George. Godfrey 1881-1886 (promoted to Superintendent Chatham)
William Ventham (j.1863) 1888 - 1895 (rtd) (originally dockyard Pc at Pembroke)	Michael Money (1862) 1888 -1894 (rtd)
James Carter 1898 – 1907 (rtd)	William Ventham 1883-88
James Last 1910-1914 (rtd)	James Carter 1895 – 1898 (To Supt Portsmouth)
Fredrick Spencer 1915 – 1923 (rtd)	James Last 1894- 1897 Arthur Waddell 1897-1901 (To Chatham)
David Sewell 1924 -1928 (rtd)	George Dixson –1901-1905
John George Parsons (87860) 1928- 1933 (rtd)	Henry Wickes 1905 Thomas Kraze 1910 Charles E. Sly (1912-3) David Sewell 1914-15 Thomas Peel 1917

322

Portsmouth Dockyard remained in the control of the Metropolitan Police from October 1860 until 1934 when they were replaced by a dedicated Dockyard Force. The Police were not only responsible for the dockyard but also for Gosport Victualing Yard; Gunboat Yard, Haslar; Haslar Naval Hospital; Gun Wharf, Portsmouth Naval Depot; Portland Magazines; Priddys hard; Floating Magazines, Portsmouth Harbour; and the Magazine at Marchwood [58]. These were referred to as War Department (Military) Stations located in the dockyards and the instruction to supervise the dockyards took effect from 7th November 1862. At the same time there was an increase of Police Officers at Portsmouth by 1 Sergeant and 12 Constables[59]. Some of the first Constables transferred to Portsmouth from London Divisions (all unmarried) consisted of Constables Neale, Blackman, Ely, Costello, Cogger, Peacock, Rayment, Savage, Lock, Clarke, Childs, Christmas and Stribling.

Superintendent Henry Guy had been asked by the Commissioner to compile a list of married Police Officers who resided outside the dockyard and who lived more that 5 minutes away. The Commissioner noticed that 23 Constables and Sergeants lived over a mile away from the dockyard. Concerned that they may not be able to make it back to the dockyard (in their own time for which they were not paid) should a fire alarm occur the Commissioner reminded Guy and the other Superintendents that in future not to allow a married officer to reside more that 1 mile from the dockyard[60].

In 1869 when Portsmouth was being established the dockyard strength included four 1st class Inspectors, one Detective Sergeant, four Water Sergeants, seven 1st class Sergeants, 106 1st class Constables, 24 2nd class Constables and one 3rd class Constable[61]. Later this was adjusted and became one Superintendent, seven Inspectors, 24 Sergeants and 133 Constables. Records show that Henry Guy remained the Superintendent until 1869[62] and he remained so until Admiral Sir Thomas Paisley, who was Admiral Superintendent of the dockyard, was replaced. The Admiral highly commended Superintendent Guy and his men for their tact and ability together with Inspector Sherlock of the Water Police who was always prompt with assistance[63]. Sherlock was a trusted and responsible Police Officer who was in charge of duties outside the dockyard that not only included the Water Police but the Detective Police, contagious disease prevention duties, prisoner transport, and apprehension of stragglers, deserters and disorderly seamen and marines[64]. The strength at

Portsmouth in 1873 was 1 Superintendent, 8 Inspectors, 24 Sergeants and 127 Constables[65].

By 1877 Mr Archibald McDonald was the Superintendent and was assisted by Robert Martin as Chief Inspector[66]. The Inspectors were Daniel Godden, William Jones, William Connell, George Morsman, George Coppen, Joseph Wooton, John Camac and William Briggs[67].

The Dockyard Police were responsible for the supervision of Royal Navy Hospitals and Haslar was a designated Inspector Station with an office situated near the entrance gate. The Inspector was responsible for patrolling the hospital at least once each shift, supervise and take charge of the front gates and compile daily reports to the Superintendent[68]. Women and children of seamen and marines were allowed to visit the hospital for treatment and to use the dispensary. Passes for medicine would be inspected at the main gate prior to anyone leaving the hospital grounds[69]. Visitors were allowed to visit the museum and to inspect the building and the grounds at allotted times. Those visitors were allowed in after verification and once they had signed the visitors' book. Visitors to patients were stopped and often searched in an effort to find tobacco, fruit, cake or alcohol of any kind as none of these were permitted by the Captain Superintendent and confiscated.

Passes issued by the Medical Examiner for others to enter would be collected and returned to the Captain Superintendent. Any strangers, people of known bad character and those discharged for misconduct were not allowed to enter the yards. When dockyard workers and male nurses left the hospital at mid day and in the evening the Inspector in charge would be present and decide whether anyone should be searched or not. Constables supervised smoking arrangements of the building since smoking only took place in the outer airing ground and the back of the hospital square between 10am and 12 noon and 1 until 3pm. The picture at left shows the bell which was sounded on the instructions of the Admiral Superintendent, normally for calling dockyard trades to work, to dinner, and when to vacate the yard.

The Dockyard bell which was sounded calling people to work.

At other times the bell would be used to alert people to a fire in the yard and rung only with special authority[70].

There was also a list of duties for Police staff manning the Main Gate, Factory Gate and East Gate to the Dockyard. For example, staffing of the Main Gate at Portsmouth consisted of 1 Inspector, 1 Sergeant and two Constables with similar arrangements for the other gates. The Inspector was required to be present at all times unless relieved by the Sergeant. The Constables' function in all instances was to stop and question all strangers, visitors and others before being allowed in or out[71]. An Inspector, or Sergeant acting for him whilst he was away, was also responsible for duties outside the gates meaning, supervision of the Water Police, Detectives, duties under the Contagious Diseases Prevention Act, conveyance of prisoners to Lewes Gaol and apprehension of disorderly Sailors and Marines[72]. The Inspector would be on duty from 8am until 6pm and was responsible for parading the Dockyard Police Officers for duty at their fixed hours, inspecting their appointments, reading out the list of absentees from the dockyard and any other relevant information. He would then supervise Police employed at the wharves, landing places, railways and afloat and inspecting the Police Ship and cells[73]. The Inspector also needed to complete entries in the occurrence book of matters connected with his duties, compile the daily report to the Superintendent by 8am and attend the Divisional Office when required to do so. The conveyance of prisoners to gaol with the appropriate Constable acting as escort was another feature of dockyard life. Prisoners were transferred along the coast from Portsmouth to Lewes by train. Expenses were paid to Police in advance[74].

Dockyard constable circa 1870

The picture above right shows a Dockyard Police Officer circa 1870 complete with summer-wear ceremonial gloves. They were required to wear gloves all year round, wearing thick dark woollen gloves in winter[75]. There was no discretion in those days for supervisors to instruct their staff to wear shirt sleeve order during hot weather. They generally wore a tee shirt underneath a tunic which buttoned up to the neck.

Portsmouth Dockyard had a long reputation for losing or having property stolen from its stores. This came to light in 1796 through Colquhoun's review of the Police of the Metropolis and asserted that nearly one million Pounds sterling was lost in time of war, and half that in peacetime, through fraud, plunder or pillage. Ensuring the security of property over such an extensive and complicated site as Portsmouth was a big problem for the Dockyard Police. Inspector Horne was rewarded with £5 on the personal directions of Sir Richard Mayne, the Chief Commissioner, for his actions in discovering stolen property being removed from the dockyard[76].

Honesty was always the best policy but lying to a senior officer was always unforgivable and treated harshly. Police Officers worked 7 days a week and had no day off. Senior officers also had to be vigilant when presented applications for leave based on the un-corroborated facts on family matters. For example Constable 48 Boxall attached to the dockyard sought leave to visit his dying mother. He was sacked when it was found that this was not the case[77] and she was not in imminent danger of death. Not the first example nor would it be the last of a Police Officer wanting leave and giving a dubious reason.

Portsmouth Dock yard in about 1915

In 1875 the Superintendent in charge submitted to the Commissioner in his annual report that 29 cases of embezzlement had been detected, with convictions obtained in each case and all outstanding property recovered[78]. The Dockyard Fire Brigade and Police Officers had been vigilant in 1875 as there were no reports of fires in the dockyard but they helped fight three fires in the neighbourhood[79].

The picture on the previous page shows a view across the dockyard taken after the Semaphore Tower had been burnt down in 1913.

By 1879 the strength at Portsmouth had increased to 202 Police Officers and a new Section House was built near Unicorn Gate to accommodate 2 Inspectors, 2 married Sergeants and 35 single Constables. It was occupied in the same year[80]. Inspector Connell was a dockyard Officer through and through. He retired from the dockyard after 43 years Police service having spent 21 years at Portsmouth, the last ten years of which he was in charge of the Clarence Victualling Yard, Gosport. Inspector Connell was a trusted Officer and had also been responsible for the police arrangements on the many occasions the Queen and her entourage passed through the yard[81], often on the way to Osborne house on the Isle of Wight. The photograph at the end of this section (chapter?) shows the Section House contingent in 1914.

Inspector Coppen, aged 43 years and originally from Linton in Kent, resided at the Royal Naval Hospital, Haslar, with his wife Sarah and their six children[82]. Coppen had joined the Police in 1868 and within three years was a Dockyard Inspector, a rank in which he remained until he retired in 1894.

A picture showing dockyard workers leaving Portsmouth main gate.

The picture above is of a typical scene at the main entrance to Portsmouth Dockyard and shows workers making their way home after a hard day.

There was a social side to policing which was not only reflected in the Dockyards Divisions but on the London Divisions as well. The Police family included the wives, children and the Officer's other relatives. For example, a social club was in place at most Police Stations and Christmas parties for the children have long been a tradition, even up to today. In 1894 the fifth annual Portsmouth Dockyard event for the children of Police, took place. This not only included the children of serving Dockyard Police but also Police orphans and children of retired Police Officers. The show lasted three hours and took place in the dining hall of the Workman's restaurant near Unicorn Gates and included Herr Wingard, a magician. A bun, an orange and sweets were provided to each child as they left[83].

The issuing of a Police Order in 1894 that prevented Dockyard Police from working in yards where their relatives were also employed caused considerable concern among the Police Officers. The effect of this order, originating from the Home Secretary, suggested that Dockyard Police Officers would be re-assigned to other postings if found working with or near relatives. In Portsmouth and Gosport this affected some 50-60 Police

Superintendent Carter and his Dockyard Fire Brigade 1902

Officers alone and such was their concern that Assistant Commissioner

A. C. Howard had to visit to dispel anxieties. The result was that a liberal interpretation was applied to the general satisfaction of those affected[84].

The picture below shows the Dockyard Fire Brigade with fire engines, ladders, and Divers in their breathing equipment. Notice that there is very little specialist equipment for fire fighting. Superintendent Carter in flat kepi is standing proudly forth from the left.

Inspector Michael Money resided at 4 Dockyard Extension Police Station with his wife Sarah in 1881. Money, originally from Ireland, was 40 years old although his wife was some eight years younger. Money had joined the Police in 1862 and by 1869 had become an Inspector at Woolwich Dockyard where he stayed until 1881 when he was transferred to Portsmouth in the same rank. He was promoted to Chief Inspector at Portsmouth in 1888. He retired from the Dockyard Police in June 1894 and was presented with a cheque, a handsome gilt clock and ornaments for 32 years service[85]. Money had been transferred at a time when Superintendent Macdonald was quite unwell and it was felt that Money could support the ailing Superintendent. Archibald Macdonald had become Superintendent of the dockyard in 1869 however in 1882 he unfortunately died in service from a cancerous tumour.

The picture below shows the Haslar Naval Hospital gates with Police

| The Haslar Naval Hospital was a busy place and only people who had business inside were allowed in by police. |

Officers at their posts.

In March 1895 Superintendent Ventham also retired, moving a short distance to St. Denys, Southampton. Ventham originally started at Pembroke as a Constable in 1863 and had worked his way up the ranks. He had been in charge of the dockyard at Portsmouth for 7 years. The Commissioner moved Superintendent Carter (shown right) from Chatham Dockyard to take over in his place. Ventham was held in very high regard by his men. Although he was a strict disciplinarian he was also described as being courteous and obliging to all he had contact with. He spoke two foreign languages, French and German; a great asset bearing in mind the many different nationalities he would meet in the course of daily business in the dockyard[86].

Sport amongst the Police Officers was always encouraged by senior Officers and the differing sporting events also provided constant

Unicorn Gate, Portsmouth Dockyard at leaving time.

entertainment for off duty Officers, some of whom from the dockyard in Portsmouth took part in a game of cricket with Portsmouth Borough Police. The Dockyard Police won by three runs[87], however in the return match a short while later the Borough Police won by six runs making matters all square[88]. One of the Dockyard gates at Portsmouth, Unicorn Gate is shown above.

In May 1895 Inspector Chubbock also served notice of his intention to retire after 25 years of service. He was presented with a 'handsome marble timepiece' as a token of esteem and goodwill[89]. Chubbock had joined in 1869 and been a Dockyard Inspector from 1888 until he retired.

One of the first presentations that Superintendent Carter attended was of the retirement of a Constable who had completed 38 years in the Police. This was a considerable length of service by the standards of the day.

Constable F. Lane retired on pension and Carter presented him with a silver mounted walking cane and a pipe. Kind words were expressed by Inspector Goss, Chief Inspector Last and Det. Sergeant Smallbridge[90].

Superintendent Carter 1898-1907

The picture above shows Superintendent Carter dressed in his ceremonial uniform and with his medals. Carter had been the Superintendent at Portsmouth since 1898 until he retired in 1905. Before that he had been Chief Inspector at Portsmouth from 1895 after being transferred from Pembroke where he had served as the officer in charge. Carter had joined the Woolwich Dockyard as Inspector in 1885 where he progressed well and earned the respect of his superiors.

Portsmouth Dock yard Sergeants posing with their medals in 1897

331

The picture on the previous page shows the Sergeants of Portsmouth Dockyard in receipt of their 1897 Jubilee medal which they are proudly displaying.

The medal at left shows the detail of the front. This medal was identical to the 1887 Jubilee medal save for some minor alterations and date changes. Those Police Officers who were awarded the 1887 medal and were also on duty for the 1897 celebrations were later awarded a clasp to attach to their medal.

The 1887 Jubilee medal

The picture below shows Portsmouth and Gosport Police circa 1902. Superintendent James Carter is shown seated in the centre 2nd row.

Police Officers were trained in fire fighting techniques and those who were either on or off duty had to go and help put out any fire that should

Portsmouth and Gosport Dockyard Police 1902

occur. Whilst there was no standing brigade available at Portsmouth it depended solely on availability. One Police Officer or another member of the dockyard workforce was normally posted to the fire engine and remained with it in case an alarm was sounded. The Dockyard Inspector General was responsible for overseeing the safety of all people working within the docks. He recognised the efficiency of the Police Fire Brigade when he commended Inspector Rogers and his Police Officers for their promptitude in extinguishing a potentially serious fire in the Haslar Hospital[91] in 1896. Inspector Rogers was a prominent and respected

Dockyard Inspector, later becoming Sub-Divisional Inspector in 1897 and Chief Inspector at Woolwich. He was also a member of the Dockyard Cricket Club whose annual luncheon was held in the Recreation Room at Marlborough Gate and which was attended by 60 people in November 1896. The Chairman Superintendent Carter was presiding with Chief Inspector Last and Inspectors Short, Rogers and Butler also in attendance[92]. Speeches were normally made by the various Officers of the Club.

In 1908 whilst out on inquiries Detective Sergeant Alfred Barton was found drowned in the dockyard[93]. Another case of an unexplained death on duty which almost never ended in prosecution.

RHS Medal

The photograph below shows Pc 443 Charles Burton who, in 1916, was presented with the Royal Humane Society Medal by Rear Admiral Superintendent A. A. Weymouth[94]. Constable Burton, whilst on night duty the November before, had jumped fully clothed into the tidal basin to rescue a stoker (standing next to the Constable) who had fallen overboard from his vessel which had been moored alongside the quay. He was further rewarded by Sir John Dickenson, Magistrate at Bow Street, with a reward of £10 from the Hero Reward Fund. Superintendent Fredrick Spencer is standing facing the recipient after having given his speech. He is seen still holding his notes in his hand. The medal shown above is the bronze version as given to PC Burton.

The 1916 awards ceremony for Constable Burton and the stoker he saved

Saturday 20th December 1913 was a particularly memorable day in the life of the dockyard as what occurred then had serious consequences for

An artist's impression of the Fire at Portsmouth dockyard in 1913

years to come. A fire, which quickly got out of hand, broke out and destroyed one of the central features that dominated the sky line and helped guide ships into the docks. The Semaphore Tower was completely destroyed. An investigation into the cause of the fire was undertakern by the Superintendent Last who reported the results to the Admiral Superintendent. The investigation required a report from witnesses and workers who were in the area prior to the fire breaking out. All the facts were taken down and anyone who could be blamed for the fire would be the subject of disciplinary action by the Admiral Superintendent. Artists and illustrators were busy attempting to recreate the scene in order to sell the images as postcards to an interested public.

Like the card above, the card below was one produced for sale to the general public. All the dockyard Police were summoned together with others workers from the dockyard to fight the fire and it took some considerable time to put out. This was a talking point for some time and finding out how it happened was a primary concern for the Police Superintendent in charge. The charred remains of the Semaphore Tower are evident in the picture on the next page which was taken by a local photographer the next day.

The dock yard fire showing charred times and ruins of the Semaphore Tower

Access to take such pictures was strictly regulated as this was an embarrassment to the Authorities. There is a slim chance that the picture was taken by a workman, dock worker, sailor or even a Police Officer and then sold on later.

Portsmouth was a very busy port and there was much to see and supervise. In 1905 Portsmouth Dockyard was responsible for building

The patrol of a Dockyard Constable on duty at Portsmouth in about 1910.

and launching the Dreadnought Class Battleships, a prelude to an arms

335

race with Germany that ended with the start of the First World War. Thousands of workers were needed to help towards the war effort

Vigilance was an essential skill for the many Police Officers who were sent to the dockyards to supplement the dwindling numbers. It had been felt that Germany would spy on British efforts to get ahead in this race and Police Officers were constantly aware of the threat. Arrests were made on a number of occasions.

The Sergeant at left shows a Dockyard Officer wearing the 1887 Jubilee Medal with bar (1897) and the 1902 Coronation Medal. On the table is the officer's helmet with its badge, a copy of which is shown on the right.

Dock yard Sergeant circa 1904

The photograph below shows the helmet plate badge worn by constables and sergeants on the dock yard divisions. It is the same plate as shown in the picture at left and was worn for service between 1902 and 1936 when a new plate was issued.

The group photograph below shows Constables, Sergeants and the Sub-Divisional Inspector of the Unicorn Section House at Portsmouth Dockyard in 1914. Although there were exceptions it was taken just as the United Kingdom was preparing for war. The Sergeants and the Sub-Divisional Inspector would not have been occupants of the Section House as they would have occupied married quarters within the dockyard itself. Portsmouth Dockyard became extremely busy

Dockyard helmet plate 1902 - 1935

during this time and often the Dockyard Divisions were augmented with more Police Officers to combat the level of spying and the taking of pictures which may have aided an invader. Many of the Police Officers are proudly displaying their 1912 issued Coronation Medals. The Unicorn Gate was another of the dockyard entrances.

In 1924 Portsmouth Dockyard Police had the largest complement of men

Unicorn dockyard Section house 1914

with 211 Officers, Sergeants and Constables with Superintendent D. Sewell in charge[95]. By 1932 the dockyard strength was being reduced with 6 Constables being transferred to Town Divisions back in the Metropolitan Police area[96]. The remaining Metropolitan Dockyard Police were all transferred back to London in 1933.

The Portsmouth Championship Dockyard Cup 1922

The cup shown above is the Metropolitan Police Portsmouth Challenge Cup which was presented in 1922 by the Admiral Superintendent to the winning sports team from the Dockyard.

Devonport Dockyard or 3rd Division

Superintendents	Chief Inspectors
Robert Bray 1860-61 (transferred to R)	William Crook (1840) 1868 -76
John Baxter 4/1861-1869	William Ventham 1877-78 (Pc 18 at Pembroke in 1862)
William Wakeford 1869-91 rtd Transferred to Devonport as Inspector in 1860 1869-1891 Customs Inspector Pembroke 1860 -1865 later 1865- 67 superintendent at Pembroke	J. Willmott 1885-1888 (To Woolwich) George Harding 1891- 1894
Josiah Hobbins 1891 -1894	Charles Wall 1894 -1899
Edwin Smith 1897 – 1905	George Dixson -1901 - (transferred to Portsmouth) –
George Dixson 1910 - 1913	William Tett (trans from 'M' to C/I) 1902 -05
Thomas Evans (68285) 1913 - 1918 (rtd)	Albert Keys 1910-17
Albert Keys 1923 (rtd)	Down (1911)
David Sewell 1923-1924 (To Portsmouth)	Alford Hunt (86548) 1927 (Later Superintendent 'N' Division)
Owen Webb 1924-1930 (rtd)	

Devonport dock yard gate

Devonport is situated in the docks at Plymouth. The police responsibility at Devonport not only included the Devonport Dockyard – South and Devonport Dockyard - North but also Keyham Factory Yard, Stonehouse Victualling Yard, Stonehouse Naval Hospital, Gun Wharf, Floating Magazines, Hamoaze, Turnchapel Coal Depot and St Georges Halland - the Royal Magazine at Bull Point[97]. These all had Inspectors in charge whilst Sergeants took responsibility for Stonehouse Naval Hospital and Gun Wharf. The picture left is the Naval Barrack gate. A number of Constables had been sent for duty at Devonport but all were quickly promoted or reallocated different roles. PCs Anniss (later Inspector at Portsmouth), Chaplin, Bates and Looker were all promoted to Sergeant whilst PCs Huxtable, Pearn and Angear were re assigned to the

338

Water Police[98]. In 1862 eight Constables were transferred to Devonport from London as part of the increase in establishment.

Duty at Royal Hospitals varied slightly from other hospitals but generally this involved ensuring strangers, vagrants and other undesirable folk were not permitted entry. Female searchers were employed on the front gate to search women and children. No patient was allowed to leave without a discharge pass being issued and these would be inspected at the front gate before the bearer was allowed to leave. Women, children and families of the navy and marines were allowed to enter to attend the dispensary or for advice from the Medical attendant[99].

Gratuities were allowed to Police for good detection and police work. In 1860 the magistrate, in essence the Dockyard Admiral Superintendent, awarded a Sergeant a sum of money as a gratuity for his diligence in discovering stolen property being removed from the dockyard[100]. All of the authorities were keen to ensure the success of the newly installed Police and rewards were granted to Police Officers, in addition to extra pay and free accommodation, to lure them to work in the dockyards. Sergeants Brown and Anniss of the Devonport Police shared a large reward of £12 7shillings and 8 pence each, which was the residue of a fine of £50 imposed by the Navel Dockyard Superintendent on Richard Pascoe[101]. Such rewards provided a valuable incentive to Police Officers to be diligent in their duties.

The picture at left is the Royal William Yard Gate, Devonport. In 1864 Superintendent John Baxter[102], who was in charge of the dockyard had the sad task of dealing with Charles Pearce, a dockyard Constable who was on normal patrol in a Police launch and fell into the estuary and drowned[103]. Baxter was followed by Superintendent William Wakeford in 1869 that remained in charge of Devonport for 22 years until he retired. This was the longest period of time spent not only as a Superintendent in the same post but also without a move to another dockyard. Wakeford clearly had the confidence of the Commissioner who had decided to leave him in situ.

Royal William Yard gate Devonport

The fortunes of people can change in an instant, especially when some failure of duty was discovered. In August 1873 Inspector Bradley was suspended from duty. An investigation was carried out by Superintendent William Wakeford who submitted a report that was forwarded to the Commissioner Col. Henderson. It was not known exactly what Bradley did, but it was serious enough for him to be dismissed from the Force on 30th August. Bradley and his family were required immediately to vacate their subsidised lodgings in the dockyard[104]. There would have been a great deal of sympathy amongst his fellow Police Officers and to be sacked in this way was very harsh especially given his circumstances. Often a collection was raised amongst the Officers and families to tide them over.

The Victorian shaving mug measuring 12 cm across and bearing the fouled anchor of the Dockyard Police was unearthed in the garden of a house once occupied by a Dockyard Constable in 1890. It shows that even the dockyards produced china-ware for their own purposes.

Devonport Dockyard shaving mug

In 1869 the Dockyard Police established strength was 1 Superintendent, 8 Inspectors, 20 Sergeants and 133 Constables. One Inspector was responsible for the duties outside the yards and he was stationed in the Police Reserve Room at St. Georges Hall, Stonehouse. Care was to be taken in inspecting the ships held in reserve by the Admiralty and located in the estuary at Hamoaze. The Inspector was also to ensure of at least three visits to the ships by the Water Police in each 24 hour period, although going aboard would only be undertaken if something irregular was going on[105]. The Water Police had their own Station aboard the hulk 'Leda' which was also fitted out as a residence for officers and men[106]. This had replaced the unserviceable and condemned ship 'Igeria' which had been removed. Inspector Anniss and his family occupied 4 of the stern cabins whilst Sergeant Angear was instructed to live in No. 1 Suite which consisted of 3 cabins with one entrance[107]. There were 17 houses in Pitt Street, Portsea, which were the property of the War Department and because of a shortage of living accommodation for Police these were handed over for their use until such times as they were required again for public service[108].

A new steam fire engine was delivered to the dockyard not only to replace one of the manual engines but also to ensure the fire engine was properly looked after and accordingly the Commissioner instructed Superintendent Strength on the deployment arrangements for the new engine[109] once it was delivered.

Dockyard Constable 96 Hollins was handsomely rewarded for his courageous conduct in the rescue of RN Lieutenant MaCauley's brother-in-law from drowning when he fell into the dock basin. Hollins received a solid silver watch and chain as a reward[110].

In November 1867 Superintendent Baxter retired from the dockyard on an annual pension of £153, 6s[111]. A Constable would receive an annual pension in the order of £30. In 1877 Baxter was succeeded by William Wakeford who was assisted by Chief Inspector William Ventham, and Silas Anniss, Edwin Smith, Henry Smale, Neil McCrimmon, Leonard James, Aubrey Hann, Thomas Wonnall and William Potts as Inspectors.

In 1894 Inspector C. Wall was promoted to Chief Inspector[112] until 1899 when Sub-Divisional Inspector Moorman took his place and was promoted to Chief Inspector[113]. The Devonport Police Dockyard Social Club took its annual outing to Oakhampton in Devon on the 10th July and a good time was had by all. This outing by charabanc (an open topped long wheel based bus) included not only the Police Officers but often their wives and children as well. Only those Police who were off duty were able to take advantage of the trip[114].

Superintendent Edwin Smith 1906

In August 1906 Superintendent Edwin Smith (shown at left) retired on pension from Devonport. Smith had joined the Metropolitan Police in July 1865 from his native Nottingham when he commenced 41 years of duty. He was originally drafted to Woolwich Dockyard Division and within two years he was promoted to Sergeant and transferred to

Pembroke Dockyard in Wales. Two years later he was back at Woolwich where he remained until 1887 when he was promoted to Inspector. On promotion he was transferred to Devonport Dockyard and in 1886 he was recommended for promotion again. As a Chief Inspector he was posted to Chatham moving to Sheerness' in 1893. Only one year later he was once again promoted and sent to Devonport.

Promoted to Sub-Divisional Inspector was Inspector Wedlock who stayed in situ[115]. Sergeant Rothnie was transferred to Detective duties and Inspector Burch was promoted to Sub-Divisional Inspector[116].

In 1911 Inspector Alfred Sly retired on pension after 27 years service in Devonport Dockyard. Inspector Sly had a very strong connection with Devonport since his father (who had five sons, all of whom joined the Metropolitan Police) spent all of his service stationed at the dockyard. Slys father had also been a Dockyard Police Officer.

The picture on the next page shows the Horse drawn steam fire engine at Devonport in 1903. Inspector John Wedlake is shown at left and he had overall responsibility for the engine. The Brigade consisted of Police Officers, dockyard workers and labourers On the left of the picture is a member of the Dockyard Water Police who is wearing a flat hat and there are ten civilian members all wearing an assortment of hats.

Sub Divisional Inspector Alfred Sly in 1911

There was discontent expressed anonymously in the Police Review from the Constables in the dockyard who had not been allowed their weekly rest day from March until July 1896.

The dockyard strength had been increased by 4 Constables at that time so it was felt by the men that there was no reason not to allow their leave, Weekly leave days could not be accumulated so they were lost[117]. This must have been resolved since nothing further was reported about the problem in the paper.

342

Devonport Dockyard Fire Brigade in 1903

The picture below shows the Devonport Police Band in 1912 with the

Devonport Dockyard band 1912

Dockyard Superintendent George Dixson in the centre. To his right is Chief Inspector Albert Keys, who later took Dixson's place as Superintendent. Many Police Officers learnt to play an instrument as it meant that they would be present at every ceremonial event or even playing at the local bandstand on a Sunday afternoon. Senior officers encouraged this since it promoted team spirit and a sense or camaraderie. In the same way sport was also promoted amongst the Constables and Sergeants as it was prestigious for senior officers to have the winning team. Games played between Police teams included football, rugby, cricket, hockey, tug of war and swimming. There was even a water tug of war event.

Devonport Dockyard Rifle Team 1913

The picture above shows the Devonport Police Rifle Team, who in 1913 won the cup shown on the table following an open rifle shoot. The five man winning squad consisted of Sergeants Frewin, back row standing left to right, Constable Lack, Constable Hill, Clerk Sergeant Wakefield and Station Sergeant Thompson (seated front row left). Superintendent Evans is shown seated front left. The cup was presented by the wife of Admiral Superintendent Stokes. In the prelude to the 1st World War such competitions were encouraged especially at the Dockyard Divisions since there were time when police officers would need to be armed especially on sentry duty.

Following events of the First World War when the Germans employed mustard gas and other similar substances to overcome their opponents the Government and Police developed anti–gas schools to teach their officers the dangers associated with gas attacks. They were particularly concerned that German bombers or Zeppelins could deploy gas bombs, especially on

Devonport Dockyard Gas Training School

dockyards, and cripple their operations. They taught them about the substances that were available to be used and how to use the House hold Respirator. The picture above shows the school at Devonport with their gas masks and respirators correctly deployed.

By 1924 Devonport had 198 Police Officers and Superintendent Owen Webb was in charge[118]. Webb retired in 1930 and was not replaced as superintendent.

In 1934 instructions arrived for the vacation of the Devonport Dockyard by the Metropolitan Police and control to be handed over to the newly appointed Marine Police. By 20th August 1934 Inspector (97240) Turner, 2 Station Sergeants, 3 Sergeants and 23 Constables had left the dockyard and returned to London[119] after handing over duties to their replacements. Thus, ended the long association and co-operation between the Metropolitan Police and Devonport dockyard.

Chatham (and Sheerness) Dockyard or 4th Division

Superintendent	Chief Inspectors
Thomas Richardson 1863-4 customs demoted to Inspector and transferred away from the dockyard to N division. He never returned	
John Strength (joined in 1842) 1864- 1871	
John Smith 1872-86 (died in post)	
George Godfrey (j1860) 1886-1894 (rtd) Inspector at Woolwich 1873–1881. Chief Inspector Portsmouth 1881-1885	
G. Hornsby 1897 -1900 Transferred on promotion from K or Bow Division (No previous dockyard experience)	
William. Smith 1902 - 1910 Chief Inspector at Chatham 1893 – 1907 (to Sheerness Dockyard from Chatham)	
William Tett 1910 - 1919(trans from 'M' to C/I) to Devonport 1902 - 10 No previous dockyard experience	
Charles E. Sly 1920 – 1929 (74318) Chief Inspector at Chatham 1914 – 15 and later Chief Inspector at Pembroke in 1917	
	Chief Inspector John Kane 1927-32 (Last senior officer to leave Chatham Dockyard) Transferred to Devonport

Chatham Dockyard was located in county of Kent on the Thames and situated outside the jurisdiction of the Metropolitan Police, although the London Police took control over Chatham from December 1860 until 1932. Once the Metropolitan Police had left in 1932 the security for the dockyard was handed over to the Royal Marine Police[120] a substantially cheaper option.

Prior to this, duties at Dockyard Divisions meant officers had to ensure the security and protection of property owned by the government by preventing theft and burglary. Records show that security at the dockyard in 1574 was undertaken by 'men with mastiff dogs who patrolled the boundary hedges at night'[121].

Later in 1628 Porters were recruited to man the gates and take charge of the keys when not in use[122]. Experience had been gained when Samuel Pepys, the famous diarist who became the Secretary to the Admiralty, saw the depredations taking place at Deptford and Woolwich Dockyards[123]. The Porters stayed until 1686 when they were joined by Rounder's and Warders[124]. This marked the first organised protection of Chatham Dockyard, a factor which continued unbroken until 1983 when the yards closed.

Lieutenant William Hubbard (RN) was the first Superintendent in charge at Chatham in 1838 and he originally took charge of Dockyard policing until the Admiralty felt that a more efficient form could be developed. The Superintendent's Divisional Headquarters were situated at Chatham Dockyard whilst the Police Stations were located at Chatham Dockyard; Sheerness Dockyard; Upnor Powder Magazines; Sheerness Gun Wharf; Royal Naval Hospital, Chatham; Chatham Gun Wharf; Chattenden Naval Ordnance; Powder Magazines, Chattenden; Submarine Mining Establishment, Field Park, Chatham; Field Park and Upnor and Brennan's Factories, Chatham[125]. Initially Inspector Burke was promoted to Chief Inspector and placed in charge of Sheerness Dockyard[126].

Superintendent F. M. Mallalieu was best placed to supervise the Chatham Dockyard as he had become the 'R' Divisional Superintendent back in October 1835 and was experienced in the supervision of dockyards; 'R' Division was responsible for Woolwich and Deptford docks. His experience with the dockyards made him the natural advisor especially when the Metropolitan Police were given security responsibilities for all the Royal dockyards.

In 1859, in addition to his own Divisional responsibilities, Mallalieu took operational charge of Chatham from Lieutenant Thomas Pearse who was at that time the director of the Dockyard Police. Many ex-Dockyard Police were retained by the Metropolitan Police and allowed to keep their uniforms as they were similar to the Metropolitan Police's swallow tail coats, but they had to pay to have their collars altered and buttons replaced[127]. Sergeants had been allocated numbers from 26'R' to 39'R' whilst Constables started at 243'R' to 301'R'[128]. The numbering of Police Officers later changed and the Divisional letter was removed.

In March 1861 Mallalieu gave up charge of 'R' Division but kept his responsibilities for the Dockyards by becoming Inspecting Superintendent, a position he kept until January 1870 when he was retired on pension for being 'worn out'[129]. In fact he had been seriously ill for some time and once pensioned he did not live very long to enjoy his retirement. Because 'R' Divisions' association with the dockyards of Woolwich and Deptford it was felt that this Land Division should have an experienced Dockyard Superintendent in charge. Accordingly Superintendent Bray was transferred from Devonport Dockyard to take over from the departing Mallalieu[130]. It was clear that apart from his Divisional responsibilities Bray was also in charge of Chatham while Mallalieu established his Dockyard Divisions throughout the country. In 1863 Bray handed over to Superintendent Richardson who then took control[131].

The photograph below shows the main entrance to the dockyard taken between 1865 and 70 as the Constables are wearing cox-comb helmets with badges.

The Gatehouse at Chatham in 1865

In the early days, apart from Chatham and Sheerness Dockyards which were supervised by Inspectors, Sergeants were responsible for Chatham (Melville) Naval Hospital and Chatham Gun Wharf. Married and single residents of dockyards who were off duty, had to hold themselves in a general state of readiness for action at all times. In other words, they were a sort of instant reserve that the Superintendent could call on at any time. Permission was required in advance from the Superintendent or his deputy for Police to be absent from the dockyard for more than three hours[132]. Off duty Police were to be in their residences by 11pm, except when coming off duty at 10pm when the time of 11.30pm was allowed, as this was the time for gas to be shut off at the meter[133]. The probable reason for this was to prevent fire. One particular responsibility for the early shift at Gun Wharf, Chatham, was the extinguishing of the gas street lamps[134]. Police Orders published the lighting-up times and gave instructions for the time at which those lamps should be put out and a designated Police Officer would walk around and turn the gas taps off.

The picture shows Pc Rogers of Chatham Dockyard circa 1881 wearing the star pattern helmet plate.

Mallalieu gave the Dockyard Superintendents permission to suspend Inspectors, sergeants and Constables from duty. He also authorised them to hear minor disciplinary infractions against Sergeants and Constables which he stipulated could be dealt with locally and with a maximum deduction of up to one days pay. Appeals against this punishment could be made in writing by the defaulter to the Commissioner or to Inspecting Superintendent Mallalieu who would hear the appeal when visiting the dockyard concerned[135].

Pc 132 Rogers Chatham Dockyard

To ensure that proper order and supervision was maintained the senior Police Officers were given married quarters in main parts of the dockyards. For example, at Sheerness the main gatehouse was occupied by Inspector Court and his family whilst Inspector Still was located in rooms a short distance away[136]. Inspector Still was an original dockyard officer at Chatham who was taken on after 1860 by the Metropolitan Police however he had retired on a medical pension in 1865, the Chief Police Medical Examiner having described the reason for Inspector Stills retirement as being 'worn out'[137]. His pension was paid for by the Admiralty and amounted to £79 and 2 shillings which was less than the pension that a retiring Metropolitan Inspector leaving under similar circumstances would receive. Inspector Payne was stationed at Sheerness and his quarters were situated on the Police Ship the 'Etna' where he was expected to reside with his wife and family[138]. Police officers stationed on ships (Etna, Juno and Leda) were not normally charged for rent of their cabins and this was waived by the War Department. Those Police Officers with accommodation ashore were required to pay rent on an agreed scale[139].

A commendation was received by the Commissioner from Rear Admiral Hall when he was replaced as Admiral Superintendent of Sheerness Dockyard in 1869. He praised the work of Chief Inspector Burke and his men for the zealous and satisfactory manner in which they carried out their duties at the dockyard[140].

A new uniform had been introduced into the Metropolitan Police in 1863 and the stove pipe top hats were replaced with a cox-comb helmet with a badge containing the Officer's divisional number and anchor. On either side of the Police Officer's collar was his divisional number together with and fouled anchor and a queen's crown. Notice also that the anchor denoting dockyard duty is shown above the number.

Dockyard helmet Plate 1863 - 1870

Smoking was strictly forbidden in dockyards except for concessions that had been made by the Captain Superintendent for workmen at Chatham and Sheerness Dockyards. The instructions were for Police to ensure that these concessions, which operated only during dinner time and in places allocated, were not abused by them. The supply and sale of alcohol was also strictly regulated and banned from sale in any premises. Supply in the canteens was, with permission and under certain circumstances, agreeable[141].

All store house and timber shed keys would be deposited with the Superintendent or his deputy when working hours finished and they would have been responsible for their safety. Access to these premises would normally be gained only in the event of a fire[142].

Regulations were established by the Captain Superintendent to ensure that fire engines, with their boilers left on, and fire fighting equipment were readily available at all times. Inspections by Police of the rope store and spinning loft were also important, although daily reviews were replaced by Saturday evenings and prior to public holiday's reviews only[143]. At the front gate of Sheerness Dockyard was a sign on the wall which stated that 'Lucifer' matches must not be taken into the dockyard. Inside the yards all fires in foundries or anywhere else were to be extinguished before workers could leave to go home.

In 1863 a new slaughter house for the killing of oxen was erected by the Admiralty at Sheerness. The security was immediately handed over to the Dockyard Police at Chatham[144].

Discipline was strict and failing to comply with instructions was a serious matter. Constable 103 Doust had settled himself at the dockyard and was happy in his duties there. However he was transferred without warning and instructed in Police Orders to move to Pembroke Dockyard from Chatham, he took great exception to the move and refused to go. He quickly appeared before the Commissioner, Sir Richard Mayne, who ordered that he be required to resign forthwith[145]. Arguing with Senior officers and especially the Commissioner lost Doust his job.

Pc 69 George Collins 1865 Sheerness Dockyard

The picture at left is PC 69 George Collins who joined the Metropolitan Police in 1865. The photograph was taken at Sheerness in 1869 when he was appointed to the Dockyard Police at Sheerness. He is shown proudly wearing his new uniform with a cox-comb helmet and his number in the plate, as can be seen from the illustrated helmet plate above. Collins had been attached to the Water Police and the winter weather had been extremely wet and cold. He tragically died in January 1874 of bronchitis having been confined to the Melville Hospital, Chatham for 23 days, although Police Orders report the death unsympathetically by saying – 'pay to 14th'[146]. No entry of the death was recorded in the Commissioner's Annual Report for that year, which would have been the usual practice. As can be seen from the list of Police Officers in Dockyard Divisions at this time, many retired on grounds of ill health mainly from bronchitis one of the many causes of death as it rapidly developed into pneumonia.

In 1864 scandal rocked the dockyard when Superintendent Richardson was bizarrely suspended from duty[147]. Details are sketchy but this was a serious enough situation to put ex-Dockyard Superintendent Mott (now in charge of 'N' Division) temporarily in charge of the dockyard whilst the matter was investigated. The result of the disciplinary inquiry reported that Richardson was reduced in rank to Inspector and removed to 'N'

Division away from Dockyard supervision so that he received closer supervision from Superintendent Mott[148]. Mott knew only too well about being suspended as in the previous year Sir Richard Mayne had seen fit to briefly suspend him for failing to follow an agreed line of route for a Royal procession between Hyde Park and Marble Arch[149]. Harsh discipline prevailed not only for the lower ranks but for supervisory officers as well.

On promotion from Portsmouth Dockyard John Strength took over as Superintendent to replace the disgraced Richardson[150]. Superintendent Strength, a Dockyard officer through and through, was obviously held in high regard when he was chosen to take over this prestigious posting. He had joined the police in 1842 and by 1860 was a Dockyard Inspector at Portsmouth. Just 4 years later he was promoted to Superintendent.

By 1868 instructions had been issued to the Superintendent to allocate 2 Constables to a detached post in the newly built extension to the Sheerness Dockyard. This was the Royal Engineers Establishment that was situated in the extension works and was to be visited once in each shift during the night[151].

There had been some problems with housing Police Officers and their families at Chatham. The Admiralty had been kind enough to loan a number of quarters to the Police and the Commissioner decided that any new incumbents should be charged an enhanced rental for these premises.

In order to ensure that proper importation of goods from foreign destinations took place and that any prohibited materials were confiscated, a number of Police Officers of varying ranks from Superintendent to Constable were made Customs Officers. These functions were added to their normal duties at no extra pay. Proper declaration could now be allowed to be made by travellers, sailors and other people when coming ashore or when challenged by those in authority. Ordinary Police sometimes came across boats and ships carrying suspicious goods, but these could only be searched and items seized by a Police Officer with a Royal Customs warrant. In 1869 there was a staff totalling 128 Police Officers including 1 Superintendent, 7 Inspectors, 14 Sergeants and 106 Constables. Within two years the strength had increased to 160 Police Officers.

Constable George Potts was found drowned in the docks at Chatham on 15th August 1870[152], although his death was not treated as suspicious at the time. Many people, let alone Dockyard Police, could not swim so even if they fell into the water they could get into difficulties very quickly. Dockyards are dangerous places and many Dockyard Police Officers perished in this way either by accident, suicide or murder.

John Smith was the Superintendent in 1877, Joseph King the Chief Inspector and Inspectors were William Oaks, James Atkins, Thomas Borsberry, Charles Hallett, William Capon, and Josiah Hobbins (Later himself to become a Superintendent in the Dockyard Divisions). John Smith was aged 49 at the time of the 1881 census and these records show he was from Warbstow in Cornwall. He lived at the dockyard with his wife Lavinia, aged 50, interestingly from Devonport in Devon, together with their six children. The Superintendent knew his men and when he took charge of Chatham he had inherited a number of old Dockyard Police who had been there for some years. He drew to the attention of the Commissioner an injustice which Old Dockyard Police Officers were likely to suffer - the fact that even if they were to complete 40 years service they would not be entitled to a pension of the same order as his other Metropolitan Dockyard Police Officers retiring with 24 and 28 years service[153]. The Commissioner resolved the problem by requesting the Admiralty to supplement the pension of these old Dockyard Police.

Sadly Superintendent Smith died in office in November 1886 and such was the regard in which he was held that a memorial from his men was erected in the old cemetery next to Gillingham church where it can be seen today. John Smith was succeeded by William Wakeford.

Below on the next page is Superintendent 44292 Josiah Hobbins in full uniform. In 1881 he was an Inspector aged 35 years and resided in the Dockyard with his wife Fanny and five children. Hobbins had been born in Portsmouth in 1846 and within a year of joining the Metropolitan Police on 'C' Division in 1863 he joined the Dockyard Divisions. Hobbins had been to the USA by the time he was 12 and worked on ships as a cabin boy. Such were his survival skills and tenacity that he lived through the traumas of being ship–wrecked twice.

His first dockyard posting was to Woolwich from 1864 -1867. In 1866 he became Acting Sergeant due mainly to his skill with a cutlass which resulted in his becoming the Divisional Instructor. In 1867 he became a Sergeant and transferred back to his home town of Portsmouth. Whilst there he served most of his time in the Water Police and was commended on a number of occasions, even occasionally receiving a reward for his services. On one occasion he was lowered into the burning hold of HMS Argus to locate the fire.

1870 saw his rapid promotion to Inspector and then being posted to Thames Division for a short period. He also held a Customs Warrant enabling him to act as an Excise Officer. In 1874 he transferred to Chatham where he re-wrote Dockyard Standing Orders [154].

The census shows that 33 single Constables lived in a Section House within the dockyard, but a number of others lived on ships. These not only included ten single Constables but also a married Constable by the name of William Huggin, his wife Louisa and their two children. Louisa's job title was described as the 'ship's cook to mess' which meant that she prepared the meals for the ten single Constables as well as for her family.

Inspector William Oaks 1860 - 1879 (rtd) had been an Inspector in the original Dockyard Police at Chatham before the London Police took control. He had spent some time at Chatham and it was felt that a change was necessary so he was transferred to Sheerness in 1869. He was a senior Inspector who could be trusted and was well regarded; however, an incident occurred at Sheerness just after his transfer which brought his judgement into question by the Commissioner, Sir Richard Mayne.

Superintendent Josiah Hobbins

The Commissioner felt from a report to him that a navy rating, who had obstructed the police during an incident, should have been arrested. Oaks, who was present at the time, was cautioned for this error [155], a fact which would have been recorded on the Inspector's defaulter's sheet.

The picture below shows Sheerness Dockyard from the air in about 1925. The North Gate and Gatehouse are shown because the Police Office was situated there so that people coming in and out could have their passes checked and could also be searched if suspected of taking property from

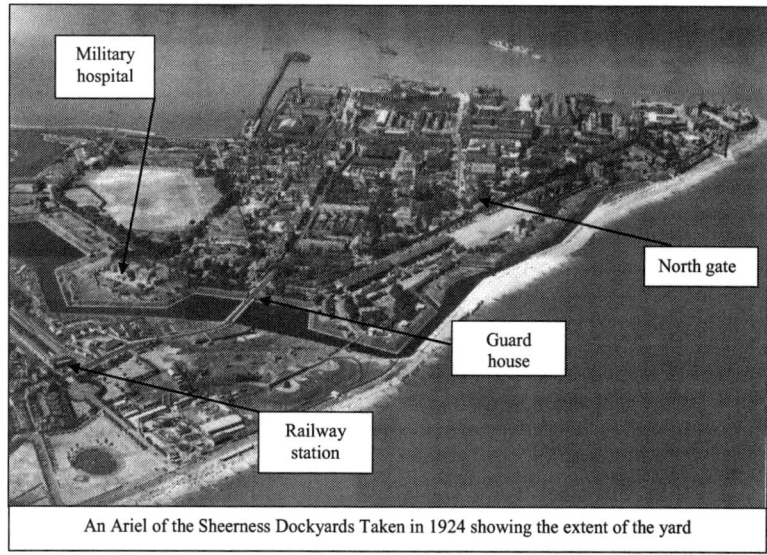

An Ariel of the Sheerness Dockyards Taken in 1924 showing the extent of the yard

the dockyards. The picture shows that the ships arriving at the pier can extricate injured sailors and military personnel to the hospital quickly.

Senior officers and men of Chatham Dockyard in 1896

The picture on the previous page shows Chatham Dockyard senior officers and men in 1896. This was the year that Superintendent Godfrey retired and he is seated in the centre in plain clothes wearing a bowler hat. He is flanked either side by Chief Inspectors Smith and Cavell.

Superintendent Smith had the sad task of dealing with deaths on duty and this was a particular problem for Dockyard Police since an accidental fall into a dock was often fatal. Such was the case in 1879 when PC William Stevens Nazer fell from the quayside whilst on patrol and drowned[156]. PC John Beer was retired on pension in 1887 but subsequently died of injuries he received whilst serving as a Dockyard Constable at Chatham[157].

In 1892 the Dockyard Superintendent had been replaced by William Wakeford, however by 1897 Superintendent G. Hornsby was in charge and Chief Inspector W. Smith was his deputy[158]. Chief Inspector Smith had been a Dockyard Inspector at Portsmouth Dockyard and successfully passed a stiff examination for the post in 1893[159]. He was later promoted to Dockyard Superintendent on Hornsby's retirement in 1910. Smith was assisted by Chief Inspector Cross, Sub-Divisional Inspector R. Hayter and Inspectors T. Bamber, C Bryant, J Green and J. Judge. Sergeant Charles Stubbington retired from the Police at Chatham Dockyard having completed 26 years service. On behalf of the officers and men of Chatham Dockyard Division Superintendent Godfey presented the Sergeant with a beautiful clock to mark his retirement[160].

Chief Inspector William Kemp in 1899

In 1899 the respected Chief Inspector, William Kemp, stationed at Chatham Dockyard, retired with 28 years service; his last three years having been spent there. Such was the esteem with which this officer was held that his retirement was published in the Police Review and Parade Gossip. The comments about him were positive and complementary, including about having remained for all of his service on Division but never having been a Dockyard Officer. Kemp had attained 25 years service and was expected to retire but he wanted to stay so he was transferred to a less favourable and possibly quieter posting out of London to a Dockyard Division[161]. In 1895 a rather strange event occurred referring to voting principles by Police in the Dockyard Division at Chatham. The Liberals had protested on the grounds that for single Police Officers who resided in cubicles in the Section House, it did not constitute a residence of separate occupation. This meant that these Officers were struck off the voters register and therefore could not vote in General Elections[162].

In 1917 the Superintendent had another unpleasant task to perform - the investigation into the death of a Dockyard Constable on duty. During a rather stormy night duty Constable Michael Donovan, whilst on patrol, fell into the dock and drowned[163]. An investigation tried to establish whether this tragic event was an accident or not, however there appears to have been insufficient evidence to justify a full scale murder investigation.

By 1924 Chatham had 164 Police Officers and Superintendent C. Sly was in charge[164]. On 26th January 1932 instructions were issued for the removal of the Metropolitan Police contingent with effect from the 1st February 1932[165]. Chief Inspector Kane and Inspector Harold Nightingale led their men, including 2 Station Sergeants, 22 Sergeants and 49 Constables from the dockyard, their places being taken by the Marine Police. Some of the dockyard officers like Chief Inspector Kane were transferred to other dockyard duties at Devonport and Portsmouth (ibid).

The 600 acre Chatham Naval Dockyard site was eventually closed in March 1984[166].

Pembroke Dockyard or 5th Division

Pembroke Dockyard became the responsibility of the Metropolitan Police in December 1860 where they remained until 1926. Initially Inspector Thompson was transferred from K Division to take up the position as Acting Superintendent together with 10 Constables who were taken from a variety of divisions on 15th December 1860. To supplement the strength later in the month 2 Inspectors and 4 Sergeants all on promotion were transferred two weeks later.

This was by far the smallest dockyard and operationally this was an Inspector-designated Station although in reality a Chief Inspector was in charge. In addition to the Chief Inspector there was one other Inspector who acted as deputy, 3 Sergeants and 21 Constables. Alexander Thomson who had considerable experience of dockyard duty had been transferred on promotion from 'K' Division in 1860 and placed in charge of the dockyard. By 1864 he had been rapidly promoted to Superintendent[167] and remained in command until Archibald Macdonald was transferred there. Macdonald later transferred to Portsmouth 1867- 1869 when Dockyard supervision reverted to Chief Inspector level probably to save money. His deputy was Inspector Daniel Collins[168] who was promoted to Chief Inspector in 1869. His deputy was Inspector George Harding. The overall police responsibility was for Pembroke Dockyard; Hobbs Point[169]. It was recognised by senior officers at the dockyard that there was a significant amount of property belonging to the Admiralty that was being stolen so Alexander Thompson, the Superintendent, encouraged his officers to stop and search workers leaving the premises and rewards were recommended for good police work.

One of the exceptional Police Officers at Pembroke at the time was PC 18 Ventham and he would later become one of the dockyard's most famous senior officers. Ventham had learnt all the duties, including the art of a Dockyard Constable. and he worked hard at it. He became a respected Constable because he was able to apprehend offenders and confiscate stolen property. He was often recognised by the Commissioner and in December 1862 rewarded with 10 shillings for his diligence[170]. The following month another good piece of police work at the docks was rewarded by Superintendent Thompson when he recommended a reward to 4 of his Constables. PC 9 Goddard, PC 20 Tunbridge, PC 14 Thomas and PC 27 Emerson were presented with 5 shillings each [171].

The Constables and Sergeants were paid in accordance with the class they were in. There were 4 classes of Constable, 1st class to 4th class, and their pay was 25shillings for 1st class, 23shillings for 2nd, 21shillings for 3rd and 19 shillings for 4th. Only 1st class Constables were on Water Police duties; Detectives in the dockyards were paid 30 shillings per week[172]. There were no 4th class Constables because becoming a Dockyard Constable would mean an automatic advance in class. This automatic advancement was an incentive which would attract Constables to the dockyards.

Workers leaving Pembroke Dockyard after a hard day's work.

The postcard above shows the dock workers leaving to go home after a day's work at the Pembroke Dock.

It was important to ensure fires were prevented or put out when started. Four manual engines together with 6 hose reels were placed in the charge of police together with an auxiliary plant of a steam fire engine and fire float which was the responsibility of the Chief Engineer[173]. So keen was the Commissioner to encourage Constables and others to move to the dockyard he offered incentives such as double pay for 9 days which attracted PCs Bonbery and Edwards of 'R' Division who transferred to Pembroke in 1860[174].

Police Orders showed that Sergeant's Wakeford 'A' and Collins 'R' (both later Superintendents) who were transferred at the same time did not receive the extra pay but they were promoted to Inspector later in December as their reward[175]. Both of these Police Officers became senior officers within the dockyards and remained there for the duration of their service. So desperate was the Commissioner that he asked for a Constable from each division except 'R' to present himself at Scotland Yard with reports of who was willing to transfer[176]. As already mentioned both Wakeford and Collins had been promoted to Inspector and in 1864 Inspector Wakeford was placed in charge of the dockyard whilst Superintendent Thomson was ill. Once Thomson returned from his period of sickness he was transferred back to Woolwich to take charge there on the retirement of Superintendent Kingston Mark[177]. Wakeford retained supervision of Pembroke on his promotion to Superintendent and had to move from his police premises into the more prestigious Superintendent's accommodation vacated by Thomson and his family.

Police pay was a weekly responsibility of those in charge of dockyards. Estimates of pay, returns and pay sheets had to be prepared the previous week and sent to the Executive Officer (usually an Inspector but later a Superintendent) at Scotland Yard for checking and ratification. These would be agreed and Superintendents would personally attend the bank in their area and draw monies which they would carry in a secure case back to the dockyard. Often they would be on horseback and accompanied by another member of the dockyard staff to provide extra security. Once back at the dockyard the Administration Sergeant would ensure that pay packets were prepared and that monies distributed as instructed. A pay parade would take place once per week and Police Officers (on or off duty) would attend to collect their pay at a certain hour. When they had been paid they had to personally sign their names on the pay list on receipt of their pay. In the early days police officers would receive their pay from a wooden cup as their pay would all be in coins as there was no paper money available although later this gave way to pay packets, but in any event the police officers had to individually check that their pay or contents were correct. Any later accusation that their pay was short was dealt with very dimly.

Duties at the dockyard included pursuing and apprehending stragglers and deserters from the Navy and the conveyance of naval prisoners to either the County Prison at Haverfordwest or the Naval Prison at Lewes in Sussex. The Chief Inspector made daily reports to the Captain Superintendent at the dockyard.

Pembroke had four manual fire engines together with six hose reels which were in the possession of the Police whilst an auxiliary engine and a fire float was the responsibility of the Chief Engineer of the yard[178].

In 1871 Pembroke became the centre for an epidemic of smallpox which caused the dockyard senior officer to ensure that all his men were vaccinated against the illness[179]. A number of fires occurred in the dockyard during the year and a small fire was discovered in the saw pits of the largest building in the yard in December. The result was that the fire was extinguished within ten minutes but had it not been discovered for another half an hour the whole building would have been destroyed[180]. Rewards for preventing crimes and discovering stolen property was a significant and well publicised fact of working in the dockyards. Recommendation for a reward was made at the discretion of the Superintendent once a report had been made to him. Inspector Crook and Sergeant Ingar were rewarded with 10 shillings each for preventing the theft of government property from the dockyard in 1864[181].

Police Officers in dockyards had to acquaint themselves from time to time with the names and faces of senior commissioned officers of the army and navy and senior dockyard officers. All Police Officers were required to salute these officers whenever they were in port and wearing their swords[182].

Senior officers from Scotland Yard would pay periodic visits for inspection purposes. In September 1893 the Assistant Commissioner A.C. Howard inspected the Police stationed at Pembroke Dockyard and was pleased to see the Constables put through their paces on the drill square by Inspector Young[183].

The dockyard now had 33 police officers stationed there and Chief Inspector Kane was in charge[184].

Senior Officers proudly showing off their new Fire Engine in 1924

The senior officers at Pembroke are proudly displaying in 1924 the new fire engine of which they have taken delivery. Notice that the engines are no longer horse drawn but have a steam engine. They are now fully mechanical and have large water pipes which are powered by the engine so they can play sufficient water on to a fire.

The picture below shows Constable William Shepherd (wt. no. 100865) who joined the Metropolitan Police in June of 1911 as 865 'N' Division. He transferred to the 5th Division at Pembroke as PC53 Dockyard (Water Police) in July 1914 just as the war was beginning. He was transferred to Chatham docks in April 1915, and by 1919 he was moved as PC214 'C' Division then as PC122 TA (Thames Division) in September of 1924. He was pensioned from C Division as 355 'C' in May 1935.

The Water Police wore different jackets than their land based colleagues; they kept them warm and were mostly waterproofed. The Constable's number is shown on the collar and also shows the fouled anchor and crown denoting dockyard service. The flat cap was also a feature of the Water Police and had a chin strap which could help fasten the cap and keep it from blowing away in windy weather.

In 1926 Inspector (89805) John Kane was transferred from Pembroke to Chatham. He had supervised the handover of responsibilities to the Marine Police and clearly done a good job in the eyes of his supervisors. Some 15 Constables, 6 Sergeants and the CID Officer were all transferred out at the same time. Later, Kane as the Chief Inspector was also to supervise the transfer of the Police from Chatham and later Devonport.

Constable William Shepherd taken in 1914

Rosyth Dockyard.

The Government decided to build another Royal Dockyard as part of the war effort and the authorities asked for the Metropolitan Police to continue its function and guard this dockyard in Scotland as part of their duties; they took control from 1914 until 1926. Their duties required policing both the Royal Rosyth Dockyard and the naval base.

Chosen for its ideal docking facilities Rosyth was not only designed to withstand attack but positioned much closer to essential facilities such as the iron foundries and coal fields of the north. It was situated 16 miles inland from the mouth of the Firth of Forth and out of reach of most modern artillery; it was completed in March 1916. The Metropolitan

The combined police of the Rosyth dockyard in 1918 with Superintendent Keys seated centre with flat hat.

Police were also responsible for Invergordon Dockyard.

The 1918 picture above shows Rosyth Dockyard Police, a mixture of Land Police (with helmets) and Water Police (with flat caps) and includes Superintendent Keys who is wearing his flat hat and sitting in the centre of the second row from the front.

Chief Inspector Charles Sly was initially placed in charge of the dockyard whilst a search was made for a suitable Superintendent to take overall control. Sub-Divisional Inspector James Keith was posted there together with Inspectors Henry Urban, John Wannop and John Sutherland. In 1915 the Officer in Charge was Albert Keys who had been a Chief Inspector at Devonport before he was transferred on promotion to Rosyth.

Apart from duties on land Rosyth also had a Water Police who patrolled in launches to detect crime and recover stolen Government stores. The painting below depicts the new dockyard and is showing the threats of a German aerial assault by Zeppelins and Gotha bombers that actually happened.

Artist's impression of the Rosyth dockyard showing the threat of zeppelin and Gotha bomber attacks

Police fatalities were fairly common-place in Dockyard Divisions as they were dangerous places especially when dockyard personnel, visitors and Police Officers themselves may not have taken proper care. In 1916 Rosyth Dockyard Constable 100867 Herbert Archer, who had been on duty for 7 hours, was awarded the King's Police Medal for rescuing a boy who could not swim from a caisson chamber at 5.20am on a very cold March morning. The boy had fallen into the dock some 40 feet below and Archer, having removed his helmet and outer clothing, jumped in. It was still dark but he found the boy after hearing splashing nearby. A rope was lowered and the Constable, holding the boy, was pulled up, however the person pulling in the rope had to let go because of the weight and they plunged back into the icy water. The Constable, still holding of the boy, swam to the end of the caisson where they were helped out of the dock without further incident. Archer also received an award from the Carnegie Hero Trust Fund and the Royal Humane Society Medal and Certificate[185]. However, other dangers existed and in 1917 Constable Lawrence James Quibell was killed in a road traffic accident whilst on a training exercise with the fire brigade[186]. By 1924 the complement of Police stood at 91 Constables with Chief Inspector R. Gadd in charge[187].

The Metropolitan Police dockyard contingent left Rosyth on 1st October 1926. Both Inspector (84294) Robert Allen and Inspector (92415) Thomas Pearce were returned to London Divisions along with 51 Constables, 8 Sergeants and 1 Station Sergeant[188].

---

[1] Weightmand, G and Humphries, S.. (1983) The Making of Modern London 1815 - 1914. Sidgewick and Jackson, London
[2] ibid
[3] Salter, A.R. (1983) The Protection of Chatham Dockyard throughout the Ages. Gillingham Local History Series No.12. Kent County Library.
[4] ibid.
[5] Salter, A.R. (1983) The Protection of Chatham Dockyard throughout the Ages. Gillingham Local History Series No.12. Kent County Library.
[6] Salter, A.R. (1983) The Protection of Chatham Dockyard throughout the Ages. Gillingham Local History Series No.12. Kent County Library.
[7] ibid
[8] Metropolitan Police Orders dated 31st January 1871
[9] Metropolitan Police Orders dated 22nd January 1863
[10] Hadaway, D. (1985) Eltham Police Station; The First Hundred Years. Latter Books, Sussex
[11] The Police and Constabulary List (1844) Parker, Furnival and Parker, Whitehall.
[12] Kirchners Almanac 1907
[13] Wynne, H. (1998) Extracts taken from the Metropolitan Police Orders 1873 (Dockyard Divisions). Friends of the Ministry of Defence Museum.
[14] ibid
[15] Wynne, H. (1998) Extracts taken from the Metropolitan Police Orders 1873 (Dockyard Divisions). Friends of the Ministry of Defence Museum.
[16] ibid
[17] Wynne, H. (1998) Extracts taken from the Metropolitan Police Orders 1873 (Dockyard Divisions). Friends of the Ministry of Defence Museum.
[18] Metropolitan Police Orders date 5th January 1859
[19] Hadaway, D. (1990) The Metropolitan Police in Woolwich.
[20] Commissioners Annual Report 1871
[21] Metropolitan Police Orders dated 2nd February 1863
[22] Metropolitan Police Orders dated 30th April 1863
[23] Metropolitan Police Orders dated 10th November 1862
[24] Police and Constabulary Almanac 1864
[25] Metropolitan Police Orders dated 11th September 1862
[26] Metropolitan Police Orders dated 6th January 1864
[27] Metropolitan Police Orders dated 4th October 1864
[28] The Mess was the latter day canteen where one of the duties was cooking for single men in the section house. This was often undertaken by Mess women- the wives of police officers who would have received either a reduction on the rent paid for married quarters or wages.
[29] Metropolitan Police Orders dated 4th January 1864

[30] National Police Officers Roll of Honour. http://www.policememorial.org.uk accessed 12th March 2002
[31] Metropolitan Police Orders dated 6th November 1866
[32] Metropolitan Police Orders dated 22nd May 1868
[33] ibid
[34] Commissioners Annual Report 1869
[35] Metropolitan Police Orders dated 3rd September 1868
[36] Commissioners Annual Report 1871
[37] Wynne, H. (1998) Extracts taken from the Metropolitan Police Orders 1873 (Dockyard Divisions). Friends of the Ministry of Defence Museum.
[38] Metropolitan Police General Orders and Regulation 1873
[39] Metropolitan Police Instructions. Dockyards and stations of the War department 1873
[40] Metropolitan Police Orders dated 25th October 1864
[41] Metropolitan Police Orders dated 7th August 1869
[42] Metropolitan Police Orders dated 22nd February 1869
[43] Metropolitan Police Orders dated 24th July 1865
[44] Commissioners Annual Report 1870
[45] Metropolitan Police Instructions. Dockyards and stations of the War department 1873 p27
[46] Commissioners Annual Report 1875
[47] ibid
[48] Commissioners Annual Report 1869
[49] Metropolitan Police Inspection of Police Premises 1881 p105
[50] The Police and Parade Gossip 30th October 1893
[51] The Police and Parade Gossip 26th January 1894 p40
[52] The Police and Parade Gossip 30th October 1893 p527
[53] The Daily Mail Map of Zeppelin and Aeroplane bombs on London 1914 - 1918
[54] National Police Officers Roll of Honour. http://www.policememorial.org.uk accessed 12th March 2002
[55] The Police mans pocket almanac and diary 1924
[56] HO45/11016/372290. LG date 1.1.1920.
[57] Metropolitan Police orders dated 23rd December 1926
[58] Kirchners Almanac 1907
[59] Metropolitan Police Orders dated 12th November 1862
[60] Metropolitan Police Orders dated 25th September 1868
[61] Metropolitan Police Orders dated 17th July 1869
[62] Police and Constabulary Almanac 1864
[63] Metropolitan Police Orders date 10th April 1869
[64] Metropolitan Police Orders dated 30th August 1865
[65] Metropolitan Police General Orders and Regulation 1873
[66] Police office London Directory 1877
[67] ibid
[68] Wynne, H. (1998) Extracts taken from the Metropolitan Police Orders 1873 (Dockyard Divisions). Friends of the Ministry of Defence Museum.
[69] Wynne, H. (1998) Extracts taken from the Metropolitan Police Orders 1873 (Dockyard Divisions). Friends of the Ministry of Defence Museum.
[70] Metropolitan Police Instructions. Dockyards and stations of the War department 1873 p40
[71] Wynne, H. (1998) Extracts taken from the Metropolitan Police Orders 1873 (Dockyard Divisions). Friends of the Ministry of Defence Museum.
[72] Wynne, H. (1998) Extracts taken from the Metropolitan Police Orders 1873 (Dockyard Divisions). Friends of the Ministry of Defence Museum.
[73] ibid
[74] ibid
[75] Metropolitan Police General Orders and Regulation 1873
[76] Metropolitan Police Orders dated 15th February 1865
[77] Metropolitan Police Orders dated 13th December 1860
[78] Commissioners Annual Report 1875
[79] Commissioners Annual Report 1875
[80] The Commissioners Annual Report 1879
[81] The Police and Parade Gossip 12th January 1894

[82] Census records 1881
[83] The Police and Parade Gossip 19th January 1894
[84] The Police and Parade Gossip 11th May 1894 and The Police and Parade Gossip 18th May 1894
[85] The Police and Parade Gossip 22nd June 1894
[86] The Police and Parade Gossip 1st March 1895
[87] The Police and Parade Gossip 31st August 1894
[88] The Police and Parade Gossip 7th September 1894
[89] The Police and Parade Gossip 17th May 1895
[90] The Police and Parade Gossip 31st May 1895
[91] The Police and Parade Gossip 29th May 1896
[92] The Police and Parade Gossip 27th November 1896
[93] National Police Officers Roll of Honour. http://www.policememorial.org.uk accessed 12th March 2002
[94] Metropolitan Police Orders dated 15th February 1916
[95] The Police mans pocket almanac and diary 1924
[96] Metropolitan Police Orders dated 26th January 1932
[97] Kirchners Almanac 1907
[98] Metropolitan Police Orders dated 3rd November 1860
[99] Wynne, H. (1998) Extracts taken from the Metropolitan Police Orders 1873 (Dockyard Divisions). Friends of the Ministry of Defence Museum.
[100] Metropolitan Police Orders dated 17th December 1869
[101] Metropolitan Police Orders dated 7th January 1863
[102] Police and Constabulary Almanac 1864
[103] National Police Officers Roll of Honour. http://www.policememorial.org.uk accessed 12th March 2002
[104] Metropolitan Police orders dated 2nd August 1873
[105] Wynne, H. (1998) Extracts taken from the Metropolitan Police Orders 1873 (Dockyard Divisions). Friends of the Ministry of Defence Museum.
[106] ibid
[107] Metropolitan Police Orders dated 31st March 1865
[108] Metropolitan Police Orders dated 3rd September 1868
[109] Metropolitan Police Orders dated 3oth December 1866
[110] Metropolitan Police Orders dated 8th September 1869
[111] Metropolitan Police Orders dated 4th November 1867
[112] The Police and Parade Gossip 9th November 1894
[113] The Police and Parade Gossip 21st April 1899
[114] The Police and Parade Gossip 19th July 1895
[115] The Police and Parade Gossip 28th April 1899
[116] The Police and Parade Gossip 16th June 1899
[117] The Police and Parade Gossip 24th July 1896
[118] The Police mans pocket almanac and diary 1924
[119] Metropolitan Police Orders dated 7th August 1934
[120] Brown, B. (1992) 'The Maritime duties of London's Bobbies' in Bygone Kent vol.13 no.4
[121] Salter, A.R. (1983) The Protection of Chatham Dockyard throughout the Ages. Gillingham Local History Series No.12. Kent County Library.
[122] ibid
[123] ibid
[124] ibid
[125] Kirchners Almanac 1907
[126] Metropolitan Police Orders dated 10th June 1869
[127] Brown, B. (1992) 'The Maritime duties of Londons Bobbies' in Bygone Kent vol.13 no.4
[128] Brown, B. (1992) 'The Maritime duties of Londons Bobbies' in Bygone Kent vol.13 no.4
[129] List of superintendents. The Metropolitan Police Historical Collection, Charlton.
[130] ibid
[131] Police and Constabulary Almanac 1864
[132] Wynne, H. (1998) Extracts taken from the Metropolitan Police Orders 1873 (Dockyard Divisions). Friends of the Ministry of Defence Museum.
[133] ibid
[134] Metropolitan Police Orders dated 20th December 1862

[135] Metropolitan Police Orders dated 3rd December 1860
[136] Metropolitan Police Orders dated 4th January 1865
[137] Metropolitan Police Orders dated 15th November 1865
[138] Metropolitan Police Orders dated 24th September 1866
[139] Metropolitan Police Orders dated 3rd September 1868
[140] Metropolitan Police Orders dated 7th April 1869
[141] Wynne, H. (1998) Extracts taken from the Metropolitan Police Orders 1873 (Dockyard Divisions). Friends of the Ministry of Defence Museum.
[142] ibid
[143] Wynne, H. (1998) Extracts taken from the Metropolitan Police Orders 1873 (Dockyard Divisions). Friends of the Ministry of Defence Museum.
[144] Metropolitan Police Orders dated 19th June 1863
[145] Metropolitan Police Orders dated 29th June 1863
[146] Metropolitan Police Orders dated 15th January 1874
[147] Metropolitan Police Orders dated 13th January 1864
[148] Metropolitan Police Orders dated 4th February 1864
[149] Metropolitan Police Orders dated 9th March 1863
[150] Metropolitan Police Orders dated 4th February 1864
[151] Metropolitan Police Orders dated 31st January 1868
[152] Commissioners' Annual Report 1870 p14
[153] Commissioners' Annual Report 1874 p99
[154] The Review and Parade Gossip 15th September 1911 p438
[155] Metropolitan Police Orders dated 23rd November 1869
[156] National Police Officers Roll of Honour. http://www.policememorial.org.uk accessed 12th March 2002
[157] National Police Officers Roll of Honour. http://www.policememorial.org.uk accessed 12th March 2002
[158] Salter, A.R. (1983) The Protection of Chatham Dockyard throughout the Ages. Gillingham Local History Series No.12. Kent County Library
[159] The Police and Parade Gossip 20th November 1893
[160] The Police and Parade Gossip 11th December 1893
[161] The Police and Parade Gossip 4th August 1899
[162] The Police and Parade Gossip 11th October 1895
[163] National Police Officers Roll of Honour. http://www.policememorial.org.uk accessed 12th March 2002
[164] The Police mans pocket almanac and diary 1924
[165] Metropolitan Police Orders dated 26th January 1932
[166] Salter, A.R. (1983) The Protection of Chatham Dockyard throughout the Ages. Gillingham Local History Series No.12. Kent County Library.
[167] Police and Constabulary Almanac 1864
[168] Metropolitan Police Orders date 10th June 1869
[169] Kirchners Almanac 1907
[170] Metropolitan Police Orders dated 10th November 1862
[171] Metropolitan Police Orders dated 11th December 1862
[172] Metropolitan Police Orders 1st August 1868
[173] Metropolitan Police Orders date 6th January 1869
[174] Metropolitan Police Orders date 8th December 1860
[175] Metropolitan Police Orders dated 27th December 1860
[176] Metropolitan Police Orders dated 11th December 1860
[177] Metropolitan Police Orders dated 3rd May 1864
[178] Wynne, H. (1998) Extracts taken from the Metropolitan Police Orders 1873 (Dockyard Divisions). Friends of the Ministry of Defence Museum.
[179] Commissioners Annual Report 1871
[180] ibid
[181] Metropolitan Police Orders dated 12th October 1864
[182] Metropolitan Police General Orders and Regulation 1873
[183] The Police and Parade Gossip 9th October 1893
[184] The Police mans pocket almanac and diary 1924
[185] HO45/10954/306338 L. G. date 1.1.1917

[186] National Police Officers Roll of Honour. http://www.policememorial.org.uk accessed 12th March 2002
[187] The Police mans pocket almanac and diary 1924
[188] Metropolitan Police Orders dated 24th September 1926

POLICE OFFICERS MENTIONED IN THIS BOOK

Name	Rank	Date	Station	London Borough
ABBOTT H.R.	Superintendent	1960	Woolwich	Greenwich
ABBOTT Thomas	Superintendent	1928	Kennington	Lambeth
ALDRIDGE William	Constable	1839	Deptford	Lewisham
ALLEN Robert	Inspector	1926	Rosyth	Royal Dockyards
ALLEN Sislin Fay	Constable	1968	Croydon	Croydon
ANDREWS James	Sub-Divisional Inspector	1905	Wandsworth	Wandsworth
ANGEAR	Constable		Devonport	Royal Dockyards
ANNIS	Sergeant	1860	Devonport	Royal Dockyards
ANNIS Silas	Inspector	1877	Devonport	Royal Dockyards
APPLEGATE George	Constable	1881	Brixton	Lambeth
ARCHER	Constable	1864	Woolwich	Royal Dockyards
ARCHER Herbert	Constable	1916	Rosyth	Royal Dockyards
ARNUP Frederick	Constable	1899	Greenwich	Greenwich
ASHLEY Joseph	Inspector	1881	Tooting	Wandsworth
ATKINS James	Inspector	1877	Chatham	Royal Dockyards
AUSTIN William	Inspector	1905	Catford	Lewisham
AYLETT	Sub-Divisional Inspector	1928	Wimbledon	Merton
BACON William	Sergeant	1881	Greenwich	Greenwich
BAILEY Chas	Superintendent	2010	Intro	Sutton
BAILEY John Richard	Constable	1954	Mitcham	Merton
BAINBRIDGE Derek	Inspector	1968	Norbury	Croydon
BALLANTYNE	Superintendent	1937	Balham	Wandsworth
BAMBER T.	Inspector	1910	Chatham	Royal Dockyards
BARHAM William	Sub-Divisional Inspector	1914	Wandsworth	Wandsworth
BARNHAM William	Sub-Divisional Inspector	1911	Wimbledon	Merton
BARRETT J	Inspector	1879	Kennington	Lambeth
BARRETT Alfred J	Superintendent	1921	Greenwich	Greenwich
BARRETT Stephen	Sergeant	2000	West Dulwich	Southwark
BARTLE G.	Inspector	1879	Kennington	Lambeth
BARTON Alfred	Detective Sergeant	1908	Portsmouth	Royal Dockyards
BASSOM Arthur	Superintendent	1919	Bexleyheath	Bexley
BATES	Constable		Devonport	Royal Dockyards
BAXTER	Superintendent	1877	Bexley	Bexley
BAXTER John	Superintendent	1861	Devonport	Royal Dockyards
BAYNES Captain H.	District Superintendent	1871	Croydon	Croydon
BAYNES Captain H.	District Superintendent	1880	Brockley	Lewisham
BAYNES Captain H.	District Superintendent	1869	Brixton	Lambeth
BAYNES Captain H.	District Superintendent	1878	Belvedere	Bexley
BEALING Henry	Inspector	1893	Southwark	Southwark
BEER John	Constable	1887	Chatham	Royal Dockyards
BERRETT	Detective Inspector	1914	Brixton	Lambeth

POLICE OFFICERS MENTIONED IN THIS BOOK

BEVANS	Constable	1912	Norbury	Croydon
BICKNELL Thomas	Superintendent	1836	Intro	Wandsworth
BISHOP J	Superintendent	1836	Intro	Wandsworth
BLACKMAN	Constable	1862	Portsmouth	Royal Dockyards
BLANCHARD Richard	Superintendent	2010	Intro	Southwark
BONBERRY	Constable	1860	Pembroke	Royal Dockyards
BOND Joseph	Sergeant	1870	Erith	Bexley
BONNER Edward	Sub-Divisional Inspector	1893	Wimbledon	Merton
BONNER Frederick	Sub-Divisional Inspector		Croydon	Croydon
BORSBERRY Thomas	Inspector	1877	Chatham	Royal Dockyards
BOXALL	Constable	1860	Portsmouth	Royal Dockyards
BRADLEY	Inspector	1873	Devonport	Royal Dockyards
BRANNAN J	Superintendent	1891	Carter Street	Southwark
BRANNAN Jas	Superintendent	1879	Kennington	Lambeth
BRANWHITE C	Inspector	1891	Carter Street	Southwark
BRAY	Superintendent		Chatham	Royal Dockyards
BRAY Robert	Superintendent	1860	Devonport	Royal Dockyards
BRICE William	Sub-Divisional Inspector	1908	Wandsworth	Wandsworth
BRIDGWOOD Peter George	Detective Constable	1961	Morden	Merton
BRIGGS William	Inspector	1877	Portsmouth	Royal Dockyards
BRIGHT Albert	Station Sergeant	1899	Lewisham	Lewisham
BRIND Ernest	Superintendent	1930	Kennington	Lambeth
BRINE	Inspector	1865	Woolwich	Royal Dockyards
BROADBRIDGE J	Inspector	1890	Sydenham	Lewisham
BROMAGE	Constable	1870	Sidcup	Bexley
BROWN	Sergeant	1860	Devonport	Royal Dockyards
BROWN F.C	Superintendent	1960	Balham	Wandsworth
BRYANT C.	Inspector	1910	Chatham	Royal Dockyards
BURCH	Sub-Divisional Inspector	1899	Devonport	Royal Dockyards
BURDEN Cheryl	Superintendent	2010	Intro	Southwark
BURKE	Chief Inspector	1869	Chatham	Royal Dockyards
BURTON Charles	Constable	1916	Portsmouth	Royal Dockyards
BURTON Clement	Inspector	1915	Bromley	Bromley
BURTON Jeremy	Chief Superintendent	2010	Intro	Lewisham
BUSSAIN John	Inspector	1830	Wandsworth	Wandsworth
BUTCHER	Constable	1863	Woolwich	Royal Dockyards
BUTCHER	Inspector	1891	Lewisham	Lewisham
BUTLER	Inspector	1896	Portsmouth	Royal Dockyards
BUTLER Charles R	Station Sergeant	1899	Lewisham	Lewisham
BUTT	Superintendent	1869	Wandsworth	Wandsworth
BUTT Thomas	Superintendent	1879	Camberwell	Southwark
BUTT Charles	Inspector	1915	Plumstead	Greenwich
BUTT Edward	Superintendent	1861	Intro	Wandsworth
BUTT Thomas	Superintendent	1865	Lewisham	Lewisham
BUTTERS Robert	Inspector	1891	Mitcham	Merton
CAPON William	Inspector	1877	Chatham	Royal Dockyards
CARMAC John	Inspector	1877	Portsmouth	Royal Dockyards

POLICE OFFICERS MENTIONED IN THIS BOOK

CARNELLY Thomas J.	Chief Inspector	1877	Woolwich	Royal Dockyards
CARR G	Superintendent	1899	Lewisham	Lewisham
CARR Percy	Constable	1919	Woolwich	Royal Dockyards
CARTER	Superintendent	1895	Portsmouth	Royal Dockyards
CATHCART John	Inspector	1899	Catford	Lewisham
CAVELL	Chief Inspector	1896	Chatham	Royal Dockyards
CAVENDISH Albert	Sub-Divisional Inspector	1928	Wimbledon	Merton
CHANCE Wayne	Chief Superintendent	2010	Intro	Southwark
CHAPLIN	Constable		Devonport	Royal Dockyards
CHAPLIN Henry J	Constable	1851	Kennington	Lambeth
CHILCOTT Wilfred John	Station Sergeant	1940	Putney	Wandsworth
CHILDS	Constable	1862	Portsmouth	Royal Dockyards
CHILDS James	Constable	1891	Banstead	Sutton
CHIN Frank	Sub-Divisional Inspector	1902	Croydon	Croydon
CHISHOLM	Chief Inspector	1879	Kennington	Lambeth
CHRISTMAS	Constable	1862	Portsmouth	Royal Dockyards
CHRISTMAS Jesse	Constable	1917	Camberwell	Southwark
CHUBBOCK	Inspector	1895	Portsmouth	Royal Dockyards
CLARK	Constable	1862	Portsmouth	Royal Dockyards
CLARK Charles H.	Superintendent	1928	Brixton	Lambeth
CLARK R.	Superintendent	1928	Streatham	Lambeth
CLARK Charles R	Superintendent	1928	Streatham	Lambeth
CLARKE Leonard Francis	Special Constable	1940	Greenwich	Greenwich
CLEAVE	Inspector	1893	Southwark	Southwark
CLEAVE Walter	Sub-Divisional Inspector	1906	Wandsworth	Wandsworth
CLIFFORD George	Inspector	1844	Woolwich	Greenwich
CLOSE F.	Detective Superintendent	1957	Tooting	Wandsworth
COFFEY Edward	Inspector	1877	Woolwich	Royal Dockyards
COGGER	Constable	1862	Portsmouth	Royal Dockyards
COLE Harry	Constable	1994	Carter Street	Southwark
COLLIER John	Inspector	1844	Croydon	Croydon
COLLINS	Sergeant	1860	Pembroke	Royal Dockyards
COLLINS W	Superintendent	1940	Catford	Lewisham
COLLINS Daniel	Inspector	1867	Pembroke	Royal Dockyards
COLLINS George	Constable	1865	Chatham	Royal Dockyards
COLLINS John	Sub Divisional Inspector	1908	Carter Street	Southwark
COLMAN Richard	Sergeant	1829	Intro	Croydon
CONCANNON John	Sub-Divisional Inspector	1896	Lavender Hill	Wandsworth
CONGTON Robert	Inspector	1877	Woolwich	Royal Dockyards
CONNELL William	Inspector	1877	Portsmouth	Royal Dockyards
COOMBS Ernest	Sergeant	1905	Catford	Lewisham
COPPEN George	Inspector	1877	Portsmouth	Royal Dockyards
CORRIGAN John	Detective Superintendent	2010	Intro	Lambeth
COSTELLO	Constable	1862	Portsmouth	Royal Dockyards

POLICE OFFICERS MENTIONED IN THIS BOOK

COSTER Vincent	Sub-Divisional Inspector	1915	Bromley	Bromley
COURT	Inspector		Chatham	Royal Dockyards
COUSINS Edwin	Constable	1886	Greenwich	Greenwich
COWLIN John Richard	Inspector	1849	Southwark	Southwark
COXON Martin	Constable	1984	St Mary Cray	Bromley
CRABB Richard	Constable	1900	Greenwich	Greenwich
CRAWFORD Bob	Constable	2007	Earlsfield	Wandsworth
CREED Henry	Inspector	1842	Wandsworth	Wandsworth
CROFT Harry	Inspector	1891	Brockley	Lewisham
CRONK John	Inspector	1877	Woolwich	Royal Dockyards
CROOK	Inspector	1864	Pembroke	Royal Dockyards
CROOK Lisa	Superintendent	2010	Intro	Lewisham
CROOK William	Chief Inspector	1868	Devonport	Royal Dockyards
CROSS	Chief Inspector	1910	Chatham	Royal Dockyards
CROSTAN William	Sub-Divisional Inspector	1905	Greenwich	Greenwich
CUNNEEN Si	Detective Superintendent	2010	Intro	Lewisham
CUTHBERT David	Constable	1881	Wimbledon	Merton
DALE George Arthur	Constable	1968	Wimbledon	Merton
DANIEL Joseph	Sergeant	1891	Peckham	Southwark
DARLING	Chief Inspector	1893	Southwark	Southwark
DAVIES David	Constable	1919	Mitcham	Merton
DAVIES Michael John	Constable	1969	Wimbledon	Merton
DAVIS James	Chief Inspector	1879	Camberwell	Southwark
DAVIS James	Chief Inspector	1865	Lewisham	Lewisham
DAVIS W.E	Chief Superintendent	1957	Tooting	Wandsworth
DEAN Thomas	Constable	1881	Deptford	Lewisham
DEVINE J.	Superintendent	1924	Woolwich	Royal Dockyards
DICKENS Charles	Constable	1891	Brockley	Lewisham
DIGBY Charles	Superintendent	1871	Erith	Bexley
DIGBY Charles	Superintendent	1869	Wimbledon	Merton
DIGBY Charles	Superintendent	1864	Intro	Wandsworth
DIXSON George	Superintendent	1910	Devonport	Royal Dockyards
DIXSON George	Chief Inspector	1901	Devonport	Royal Dockyards
DOLBY	Constable	1899	Peckham	Southwark
DONOVAN Michael	Constable	1917	Chatham	Royal Dockyards
DOUGLAS James	Inspector	1840	Greenwich	Greenwich
DOUST	Constable		Chatham	Royal Dockyards
DOWLING	Superintendent	1830	Kennington	Lambeth
DOWLING Maurice G	Superintendent	1833	Intro	Lambeth
DOWN	Chief Inspector	1911	Devonport	Royal Dockyards
DOWSET Richard	Inspector		Wandsworth	Wandsworth
DOWTY George	Constable	1881	Wandsworth	Wandsworth
DRAPER George William	Constable	1902	Wimbledon	Merton
DUNLEAVY G	Inspector	1891	Carter Street	Southwark
DUNLOP Joseph	Superintendent	1870	Southwark	Southwark
DUNN Leonard	Constable	1920	Greenwich	Greenwich
DUNNE Patrick	Constable	1993	Sutton	Sutton
DYER Frederick	Sergeant	1905	Catford	Lewisham

POLICE OFFICERS MENTIONED IN THIS BOOK

Name	Rank	Year	Location	Division
EARWAKER George	Reserve Inspector	1888	Wandsworth	Wandsworth
EASTER	Inspector	1879	Kennington	Lambeth
EDWARDS	Constable	1860	Pembroke	Royal Dockyards
EDWARDS Charles	Constable	1881	Putney	Wandsworth
EGERTON Samuel	Inspector	1868	Battersea	Wandsworth
EITE Joseph	Constable	1868	Wandsworth	Wandsworth
ELLAMS	Inspector	1891	Gipsy Hill	Lambeth
ELY	Constable	1862	Portsmouth	Royal Dockyards
EMERSON	Constable	1863	Pembroke	Royal Dockyards
EPHGRAVE Nick	Chief Superintendent	2010	Intro	Lambeth
EVANS J	Inspector	1844	Kennington	Lambeth
EVANS T	Superintendent	1957	Tooting	Wandsworth
EVANS Thomas	Superintendent	1914	Devonport	Royal Dockyards
EWART William A	Superintendent	1928	Southwark	Southwark
FAIRFAX Frederick	Detective Constable	1952	Croydon	Croydon
FENN Septimus	Superintendent	1854	Intro	Wandsworth
FERGUSON	Inspector	1844	Kennington	Lambeth
FERGUSON Guy	Detective Chief Superintendent	2010	Intro	Sutton
FIELD Charles F	Inspector	1833	Woolwich	Greenwich
FLANAGAN John	Inspector	1891	East Dulwich	Southwark
FLYNN Thomas	Inspector	1891	Banstead	Sutton
FORD Elias	Inspector	1881	Woolwich	Greenwich
FORD James	Sub Divisional Inspector	1899	Carter Street	Southwark
FOX	Inspector	1898	Camberwell	Southwark
FOX John Thomas	Sergeant	1871	Sydenham	Lewisham
FRASER	Sub-Divisional Inspector	1899	Lewisham	Lewisham
FRASER D	A/Superintendent	1865	Brixton	Lambeth
FRASER D	A/Superintendent	1865	Camberwell	Southwark
FRASER W.	Sub-Divisional Inspector	1905	Catford	Lewisham
FREWIN	Sergeant	1913	Devonport	Royal Dockyards
FRIGHT A	Constable	1895	Knockholt	Bromley
FROUD Philip	Inspector	1849	Southwark	Southwark
FULLER John	Inspector	1888	Wimbledon	Merton
FYFE John	Inspector	1851	Gipsy Hill	Lambeth
GADD	Sub-Divisional Inspector	1915	Plumstead	Greenwich
GADD R.	Chief Inspector	1924	Rosyth	Royal Dockyards
GARLAND H	Inspector	1879	Kennington	Lambeth
GAYNOR Arthur	Sergeant	1879	Greenwich	Greenwich
GEORGE	Inspector	1968	South Norwood	Croydon
GILES Alfred John	Reserve Inspector	1944	Wimbledon	Merton
GILHAM	Sergeant	1893	Woolwich	Greenwich
GILL James	Inspector		Woolwich	Royal Dockyards
GILLIES William	Sub-Divisional Inspector	1893	Wandsworth	Wandsworth
GODDARD	Constable	1863	Pembroke	Royal Dockyards
GODDEN J	Inspector	1891	Epsom	Sutton
GODDEN Daniel	Inspector	1877	Portsmouth	Royal Dockyards

POLICE OFFICERS MENTIONED IN THIS BOOK

Name	Rank	Year	Location	Division
GODFREY	Superintendent	1893	Chatham	Royal Dockyards
GODFREY George	Inspector	1877	Woolwich	Royal Dockyards
GODFREY George	Superintendent	1888	Chatham	Royal Dockyards
GOODALL	Sub-Divisional Inspector	1897	Plumstead	Greenwich
GOODALL Walter	Inspector	1877	Sutton	Sutton
GOSLING Kate	Constable	1987	Sutton	Sutton
GOSS	Inspector	1895	Portsmouth	Royal Dockyards
GOULD George	Constable	1887	Woolwich	Greenwich
GOULD Winifred	Constable	1931	Woolwich	Greenwich
GREEN T	Inspector	1879	Kennington	Lambeth
GREEN Harry	Constable	1930	Wimbledon	Merton
GREEN J	Inspector	1910	Chatham	Royal Dockyards
GREEN Thomas	Station Sergeant	1919	Epsom	Sutton
GRIFFIN James	Superintendent	1874	East Greenwich	Greenwich
GRIFFIN James	Superintendent	1870	Sidcup	Bexley
GRINSELL D.C.	Superintendent	1844	Kennington	Lambeth
GRINSELL Samual	Superintendent	1841	Kennington	Lambeth
GUNDREY	Constable	1893	Woolwich	Royal Dockyards
GUY Henry	Superintendent	1868	Portsmouth	Royal Dockyards
HALFORD Chris	Chief Superintendent	2010	Greenwich	Greenwich
HALL Charles	Constable	1921	Bromley	Bromley
HALLETT Charles	Inspector	1877	Chatham	Royal Dockyards
HANN Aubrey	Inspector	1877	Devonport	Royal Dockyards
HAPLIN Kate	Detective Superintendent	2010	Greenwich	Greenwich
HARDING	Inspector	1867	Pembroke	Royal Dockyards
HARDING George	Chief Inspector	1891	Devonport	Royal Dockyards
HARDY James	Constable	1918	West Wickham	Bromley
HARNETT	Superintendent	1883	Southwark	Southwark
HARRIS Elias	Sergeant	1878	Mitcham	Merton
HART William	Sub-Divisional Inspector	1911	Wimbledon	Merton
HASTIE James	Constable	1846	Deptford	Lewisham
HAYES William	Superintendent	1867	Mitcham	Merton
HAYNES Henry	Sergeant	1878	Epsom	Sutton
HAYTER R.	Sub-Divisional Inspector	1910	Chatham	Royal Dockyards
HENDERSON Sir Edmund	Commissioner	1870	Sidcup	Bexley
HENRY Sir Edward	Commissioner	1909	Streatham	Lambeth
HENRY Sir Edward	Commissioner	1915	Norbury	Croydon
Henry Sir Edward	Commissioner		Earlsfield	Wandsworth
HIGGINS Samuel	Inspector	1873	St Mary Cray	Bromley
HILL	Sergeant	1913	Devonport	Royal Dockyards
HILL A.	Inspector	1891	Epsom	Sutton
HILL J	Inspector	1879	Kennington	Lambeth
HILL Thomas	Sub-Divisional Inspector	1905	Eltham	Greenwich
HILL Thomas	Sub-Divisional Inspector	1908	Greenwich	Greenwich
HINDES Thomas	Superintendent	1875	Woolwich	Royal Dockyards
HOBBINS Josiah	Superintendent	1891	Devonport	Royal Dockyards

POLICE OFFICERS MENTIONED IN THIS BOOK

HOBBINS Josiah	Inspector	1877	Chatham	Royal Dockyards
HOCKING	Inspector	1897	Plumstead	Greenwich
HOCKING George	Inspector	1891	Westcombe Park	Greenwich
HODGES Charles	Sub-Divisional Inspector	1910	Wandsworth	Wandsworth
HOLDAWAY William	Inspector	1891	Carshalton	Sutton
HOLLINS	Constable		Devonport	Royal Dockyards
HOLLOWAY William James	Inspector	1944	Croydon	Croydon
HOOPER Race	Sub-Divisional Inspector	1914	Wimbledon	Merton
HOPKINS William	Sub Divisional Inspector	1905	Tower Bridge	Southwark
HORNE	Inspector	1865	Portsmouth	Royal Dockyards
HORNSBY G.	Superintendent	1897	Chatham	Royal Dockyards
HORNSBY George	Inspector	1849	Southwark	Southwark
HOWARD Roger	Inspector	1839	Woolwich	Greenwich
HOWARD A.C.	Assistant Commissioner	1894	Portsmouth	Royal Dockyards
HOWARD A.C.	Assistant Commissioner	1893	Pembroke	Royal Dockyards
HOWARD Roger	Inspector	1844	Woolwich	Royal Dockyards
HOWE Andy	Superintendent	2010	Intro	Lambeth
HUBBARD Sally	Chief Superintendent	1988	South Norwood	Croydon
HUDSON	Sergeant	1893	Plumstead	Greenwich
HUGGIN William	Constable		Chatham	Royal Dockyards
HUNT	Chief Inspector	1927	Devonport	Royal Dockyards
HUNT Charles	Inspector	1878	Croydon	Croydon
HUNT Daniel	Detective Inspector	1865	Lewisham	Lewisham
HUNT Frank	War Reserve Constable	1944	Battersea	Wandsworth
HUXTABLE	Constable		Devonport	Royal Dockyards
HYNDS Len	Constable	1952	Rotherhithe	Southwark
INGAR	Sergeant	1864	Pembroke	Royal Dockyards
JACKSON J	Inspector	1879	Kennington	Lambeth
JACKSON John	Sub-Divisional Inspector	1893	Greenwich	Greenwich
JAMES Leonard	Inspector	1877	Devonport	Royal Dockyards
JANES J	Inspector	1891	Streatham	Lambeth
JANES James	Sub-Divisional Inspector		Balham	Wandsworth
JARRETT C	Superintendent	2001	Balham	Wandsworth
JARVIS Frederick	Chief Superintendent	1971	Worcester Park	Sutton
JARVIS Henry	Inspector	1915	Plumstead	Greenwich
JEFFREY Edward	Constable	1902	Streatham	Lambeth
JEWELL	Inspector	1883	Brockley	Lewisham
JOHNSON George	Constable	1914	Battersea	Wandsworth
JOHNSTON Andrew	Chief Inspector	2010	Greenwich	Greenwich
JONES A.H	Superintendent	1957	Lavender Hill	Wandsworth
JONES William	Inspector	1877	Portsmouth	Royal Dockyards
JUDGE J.	Inspector	1910	Chatham	Royal Dockyards
KANE	Chief Inspector	1932	Chatham	Royal Dockyards

POLICE OFFICERS MENTIONED IN THIS BOOK

Name	Rank	Year	Location	Division
KANE John	Chief Inspector	1924	Pembroke	Royal Dockyards
KANE John	Chief Inspector	1927	Chatham	Royal Dockyards
KEITH James	Sub-Divisional Inspector	1915	Rosyth	Royal Dockyards
KELL	Inspector		Woolwich	Royal Dockyards
KEMP William	Inspector	1899	Chatham	Royal Dockyards
KENDALL W.F.	Sub-Divisional Inspector	1937	Wimbledon	Merton
KEYS Albert	Superintendent	1923	Devonport	Royal Dockyards
KEYS Albert	Chief Inspector	1910	Devonport	Royal Dockyards
KEYS Albert	Superintendent	1915	Rosyth	Royal Dockyards
KING Joseph	Chief Inspector	1877	Chatham	Royal Dockyards
KITNEY	Constable	1940	Knockholt	Bromley
KNIGHTON Harry	Inspector	1899	Catford	Lewisham
KNIGHTS W.	Inspector	1891	Epsom	Sutton
KNOTT W	Inspector	1891	Epsom	Sutton
LACK	Sergeant	1913	Devonport	Royal Dockyards
LANE Charles	Inspector	1905	Catford	Lewisham
LANE F.	Constable	1895	Portsmouth	Royal Dockyards
LAST	Chief Inspector	1895	Portsmouth	Royal Dockyards
LAST James	Superintendent	1913	Portsmouth	Royal Dockyards
LAWLOR J	Superintendent	1957	Tooting	Wandsworth
LAWRENCE S.C.	Sub-Divisional Inspector	1931	Sutton	Sutton
LAWS Arthur	Constable	1930	Tooting	Wandsworth
LEE Walter	Sub-Divisional Inspector	1895	Greenwich	Greenwich
LEE Nathan Thompson	Sub-Divisional Inspector	1885	W/Common	Wandsworth
LEESON B	Detective Sergeant	1920	Kennington	Lambeth
LEMMEY William	Sub-Divisional Inspector	1898	Croydon	Croydon
LENNETT G.M.	Inspector	1879	Kennington	Lambeth
LEWIS Jack	Constable	1921	Bromley	Bromley
LEWIS Ronald	Special Constable	1940	Greenwich	Greenwich
LINKINS Herbert	Special Sub-Inspector	1940	Greenwich	Greenwich
LINVILL James	Constable	1870	Biggin Hill	Bromley
LOCK	Constable	1862	Portsmouth	Royal Dockyards
LOCKE William	Constable	1940	Greenwich	Greenwich
LOFUS Michael	Inspector	1927	Woolwich	Royal Dockyards
LONG J.	Superintendent	2009	Lavender Hill	Wandsworth
LOOKER	Constable		Devonport	Royal Dockyards
LOWE G	Inspector	1879	Kennington	Lambeth
LUCAS S.T.	Superintendent	1891	Streatham	Lambeth
LUCAS Stephen T.	Superintendent	1889	Croydon	Croydon
LUMMUS Frederick	Sub-Divisional Inspector	1921	Belvedere	Bexley
MacANDREW	Sergeant		Woolwich	Greenwich
MacDONALD Archibald	Chief Inspector	1867	Pembroke	Royal Dockyards
MacINTYRE	Sub-Divisional Inspector	1927	Woolwich	Royal Dockyards
MAINE Sir Richard	Commissioner	1850	Croydon	Croydon

POLICE OFFICERS MENTIONED IN THIS BOOK

Name	Rank	Year	Location	Division
MALLALIEU	Superintendent	1860	Intro	Royal Dockyards
MALLALIEU Francis M.	Superintendent	1835	Greenwich	Greenwich
MALLALIEU F.M.	Superintendent	1835	Chatham	Royal Dockyards
MANN Dave	Chief Inspector	2010	Greenwich	Greenwich
MANN Henry	Superintendent	1921	Carter Street	Southwark
MANN Henry	Superintendent	1930	Southwark	Southwark
MARGETSON Sir Philip	Deputy Commissioner	1934	Warren	Bromley
MARK Kingston	Superintendent	1863	Woolwich	Royal Dockyards
MARK Kingston	Superintendent	1864	Pembroke	Royal Dockyards
MARR V.	Superintendent	2001	Lavender Hill	Wandsworth
MARTIN T	Inspector	1879	Kennington	Lambeth
MARTIN George	Special Sergeant	1940	Greenwich	Greenwich
MARTIN Robert	Chief Inspector	1877	Portsmouth	Royal Dockyards
MASON William	Chief Inspector	1879	Clapham	Lambeth
MASON William	Chief Inspector	1878	Croydon	Croydon
MATHEWS Annie	Constable	1931	Woolwich	Greenwich
MAUDE Henry	Inspector	1844	Mitcham	Merton
MAY Frederick	Sub Divisional Inspector	1911	Southwark	Southwark
MAYNE Sir Richard	Commissioner	1863	East Greenwich	Greenwich
MAYNE Sir Richard	Commissioner	1863	Woolwich	Royal Dockyards
MAYNE Sir Richard	Commissioner	1865	Portsmouth	Royal Dockyards
MAYNE Sir Richard	Commissioner		Chatham	Royal Dockyards
McCARTHY Philip	Inspector	1908	Rodney Road	Southwark
McCRIMMON Neil	Inspector	1877	Devonport	Royal Dockyards
McDONALD Archibald	Superintendent	1877	Portsmouth	Royal Dockyards
McELLIOTT James	Inspector	1877	Woolwich	Royal Dockyards
McHUGO Christopher H	Superintendent	1879	East Greenwich	Greenwich
McKENNA Edward	Sub-Divisional Inspector	1895	Wandsworth	Wandsworth
McLEAN Alexander	Superintendent	1833	Camberwell	Southwark
McLEAN Andrew	Superintendent	1844	Croydon	Croydon
McLEAN Andrew	Superintendent	1841	Mitcham	Merton
McNEE Sir David	Commissioner	1981	Kennington	Lambeth
McNEE Sir David	Commissioner	1980	Croydon	Croydon
MEEHAN Leslie Edwin Vincent	Constable	1960	Greenwich	Greenwich
MEERING	Superintendent	1881	Belvedere	Bexley
MELTON Robert	Constable	1917	Camberwell	Southwark
MEWTON William	Constable	1914	Woolwich	Royal Dockyards
MILES Sidney George	Constable	1952	Croydon	Croydon
MILES Thomas	Constable	1888	Wimbledon	Merton
MONEY Michael	Inspector	1877	Woolwich	Royal Dockyards
MONEY Michael	Chief Inspector	1894	Portsmouth	Royal Dockyards
MONK Richard	Chief Superintendent	1987	Brixton	Lambeth
MONNERY William	Constable	1914	Woolwich	Royal Dockyards
MOORE Charles Henry	Constable	1941	Sydenham	Lewisham
MOORMAN	Sub-Divisional Inspector	1899	Devonport	Royal Dockyards
MORSMAN George	Inspector	1877	Portsmouth	Royal Dockyards
MOTT	Superintendent	1863	Woolwich	Royal Dockyards

POLICE OFFICERS MENTIONED IN THIS BOOK

MOTT	Superintendent	1864	Chatham	Royal Dockyards
MOWER John	Inspector	1971	Worcester Park	Sutton
MURRAY William	Superintendent	1840	Southwark	Southwark
MUSTO	Constable	1956	Carter Street	Southwark
MYERS Neil	Chief Inspector	2010	Greenwich	Greenwich
NAZER William Stevens	Constable	1879	Chatham	Royal Dockyards
NEAL T	Inspector	1879	Kennington	Lambeth
NEALE	Constable	1862	Portsmouth	Royal Dockyards
NEWMAN Sir Kenneth	Commissioner	1885	Bromley	Bromley
NEYLAN	Superintendent	1893	Southwark	Southwark
NICHOLS F	Sub-Divisional Inspector	1937	Battersea	Wandsworth
NICHOLS Henry	Sub Divisional Inspector	1910	Tower Bridge	Southwark
NIGHTINGALE Harold	Inspector	1932	Chatham	Royal Dockyards
NORTHOVER Walter	Inspector	1892	Sutton	Sutton
NOTT-BOWER Sir John	Commissioner	1956	Carter Street	Southwark
NUNAN Thomas	Chief Inspector	1893	Croydon	Croydon
OAKLEY Jo	Detective Superintendent	2010	Intro	Croydon
OAKS William	Inspector	1877	Chatham	Royal Dockyards
OAKS William	Inspector	1869	Chatham	Royal Dockyards
ODELL Francis	Sub Divisional Inspector	1914	Carter Street	Southwark
OLLETT Albany J	Inspector	1881	Battersea	Wandsworth
O'NEILL Frank	Constable	1980	Kennington	Lambeth
OWEN Henry	Constable	1887	Bromley	Bromley
PACKER Albert Ernest	Constable	1926	Greenwich	Greenwich
PADDICK Brian	Commander	2000	Balham	Wandsworth
PADGETT T	Inspector	1879	Kennington	Lambeth
PALMER Dave	Superintendent	2010	Intro	Lambeth
PALMER William	Station Sergeant	1972	Bromley	Bromley
PARKER Henry	Inspector	1877	Woolwich	Royal Dockyards
PARKINS	Constable	1936	Gipsy Hill	Lambeth
PARLETT Samuel	Sub-Divisional Inspector	1898	Croydon	Croydon
PAWLEY	Inspector	1919	Epsom	Sutton
PAYNE	Inspector		Chatham	Royal Dockyards
PAYNE G.	Inspector	1879	Kennington	Lambeth
PAYNE Edward	Superintendent	1869	Carter Street	Southwark
PAYNE William	Inspector	1877	Woolwich	Royal Dockyards
PEACOCK	Constable	1862	Portsmouth	Royal Dockyards
PEAKE Benjamin	Sergeant	1878	Wimbledon	Merton
PEARCE Charles	Constable	1864	Devonport	Royal Dockyards
PEARCE Thomas	Inspector	1926	Rosyth	Royal Dockyards
PEARMAN John	Inspector	1877	Wandsworth	Wandsworth
PEARN	Inspector	1884	East Dulwich	Southwark
PEARN	Constable		Devonport	Royal Dockyards
PEARN Charles	Inspector	1891	Epsom	Sutton
PERRY James	Chief Inspector	1881	Camberwell	Southwark
PETHERICK Frederick	Constable	1881	Nine Elms	Wandsworth
PHILLIPS William	Sub-Divisional Inspector	1903	Catford	Lewisham

POLICE OFFICERS MENTIONED IN THIS BOOK

Name	Rank	Year	Location	Division
PIERCE Enoch John	Constable	1915	Wimbledon	Merton
PINEGAR	Inspector	1845	Wimbledon	Merton
PORTER J	Inspector	1891	Carter Street	Southwark
PORTER W.H.	Superintendent	1960	Wimbledon	Merton
POTTS George	Constable	1870	Woolwich	Royal Dockyards
POTTS George	Constable	1870	Chatham	Royal Dockyards
POTTS William	Inspector	1877	Devonport	Royal Dockyards
POWELLI H	Inspector	1891	Carter Street	Southwark
PRENDARGAST Thomas	Sergeant	1850	Croydon	Croydon
PRESTON	Constable	1912	Norbury	Croydon
PREWER Harold	Station Sergeant	1921	Croydon	Croydon
PRIDE	Inspector	1884	East Dulwich	Southwark
PULLEN	Sub-Divisional Inspector	1925	Norbury	Croydon
PULLEN Arthur	Sub-Divisional Inspector	1911	Greenwich	Greenwich
PURBRICK M	Superintendent	1940	Brixton	Lambeth
PURBRICK M	Superintendent	1939	Peckham	Southwark
PYRKE John	Inspector	1870	Eltham	Greenwich
QUIBELL Lawrence James	Constable	1917	Rosyth	Royal Dockyards
QUINCEY H.C.	Superintendent	1939	Croydon	Croydon
RACE W.N.	Inspector	1891	Carter Street	Southwark
RACKHAM C.	Superintendent	1957	Wimbledon	Merton
RAYMENT	Constable	1862	Portsmouth	Royal Dockyards
RENDALL Joseph	Sergeant	1852	Greenwich	Greenwich
RICHARDSON	Superintendent	1864	Chatham	Royal Dockyards
RICHARDSON Thomas	Superintendent	1863	Chatham	Royal Dockyards
RICHARDSON William	Inspector	1845	Wimbledon	Merton
ROBERTS Adrian	Chief Superintendent	2010	Intro	Croydon
ROBERTSON A	Sub-Divisional Inspector	1937	Wandsworth	Wandsworth
ROBINS George	Sergeant	1870	Carshalton	Sutton
ROBINSON	Inspector	1893	Southwark	Southwark
ROGERS	Inspector	1896	Portsmouth	Royal Dockyards
ROGERS John	Inspector	1881	Wimbledon	Merton
ROLF Francis	Sub Divisional Inspector	1905	Carter Street	Southwark
ROTHNIE	Sergeant	1899	Devonport	Royal Dockyards
ROWBOTTOM	Inspector	1882	Carshalton	Sutton
ROYLE Joe	Chief Superintendent	2004	Sutton	Sutton
RUTT Anthony	Superintendent	1849	Kennington	Lambeth
SAICH George	Sergeant	1891	Clapham	Lambeth
SAINES David	Chief Inspector	1889	Intro	Wandsworth
SARA	Sub-Divisional Inspector	1898	Plumstead	Greenwich
SAUNDERS Robert	Sergeant	1850	Sidcup	Bexley
SAVAGE	Constable	1862	Portsmouth	Royal Dockyards
SCANTLEBURY	Inspector	1891	Knights Hill	Lambeth
SCOTT Conrad	Constable	1907	Rotherhithe	Southwark
SEWELL David	Superintendent	1923	Devonport	Royal Dockyards

POLICE OFFICERS MENTIONED IN THIS BOOK

SEWELL D.	Superintendent	1924	Portsmouth	Royal Dockyards
SHAW W.H.	Inspector	1851	Croydon	Croydon
SHEPHERD James	Inspector	1837	Wandsworth	Wandsworth
SHEPHERD William	Constable	1911	Pembroke	Royal Dockyards
SHERLOCK	Inspector	1864	Portsmouth	Royal Dockyards
SHORT	Inspector	1896	Portsmouth	Royal Dockyards
SILVEY William	Constable	1883	Putney	Wandsworth
SKINNER William	Constable		Wimbledon	Merton
SLY Alfred	Inspector	1911	Devonport	Royal Dockyards
SLY Charles	Chief Inspector	1914	Rosyth	Royal Dockyards
SLY Charles E.	Superintendent	1920	Chatham	Royal Dockyards
SMALE Henry	Inspector	1877	Devonport	Royal Dockyards
SMALLBRIDGE	Detective Sergeant	1895	Portsmouth	Royal Dockyards
SMITH A.D.	Superintendent	1914	Greenwich	Greenwich
SMITH George	Sub-Divisional Inspector	1899	Catford	Lewisham
SMITH Edwin	Superintendent	1897	Devonport	Royal Dockyards
SMITH Edwin	Inspector	1877	Devonport	Royal Dockyards
SMITH Edwin	Superintendent	1906	Devonport	Royal Dockyards
SMITH Ian	Detective Superintendent	2010	Intro	Southwark
SMITH John	Superintendent	1882	Chatham	Royal Dockyards
SMITH John	Superintendent	1877	Chatham	Royal Dockyards
SMITH W	Chief Inspector	1897	Chatham	Royal Dockyards
SMITH Wiliiam	Superintendent	1902	Chatham	Royal Dockyards
SMITH William	Superintendent	1829	Intro	Croydon
SPARROW	Inspector	1965	Chislehurst	Bromley
SPENCER Frank	Sub Divisional Inspector	1904	Carter Street	Southwark
SPENCER Frederick	Superintendent	1916	Portsmouth	Royal Dockyards
STANNARD William	Inspector	1844	Kennington	Lambeth
STEVENS Joseph	Constable	1877	Intro	Sutton
STEVENS Sir John	Commissioner	2004	Kennington	Lambeth
STEVENS Henry	Constable	1958	Bromley	Bromley
STEVENS Sir John	Commissioner	2004	Lewisham	Lewisham
STEVENS Sir John	Commissioner	2004	S	Sutton
STILL	Inspector		Chatham	Royal Dockyards
STONE Edwin	Constable	1896	Wandsworth	Wandsworth
STRENGTH	Superintendent		Devonport	Royal Dockyards
STRENGTH John	Superintendent	1864	Chatham	Royal Dockyards
STRENGTH John	Superintendent	1864	Chatham	Royal Dockyards
STRIBLING	Constable	1862	Portsmouth	Royal Dockyards
STRINGER Dave	Superintendent	2010	Intro	Croydon
STUBBINGTON Charles	Sergeant	1893	Chatham	Royal Dockyards
SUTHERLAND John	Inspector	1915	Rosyth	Royal Dockyards
SWAN	Inspector	1935	Sydenham	Lewisham
SWAN Edward William	Constable	1918	Woolwich	Royal Dockyards
SYKES George	Constable	1865	Woolwich	Royal Dockyards
SYLVESTER Bernard	Inspector	1944	Wimbledon	Merton
TANNER	Inspector	1864	Belvedere	Bexley
TAYLOR Donald	Inspector	1877	Woolwich	Royal Dockyards

POLICE OFFICERS MENTIONED IN THIS BOOK

Name	Rank	Year	Location	Division
TETT William	Chief Inspector	1902	Devonport	Royal Dockyards
TETT William	Superintendent	1910	Chatham	Royal Dockyards
THOBURN George	Sergeant	1850	Croydon	Croydon
THOMAS	Constable	1863	Pembroke	Royal Dockyards
THOMAS Ian	Chief Superintendent	2004	Camberwell	Southwark
THOMPSON Alexander	Superintendent	1842	Woolwich	Royal Dockyards
THOMPSON Alexander	Chief Inspector	1860	Pembroke	Royal Dockyards
THOMPSON Alfred	Sergeant	1895	Knockholt	Bromley
THOMSON	Superintendent	1865	Woolwich	Royal Dockyards
THOMSON James	Constable	1935	West Wickham	Bromley
TOPP William J	Inspector	1844	Kennington	Lambeth
TOTTEY James Frederick	Constable	1941	Greenwich	Greenwich
TRENCHARD Lord	Commissioner	1935	Warren	Bromley
TRENCHARD Lord	Commissioner	1930	Eltham	Greenwich
TUNBRIDGE	Constable	1863	Pembroke	Royal Dockyards
TUNBRIDGE James	Inspector	1877	Woolwich	Royal Dockyards
TURK Thomas	Inspector	1881	Deptford	Lewisham
TURNER	Sergeant	1913	Devonport	Royal Dockyards
TURNER Richard	Inspector	1830	Wandsworth	Wandsworth
URBAN Henry	Inspector	1915	Rosyth	Royal Dockyards
VENTHAM	Superintendent	1895	Portsmouth	Royal Dockyards
VENTHAM William	Chief Inspector	1877	Devonport	Royal Dockyards
WADDELL A	Inspector	1891	Carter Street	Southwark
WADE Brian	Superintendent	2001	Lavender Hill	Wandsworth
WAKEFIELD	Sergeant	1913	Devonport	Royal Dockyards
WAKEFORD	Sergeant	1860	Pembroke	Royal Dockyards
WAKEFORD William	Superintendent	1869	Devonport	Royal Dockyards
WAKEFORD William	Superintendent	1886	Chatham	Royal Dockyards
WALL Charles	Chief Inspector	1894	Devonport	Royal Dockyards
WALL Charles	Chief Inspector	1894	Devonport	Royal Dockyards
WALLACE Suzanne	Superintendent	2010	Intro	Lewisham
WALSH Emily	Constable	1934	Woolwich	Greenwich
WALSHE	Inspector	1893	Plumstead	Greenwich
WALTERS Donald	Sergeant	1881	Greenwich	Greenwich
WANNOP John	Inspector	1915	Rosyth	Royal Dockyards
WATERS Donald	Superintendent	1913	Southwark	Southwark
WEBB Charles	Superintendent	1869	Kennington	Lambeth
WEBB William Jenkins	Chief Inspector	1891	Croydon	Croydon
WEBB Owen	Superintendent	1924	Devonport	Royal Dockyards
WEDLOCK	Sub-Divisional Inspector	1899	Devonport	Royal Dockyards
WELLS Arthur	Inspector	1941	East Greenwich	Greenwich
WEST	Superintendent	1921	Brixton	Lambeth
WEST	Superintendent	1921	Brixton	Lambeth
WEST	Superintendent	1910	Southwark	Southwark
WEST	Constable	1863	Woolwich	Royal Dockyards
WEST	Superintendent	1910	Norbury	Croydon
WHATLEY W.	Inspector	1879	Kennington	Lambeth
WHELLER William James	Station Sergeant	1917	Greenwich	Greenwich
WHITE	Superintendent	1936	Gipsy Hill	Lambeth

POLICE OFFICERS MENTIONED IN THIS BOOK

WHITE H.G	Superintendent	1966	Battersea	Wandsworth
WILLIS Phil	Superintendent	2010	Intro	Sutton
WILLMOTT John	Inspector	1877	Woolwich	Royal Dockyards
WILLMOTT John	Chief Inspector	1885	Devonport	Royal Dockyards
WILSON A.	Inspector	1891	Epsom	Sutton
WILSON Henry	Sergeant	1870	Erith	Bexley
WILSON Jas	Superintendent	1928	Croydon	Croydon
WILSON Paul	Superintendent	2010	Intro	Lambeth
WISEMAN William	Superintendent	1879	Brixton	Lambeth
WISEMAN William	Superintendent	1879	Clapham	Lambeth
WISEMAN William	Superintendent	1869	Croydon	Croydon
WOLLARD	Constable	1936	Gipsy Hill	Lambeth
WONNALL Thomas	Inspector	1877	Devonport	Royal Dockyards
WOOD Richard	Detective Chief Superintendent	2010	Greenwich	Greenwich
WOOTON	Inspector	1877	Portsmouth	Royal Dockyards
WORTH	Inspector	1891	Streatham	Lambeth
WREN Walter T	Superintendent	1913	Southwark	Southwark
WRIGHT	Constable	1863	Woolwich	Royal Dockyards
WRIGHT Frederick	Inspector	1917	Camberwell	Southwark
WYBORN H	Superintendent	1900	Southwark	Southwark
YATES John	Inspector	1849	Southwark	Southwark
YOUNG	Inspector	1893	Pembroke	Royal Dockyards

Metropolitan Police Warrant Numbers 1829- 2010

When joining the Police Service Officers are given an individual warrant number which remains with them for ever. This is a general guide indicating the year in which the officer joined the Service. In recent years warrant numbers have been allocated at the recruitment stage, but the officer may not formally join until later..

Women Police Officers formally joined the Metropolitan Police in 1919, and were allocated separate warrant numbers up until the end of 1992. Thereafter both male and female officers were given a six figure warrant number.

Year	Start Male	Finish Officers	Start Female	Finish Officers
1829	1	1590		
1830	1591	5680		
1831	5681	7145		
1832	7146	8100		
1833	8101	9098		
1834	9099	10130		
1835	10131	11277		
1836	11278	12333		
1837	12334	13454		
1838	13455	14550		
1839	14551	15805		
1840	15806	17889		
1841	17890	19019		
1842	19020	19888		
1843	19889	20931		
1844	20932	21751		
1845	21752	22772		
1846	22773	23994		
1847	23995	25075		
1848	25076	26454		
1849	26455	27295		
1850	27296	28154		
1851	28155	29900		
1852	29901	30746		
1853	30747	32012		
1854	32013	33213		
1855	33214	34323		
1856	34324	35345		
1857	35346	36633		

1858	36634	37702		
1859	37703	38602		
1860	38603	40126		
1861	40127	41180		
1862	41181	43505		
1863	43506	44581		
1864	44582	45647		
1865	45648	46869		
1866	46870	47941		
1867	47942	49153		
1868	49154	51382		
1869	51383	52319		
1870	52320	53466		
1871	53467	55018		
1872	55019	56399		
1873	56400	57488		
1874	57489	58561		
1875	58562	59819		
1876	59820	61042		
1877	61043	62114		
1878	62115	63173		
1879	63174	64172		
1880	64173	65149		
1881	65150	66159		
1882	66160	67354		
1883	67355	68830		
1884	68831	69957		
1885	69958	71048		
1886	71049	72224		
1887	72225	73144		
1888	73145	74142		
1889	74143	75054		
1890	75055	76480		
1891	76481	77318		
1892	77319	78187		
1893	78188	79227		
1894	79228	80147		
1895	80148	80903		
1896	80904	81811		
1897	81812	83496		
1898	83497	84741		
1899	84742	85895		
1900	85896	86986		
1901	86987	88150		

1902	88151	89422		
1903	89423	90387		
1904	90388	91356		
1905	91357	92760		
1906	92761	94152		
1907	94153	95313		
1908	95314	96457		
1909	96458	97734		
1910	97735	99563		
1911	99564	100928		
1912	100929	102128		
1913	102129	103574		
1914	103575	104647		
1915	104648	105205	Women Police	
1916	105206	105209		
1917	105210	105212	Start	Finish
1918	105213	105235		
1919	105236	108413	1	125
1920	108414	111242	126	161
1921	111243	112137	162	168
1922	112138	112268	169	181
1923	112269	112531	182	183
1924	112532	113555	184	191
1925	113556	115085	192	221
1926	115086	116068	222	229
1927	116069	117122	230	231
1928	117123	118042	232	236
1929	118043	119309	237	241
1930	119310	120633	242	251
1931	120634	121959	252	264
1932	121960	122676	265	268
1933	122677	123179	269	279
1934	123180	123898	280	286
1935	123899	124677	287	300
1936	124678	125442	301	316
1937	125443	126591	317	350
1938	126592	127433	351	373
1939	127434	128336	374	421
1940	128337	128340	422	464
1941	128341	128342	465	505
1942	128343	128343	506	525
1943	128343	128343	526	535
1944	128344	128345	536	545
1945	128346	128347	546	551

1946	128348	130122	552	606
1947	130123	132418	607	677
1948	132419	134162	678	741
1949	134163	135258	742	819
1950	135259	136624	820	943
1951	136625	137505	944	1031
1952	137506	138816	1032	1110
1953	138817	139849	1111	1246
1954	139850	141157	1247	1346
1955	141158	142540	1347	1432
1956	142541	144298	1433	1527
1957	144299	145873	1528	1616
1958	145874	147251	1617	1689
1959	147252	148595	1690	1756
1960	148596	149657	1757	1813
1961	149658	150882	1814	1884
1962	150883	152097	1885	1953
1963	152098	153317	1954	2047
1964	153318	154373	2048	2126
1965	154374	155588	2127	2226
1966	155589	156962	2227	2322
1967	156963	158570	2323	2452
1968	158571	159825	2453	2540
1969	159826	161018	2541	2638
1970	161019	162175	2639	2765
1971	162176	163210	2766	2864
1972	163211	164320	2865	2980
1973	164321	165326	2981	3086
1974	165327	166626	3087	3319
1975	166627	168094	3320	3607
1976	168095	170080	3608	4143
1977	170081	171503	4140	4600
1978	171504	172751	4601	4916
1979	172752	174488	4917	5394
1980	174489	176305	5395	5946
1981	176306	178761	5947	6382
1982	178762	180947	6383	6718
1983	180948	182422	6719	6913
1984	182423	183493	6914	7063
1985	183494	184560	7064	7270
1986	184561	186018	7271	7562
1987	186019	187426	7563	8069
1988	187427	189205	8070	8590
1989	189206	190569	8591	9018

1990	195570	191671	9019	9343
1991	191672	192583	9344	9701
1992	192584	193264	9702	9994
1993	193268	194414		
1994	194415	195606		
1995	195607	196678		
1996	196679	197745		
1997	197746	198855		
1998	198856	200199		
1999	200200	201453		
2000	201454	202648		
2001	202649	205107		
2002	205108	208350		
2003	208351	217921		
2004	217922	220926		
2005	220927	220965		
2006	220966	224740		
2007	224741	226712		
2008	226713	229031		
2009	229032	232026		
2010	232027	232537		